Manual of Travel Agency Practice

Manual of Travel Agency Practice

Gwenda Syratt FInstTT, FInstCM
Senior Lecturer, London City College and Cavendish College

BUTTERWORTH
HEINEMANN

Butterworth-Heinemann Ltd
Linacre House, Jordan Hill, Oxford OX2 8DP

● PART OF REED INTERNATIONAL BOOKS

OXFORD   LONDON   BOSTON
MUNICH   NEW DELHI   SINGAPORE   SYDNEY
TOKYO   TORONTO   WELLINGTON

First published 1992

© Gwenda Syratt 1992

British Library Cataloguing in Publication Data
Syratt, Gwenda
  Manual of travel agency practice.
  I. Title
  388.06

ISBN 0 7506 0088 8

Library of Congress Cataloguing in Publication Data
Syratt, Gwenda
  Manual of travel agency practice/Gwenda Syratt.
  p.   cm.
  Includes index.
  ISBN 0 7506 0088 8
  1. Travel agents – Handbooks, manuals, etc. I. Title.
  G154.S94   1992
  338.4'79102373–dc20   91–31407
                                                                 CIP

Photoset by Deltatype Ltd, Ellesmere Port, Cheshire
Printed and bound in Great Britain by Thomson Litho Ltd, East Kilbride, Scotland

To Sylvia, Daisy and Frederick Plumley

Contents

Preface   ix

Acknowledgements   xi

1 **Introduction**   1

2 **Package and group tours**   3
   - Understanding booking conditions • Costing • Destinations
   - Departures • The supplements, surcharges and small print
   - Organizing your own tours

3 **Holiday centres and special interest holidays**   20
   - Holiday centres today • Costing and reservations • Locations
   and facilities • Travellers with common interests

4 **Hotels, theatres and bargain breaks**   35
   - Theatre bookings • Stopovers and bargain breaks
   - Understanding reference books • Making reservations • Types
   of accommodation • How to read the *ABC Guides* • Explanation of
   theatre bookings • The benefits of stopover and bargain breaks

5 **Coaching and incoming tourists**   51
   - Reservation procedure • Discovering advantages of coach travel
   and routings • The work involved when handling incoming tourist
   reservations

6 **Car rental**   58
   - Types of hire available • How to read manuals • Making car
   rental reservations to include calculations

7 **Car ferries**   73
   - Understanding routings • Reservations • Costings • *ABC
   Shipping Guide.*

8 **British and Continental rail and motor rail**   92
   - Understanding the timetables • The routings and benefits of rail
   and motor-rail travel

9 **Cruising** 108
   ● Location of ocean travel services ● Costing ● Life onboard
   ● Making sea travel reservations ● Understanding conditions and
   nautical terminology

10 **Introduction to airline reservations** 122
    ● IATA ● Traffic Conference Areas ● Three letter codes
    ● Aircraft types ● How to use *ABC World Airways Guide*
    ● Minimum connecting times ● Time differences and elapsed
    flying times ● Passport, visa and health requirements ● Special
    services for passengers ● Baggage and airport information
    ● Airfares ● A brief outline on understanding fare
    rules, maximum permitted mileages, and ticketing

11 **Insurance** 159
    ● Holiday insurance – why necessary? ● Understanding the
    exclusion clauses and handling claims

12 **Handling cash and cheques** 171
    ● Handling cash, cheques, credit cards, travellers' cheques and
    observing strict security

13 **Skills** 189
    ● Selling skills ● Telephone techniques ● Communicating with
    others ● Information seeking ● Product knowledge ● Tone of
    voice ● Organization

14 **Business letters** 201
    ● How to apply for a travel position ● How to write the
    curriculum vitae ● How to write business letters within the travel
    industry

15 **Business travel** 209
    ● How to give a good service to secretaries ● Types of business
    travel service offered ● Getting new business house traffic
    ● Handling buiness travel problems

16 **Handling complaints** 216
    ● Ethics ● Tourist organizations ● Problem solving – if you fail,
    who can the client turn to?

17 **Finance and planning** 220
    ● A profitable travel agency ● Sources of income ● Filing
    systems ● Passenger records and accounts procedure ● Controlling
    the finances ● Forecasting future business

Solutions to exercises 231

Glossary of terms 255

Index 257

Preface

Why are you looking at this book? Does working at a travel agency appeal to you, but you need to know more about it? This book can help you! If you enjoy meeting the public and learning something new each day, feel happy to help, and are eager to travel to faraway places with strange sounding names, you could be on your way to a fulfilling and exciting career.

Are you attending a travel and tourism course, and need retail travel operations explained in easy-to-read language? This book can *definitely* help you! It covers the syllabus of:

Institute of Commercial Management: Retail Travel Operations
City and Guilds/ABTA: Certificate of Travel Agency Competence, Level 1 495–1–02
IATA/UFTAA Operation of a Travel Agency: Unit 6
BTEC Travel and Tourism: Retail Travel Services
SCOTVEC National Certificate in Travel Studies (content currently under review)

Have you just begun work in a travel agency, but are not sure how to do a job in hand, and everyone is too busy to explain to you at the moment? This book can *most certainly* help you! It is a manual of retail travel practice, and the everyday work of a travel agency is explained step by step. It can be used as a reference book – and you may even find it light entertainment reading too!

For lecturers in travel and tourism, many of the exercises and assignments have been taken from past examination papers of ICM, City and Guilds, IATA/UFTAA, BTEC and SCOTVEC. So hopefully you will find this book helpful and time saving as well.

On a general note, the travel and tourism industry is ever changing; it would be impossible to quote up-to-date fares, for example. However, the methods of arriving at those fares and obtaining information do not change, and can be applied to current manuals.

Technology plays a large part in our industry, and is referred to on many occasions throughout the book. This manual is designed to help travel personnel on an international level, and examples will be given on a worldwide basis.

Finally, we wouldn't be in the travel business if we didn't have a keen interest in other countries, would we? There is no geography chapter, but there is a strong travel flavour running through the book, so be careful – you could soon be getting itchy feet!

I hope that you enjoy reading this book and that you find it useful. If you have chosen a career in the travel and tourism industry, I hope you really enjoy the exciting years to come.

Gwenda Syratt

Acknowledgements

I wish to thank those who helped me in the preparation of this book by supplying material for inclusion, and in particular:

ABC International Travel Guides
Butlin's Holiday Worlds
County Coaches
Enterprise Holidays
Europcar UK Ltd
Greyhound Coaches
The Institute of Travel and Tourism
The International Air Transport Association
Sealink British Ferries Ltd
Thomas Cook Publishing
Travelguard Insurance
The Universal Federation of Travel Agents Association

My thanks to George Syratt for his constant constructive support.

1 Introduction

You may have thought of working in a travel agency but you may not really be sure what this type of work entails, or whether you would enjoy life at an agency. I will try to answer some anticipated questions.

What would I do?

This is bound to be the first question. When working in a travel agency the travel consultant must be able to advise and to process business on many topics, such as package holidays, car rental, travel insurance, airline routes and regulations, ferry services, cruising, independent holiday arrangements, passport and visa requirements, hotel bookings, rail and coach bookings and air fares. The consultant must be able to deal with administrative work – and to make a good cup of tea!

The kind of work to be found in a travel agency is enormously varied. It is nearly always satisfying, mainly because you never stop learning. You will never be able to say 'Well, now I know my job', because there is so much to learn and the scene is ever changing.

A travel agency usually divides its custom between leisure travellers and business travellers, because the methods used to service the two types of travel arrangements are quite different. A travel agency can provide multipurpose services and play the role of combined tour operator and travel agent if required to do so.

What sort of person would I need to be?

First, you need to have patience. Anyone who has a job that involves working with people will say the same thing.

Unfortunately it is not a question of picking up the telephone, making the reservation, writing out the ticket and wishing your client a smooth journey. Changes are often made; reservations may be cancelled and rebooked; and there can be long delays in getting through to tour operators and airlines.

You will need to be able to take responsibility – and you *must* be accurate. As with any job, you will need to be enthusiastic. I'm sure you will be, because the travel business is the sort of job that gets into your bloodstream and doesn't let you go!

You also have to be prepared to work long hours when required, bearing in mind that the work tends to be seasonal, and there are often deadlines to meet. You cannot say to your client 'I'm sorry, your travel documents are not ready, I had to go home at 5 p.m. last night!'

In this book I hope to help you to cope with some of the situations you are bound to face at some stage in a travel and tourism career, and to remind you that there is also a lighter side to the industry. The travel industry tends to have a 'family' environment as there are many opportunities to meet other travel personnel and occasionally to have the opportunity to make educational trips to interesting places and to benefit from reduced air fares, when flights are available.

What would be the requirements?

Entry qualifications are not rigid. The most useful GCSEs or equivalents would be in English language, mathematics and geography.

What training would I be given?

Beyond school there are colleges where one can learn the technical side of the travel industry, and this background does help when looking for employment. A large travel company will provide its own training schemes throughout your career. Airline companies, in particular British Airways, have their own centres where travel agents and airline personnel throughout the world receive specialized training.

Where would I work?

The travel industry has many outlets. You could work at an airport, in a hotel, as a courier at a resort, and so on. However, as a travel agent you would probably work in a shop; you would be selling holidays. If your work dealt with business travel it would not be necessary to have a high street location; most of your business would be conducted over the telephone, so you might work in an office above street level. Some travel positions have 'in-plant' locations; this means you have your own travel office at a large factory or office site, making travel arrangements only for the employees of that particular company.

What are the promotion prospects?

Travel is a young people's industry with plenty of room to grow. If you are really interested in your job and would like to rise to the top, it is not *too* difficult. Listen to your colleagues and learn from the way they handle their work. Attend every training scheme you are offered. Assist in the everyday needs of your office, as there are many behind-the-scenes jobs to be done that are very important in the running of a smooth office.

Positions are usually notified within a company before being advertised publicly. When you feel confident, apply for a managerial position within your company at one of its branches.

After manager, the next step is regional manager; this means you would be responsible for the productivity of several shops in your area. A regional manager might occasionally rise to director and even to chairman. This is the direct line, but there are many paths that lead off and many jobs where you could no doubt find a very happy niche for yourself.

2 Package and group tours

Summary

In this chapter the following are discussed:

- package holidays;
- how to find the right package holiday for the client;
- how to read the Enterprise Winter Sun brochure;
- understanding the Booking Conditions;
- how to calculate the cost of package holidays;
- how to complete the Booking Form;
- organizing an incentive group tour oneself
- incentive travel;
- how to plan a group tour;
- how to arrive at the retail selling price;
- tests and assignments to complete.

Although there is a wonderful variety of work within a travel agency, the bulk of it probably stems from airline reservations and package holidays. What is a package tour? It is a combination of travel services, transport and accommodation, for example purchased in bulk by a tour operator and resold as part of a package at an inclusive price. There are numerous package holiday brochures from which to choose, and many offer the same destinations. So how can you help your clients to choose the right one for them?

First of all, in the UK there are actually very few independent package tour companies; one company may operate under several different names. It should also be said that many travel agencies enjoy the 'overriding commission' system whereby, for showing loyalty to a few selected package tour operators, an agency will receive a higher rate of commission above an agreed total of sales. Tour operators also offer personal incentive gains to travel consultants, such as free holidays or gift vouchers to be spent in large popular department stores. These factors could well influence the travel consultant in helping the client to choose the right package tour! The customer's choice must always come first and the traveller can also benefit from a closer working relationship between tour operator and travel agent where product knowledge is concerned.

What other elements will encourage a client to choose one package tour from another? It isn't *always* price. Certainly prices do vary for exactly the same holiday, and this is mainly due to one tour operator negotiating more favourable rates with the principals than another. The rates are usually obtained on the basis of volume of traffic: the more guests a tour operator is able to guarantee to a hotel week after week, the cheaper the accommodation becomes.

Other factors can be reputation and previous experience. The travel and tourism industry relies heavily on repeat business. The same people go on holiday year after year, often several times a year; other people stay at home. There are many reasons for loss of business. If clients suffered a bad experience when travelling with a particular tour operator and the outcome was unsatisfactory, or if they have friends who had a horrific tale to tell, there will be no repeat business from those clients. Other determining factors could be flight details, such as the airline used, the aircraft type and – very importantly flight *times*. Often a client would prefer to pay more for the holiday and have flight times that suit his or her lifestyle. Flying during the day could be important, especially for families with young children. A whole day spent at the resort waiting to board a flight at midnight can seem long and tiring, especially if the hotel room had to be vacated at midday. Many clients like to be up and away on the flight home once the last day of the holiday arrives. The airport of departure can also be important; clients may prefer to pay more to depart from an airport close to their home rather than pay less and have a long drive to the airport.

Can the information supplied in the brochure be trusted? Where conditions of booking are concerned the answer is usually yes. However, descriptions can vary. Do read as many brochures as possible and compare descriptions of the *same* hotel and the *same* resort. Learn to read between the lines; often more is learnt from what is left unsaid than from what is actually explained in the brochure. 'Lively' can mean 'noisy'; 'relaxing' can mean 'miles from anywhere'. Travel agents have a resort gazetteer giving details of the resorts and hotels. This publication will paint a more realistic picture, and should be consulted if you do not have first-hand experience of the resort. Do not trust the brochure for days of departure, flight times etc., as often there are changes. If a tour operator is not selling as many holidays as it would like on a particular departure date, it will 'consolidate'. That is, it will cancel that departure and offer the few passengers who have booked (and paid) an alternative holiday that is guaranteed to operate. The tour operator (naturally) doesn't want to operate the tour at a loss. The clients (naturally) will be very upset by the change of plans; they may be in a situation where the alternative holiday is unsuitable, and a full refund will be unsatisfactory because it will now be too late to book the same holiday elsewhere. This is where your problem solving skills are required!

Millions of people

Please do not rely only on the information you can retrieve on the computer. There will be *many* tour operators who do not subscribe to the computerized system being used by your travel company, and they should be approached before you tell the client that there is no alternative. This is where good service by experienced staff can outshine the run-of-the-mill travel consultant any day.

Millions of people travel on package holidays every year and are very happy to do so because the benefits are enormous. As previously explained the tour operators benefit from bulk buying and this reduction is passed on to the customer, so there is the financial advantage of travelling on a package tour. Then there is the 'no hassle' element, everything is arranged for the traveller, flight reservations, transport between airport and hotel on arrival, and again on the day of departure. Accommodation at a hotel, villa or apartment all confirmed and the services of a representative. The choice is also very wide: package tours are available to almost every country, providing a wide range of flight services, days of operation, flight departure and arrival times, choice of type and standard of accommodation, and many other services such as sight-seeing tours, and welcome packs (grocery packs for holidaymakers staying in apartments). We need to study as many tour operators' brochures as possible to appreciate the great choice available.

Make good use of the *ABC Holiday Guide*. What will it tell us? As always there is an introduction and advice on how to use the guide. Information is then given on the following: international telephone; telex and times; UK airports; US states and cities; international climate; skiing resort altitudes; overseas centre holidays; overseas touring holidays; overseas cruise holidays; and resorts, hotels and tour operators. It really offers a wealth of information.

Using a brochure: Enterprise

The reference material used in this chapter is taken from the Enterprise Wintersun brochure.

Begin by looking at the contents page to find information quickly. The contents include: price guarantee; what the price includes; child reductions; things you ought to know; booking conditions; insurance and claims; booking form; holiday destinations; and price and flight guide.

The questions your clients might ask, or indeed the matters you should advise them on, are as follows. Bear in mind that all the answers will be found in the brochure.

Price   What does the price include: flights, in-flight meals, half board, full board, baggage allowance, airport taxes, hotel service charge and taxes, representatives at airports and resorts, transfers between airport and hotel?

Welcome party   Will anyone be there to explain the procedures to us? When will the representative visit our hotel? What happens if we arrive at the apartment on a day when shops are closed: will a welcome pack of groceries be supplied?

Excursions   Will they be available? How much will they cost? What are the car rental rates? Are there any special festivities for Christmas and the New Year? Can I take a two-centre holiday? Are there holidays catering for guests travelling alone?

Special offers   Are there any great reductions? What is the charge for an infant? What is the reduction for children? Will the cost of the holiday be guaranteed not to increase once the deposit has been paid? What is the cancellation charge?

The only way to answer these questions and many more is to read the brochure thoroughly and to be confident of knowing where to find the answers.

Exercise 1

Please study the booking conditions extract from the Enterprise brochure. This exercise means reading a lot of 'small print' and thinking, seriously about the meaning.

BOOKING CONDITIONS

OUR COMMITMENT TO YOU

Enterprise Holidays is operated by Redwing Holdings Limited. We are committed to a policy of fair trading and make every effort to ensure that you will have an enjoyable holiday with us. Our Booking Conditions have been formulated as a result of our responsibilities under law and in no way affect your statutory rights as a consumer.

1. Your Reservation

All bookings are made and accepted subject to the terms set out in these conditions. When you or your travel agent instructs us to confirm your booking, we will do so immediately, and you must pay your deposit at that time. An invoice will automatically be raised and sent to you, and will include any appropriate holiday insurance premium.

2. Our Policy on Surcharges

We guarantee that the price of your holiday will not be subject to any surcharges, except for those resulting from Governmental action. Even in this case, we will absorb an amount equivalent to 2% of the holiday price which excludes insurance premiums and any amendment charges. Only amounts in excess of this 2% will be surcharged, together with an amount to cover agent's commission. If this means paying more than 10% on the holiday price, you will be entitled to cancel your holiday with a full refund of all money paid except for the premium paid to us for holiday insurance and amendment charges. Should you decide to cancel because of this, you must exercise your right to do so within 14 days from the issue date printed on the invoice. No surcharges will be applied within 30 days of your departure. In view of the financial risk we accept in making this guarantee we will not make any refund as a result of currency movements or reductions in costs. All prices quoted in this brochure based on rates published in the Financial Times of 27/3/90, and are as follows (in foreign currency value per £1):

USA	(Dollar)	1.6140
Spain	(Peseta)	176.60
Portugal	(Escudo)	244
Malta	(Maltese £)	0.5415
Tunisia	(Dinar)	1.4652
Cyprus	(Cyprus £)	0.7810
The Gambia	(Dalasi)	13.4170
Senegal	(French Franc)	9.3175

3. If we change your holiday

We plan your holiday arrangements many months in advance, and though it is unlikely that we will have to make any changes to confirmed arrangements, it does occasionally happen. Most changes are of a minor nature and we will advise you (or your travel agent) at the earliest possible date,if there is time before your departure. Flight timings and Carriers in the brochure are subject to change as a result of airline procedures - please check final details on your tickets. When any major change occurs, provided it does not arise from events beyond our control, you will have the choice of (a) accepting the changed arrangements, (b) purchasing another available holiday from us at its advertised price, or (c) cancelling your holiday. If you choose (a), (b) or (c) we shall pay compensation on the scale shown below. In addition, if you choose (c) we will refund all monies you have paid us. However, please see IMPORTANT NOTE below. We consider a major change to be any of the following changes made before the day of departure: change of departure airport, resort area, outward or return time of departure by more than 12 hours, or substitution of the accommodation you have booked with one of a lower price or official classification. It does not include a flight delay, since flight delay cover is automatically included in our insurance.

Based on period before scheduled departure within which a major change is notified	Compensation per full fare paying passenger (excluding infants)*
More than 56 days	Nil
55-43 days	£5
42-15 days	£10
14-8 days	£15
7-0 days	£20

* NB For children invoiced at reduced rates, compensation will be paid on a pro-rata basis.

IMPORTANT NOTE

Compensation will not be payable if we are forced to cancel or in any way change your holiday due to war, or threat of war, riots, civil commotion, industrial disputes, disaster, terrorist activities, technical or other problems with transportation, closure of airports or seaports, alteration or cancellation of scheduled services or other events outside our control.

4. If we cancel your holiday

We reserve the right, in any circumstance, to cancel your holiday. However, in no case will we cancel your holiday less than 8 weeks before the scheduled departure date, except for the reasons detailed in Conditions (3) and (7). If, due to events beyond our control, we are no longer able to provide the holiday booked, we will return to you all monies paid, or offer you an alternative holiday of comparable standard.

5. Our liability to you

We accept responsibility for the acts and/or omissions of our employees, agents, and suppliers while acting within the scope of or in the course of their employment, agency or contract of supply and we also accept responsibility for any deficiencies in the services we are contractually obliged to provide, or the failure of such services to reach a reasonable standard.

However, we do not accept responsibility in respect of death, bodily injury or illness of, or to the signatory to the contract and/or any other named person on the booking form, except when caused by the negligent acts and/or omissions of our employees, agents suppliers or sub-contractors while acting within the scope of or in the course of their employment, agency, contract of supply or sub-contract.

We shall afford every assistance to a client who through misadventure suffers illness, personal injury or death during the period of the holiday arising out of an activity which neither forms part of the foreign inclusive holiday arrangement nor forms part of an excursion offered through us. Such assistance shall take the form of advice, guidance and initial financial assistance where appropriate, up to a limit of £5,000 per booking form.

Nothing in this condition (5) shall apply where the services in question consist of carriage by air or sea, where our obligations and liabilities are limited in the manner provided by international conventions in respect of air and sea carriers.

6. Customer Service

We do try to ensure that your holiday with us is as enjoyable as possible, but occasionally plans do go wrong. If you have a problem during your holiday it is important that you advise your resort representative who will endeavour to put things right quickly. If your complaint cannot be resolved locally, your representative will ask you to complete a report form, the original of which is for you and a copy will be forwarded to our Head Office. Follow this up within 28 days of your return home by writing to our Customer Services Department at Groundstar House, London Road, Crawley, West Sussex RH10 2TB, giving your original booking reference number and all other relevant information. It is most unlikely that you will have a complaint that cannot be settled amicably between us. However, disputes arising out of, or in connection with, this contract which cannot be amicably settled, may (if you so wish) be referred to arbitration under a special Scheme, which, though devised by arrangement with the Association of British Travel Agents, is administered quite independently by the Chartered Institute of Arbitrators. The Scheme, details of which can be supplied on request, provides for a simple and inexpensive method of arbitration on documents alone with restricted liability on the customer in respect of costs. The Scheme does not apply to claims for an amount greater than £1,500 per person. There is also a limit of £7,500 per booking form. Neither does it apply to claims which are solely or mainly in respect of physical injury or illness or the consequence of such injury or illness. If you elect to seek redress under this Scheme, written notice requesting arbitration under this Scheme must be made within 9 months after the scheduled date of return from holiday (only in exceptional circumstances may it be offered outside this period). Full details are available from the Association of British Travel Agents, 55/57 Newman Street, London W1P 4AH.

YOUR CONTRACT WITH Enterprise

7. Booking and payment

The person in whose name the booking is invoiced acts on behalf of all other persons named on it and becomes primarily responsible to us for all payments in respect of the booking. Your reservation will be made definite upon payment of a deposit of £60 per person (excluding infants under 2 on the date of their return flight). It is a condition of booking that you are adequately insured on your holiday. Unless you or your travel agent have agreed alternative insurance arrangements with us, you will automatically be insured under our policy arranged with Commercial Union and the appropriate premium will be added to your invoice. We allow 7 days from confirmation of the booking for monies to reach us by post. If we do not actually receive the money within this period, our computer will automatically cancel your reservation and we cannot be held responsible if that holiday is subsequently not available. The full balance of the holiday cost must be received by us at least 8 weeks before the departure date - please note that you will not receive a reminder that final payment is due. You should post payment, or pay the balance to your travel agent, 10 weeks before departure to allow the payment to clear to our account, otherwise our computer will cancel your booking, and you would be liable to pay cancellation charges as shown in Condition (9).

Late Bookings. For all bookings made within 8 weeks of departure, the holiday is confirmed as soon as a verbal confirmation is given over the telephone or your travel agent confirms the booking via Viewdata, and therefore if you subsequently cancel your booking, cancellation charges as shown in condition (9) apply. Full payment for the holiday, including insurance premiums, must be made at the time of booking in order to secure the reservation.

8. Changes by you

Cancellation charges are detailed in condition (9). Timescales refer to the date of receipt of your instructions in writing. If you wish to change your booking, the following charges will apply:

Number of days prior to departure		Charge per booking
42 or over		£20
Less than 42	Name change only	£40*
	Any other change:	Cancellation charges as shown in condition (9) will apply.

* Name changes within 42 days on bookings involving scheduled flights incur cancellation charges. If all names change on any booking, then cancellation charges will apply.

If the number of persons booked changes, the holiday price will be recalculated on the basis of the amended party size. Any increase in price per person as a result of a part cancellation eg. underoccupancy, is not a cancellation charge and is not covered by our insurance. A separate cancellation charge will be made against the cancelled booking as detailed in Condition (9), and the booking will be re-invoiced accordingly.

9. Cancellation by you

If you wish to cancel your booking this must be done in writing from the person in whose name the booking is invoiced to the travel agent through whom the booking was made or to the Invoicing Dept, Redwing Holdings Limited, Groundstar House, London Road, Crawley, West Sussex, RH10 2TB, and sent by Recorded Delivery if you have booked with us direct. In the event of cancellation or part cancellation, the following charges will become payable:

CANCELLATION CHARGE (including deposit paid) as % total price excluding insurance premium.

More than 42 days	42-29 days	28-22 days	21-0 days
Deposit only	45%	60%	100%

CANCELLATIONS MUST BE NOTIFIED IN WRITING TO YOUR TRAVEL AGENT OR TO US IF YOU HAVE BOOKED DIRECT, AND COMMENCE FROM DATE RECEIVED BY US

Please note that if the reason for cancellation falls within the terms of the holiday insurance policy, then any such charges will normally be refunded to you by the insurance company. The insurance premium is forfeited on cancellation.

10. Travel Insurance

It is a requirement when booking your holiday, that you accept our special travel insurance unless you or your travel agent have agreed alternative insurance arrangements with us.

11. Brochure Prices

The prices and offers printed in this edition are valid at time of publication in April 1990. We reserve the right to increase or reduce any of these prices or amend these offers at any time after publication and in future editions of this brochure. You will be advised of any change at time of booking.

12. Miscellaneous conditions

Civil Aviation regulations specify that both the outbound and inbound sections of the air ticket must be used. In the event that the outbound flight is not used the person concerned will not be allowed to return on the inbound charter flight.

Should anyone arrive less than 45 minutes before the ticketed departure time admission to the flight is likely to be refused.

Should anyone be refused admission to the flight or to the destination country by the airline or government authority then we are powerless to assist and cannot be held responsible. In all such cases we will not be responsible for any costs involved. When you travel with a carrier, the Conditions of Carriage of that carrier apply, some of which limit or exclude liability. Such conditions are often the subject of international agreements between countries and copies of the Conditions which apply to your holiday/flight/sailing are available for inspection at the travel agent where you book your holiday or any of our offices. This brochure is the responsibility of the tour operator. It is not issued on behalf of, and does not commit, the airline(s) mentioned therein, or any airline whose services are used in the course of the tour(s).

Please note that to be classed as an infant, in accordance with Air Navigation Article 34, a child must be under 2 years of age on the date of their return flight.

This contract is made on the terms of these Booking Conditions which are governed by English law and both parties shall submit to the jurisdiction of the English courts.

IATA

ABTA 95301

OUR COMMITMENT TO YOU explains Enterprise Holidays is operated by a company called Redwing Holdings Limited and confirm their booking conditions are responsible and within the law of the country and will not affect the customer's statutory rights. We have an OFFICE OF FAIR TRADING in the United Kingdom providing certain conditions and businesses are committed to work within those guidelines.

YOUR RESERVATION confirms any instruction to book a holiday must be accompanied by a payment (deposit) – this is a commitment.

OUR POLICY ON SURCHARGES explains about increases that may

CHILDRENS REDUCTIONS

Enterprise offer an excellent choice of family holidays. There are generous child discounts - up to 70% off. Even during high season like Christmas and Easter, you'll still get some discount off our brochure price.

TO QUALIFY

★ Discounts apply only to children aged between 2-11 inclusive on the date of departure.

★ The reductions as detailed in the price panel are applicable to a child when sharing a room or apartment with two full fare paying passengers.

★ These reductions apply to the basic holiday price and flight supplements. Any applicable room or meal supplements (if booked) are then added in full.

ADDITIONAL CHILDREN

Additional children sharing the same room or apartment with two full fare paying passengers qualify for the following reductions:

Departures on or between - All durations

17 Oct - 25 Nov
19 Dec - 31 Dec } 10%
13 Feb - 23 Apr

26 Nov - 18 Dec } 25%
1 Jan - 12 Feb

INFANTS

A charge of £15 is made for infants under two years.

★ Infants must be under two on the date of their return flight.

★ No deposit required.

Subject to availability at your hotel or apartment, we can order a cot to be placed in your room. The price of meals and cots should be paid direct to the hotelier.

YOUR FLIGHT

Flights will be operated by either British Airways, Caledonian Airways or other leading British and foreign airlines.

For example, the following airlines and aircraft types are used: Caledonian Airways (737, 757, L10-11), British Airways (1-11, Airbus, 737, 757, 767, Tri Star, DC10, 747), Air Europe (757, F100, 737), Monarch (737, 757, Airbus), Dan Air (737, 1-11, 727, 146), Air 2000 (757, 737), Britannia (737, 767), British Midland (DC9, 737), Cyprus Airways (Airbus), TAP/Air Atlantis (Airbus, 727, 737), Air Malta (737, Airbus), Iberia (727, 737, DC9, Airbus), Spanair (MD-83), Inter European Airways (737, 757), Nortjet (MD83), Viva (737), Ryanair Europe (1-11), LAC (MD83), Oasis (MD83), Air Sur (MD83), Loganair (146), TEA (737), Air Columbus (727).

Alterations to your flight details sometimes occur for operational reasons and we reserve the right to make these when the need arises. Flights are planned many months in advance, but alterations to these may be made by the IATA scheduling committees which regulate the movements of all international air traffic. Further alterations may be made by airport authorities or airlines later than this. This may mean that timings change from those originally published, and we also reserve the right to substitute airlines wherever necessary. In general, only a minority of holidays are affected in this way, and most changes to the published arrangements are small. Wherever possible, these changes will be advised at the time of booking or as quickly as possible after they occur. When there are major changes, compensation will be paid as detailed in our Booking Conditions.

Timings shown are local times based on the 24 hour system and may change during certain periods according to the individual country's daylight savings time policy. Immigration regulations specify that the names on the passport and tickets held by customers must be the same. During your international flight you can relax with a drink from the duty-free bar, and meals or light refreshments will be served according to the time of day. Duty-free goods will be available for sale (on some flights these may be restricted though).

It is not normally possible to change your return flight arrangements once you are in the resort. This is due to airline regulations over which Enterprise has no control. Should a passenger wish to curtail or extend his or her stay, this is usually possible only by contacting our local representative, purchasing a new air ticket and paying locally. In the event of a passenger having to return earlier, or later, for medical reasons, the procedure is the same except that in the case of insured passengers, they may claim any money paid out from the insurance company.

Please note: It is important to check your flight details and timings upon receipt of your tickets. Last departure date shown is for 7 nights. 14 nights stop one week earlier.
Only 14 night holidays are available before 25 October.
S – denotes a scheduled flight.

KEY TO ABBREVIATIONS

B	bath
sh	shower
balc	balcony
pv	pool view
terr	terrace
ssv	side sea view
sv	sea view
fsv	full sea view
SGL	single
RO	room only
AO	accommodation only
BUNG	bungalow
BB	bed/breakfast
HB	half board
FB	full board
SUP	superior

TENERIFE (Flights to Reina Sofia Airport)

Departure airport & duration of flight	No of nights	Departure day/time	UK arrival day/time	First/last departure	Supplement per person
Gatwick (4 hrs 15)	7/14	Tue 0855	Tue 1805	6 Nov/23 Apr	£0
	7/14	Fri 0800	Fri 1830	19 Oct/19 Apr	£0
	10	Tue 0855	Fri 1830	6 Nov/16 Apr	£0
	11	Fri 0800	Tue 1805	19 Oct/19 Apr	£0
Heathrow (4 hrs 20) S	7/14	Tue 1445	Tue 1330	6 Nov/23 Apr	£58
S	7/14	Sat 1445	Sat 1330	3 Nov/20 Apr	£87
Luton (4 hrs 15)	7/14	Fri 0825	Fri 1735	19 Oct/19 Apr	£0
Bristol (4 hrs 30)	7/14	Fri 1425	Fri 1325	19 Oct/19 Apr	£8

Departure airport & duration of flight	No of nights	Departure day/time	UK arrival day/time	First/last departure	Supplement per person
Birmingham (4hrs 20)	7/14	Fri 1345	Fri 2330	19 Oct/19 Apr	£12
Manchester (4 hrs 30)	7/14	Tue 0855	Tue 1805	6 Nov/23 Apr	£14
	7/14	Fri 0830	Fri 1815	19 Oct/19 Apr	£14
	10	Tue 0855	Fri 1815	6 Nov/16 Apr	£14
	11	Fri 0830	Tue 1805	19 Oct/19 Apr	£14
Newcastle (4 hrs 50)	7/14	Fri 0900	Fri 1830	2 Nov/19 Apr	£22
Glasgow (5 hrs)	7/14	Fri 1005	Fri 2040	19 Oct/19 Apr	£28

TENERIFE: SEE WINTERSUN BROCHURE PAGES 22-25

Accommodation	MONOPOL			FLORIDA			PARQUE SAN ANTONIO			TENEGUIA			OASIS MOREQUE			SANTIAGO			PARADISE PK. APTS.			PARADISE PK. HOTEL		
Holiday Number	BCTFS6648			BCTFS1103			BCTFS1100			BCTFS1102			BCTFS5935			BCTFS1108			BCTFS6616			BCTFS6616		
Prices include	Twin Bath/HB		Child Red	Twin B balc/HB		Child Red	Twin B balc/HB		Child Red	3 persons/studio/BB		Child Red	Twin B balc/BB		Child Red	Twin B balc/BB		Child Red	3 pers/1 bed/4 pers/Duplex/BB		Child Red	Twin B balc/BB		Child Red
No. of Nights	7	14		7	14		7	14		7	14		7	14		7	14		7	14		7	14	
17-24 Oct	—	—	—	—	399	25%	—	481	25%	—	—	—	—	430	25%	—	467	25%	—	—	—	—	—	—
25-31 Oct	—	—	—	295	387	25%	331	504	25%	—	—	—	299	406	25%	320	452	25%	—	—	—	—	—	—
1-11 Nov	327	471	20%	274	359	35%	347	517	35%	249	307	20%	281	377	35%	303	437	35%	297	405	35%	315	443	35%
12-18 Nov	323	456	20%	255	344	35%	333	500	35%	226	290	20%	264	367	35%	293	419	35%	280	390	35%	297	426	35%
19-25 Nov	304	450	25%	244	338	45%	321	492	45%	217	282	25%	250	357	45%	279	412	45%	264	384	45%	281	419	45%
26 Nov-11 Dec	280	425	30%	219	305	55%	297	467	55%	192	257	30%	226	331	55%	255	386	55%	239	362	55%	252	397	55%
12-18 Dec	276	512	30%	204	544	55%	292	723	55%	187	377	30%	217	507	55%	252	621	55%	235	653	55%	252	590	55%
19-24 Dec	423	602	10%	401	619	10%	507	837	10%	307	387	10%	407	611	10%	447	687	10%	477	744	10%	492	772	10%
25-31 Dec	407	572	10%	419	559	10%	532	742	10%	289	362	10%	426	541	10%	447	606	10%	480	619	10%	494	650	10%
1-24 Jan	317	487	30%	281	428	55%	344	544	55%	222	306	30%	264	389	55%	289	437	55%	289	445	55%	307	481	55%
25 Jan-12 Feb	331	494	25%	292	434	45%	352	547	45%	237	312	25%	281	415	45%	307	465	45%	302	454	45%	321	490	45%
13-20 Feb	360	521	15%	303	442	25%	382	575	25%	267	343	15%	318	443	25%	335	494	25%	330	475	25%	349	514	25%
21 Feb-9 Mar	344	505	20%	305	444	35%	366	559	35%	250	324	20%	299	430	35%	326	481	35%	317	465	35%	335	501	35%
10-16 Mar	346	507	20%	307	447	35%	367	566	35%	252	327	20%	301	432	35%	327	482	35%	319	467	35%	337	502	35%
17-23 Mar	349	532	20%	311	454	35%	377	607	35%	257	369	20%	302	443	35%	331	507	35%	322	486	35%	340	507	35%
24-31 Mar	372	521	10%	319	425	10%	407	542	10%	292	357	10%	332	421	10%	357	470	10%	337	432	10%	367	475	10%
1-13 Apr	349	507	15%	274	377	25%	312	439	25%	257	327	15%	274	371	25%	302	426	25%	282	384	25%	297	419	25%
14-23 Apr	344	502	15%	269	372	25%	302	429	25%	257	320	15%	267	367	25%	297	421	25%	275	377	25%	292	414	25%

Supplements per person/per unused bed per night	Rooms	+ balc £1.25 SGL Bath £1.25 (p.p.p.n.)	SGL Bath £12.25 (p.p.p.n.)	SGL B balc £10.50 (p.p.p.n.)	Per unused bed per night £11	+ SV £2 SGL B balc £7 (p.p.p.n.)	SUP twin £3.50 SGL B balc £7.50 (p.p.p.n.)	Per unused bed per night £20 (Duplex); £22 (1 bed)	
	Meals	—	FB £4	FB £3.50	—	HB £6	HB £6.75	HB £8.75; FB £12 (p.p.p.n.)	HB £8.75; FB £12

LONG STAYS – DEPS. ON OR BETWEEN

	MONOPOL	FLORIDA	PARQUE SAN ANTONIO	TENEGUIA	OASIS MOREQUE			
17 Oct-25 Nov & 10-16 Mar & 1-23 Apr	£154	£102	—	£74	£116	—	—	—
26 Nov-11 Dec	£190	£212	—	£85	£199	—	—	—
1 Jan-9 Mar & 17-31 Mar	£172	£151	—	£79	£139	—	—	—

TENERIFE: SEE WINTERSUN BROCHURE PAGES 26-27

Accommodation	CLUB BONANZA					PARQUE DE LA PAZ					COLON II			CLUB PARAISO		
Holiday Number	BCTFS1113					BCTFS1114					BCTFS5501B			BCTFS1112		
Prices include	2 pers/studio/4 pers/1 bed/AO				Child Red	4 pers/1 bed/AO				Child Red	2 pers/studio/3 pers/1 bed/AO		Child Red	3 pers/studio/4 pers/1 bed/AO		Child Red
No. of Nights	7	10	11	14		7	10	11	14		7	14		7	14	
17-24 Oct	—	—	—	239	15%	—	—	—	261	15%	—	—	—	—	307	25%
25-31 Oct	207	—	—	249	15%	217	—	—	264	15%	—	—	—	240	295	25%
1-11 Nov	210	222	227	248	20%	214	225	229	257	20%	260	337	20%	217	281	35%
12-18 Nov	202	217	219	236	20%	207	219	225	242	20%	243	322	20%	213	266	35%
19-25 Nov	186	199	205	229	25%	191	204	209	236	25%	231	316	25%	201	256	45%
26 Nov-11 Dec	162	176	181	202	30%	167	179	185	210	30%	206	289	30%	176	229	55%
12-18 Dec	157	229	—	329	30%	162	219	—	327	30%	201	367	30%	173	367	55%
19-24 Dec	279	—	296	339	10%	287	—	294	345	10%	307	397	10%	302	376	10%
25-31 Dec	268	—	285	316	10%	277	—	285	322	10%	227	374	10%	291	352	10%
1-24 Jan	191	209	215	250	30%	197	215	223	259	30%	225	316	30%	205	271	55%
25 Jan-12 Feb	201	216	221	251	25%	211	228	233	267	25%	240	325	25%	217	280	45%
13-20 Feb	222	226	231	269	15%	237	242	247	293	15%	266	349	15%	245	307	25%
21 Feb-9 Mar	209	228	233	256	20%	224	244	251	277	20%	253	336	20%	232	295	35%
10-16 Mar	213	229	235	257	20%	227	246	253	281	20%	255	337	20%	235	297	35%
17-23 Mar	216	232	237	286	20%	230	248	255	307	20%	259	384	20%	237	340	35%
24-31 Mar	239	249	249	272	10%	255	256	261	286	10%	296	373	10%	279	304	10%
1-13 Apr	214	229	235	254	15%	217	228	234	254	15%	259	337	15%	232	277	25%
14-23 Apr	208	224	229	245	15%	211	223	229	247	15%	252	267		222	267	25%

Supplements per unused bed per night	Rooms	£11 (Studio); £10 (1 bed)	£8.50	£14.50 (Studio); £12 (1 bed) NB £5.50 Supp per studio per nt.	£9.50 (Studio); £8.50 (1 bed)
	Meals	B'fast £2.75; HB £6.75 (p.p.p.n.)	—	BB £2.75; HB £9.50 (p.p.p.n.)	

LONG STAYS – DEPS. ON OR BETWEEN

	CLUB BONANZA	PARQUE DE LA PAZ	COLON II	CLUB PARAISO
17 Oct-25 Nov & 10-16 Mar & 1-23 Apr	—	—	—	£63
26 Nov-11 Dec	—	—	—	£83
1 Jan-9 Mar & 17-31 Mar	—	—	—	£69

NEW! 10 & 11 NIGHT HOLIDAYS TO TENERIFE

RESERVATIONS HELP LINE: 0293 519151   TAILOR MADES: 0293 612122
AGENTS VIEWDATA: ISTEL - 59#   FASTRAK SUN   PRESTEL *RV2#

Enterprise

occur after the brochure has been printed. Changes in exchange rates and the increase in the cost of fuel could affect the cost of the holiday. The exchange rates used at each destination have been given.

IF WE CHANGE YOUR HOLIDAY explains the conditions regarding cancellation and compensation made by the tour operator.

IF WE CANCEL YOUR HOLIDAY – occasionally there are reasons beyond the tour operator's control for cancelling the holiday.

OUR LIABILITY TO YOU confirms the responsibilities accepted by the tour operator.

CUSTOMER SERVICE explains the complaints procedure.

BOOKING AND PAYMENT explains confirmation of the holiday, the deposit, and late bookings (reservations made within 8 weeks of departure).

CHANGES BY YOU explains the fee charged for the customer changing his/her mind!

CANCELLATION BY YOU clearly explains the cancellation charges.

TRAVEL INSURANCE is compulsory: this is to prevent problems at a later date. The tour operator can be caused great problems if the client should suffer an illness or loss whilst on holiday and is not insured and does not have sufficient funds to pay for treatment, for example. Therefore to safeguard everyone's interests, holiday insurance is mandatory.

BROCHURE PRICES explains Enterprise have the right to change the prices but will advise the client at time of booking.

MISCELLANEOUS CONDITIONS refers mainly to regulations concerning the aviation industry.

Take your time, read and digest, then try to find the answer to the following questions:

(a) Today is 14 October. Mr Jimain and family are due to depart for their holiday on 3 November. Could they be asked to pay a surcharge increase?
(b) The Kamino family of four adults has booked a holiday with a basic cost of £450.00 per person, and has now been advised of a 10 per cent surcharge increase. (i) give the total amount that has to be paid. (ii) Can the Kamino family decline to pay, cancel the holiday and receive a full refund?
(c) Give the amount to be paid as deposit to secure the booking.
(d) Miss Sanchez and friends are due to depart on their holiday on 24 October. When should the balance be paid?
(e) Today is 20 September. Mr James has decided to cancel his holiday and was due to travel on 7 October. What will be the cancellation charges?

Flight details and holiday costs

Please study the extracts from the Enterprise brochure concerning flights and the tariff for holidays to Tenerife.

Here are a few guidelines. The airports of departure are Gatwick, Heathrow, Luton, Bristol, Birmingham, Manchester, Newcastle and Glasgow. The airport in Tenerife is called Reina Sofia, and the flight takes 4 hours 15 minutes. The times, dates and supplement charges are given. You will notice that for departures from Heathrow there is a supplement of £58.00 for a Tuesday departure and £87.00 for a Saturday departure. In addition, for Heathrow the letter S in heavy print denotes that a scheduled flight is used, not a charter flight as from the other airports.

Take your time; read the extracts carefully; remember to be sure about per person or per night charges; think about it; then check the following example:

Booking Form — Enterprise WINTERSUN

TO BE RETAINED BY TRAVEL AGENT

HOLIDAY DETAILS

Departure date	Departure Airport	Country/Island	Option No:
No of nights	Destination Airport	Resort	Holiday No:

ACCOMMODATION DETAILS

Hotel/Apartment/Villa	
Two centre: 2nd Resort	2nd Hotel/Apartment/Villa

PASSENGER DETAILS

Room Type	Mr/ Ms	Initial	Surname	Age if under 12	✓ if cot required	Board basis	Extra facilities	Infants @ £15 each	Total No. in Party

CAR HIRE	SPECIAL OFFERS		OTHER REQUESTS
Group:	Singles Holidays	☐	
Resort:	3 weeks for price of 2	☐	
From: To:	Special board (specify)	☐	
Pickup Point	Other (specify)		

ROOM TYPE CODE

S - Single   Q - Quad
TW - Twin   SU - Suite
TR - Triple   APT - Apartment

BOARD TYPE CODE

FB - Full board   HB - Half board
BB - Bed & Breakfast
AO - Accommodation only
All party members must take the same
board arrangements

EXTRA FACILITIES CODE

BAL - Balcony   SR - Superior room
B - Bath   MB - Main building
SV- Sea view   Other - (Please Specify)

PAYMENT DETAILS

Initial Payment Enclosed £

(Full payment, including insurance premium, if within 8 weeks of departure).

Holiday deposit £60 per person (excluding infants). Holiday insurance is arranged automatically unless you or your travel agent have agreed alternative insurance arrangements with us and the appropriate premium will be added to your invoice. Infants (age 2 or under on date of return) pay a standard £15 holiday charge and are insured free. For details of premium and cover, see brochure page 107.

I certify, on behalf of the person(s) included on this form, by whom I am authorised to make this booking, that I/we have read and agree to the Booking Conditions in the above-named brochure, and the conditions of insurance, and that my/our booking is made and is subject to those conditions and that I am over 18 years of age.

Signature   **Date**
(of lead name)

ENTERPRISE WINTERSUN
Groundstar House, London Road, Crawley, West Sussex, RH10 2TB.

Reservation Help Line: (0293) 519151   Switchboard: (0293) 560777
Group Bookings: (0293) 517866   Tailormade Bookings: (0293) 612122
Telex: 878791 WING G Fax: (0293) 25225

Agents Viewdata
ISTEL –59# FASTRAK SUN PRESTEL ∗RV2#

TRAVEL AGENT'S STAMP

All holidays in this brochure are operated by Redwing Holdings Ltd., trading as Enterprise Holidays, Registered in England No. 2357936, and subject to availability.

IATA   ABTA   ABTA 95301

Two adults are to depart from Birmingham on Friday 22 November, staying 14 nights at the Florida Hotel on a half board basis. The costs are as follows:

Basic cost £338.00 × 2	£676.00
Supplement for Birmingham £12.00 × 2	24.00
	£700.00

Insurance premium is to be added.

Exercise 2

Please study the extracts from the Enterprise brochure again, and then calculate the costs for the following holiday:

Two adults, two children ages 7 and 9 years plus an infant all sharing the parents' room, are to depart from Gatwick on Tuesday 4 April, staying at the Monopol Hotel on a half board basis for 7 nights. The clients would like a balcony.

Exercise 3

Using the Enterprise brochure extracts in this chapter, answer the following:
(a) Name the currency used in Spain.
(b) What should be the first step to take for a client dissatisfied with the hotel accommodation on arrival at the resort?
(c) Give the maximum age for a person classed as an infant.
(d) Give the day of departure for a flight from Glasgow to Tenerife.
(e) You have made a reservation on your computer (option number TNR 270390) for Mr R. Armstrong and Mrs S. Armstrong. Calculate the cost for accommodation at the Club Paraiso, Playa de las Americas, for a studio apartment with breakfast (BB) departing from Newcastle on Friday 27 March for 14 nights. The cost is to include insurance at £18.00 per person.
(f) When you have calculated the cost, decide the amount to be collected from your client. Today is 2 February.
(g) Complete the booking form. Supply the information requested in each 'box'. An example of a completed booking form can be found in Chapter 3. Please study that booking form, if necessary, before checking the answers at the back of the book.

Making a reservation

This can be done either by telephoning Enterprise Holidays or by calling up the details on your computer, checking the availability and making the reservation. You will need the following information at hand:

> names of passengers;
> accommodation required;
> holiday number (found in brochure);
> number of nights;
> name of departure/arrival airport;
> name of resort;
> ages of any children/infants;
> any special requests.

Enterprise will confirm the reservation by sending a confirmation/invoice to your agency. When this is received it must be checked by you to ensure that the details are as booked. It should then be forwarded to your clients advising them when to pay the balance. If full payment has been collected, the confirmation/invoice will reflect this. Tickets will be sent to your agency approximately two weeks before the passengers are due to travel. The reason tickets are not issued months in advance is because there could be changes in flight times etc. and a tour operator would have to reissue perhaps 500 tickets – a waste of time and money!

Conclusions

Let's just go through the procedure once again:

1　Read the tour operators' brochures from cover to cover; get to know the destinations and accommodation well.
2　Check the surcharges and supplements.
3　Understand the booking conditions.
4　Help your client with information on the resort.
5　Check visa and health requirements.
6　Understand the cancellation charges
7　Have all the details ready before making the booking.
8　Be sure the details are correct: clients' names spelt correctly, ages of children, special requests and any extra payments required.
9　Do try alternatives if the clients' first choice is not available.

Don't forget late bookings. Rather than send an aircraft on its way with perhaps 50 per cent occupancy, a tour operator will have special last-minute reductions to the package holiday prices to encourage sales. There are many tourists who rely on these reductions; they are prepared to accept the dates, destinations and accommodation that are available at short notice. Many travel agents display these holiday details in their windows, and they must be kept up to date.

Indeed, travel agents must always keep up to date with special offers, incentives, improved standards – everything and anything to do with travel. It is embarrassing when a client knows more about recent changes than we do; we should be advising them! As you continue through the chapters of this book you will realize that there are many situations that can be embarrassing. The travel industry reminds me of a minefield: we have to tread very carefully to avoid an explosion. Let's hope we manage to do that together!

Group travel

We first briefly consider conferences and incentive travel. A large part of the work involved will be in organizing arrangements for your clients travelling as part of a group, and we will discuss arranging group tours in a moment.

Conferences

We are always looking for new, interesting and comfortable venues for conferences, trade fairs, exhibitions and the like. The business traveller needs space, amenities such as meeting rooms, secretarial services, relaxation facilities such as health suites, and easy access to surrounding areas. Many articles are written in newspapers, magazines and travel trade journals to help keep us up to date with new locations. Many countries and pleasant islands have studied this market and have developed this side of tourism, offering all the amenities and at very competitive rates. The *Travel Trade Directory* will list tour operators who specialize in this operation and offer a good service. The benefits for the client to attend trade fairs and conferences is to exchange ideas, meet other business colleagues and keep up to date, and hopefully his own company will benefit from the trip.

Incentive travel

What is incentive travel, and what are the benefits? This is travel offered to employees as a reward for good results in their work.

Why should a holiday given as a prize have more motivating power than rewarding the employee with a gift of cash? First, the employee likely to respond to this offer enjoys a challenge, welcomes competition, and has a position in a company that demands personal achievement. If the employee is offered cash as a reward it can be reduced by taxation deductions, spent on mundane items at home, or paid quietly into the bank; none of this is very exciting. A free trip to somewhere the employee would never have thought of holidaying, with colleagues from work whose company is enjoyed but is not usually shared out of office hours, and time allowed for the trip that doesn't come out of the annual leave, can add a sparkle to the award. The opportunity to take one's family, together with the prestige of being offered an exotic trip for achieving results, make incentive travel very attractive. We said earlier that many travel agencies are multipurpose often organizing their own tours, and it is possible you would be involved in this type of work.

Planning a group tour

How would we go about organizing group travel? We would begin with market research. Who will be travelling as a group – our business clients? Perhaps a company has requested us to organize a three-day conference for 20 executives on the island of Majorca. Perhaps we have contacted all the local sports clubs and can see a need for a tennis holiday in Portugal; here is a special interest.

Let's imagine we have been asked to organize a 21 day tour to America departing from London for employees of one of our business account companies as an incentive holiday.

We would need to do a lot of research – find out information – on the clients themselves: what they would like to do; whether business is to be mixed with the pleasure trip; the number of employees participating; how many rooms are required; and the amenities requested. We would need to research the airline to be used, the group air fare to be charged, the places to be visited, the standard and location of the hotels, the climate, the health requirements and the visa regulations. Absolutely *everything* we need to know about the trip has to be researched. When planning the itinerary, study the Atlas and arrange each stop in the most logical order.

The next step is to set up contracts with the principals in the US – the hoteliers, the airline companies and the tour operators (for sight-seeing tours). We would establish the cost of the services and the amount of commission our agency would receive. As we are planning travel arrangements for a group of tourists travelling together, we can expect to benefit from cheaper tariffs for every service used.

We need to establish the cost of the tour, and we will be working in two currencies, US dollars and UK pounds. We may like to have a brochure printed giving details of the tour and making it personalized. (We will not have to advertise the holiday as it is a gift to the employees of a particular company.) We will have to organize the documentation, and this may mean reshuffling staff at our own agency to help with the extra work involved.

So! We will say that we have done our research, set up contracts with the principals, and booked the flights, city tours, hotels and transfers as shown on the accompanying itinerary.

Itinerary for 21 day tour to United States

Day 1	London	0830	Check in at London airport terminal 3
		0955	Departure by Transworld Airlines flight TW709
		1200	Arrive New York. Transfer to Tulip Hotel
Day 2	New York	0930	City sight-seeing tour. Afternoon and evening free
Day 3	New York	1900	Day at leisure. Evening excursion to theatre followed by dinner
Day 4	Washington	0930	Full day tour to Washington
Day 5	New York		At leisure
Day 6	Miami	0630	Transfer to airport to board Transworld Airlines flight TW 17 to Miami
		0845	Depart New York
		1200	Arrive Miami. Transfer to Sheraton Hotel
Day 7	Miami		At leisure
Day 8	Miami	0930	Depart for full day tour to Everglades National Park
Day 9	New Orleans	1200	Transfer to airport to board American Airlines flight AA 1296 to New Orleans
		1405	Depart Miami
		1515	Arrive New Orleans. Transfer to Hotel Trust House Forte
Day 10	New Orleans		Enjoy Mardi Gras (own arrangements)

Day 11	New Orleans	1900	Day at leisure. Evening jazz concert
Day 12	Los Angeles	1700	Day at leisure. Transfer from hotel to airport to board Continental Airlines flight CO 835 to Los Angeles
		1825	Depart New Orleans
		2035	Arrive Los Angeles. Transfer to Hotel Barron
Day 13	Los Angeles	0930	City tour including full day visit to Universal Studios, Beverly Hills and Hollywood
Day 14	Los Angeles	0930	Full day tour of Disneyland
Day 15	Los Angeles		At leisure
Day 16	San Francisco	1600	At leisure. Transfer from hotel to airport to board United Airways flight UA1040 to San Francisco
		1730	Depart Los Angeles
		1838	Arrive San Francisco. Transfer to Hotel Hollywood Roosevelt
Day 17	San Francisco	0930	Morning tour of city. Afternoon at leisure
		1900	Evening tour of Chinatown
Day 18	San Francisco	0930	Visit to Fisherman's Wharf, morning tour
Day 19	San Francisco		At leisure
Day 20	San Francisco	1630	Morning at leisure. Transfer from hotel to airport to board British Airways flight BA 286 for London
		1820	Depart San Francisco
Day 21	London	1230	Arrive London

Costing a group tour

We have established the itinerary, the contracts with the principals, the cost of each service included in the tour, the net costs, (these are the costs *after* deductions i.e. commission earned) the gross costs, (these are costs *before* deductions) the commission earned on each service and the bank rate of exchange (remember, we said we would be working in US dollars and UK pounds). We can now calculate the cost of this tour on a per person basis.

Please study the information you have been given on the cost of each item on the costing sheet. The sheet will help to put your thoughts in order and make calculations clear and straightforward.

The rate of exchange we will use is US$1.82 to UK£1.00.

We will say that this trip involves two air fares. The first is for the journey from London to New York and from San Francisco to London; the cost is £584.00. The second fare is a special fare enabling tourists to travel around the USA at a reduced rate; the routing is New York, Miami, New Orleans, Los Angeles and San Francisco, and the cost is $420.00. The cost of the transfers between airports and hotels is $20.00 per transfer.

The tour costs are: for a half day tour $20.00; for a full day tour $40.00; and for an evening excursion $50.00.

Description	Fare/rate (US$, UK£)	Total (US$)	Gross (UK£)	Commission (%)	(UK£)	Net (UK£)
Transportation						
Air:						
London/New York/San Francisco						
London	£584.00		584.00	9	52.56	531.44
New York/Miami/New Orleans						
Los Angeles/San Francisco	$420.00		230.76	9	20.76	210.00
Transfers (10)	$ 20.00	200.00	109.89	10	10.98	98.91
Tours						
Half day (3)	$ 20.00	60.00	32.96	10	3.29	29.67
Full day (4)	$ 40.00	160.00	87.91	10	8.79	79.12
Evening (3)	$ 50.00	150.00	82.41	10	8.24	74.17
Accommodation (nights)						
Tulip (5)	$ 40.00	200.00	109.89	8	8.79	101.10
Sheraton (3)	$ 65.00	195.00	107.14	8	8.57	98.57
Trust House (3)	$ 88.00	264.00	145.05	8	11.60	133.45
Barron (4)	$ 85.00	340.00	186.81	8	14.94	171.87
Roosevelt (4)	$ 77.00	308.00	169.23	8	13.53	155.70
Insurance						
Atlas	£ 40.00		40.00	35	14.00	26.00
		$1897.00	£1886.05		£176.05	£1710.00
				Mark-up 15%	£256.50	256.60
				Profit	£432.55	£1966.50 retail selling price

The accommodation costs per night are as follows:

Tulip Hotel	$40.00
Sheraton Hotel	$65.00
Trust House Forte	$88.00
Barron Hotel	$85.00
Hollywood Roosevelt USD	$77.00

The commission earned is: air 9 per cent; transfers 10 per cent; tours 10 per cent; hotels 8 per cent. We also include travel insurance (Atlas Insurance) at £40.00, with commission earned 35 per cent.

Please study the costing sheet carefully. We are going to calculate this step by step. The secret of accuracy is to read the itinerary *thoroughly*: take your time, and read this section again if you are not really clear.

You will see that on the costing sheet the first column is headed 'Description'. Here we enter the products being used. The travel arrangements comprise flight tickets, transfers between airport and hotels, tours in America, and hotel accommodation. These are listed with the numbers of transfers, tours, and nights at each hotel. So immediately we need to read the itinerary again and count those numbers of transfers, tours and nights at each hotel. Please check the totals given on the costing sheet.

The next column has the heading 'Fare/rate'. In this column we enter the actual cost. Note that fares and rates are quoted in the relevant currency. The air fare originating in the UK has been quoted in sterling (UK£). The air fare for the journey commencing in New York has been quoted in US dollars (US$). As this is a tour of the USA, most of the items are given in US dollars.

The third column is headed 'Total', and here we add the total when necessary. Check the transfers. The cost of one transfer is $20.00; we have 10 transfers, so $20.00 × 10 = $200.00. Now look at the accommodation. We have booked four nights accommodation at the Barron Hotel; the cost for one night is $85.00, so $85.00 × 4 = $340.00.

The next column is headed 'Gross (UK£)'; this means the full amount in sterling. We have arrived at these totals by converting the dollar amounts into pounds. The rate of exchange was given as $1.82 to £1.00. Our first converted entry is the air ticket for the journey within the USA; it costs $420, so divide by the rate of exchange (1.82) to give £230.76. Let's try another one: five nights at the Tulip Hotel cost $200, so divide by the rate of exchange to give £109.89.

The next column is headed 'Commission'. Here we deduct the amount of commission we will earn from each transaction. Look through the column and compare the totals earned.

The final column is 'Net (UK£)'; this is the total after the commission has been deducted.

We then total the columns. We are able to see at a glance the amount of money leaving the country, the amount earned on each item and the amount of profit we hope to make on this particular group tour.

To the net total we add a 15 per cent mark-up; this means profit margin. We would sell this tour at the total of £1966.50. The client pays the *net* costs plus the mark-up total. We can add together the mark-up and the commission earned, making a total of £432.55. This may seem a lot of profit, but expenses have to be deducted from that total: telephone bills, heating, electricity, taxes, rents, stationery, advertising when appropriate, research, brochure production, staff salaries and many more.

As you are organizing the tour, you would not have to keep to a 15 per cent mark-up; this could be adjusted, depending on the tariff your competitors are using for tours to the USA. Are their itineraries more interesting? Is the accommodation used on your tour superior? Are competitors including more sight-seeing tours and excursions? Are they gaining more favourable rates with the principals? There are many reasons why similar tours can have a wide range of tariffs.

Summary of group tour organization

Let's work our way once again through the jobs to be done when organizing a group tour. There is of course a great deal more to learn about tour operating. In this chapter the aim has been to give you the basic knowledge required when starting your travel agency career.

1 Research: obtain as much information as possible.
2 Decide on dates and itinerary.
3 Negotiate with principals.
4 Establish contracts with the principals.
5 Calculate the selling price.
6 Have brochure printed.
7 Promote the tour (in this case a cocktail party could be held for the fortunate winners of the incentive travel award).

8   Issue travel documents (air tickets, hotel vouchers etc.), making sure all documents are accurate and up to date.

Exercise 4

Recap by checking again through the itinerary and calculations for the US tour. Then try calculating the costs for a tour to Holland with the following itinerary and details. Draw up a table similar to that for the US tour.

Day 1	Stansted	1700	Depart on flight UK 714
		1800	Arrive Amsterdam. Transfer to Hotel Amber
Day 2	Amsterdam	0900	City sight-seeing tour (half day) visiting Rijks Museum and diamond works. Afternoon at leisure. Evening tour: candlelight dinner on canal cruise
Day 3	Amsterdam	0930	Full day tour visiting fishing village of Marken. A cheese market and flower market. Evening excursion to Indonesian restaurant
Day 4	Amsterdam	2000	Day at leisure. Evening excursion to Dutch restaurant for a meal followed by folk dancing
Day 5	Amsterdam	1700	Day at leisure. Transfer from Hotel Amber to airport
		1900	Depart Amsterdam
		2000	Arrive Stansted

Air fare Stansted/Amsterdam/Stansted UK £120.00 return
Hotel Amber guilder/florin (DFL) 92.00 per person per night
Tours: half day DFL 64.50; full day DFL 90.00; evening DFL 170.00
All transfers DFL 25.00 per transfer
Atlas Insurance UK£17.00 per person
Commission rates: airline ticket 9 per cent; transfers 10 per cent; hotel accommodation 8 per cent; all tours 10 per cent; insurance 30 per cent
Mark-up for this tour 15 per cent
Rate of exchange: DFL 3.20 to UK£1

Assignment 1: getting to know your package tour brochure

Collect six different package tour brochures. Analyse and compare the brochures in respect of the following topics, and write a report on your findings:

1   Descriptions of hotels.
2   Descriptions of resorts.
3   Simplicity in presentation.
4   Child reductions.
5   Choice of airports.

6 Costs for *exactly* the same holiday.
7 Insurance details and value for money.

Assignment 2: taken from an ICM Examination Paper

Jim Waterman has the opportunity to organize a tour to America for the local Golf Club. Outline the steps he must take to make his tour successful.

When writing an ABTA/CITY and GUILDS COTAC level one examination on the subject of package holidays a tour brochure is provided and you would be requested to calculate the cost of specific holidays, provide flight information, and complete a booking form.

You would be expected to be proficient in the following tasks, so for this assignment, please collect various operators' brochures relating to package holidays and follow the ABTA requirements.

1 Know basic travel geography concerning the main resorts and tourist attractions in the area outlined in the brochures of your choice.
2 Explain the procedure for making reservations.
3 Explain the operator's regulations and requirements and process a booking in accordance with them.

Assignment 3

By using the SHORT GLOSSARY OF TERMS, explain the following questions taken from the IATA/UFTAA TRAVEL AGENTS' DIPLOMA COURSE (STANDARD LEVEL):

1 What is a tour?
2 Describe the role of the TOUR OPERATOR: SUPPLIER: RETAIL AGENT.
3 Explain the meaning of incentive travel and why it can have a higher motivating power than cash.
4 Explain the expenses to be deducted from the 'mark up' earned when arranging your own group tour.

3 Holiday centres and special interest holidays

Summary

In this chapter we are going to discuss:

- the development of Holiday Centres;
- a description of Holiday Centres today;
- considerations for choosing a centre;
- learning to read the Butlins' brochure;
- costing a holiday;
- making a reservation;
- travellers with a common interest – Special Interest Holidays;
- exercises and assignments to complete.

What is a holiday centre?

There are many different types of holiday centre in almost every corner of the world. Each offers different kinds of entertainment and accommodation (some are non-residential), but all answer the needs of the holiday-maker or excursionist. Theme parks have been established for many years, and their growth, popularity and originality are going from strength to strength as more inventive sports and entertainments are developed.

Let's take a quick look into the past to see how holiday centres have developed in the United Kingdom. The first holiday centres were opened in the 1930s by Butlins and Warners because there was a need for all-weather entertainment complexes. Can you imagine families spending a holiday by the seaside in Britain with its unpredictable summer weather, and walking around in the wet and cold with nowhere to go? That's not much of a holiday! So the first all-weather entertainment centre was opened by Bill Butlin at Skegness in 1936. World War II interrupted the growth of the holiday centres; in fact they were taken over by the troops during the war and used as training centres.

After the war, families wanted to be together on holiday. This is when holiday centres became very popular; they reflected the lifestyle of the British people at that time. They needed good value for money; something to interest all members of the family, whatever their ages; and no worries, with everything included in the one price. During the 1950s and 1960s the holiday centres were very basic, large and organized. There have been vast changes since then, which mainly began in the 1970s and are still going strong! Millions of pounds are invested every year in improving the holiday centres.

Accommodation   There is now a great choice of very comfortable and pleasant accommodation ranging from deluxe caravans to suites.

Catering   Holiday centres now offer full board, half board or self-catering. There are varied menus from which to choose the meals, and restaurants provide a wide catering choice throughout the day and evening.

Entertainments   These really have kept up to date with all that children and adults alike are seeking.

Sports facilities   The very latest equipment and a wide variety of sports are available.

Location   Many of the holiday centres are surrounded by acres of beautiful gardens and countryside, and are situated in interesting areas for sightseeing trips.

Staff training   Excellent training schemes are offered to employees as the demands and expectations of the public have increased. The results of the in-depth training are evident as the centres become increasingly more sophisticated.

Helping the clients

There are many holiday centres from which to choose. So how do you help your clients to choose the *right* one? It means putting on those shoes again! Find out your clients' likes and dislikes; discover what they are really looking for when they go on holiday.

Information on holiday centres can be obtained from tourist offices throughout the world, and many holiday centre companies will send their own manuals to a travel agency. Dare we say it again? Collect as many brochures as possible and take them home to *read*!

What are the considerations?

Size of centre   There is a great choice. Some centres hold just a few hundred guests and are managed by a family. Others are enormous, accommodating 16,000 to 17,000 guests, making a village seem more like a town. The larger the holiday centre, the more facilities are offered: more choice, more people, more noise pollution! Therefore check to see what your clients are really seeking – a large lively centre or a small quiet location.

Age group   If your clients are elderly, would they like to stay at an adults-only centre? This is possible, as there are several catering for adults only. If your clients are young and looking for lots of nightlife and sports facilities, it is equally easy to accommodate them.

Location   Is the location important? In which part of the country would your clients like to stay?

Accommodation   Are your clients looking for self-catering or full board? What kind of accommodation is required?

Special reductions   Is cost important to your clients? Compare prices and the many special reductions available: are they applicable to your clients' circumstances?

Using a brochure: Butlin's

It would be impossible to study every brochure during the course of this book. Although each has its own style, they all give basically the same information. We are going to study the Butlin's brochure.

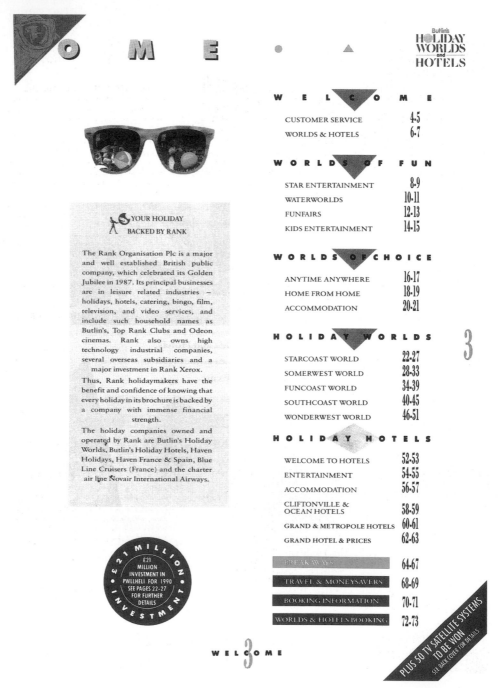

Butlin's HOLIDAY WORLDS and HOTELS

YOUR HOLIDAY BACKED BY RANK

The Rank Organisation Plc is a major and well established British public company, which celebrated its Golden Jubilee in 1987. Its principal businesses are in leisure related industries – holidays, hotels, catering, bingo, film, television, and video services, and include such household names as Butlin's, Top Rank Clubs and Odeon cinemas. Rank also owns high technology industrial companies, several overseas subsidiaries and a major investment in Rank Xerox.

Thus, Rank holidaymakers have the benefit and confidence of knowing that every holiday in its brochure is backed by a company with immense financial strength.

The holiday companies owned and operated by Rank are Butlin's Holiday Worlds, Butlin's Holiday Hotels, Haven Holidays, Haven France & Spain, Blue Line Cruisers (France) and the charter air line Novair International Airways.

£21 MILLION INVESTMENT IN PWLLHELI FOR 1990 SEE PAGES 22-27 FOR FURTHER DETAILS

WELCOME

CUSTOMER SERVICE	4-5
WORLDS & HOTELS	6-7

WORLDS OF FUN

STAR ENTERTAINMENT	8-9
WATERWORLDS	10-11
FUNFAIRS	12-13
KIDS ENTERTAINMENT	14-15

WORLDS OF CHOICE

ANYTIME ANYWHERE	16-17
HOME FROM HOME	18-19
ACCOMMODATION	20-21

HOLIDAY WORLDS

STARCOAST WORLD	22-27
SOMERWEST WORLD	28-33
FUNCOAST WORLD	34-39
SOUTHCOAST WORLD	40-45
WONDERWEST WORLD	46-51

HOLIDAY HOTELS

WELCOME TO HOTELS	52-53
ENTERTAINMENT	54-55
ACCOMMODATION	56-57
CLIFTONVILLE & OCEAN HOTELS	58-59
GRAND & METROPOLE HOTELS	60-61
GRAND HOTEL & PRICES	62-63
BREAKAWAYS	64-67
TRAVEL & MONEYSAVERS	68-69
BOOKING INFORMATION	70-71
WORLDS & HOTELS BOOKING	72-73

3

PLUS 50 TV SATELLITE SYSTEMS TO BE WON
SEE BACK COVER FOR DETAILS

WELCOME 3

Please look at the contents page; this is the best way to find just the information you need. Then read the information given on Starcoast World, which is in Pwllheli, North Wales. You will read that £21 million is being spent on this particular holiday centre, and the brochure explains how it will be spent.

The new Bardsey Village will be similar to Burns Village at Wonderwest World.

A great new foodcourt is being built similar to The Plaza at Southcoast World.

CHOICE

STARCOAST WORLD is the latest Butlin's investment story, completing the Holiday Worlds family. It will offer an unbeatable combination of spectacular holiday fun in beautiful surrounds.

A massive **£21 MILLION** will have been spent by the Spring of 1990 to bring you:-

★ STARSPLASH – a fabulous *NEW* subtropical waterworld of spiralling flumes, rushing rapids, whirlpools and waves for all the family to enjoy. Starsplash will be developed on a similar scale to Funsplash at Funcoast World (featured opposite), and many of the key features will also be similar to those in Aquasplash at Southcoast World.

★ THE COURT – an impressive *NEW* Foodcourt will be developed, similar in style to the Plaza Foodcourt at Southcoast World (as featured). The Court will have eight serveries, Chinese, Fish 'n' Chips, a la Carte bistro, Cafeteria, Pizzeria, Bakery, Ice Cream parlour and Fast Food servery. With a separate new dining room for ★ ★ ★ County Suite Half Board guests.

★ 'STARS' – The Gaiety theatre has been transformed into STARS a completely new entertainment experience, with cabarets, top star entertainment, films and disco's – day and night.

★ NEW ACCOMMODATION
Bardsey Village with ★ ★ ★ County Suites for Half or Full Board and Self Catering guests (similar design to Burns Village at Wonderwest World as featured).

Harlech Village with ★ ★ ★ County Suites and ★ ★ Standard accommodation units.

★ NEW SHOPPING FACILITIES.

★ A NEW 'SPAR' CONVENIENCE STORE – ideal for self catering guests.

From children's Theatre Shows to late night Cabaret, Discos to Darts, you'll find the biggest stars, the best entertainment and all the great Butlin's value you'd expect at STARCOAST WORLD – where nearly everything is *FREE!*

───── PHOTOGRAPHIC REPRESENTATION ─────
Some of the photographs on the Starcoast World pages have been sourced from other Holiday Worlds. They have been included to convey a visual impression of the intended results of the investment programme.

STARCOAST WORLD

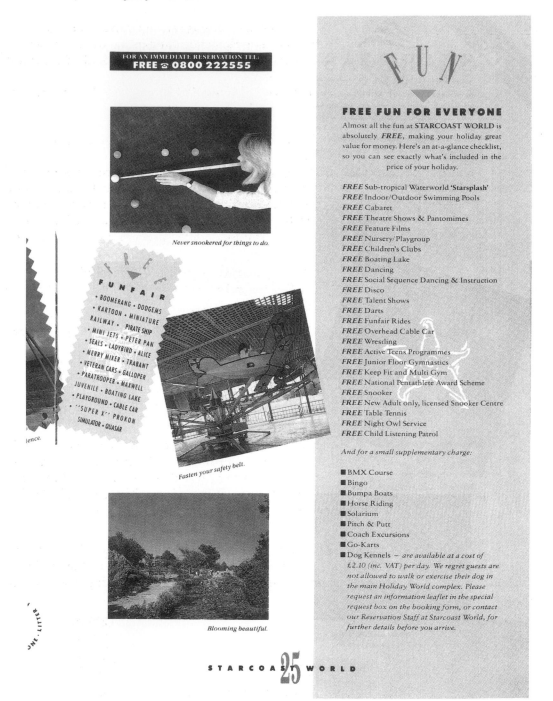

FOR AN IMMEDIATE RESERVATION TEL:
FREE ☎ 0800 222555

Never snookered for things to do.

FREE

FUNFAIR

• BOOMERANG • DODGEMS
• KARTOON • MINIATURE
RAILWAY • PIRATE SHIP
• MINI JETS • PETER PAN
• SEALS • LADYBIRD • ALICE
• MERRY MIXER • TRABANT
• VETERAN CARS • GALLOPER
• PARATROOPER • MAXWELL
JUVENILE • BOATING LAKE
• PLAYGROUND • CABLE CAR
• "SUPER X" PROKON
SIMULATOR • QUASAR

Fasten your safety belt.

Blooming beautiful.

FUN

FREE FUN FOR EVERYONE

Almost all the fun at **STARCOAST WORLD** is absolutely *FREE*, making your holiday great value for money. Here's an at-a-glance checklist, so you can see exactly what's included in the price of your holiday.

FREE Sub-tropical Waterworld **'Starsplash'**
FREE Indoor/Outdoor Swimming Pools
FREE Cabaret
FREE Theatre Shows & Pantomimes
FREE Feature Films
FREE Nursery/Playgroup
FREE Children's Clubs
FREE Boating Lake
FREE Dancing
FREE Social Sequence Dancing & Instruction
FREE Disco
FREE Talent Shows
FREE Darts
FREE Funfair Rides
FREE Overhead Cable Car
FREE Wrestling
FREE Active Teens Programmes
FREE Junior Floor Gymnastics
FREE Keep Fit and Multi Gym
FREE National Pentathlete Award Scheme
FREE Snooker
FREE New Adult only, licensed Snooker Centre
FREE Table Tennis
FREE Night Owl Service
FREE Child Listening Patrol

And for a small supplementary charge:

- BMX Course
- Bingo
- Bumpa Boats
- Horse Riding
- Solarium
- Pitch & Putt
- Coach Excursions
- Go-Karts
- Dog Kennels – *are available at a cost of £2.10 (inc. VAT) per day. We regret guests are not allowed to walk or exercise their dog in the main Holiday World complex. Please request an information leaflet in the special request box on the booking form, or contact our Reservation Staff at Starcoast World, for further details before you arrive.*

STARCOAST 25 WORLD

Under the heading 'Free fun for everyone', details are given of all the things your clients can enjoy that are free of charge and those that carry a small supplementary charge. It really is ideal for Mum and Dad not to have to carry money around with them each day. The family are able to enjoy so much because most of the activities are included in the cost of the holiday.

Looking at the list, you will notice there is a free Night Owl Service (for children under 9 months) and a Child Listening Patrol. This means that parents can enjoy an evening together, feeling confident that their children are in good care. However, the Night Owl Service is not a baby sitting service (this can often be arranged at additional cost), and the Child Listening Patrol is not meant to replace parental supervision.

Still looking at the list, you may wonder what Children's Clubs offer. The children are divided into age groups, as they are then able to share similar interests.

Whizzy Worlds Club is for 6–9 year olds. They enjoy talent shows, competitions, gymnastics, swimming instruction, discos, cartoon and film shows.

Teamsters Club is for 9–13 year olds. They enjoy archery, trampolining, soccer coaching and competitions. There is the opportunity to participate in the National Pentathlete Award Scheme. In this scheme, bronze, silver and gold certificates are awarded for achieving the required standard in five sports, chosen from athletics, canoeing, hockey, table tennis, netball, jogging, basketball, football, archery, trampolining, fitness and swimming, and qualified instructors provide all tuition.

Bandido's Club is for 13–17 year olds. Here young adults and teenagers can mix and make friends at Bandido's. There is fun with sports and outings, some weird and wonderful competitions, and of course a disco!

All sports and entertainments are supervised by the entertainments team, easily recognizable by wearing a red jacket.

Costing holidays at Starcoast World

Please look at the Starcoast World tariff page, and take time to read it carefully. There is a 17½ per cent service tax (VAT) in the United Kingdom, and you will notice that the prices quoted include the tax. The prices are for one week, starting on a Saturday and finishing on a Saturday. Our client has a choice of half board (two meals a day) or self-catering. The tariff is shown in date order and type of accommodation.

Let's try costing a holiday together:

Two adults and two children aged 14 and 9 years, for one week commencing 16 June, staying in budget accommodation on a half board basis. Note the information given on the children's tariff: children aged 2–14 years are half price when on a half or full board holiday. The costs are as follows:

Adults at £110.0 × 2	£220.00
Children at half price £55.00 × 2	110.00
	£330.00

Let's try one more. The same family have decided to travel on the same date but to stay in budget self-catering accommodation. Here we cost the apartment, which holds up to four persons. Two adults and two children for the week commencing 16 June in budget accommodation pay a total of £228.00. So it would cost the family less to stay in self-catering accommodation (the saving is £330.00 − £228.00 = £102.00) but they would need to buy food for one week.

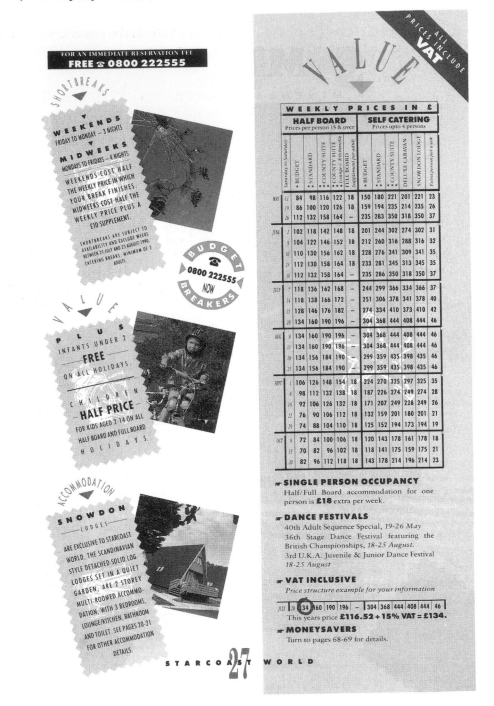

Exercise 1

Please read carefully the extract from Butlin's brochure concerning British
Rail travel savers and money savers. You will see that there are benefits for

clients wishing to travel to a holiday centre by train, and money saving offers for senior citizens and clients travelling in groups.

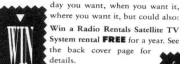

Standard British Rail return ticket from any British mainland rail station to any Butlin's Holiday World or Hotel is only **£17.25** per adult and **£8.65** per child (aged 5 to 14 years inclusive).

TICKET INFORMATION

☞ The ticket prices of £17.25 per adult, £8.65 per child are only valid when used in conjunction with a Butlin's Summer 1990, Saturday to Saturday holiday.

☞ Children under 5 travel free. The age at time of travel must be stated on the booking form.

☞ The ticket is valid from any B.R. station in Britain, to the nearest station to your holiday destination.

☞ For Somerwest World, (nearest B.R. station **Taunton**) and Starcoast World (nearest B.R. station **Bangor**) a Butlin's coach transfer service operates on Saturdays and is included in the price of your ticket. Please note the last bus from Taunton is at 7.45p.m.

☞ Butlin's Limited cannot be held responsible for any train delays, strikes or cancellations. All travel will be subject to the normal British Rail conditions of carriage.

☞ There is no refund available on tickets issued and they are not transferable.

☞ One ticket is issued per booking, passengers must travel together.

☞ Butlin's Limited are unable to assist in any enquiry relating to British Rail timetables or the British Rail network. Provision of reservation, sleepers etc., must be arranged directly with British Rail.

☞ Please state on the booking form the date you intend to commence rail travel.

☞ Tickets will be issued after the balance has been paid for your holiday.

☞ Offer is subject to availablity.

☞ Please note all booking forms must be received at your chosen Holiday World or Hotel at least 3 weeks before your holiday commencement date so that tickets can be returned by post.

☞ The offer does not apply to Breakaways.

It pays to book early in so many ways – Book before 31st January 1990 and not only will you be more certain of getting the holiday you want, when you want it, where you want it, but could also:

Win a Radio Rentals Satellite TV System rental **FREE** for a year. See the back cover page for details.

Book two consecutive weeks in the same holiday location and accommodation and we will take **10% OFF** the cost of your holiday *(min. 2 adults on Catering Holidays)*.

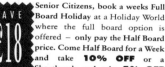

Senior Citizens, book a weeks Full Board Holiday at a Holiday World where the full board option is offered – only pay the Half Board price. Come Half Board for a Week and take **10% OFF** or a Shortbreak and take **5% OFF** *(min. 2 adults)*.

Single Parents can bring the first child **FREE** on Catering Holidays in May, June and up to week commencing 14 July 1990 *(max. one adult)*.

GROUP BOOKINGS

Why not get together with friends, relatives or workmates and **SAVE MONEY** by booking your holiday together.

SAVE 10% off your holiday cost for groups of 15+ persons (with a minimum of 10 adults on catering holidays). Just ring our usual reservations number.

EVEN BIGGER SAVINGS – For groups of more than 30 ring (0883) 626647/8 and our Group Sales Organiser will be ready to discuss your booking requirements.

CONDITIONS

Moneysavers will be deducted from your total holiday price **INCLUDING VAT** but excluding Travelsavers.

Moneysavers are subject to availability and are not available for Breakaways.

Moneysavers cannot be used in conjunction with any other Butlin's Limited discount or special offer including other Moneysavers. Only one Moneysaver per booking.

TO ENSURE YOU GET YOUR MONEYSAVER PLEASE REQUEST IN THE SPECIAL REQUEST BOX ON THE BOOKING FORM.

Now please read the pages giving details on holiday payments and holiday insurance.

HOLIDAY INSURANCE

Butlin's Limited offer a special insurance scheme for our guests, through **TIA** (a subsidiary of Commercial Union). This provides you with the reassurance that if for any unforeseen reason covered by the policy your holiday is threatened, before or during your stay, financially you will not have to worry. **It is the minimum protection necessary to cover guests in the event of problems arising. Please note Booking Conditions 9 and 11.**

All persons booking will be covered by the TIA insurance listed below, unless otherwise indicated on the booking form. If not required please enclose the name of your insurer with your booking form.

Cost per Adult **£3**,
Cost per Child (under 15) **£1.50.**

Insurance is only offered where the full booking party wish to be covered. **Cover for individuals in a booking party, not all taking TIA insurance, should be arranged with your own Insurance Company.**

INSURANCE COVER:

Transport/Accommodation following injury or illness sustained during the holiday – **up to £400**

Personal luggage and money. (Money limit £75, Valuables limit £75, Single articles limit £75) – **up to £500**

Personal Accident – **up to £5,000**

Public Liability – **up to £1,000,000**

Cancellation or Curtailment – due to certain factors including illness, injury or redundancy (under the terms of the Employment Protection (Consolidation) Act 1978) in respect of the Person – Insured, his/her spouse or friend with whom the Person – Insured is travelling UP TO THE INVOICED HOLIDAY COST.

FULL DETAILS OF THE COVER AND EXCEPTIONS WILL BE SENT WITH YOUR DEPOSIT RECEIPT BUT ARE AVAILABLE EARLIER ON REQUEST.

CONDITIONS OF RESERVATION

The Company will endeavour to provide all facilities advertised in the Brochure or elsewhere but reserves the right to make changes to those facilities. All information, transparencies, accommodation descriptions and inventories have been compiled from the most accurate information available at the time of going to press. Photographs of the Holiday Worlds and Hotels are illustrative, not all items shown will be identical in all the Holiday Worlds or Hotels. A contract is made upon acceptance of the booking by Butlin's Limited and is subject to the following conditions:

1. Signatory – The person signing the booking signs on his/her behalf and on behalf of all other applicants (i.e. persons named on the booking) as if they were

contracting parties. The person signing must be aged 18 years or over. Failure to disclose all material facts as required may lead to termination of the contract.

2. Arrival – Accommodation will be available from 5.00 pm on the stated date of arrival. Applicants arriving earlier may be allowed access to their accommodation at the discretion of the management but may find that it is not cleaned and ready until this time.

Fully paid reservations will be held until the day following the date of holiday commencement. Part or unpaid holidays will not be held after 10.00 pm on the day of holiday commencement unless prior arrangements have been made with Butlin's.

3. Departure – Accommodation must be vacated by 10.00 am on the stated day of departure. Applicants should leave the premises by 12 noon.

4. Occupation By Applicants Only – Only the applicants may occupy the accommodation. If any other persons are found in occupance, Butlin's may terminate the booking and the applicants and unauthorised persons will be required to leave the premises immediately. If they remain after this time they will be trespassing.

5. Nuisance – Butlin's reserves the right to decline a booking if, in the opinion of the Butlin's Management, the constitution of that booking party may lead to a situation that could prejudice the service or safety of other guests or staff.

The applicants will not do anything which in the opinion of the World or Hotel Management constitutes a nuisance or interferes with the quiet or general comfort of other guests. If applicants fail to comply with this condition their booking may be terminated and they will be asked to leave the premises. After this time they will be trespassing.

6. Pets – Dogs (with the exception of Starcoast World), Cats or other pets cannot be permitted at any Holiday World or Hotel. Guide dogs for blind guests are accepted.

7. Competitions – Applicants must have booked for at least one week's holiday in order to qualify for entry to any of the following competitions:
Glamorous Grandmother, The National Holiday Princess.

8. Clubs – The booking form contains an application for membership of the Butlin's Holiday Social Club. Completion of the form is an application for membership. The club is open to guests over 18 years old. The applicants warrant that the information contained on the form regarding personal details and age is true and correct.

9. Loss, Damage and Personal Injury – Applicants undertake to treat the accommodation, its furnishings, fittings, utensils (where appropriate) and other items provided by Butlin's such that on leaving they remain in a reasonable condition. Applicants will make good or pay for any damage, loss or breakages.

Butlin's, its servants and agents, will not be liable for any personal injury, death or loss or damage sustained by the applicants or their property unless it arises from negligence of Butlin's, its servants or agents. **Holiday insurance is available and recommended (see Holiday Insurance).**

10. Deposit/Payment – The appropriate deposit must accompany this booking. **Payment of the balance must be made prior to 49 days before the commencement date of the holiday.** Applicants will lose all their deposit if the holiday is cancelled before the balance is paid or if the applicants fail to pay the balance when due. Butlin's will treat this as a cancellation.

11. Cancellation Within 49 Days – Cancellations must be made in writing addressed to the Reservations Manager at the relevant Holiday World or Hotel. If the applicants cancel within 49 days of the commencement date of the holiday they will be liable to pay to Butlin's a proportion of the total holiday cost (which will include the deposit) in accordance with the following scale:

1. Cancellation between 49 and 14 days before commencement – 30%

2. Cancellation between 13 and 1 day before commencement – 60%

3. Cancellation on day of arrival or afterwards for Half or Full Board Holidays – 80%
Self Catering Holidays – 100%

12. Amendments to Bookings – Changes or amendments will be accepted subject to availability. Full details of charges are shown in the information section "Changing Your Booking".

13. Closure of Holiday Worlds and Hotels – If a Holiday World or Hotel is not open for any reason for the period during which the company has accepted a booking, such bookings will be transferred to an alternative date or Holiday World or Hotel acceptable to the applicants at no extra cost, or at the applicants' option, any monies paid in advance will be refunded.

14. Delayed or Missed Holidays – The Company will not accept any liability to applicants where Holidays are delayed or missed as a result of strikes or other forms of industrial action, which affect coach or train schedules etc. Information is available from local British Rail or National Express Information Offices.

15. Child Listening Patrol – This is not a babysitting service. It does not replace parental supervision and is not suitable for the care of young children.

71

When you feel ready, try to answer the following questions. They are typical of those you would be expected to answer when working at a travel agency. You need to read the small print carefully and so feel confident to advise your client.

(a) At what time are rooms available on the day of arrival?

(b) Who owns Butlin's Holiday Worlds and Hotels?

(c) What will it cost to be insured for a one-week holiday?

(d) On which page will you find all the information about children's entertainment?

(e) Name five facilities to be found at Starcoast World.

(f) Can Mrs Jones take her dog Rover with her to Starcoast World?

(g) Two adults and two children have booked with you to spend a week at a centre on a full board basis. What is the total of the deposit you must collect?

(h) Starcoast World has a Starsplash. What is it?

(i) What can be found at The Court at Starcoast World?

(j) Calculate the cost of the following to include insurance. You will note from the information given on insurance that the entire party travelling together must all accept the insurance, or make their own arrangements.

Two adults and one child aged 5 years, commencing 1 September, staying for one week in standard accommodation on full board basis.

(k) (i) Your clients intend to travel to Starcoast World by train. Which is the nearest station to their destination?
(ii) Travelling from Brighton in Sussex to Starcoast World, what would the return rail fare cost?

(l) You have 20 adults from the local golf club wishing to stay at Starcoast World, commencing 26 May for one week, staying in standard accommodation on a half board basis; all require insurance. Please advise them of the cost.

Exercise 2

Let's try to complete a booking form. The details are as follows:

The clients are Mr Joseph De Silver, aged 41, and Mrs Maria De Silver, aged 40. The grandparents will be with the family; they are Mr Antoni De Silver, age 68, and Mrs Sofia De Silver, aged 66. There are two children, Miss Angela De Silver, aged 12, and her friend Miss Sara Vickery, aged 11. The De Silvers live at 44 Sea View Road, Brighton, Sussex, BT13 6SX, and Sara lives nearby at 33 The Drive, Brighton, Sussex, BI14 7SX. They will be staying at Starcoast World in County Suite accommodation on a self-catering basis. The holiday dates are from Saturday 1 September to Saturday 8 September. They will require return rail tickets from Brighton to Starcoast World. They require Butlin's insurance. They will pay the deposit to secure the booking with cheque number 950. They have a special request to be accommodated close together and to be near the swimming pool. You have booked the holiday on your computer, and the Butlin's reservation confirmation number is SCW/019/LPA. Mr Joseph De Silver will sign the booking form, and his telephone number is 0702 77329.

Butlin's HOLIDAY WORLDS

BOOKING FORM

To make a reservation telephone **0800 222555** or see your Travel Agent. Our staff will give you a provisional booking reference number. Write the reference number in the box below marked Provisional Tel. Ref. We will hold your reservation for 5 days, to give you time to send your booking form and deposit. This booking form is an application for Butlin's Holiday Social Club. Please read the information section carefully before filling in the booking form. PLEASE USE BLOCK LETTERS.

Provisional Tel. Ref.

FOR AN IMMEDIATE RESERVATION PHONE: FREE ☎ 0800 222555

1 WHO WILL BE COMING

Please enter the Principal booking name in line 1. Will the Principal please indicate year of last holiday at Butlin's Holiday World___
If there are more than 6 persons, use an additional sheet of paper and attach to the booking form.

	Title	First Name	Surname	Address	Postcode	Husband · Wife · Son · Daughter · Friend	Age on Arrival for room allocation	HH	GC
1									
2									
3									
4									
5									
6									

Age on Arrival. *Please indicate the number of people in the appropriate box's*

Senior Citizens ☐   Adults ☐   Children 5-14 ☐   Junior 2-4 ☐   Infants under 2 ☐   No. of Cots required ☐

2 WHICH HOLIDAY

Please tick the appropriate accommodation under your choice of Holiday.

☐ **FULL**   ☐ **HALF BOARD HOLIDAY**   ☐ **SELF CATERING HOLIDAY**

★★★ County Suite with Lounge & Kitchenette ☐   ★★★ County Suite ☐   Deluxe Caravan ☐
★★★ County Suite ☐   ★★ Standard ☐   Snowdon Lodge. *Starcoast World only* ☐
★ Budget ☐   Single Person Accommodation ☐   ★★ Standard ☐   ★ Budget ☐
(supplement will apply)

FOR TRAVEL AGENTS
Travel agents must enter the full lead names and address of clients, otherwise bookings cannot be accepted.

Travel Agent's Stamp including ABTA Agency Number

3 WHERE & WHEN

Please tick your Choice of Holiday World then insert your arrival and departure date.

Starcoast World ☐   Somerwest World ☐   Funcoast World ☐
Southcoast World ☐   Wonderwest World ☐

Arrive after 2.00 p.m. Day___Month___Year___   Depart by 10.00 a.m. Day___Month___Year___

I enclose Cheque- Please charge to my account* (Authorised Credit Agents only) *Delete not applicable

the amount_____confirming this booking on behalf of

Client's Name

ABTA Number |___|___|___|___|___|

Agent's Reference

4 TRAVEL SAVERS

The cost of your Ticket will be added to the cost of your holiday. See page 70/71 for details.

National Express ☐   *Please do NOT include children under 5 who are not occupying seats*
British Rail ☐   *Your ticket is valid from 7 days prior to your holiday start date*

Total Number Travelling_____ Adults 15+_____   Children 5-14 years_____

NE/BR Station of Departure_____   Date of Travel departure____ ___ 90

FOR OFFICE USE ONLY

FORM	DEP	RJ

BF CODE	DATE REC'D
61	

PTY	SC	AD	CH	INF	JN	COTS	CODE	NO

CODE	AMT	A/P

5 DEPOSIT PAYMENT

Half/Full Board Deposit

No. of Adults   x £15 = £_____
No. of Children   x £6 = £_____
Total Amount enclosed   £_____

Self Catering Deposit

No. of units   x £25 = £_____

Please enclose the name of your insurer if you do NOT want Travel Insurance arranged by Butlin's Ltd.

I enclose Cheque/Giro order No._____

Name & Address if different from Principal Booking Name_____
_____Postcode_____

Credit Card Payment

Please complete the following if you wish to pay by Credit Card.

Tick appropriate box ☐ Access   ☐ VISA

Card No. |___|___|___|___|___|___|___|___|

Expiry Date_____

Signature_____

LKT	
RIT MSG	

DRY	

DH	

6 SPECIAL REQUESTS

We regret that these cannot be guaranteed.

7 DECLARATION

The principal booking name in (1) above signs on behalf of his/her party and accepts the Conditions of Reservation.

Principal Signature_____   Daytime Tel. No._____

AL	

There are several points to keep in mind. We will need two County Suites because the tariff page explains 'up to four persons' per unit. The deposit to collect is £50.00 because on the booking form it says £25.00 per unit (we have booked two units). Why do you think Butlin's need to know our clients' ages? So they can be accommodated with similar compatible age groups. Is there an age restriction on the person who signs the booking form? Yes, look at the notes on the conditions of reservation: you will see that the minimum age is 18 years. This is a very important point to remember if booking a group of teenagers at a holiday centre.

Complete the booking form double checking the details as you go along.

Now calculate the cost of this holiday for the De Silver family.

Special interest holidays

The Association of British Travel Agents produces a *Guide to Special Interest Holidays*. Many articles can be read in magazines and newspapers, and there are books to be found at the bookshops giving details of companies that provide specialist holidays. There are over 150 different types of special interest holiday. People enjoy coming together to share a common interest, or to take the opportuinty to learn something completely new to them. A special interest holiday can add zest to the vacation for the tourist who is looking for more than sun, sand and sea.

Here are a few different types of special interest holidays to consider.

Antiques A fascinating hobby, delving back into our past, actually touching elegant pieces of history.

Archaeology 'Dig' further back into the past, in countries such as Greece, France, Germany and Peru.

Athletics Try the World Wide Marathon on Barbados and in London. Train for the event at La Santa on Lanzarote, Canary Islands, which has Olympic training facilities.

Bird watching Virtually all countries offer this peaceful and fascinating hobby, but imagine bird watching in Kenya, Ecuador, the Scottish Hebrides or the Seychelles Bird Island. What beautiful birds are to be seen!

Botany/Flowers Most countries offer the beauty of flowers, but perhaps Holland's spring bulbs or Jersey's flower festival come first to mind.

Castles Have you clients who are interested in castles? These are to be found in most countries, especially in Europe, but perhaps we think first of Germany and Austria for this type of special interest holiday.

Cookery/food Cooking is something we do every day. However, perhaps the clients would like to learn how to make entertaining easy, or to gain more knowledge on vegetarian cooking, or perhaps to explore something completely different for them, such as Italian, Chinese or Indian cooking. Perhaps they would enjoy a 'gourmet delights' holiday, where guests do not do the cooking but just enjoy eating! Perhaps a visit to a food festival in Hong Kong would appeal, combining discovering a new destination with a hobby.

Dinghy sailing Learn to sail a small boat, or improve on this skill. Where better than around the islands of Greece and Turkey!

Fishing Many countries offer fishing holidays, whether in sea or lakes and rivers, where peace or excitement, solitude or companionship can be found.

Gambling It has to be Las Vegas in America!

Golf So many countries offer golf holidays, to learn or improve, to enjoy beautiful courses or to follow the stars. There are golfing locations in the United States, the Caribbean, the United Kingdom, Hong Kong, Singapore, Thailand, Spain, Portugal, Austria and many more.

Health/keep fit/beauty   Most of us probably need some type of holiday along those lines! Many countries offer health farms or spas with healing waters. Many clients just like to set aside a week or even a few days to concentrate on trying to get fit or to improve their fitness condition. It is lovely for women to spend a few days feeling treasured at a health and beauty farm. Most of them are converted stately homes and stand in magnificent grounds, offering peace, luxury and an opportunity for self-improvement that time does not permit in our everyday routine.

Horse riding/pony trekking   Again these are offered by most countries, perhaps to learn or improve or just to enjoy being close to these sensitive animals. For clients not wanting to ride there are horse-drawn caravan holidays, on which they can travel at a slow pace and enjoy the countryside.

Motor racing   Holidays can be arranged to the Worldwide Grand Prix circuits. This special interest has a great following.

Music   What a tremendous range worldwide. The type of music can determine the venue: jazz, classical, country and western, 50s and 60s music, the Glen Miller sound, opera, ballet – the variety is endless. There are many festivals throughout the year, and we think of Vienna and Milan in particular.

Painting   On canvas, paper, china or cloth, indoors or outdoors, in every country – the choice is endless. Clients can study by attending lectures, or try a new experience where beginners are welcome, or improve and perfect a recognized gift.

Parachuting/jumping   Do you have a client with the courage and adventurous spirit to go on this special interest holiday? Be sure to collect full payment before they go!

Skiing   Skiing is an exhilarating holiday for active holiday-makers. We think of the ski resorts in Europe, but of course many countries with mountains offer this special type of holiday. A few lessons on dry ski slopes at home can speed up learning to ski during the holiday.

Survival   This is an adventure holiday for children and adults. Try a Robinson Crusoe holiday on an uninhabited Greek island, or survival training on an uninhabited Scottish island; there is always something different.

Walking   Walking is a great favourite for all ages. Ramblers Holidays and Holiday Fellowship Holidays are well organized and offer a wide range of destinations.

Only 20 different types of holiday have been mentioned. Can you think of the remaining 130? The assignment at the end of this chapter tests your skills further.

Selecting and booking special interest holidays

Special interest holidays can be divided into certain groups by age; for example, there are many holidays available for the over 55s. There are destination interests; for example, Iceland may be a very special destination, offering something quite different from the usual type of holiday choice. The venue can also be different; many universities are available to holiday-makers during the summer months when not being used by students, and hotel groups offer weekend or midweek special interest breaks.

Special interest holidays provide a good source of revenue for the travel agency. Often your clients will be travelling as a group. Consider the clubs and associations in your area and make contact; there could be a lot of untapped business there.

Reservation systems differ. Your agency could be using computers, and the holiday centres and tour operators will be subscribing to the system. Alternatively you may need to telephone the companies to make the reservation. We will need the facts to hand:

name of passengers travelling;
choice of holiday;
destination;
length of stay;
ages of children (infants);
type of accommodation required;
holiday number;
special requests;
date of travel.

Once the reservation has been made, a deposit will be collected from the client to secure the booking. The reservation booking form must be signed; by doing this, the client is agreeing to the tour operator's booking conditions. Payment will then be sent from the travel agency to the tour operator. Again, systems vary. Your travel agency may have a credit agreement with the tour operator, with payments sent at the end of each month for all reservations made. Alternatively it may be necessary to send the payment as each booking is made, deducting the amount of commission earned for making the reservation.

Conclusions

It will be difficult to remember all you need to know about every holiday centre and special interest holiday. However, it will improve your service greatly if you contact the operators (details are in the travel manuals), obtain the brochures – and take the brochures home to read! This will open up a new world. You will find holidays available that you never knew existed, and – who knows? – you may get involved in a different, very special interest yourself.

Assignment: special interest holidays

Select a number of special interest holidays, list them, and then match them with the types of tourist that might find them suitable.

Second assignment, taken from the BTEC travel and tourism course

You have been appointed as a travel consultant to a Tour Operator that specializes in Special Interest Holidays in the United Kingdom and Worldwide.

You have been given the task of organizing a holiday for a group of six tourists.

Task 1

Using a brochure promoting special interest holidays, choose one of these for your clients and explain the appeal of this type of holiday.

Task 2

Explain the following concepts to your clients and why they are important requirements for special interest holidays: travel insurance; passports; visa and health requirements; special clothing and equipment; and climate.

Task 3

Complete the booking form and find the cost of the holiday per person.

Task 4

Explain how the customers can pay for the holiday i.e. how much deposit they must pay and when this has to be paid. When final payment must be received and the various methods of payment. Also explain what would happen if their final payment is late or if they cancel their booking.

4 Hotels, theatres, stopovers and bargain breaks

Summary

In this chapter we will discuss:

- various types of accommodation and their facilities;
- how to read the ABC Hotel Guide;
- where hotel reservations may be made;
- theatre reservations explained;
- blank theatre ticket to complete;
- airline stopover holidays and their benefits;
- bargain/short breaks and their benefits;
- exercises and assignments to complete.

Choosing hotels

Hotel accommodation: what a choice – and what a disaster it can be if we make the wrong one! Let's consider our clients' needs once again.

Is the location important? Must the hotel be close to the sea, the city centre, a conference centre or a factory site? Are the facilities important? Should the hotel be large enough to have a swimming pool and a health centre, or perhaps conference rooms? Are our clients looking for accommodation that is small and friendly, perhaps family owned and managed? The choice is enormous, and many manuals have been published to assist the travel consultant in gaining product knowledge. In this book we are using extracts from the *ABC Worldwide Hotel Guide*.

Hotel types

First we will discuss some of the different types of hotel available. As you listen to your client a picture will soon form as to which type is required.

Holiday resort hotels   Usually the location is very important. If the resort is a beach resort, tourists usually prefer to be very close to the beach front. The hotel can be located in a beautiful scenic area or close to special facilities, perhaps a golf course or ski slopes. Many of these resort hotels have an excellent entertainment programme and sports facilities for all the family.

Motels   These have enjoyed an increase in business in recent years with the rise in the numbers of private car owners. A motel is a hotel mainly for motorists, and is located conveniently near a major road.

City hotels   These are used by business travellers and tourists alike. Often tourists require a hotel in the centre of the city, convenient for sightseeing but not necessarily expensive. The business traveller will also need the convenient location, but may require particular facilities.

Pensions   Pensions or guest houses are very popular with tourists who do not want a large hotel with many facilities that they may never use. They are looking for a more personal place to stay which will cost less and have a home-from-home feeling.

We are not restricted to booking hotels, motels and pensions for our clients. Other interesting accommodation can include castles and stately homes, of which there are many in Europe in particular, where guests can experience the life of the nobility. A game lodge can be a very peaceful venue; it is often designed and built to merge with a game reserve, offering a tranquil watering-hole for humans! There are floating hotels, youth hostels, camping and caravan sites, rooms in taverns, holiday centres and many more. A good way to keep up to date is to read the newspapers and magazines, which often give details of new and exciting venues.

Accommodation

The accommodation available at hotels can range from very small rooms to very large suites, with bedrooms and living rooms extending to balconies and patios. The price ranges accordingly, and you will need to find out whether your clients are looking for very cheap accommodation, for absolute luxury on a special occasion, or (like many tourists) for something in the middle range.

   Let's look at the terms used for different types of room:

Single   A room to be occupied by one person.

Twin   A room with two single beds for two persons.

Double   A room with one large bed for two persons.

Twin double   A room with two double beds for two, three or four persons.

Suite   A living room connected to one or more bedrooms.

Duplex   A two-storey suite (sitting room and bedrooms) connected by a stairway.

Connecting rooms   Two or more rooms with private connection doors, permitting access between rooms without going into the corridor (ideal for families).

Efficiency   An accommodation containing some type of kitchen facility. Could also be known as a *studio apartment*.

Cabana   A room adjacent to the pool area, with or without sleeping facilities; often separate from the hotel's main building.

Food service

We also need to be familiar with the terms used for food service:

American plan (AP)   The tariff includes three meals per day, breakfast, lunch and dinner; often known as *full board* or *full pension*.

Modified American plan (MAP)   The rate includes breakfast, dinner and room; also known as *dinner, bed and breakfast* or *half board* or *half pension*.

Continental plan (CP)   The rate includes only a continental breakfast and room.

European plan (EP)   No meals are included in the room rate; also known as *room only*.

Continental breakfast   Consists of juice, toast, roll or pastry, and coffee, tea or milk. In some countries it includes coffee and roll only.

English breakfast   Usually includes hot or cold cereal, bacon and eggs, sausages, tomatoes and fried bread, toast, jam or marmalade, and tea or coffee. A good English breakfast can save time and money for the remainder of the day. The tourist need only stop for a light snack at lunch time.

ABC WORLDWIDE HOTEL GUIDE

INCORPORATING A-Z WORLDWIDE HOTEL GUIDES

CONTENTS

PUBLISHER'S INTRODUCTION 5
   HOW TO USE ABC WORLDWIDE HOTEL GUIDE 8
   NINE LANGUAGE SAMPLE LISTINGS 8
   INTERNATIONAL TELEPHONE/TELEX CODES & TIME ZONES ... 10

RESERVATION OFFICE CODES 13

RESERVATION OFFICES 19

WORLDWIDE HOTEL LISTINGS 65

AREA MAPS
   ASIA/PACIFIC AREA 454
   AUSTRALIA 68
   BAHAMAS 109
   CANADA 139
   CARIBBEAN 160
   CYPRUS 188
   LOS ANGELES AREA 676
   PACIFIC OCEAN (ISLANDS) 451
   UNITED STATES 650

HOTEL LOCATION MAPS

Abu Dhabi	583	Funchal	474	Nassau & Paradise Island	110
Acapulco	408	Gatwick Area	596	New Delhi	315
Amsterdam	426	Geneva	548	New Orleans	806
Antwerp	116	Hamburg	271	New York City	852
Athens	289	Helsinki	206	Nice	230
Atlanta	760	Hong Kong & Kowloon	298	Orlando/Disneyworld	754
Bali-Kuta & Sanur	318	Houston	910	Osaka	379
Bangkok	570	Island of Hawaii	766	Oslo	447
Barbados	164	Island of Kauai	770	Palm Springs Area	693
Barcelona	507	Island of Maui	771	Paris	234
Basle	543	Island of Oahu	776	Pattaya Beach	573
Berlin-West	258	Istanbul	579	Philadelphia	892
Bermuda	124	Jamaica	172	Phoenix	656
Beverly Hills	678	Jerusalem	331	Phuket Island	574
Birmingham	587	Kuala Lumpur	404	Rio de Janeiro	132
Bombay	312	Kyoto	374	Rome	354
Boston	812	Las Vegas	837	San Diego	697
Brussels	119	Lisbon	470	San Francisco	700
Budapest	308	London	606	Sao Paulo	135
Cairo	202	London Airport ·		Seoul	496
Chicago	784	Heathrow	623	Singapore	482
Copenhagen	195	Los Angeles Downtown	680	Stockholm	539
Costa del Sol	511	Los Angeles International		Sydney	74
Dallas	906	Airport	689	Taipei	565
Disneyland Area - Anaheim	668	Madrid	516	Tampa/St Petersburg	749
Dominican Republic	168	Manila	463	Tel Aviv	333
Dubai	584	Melbourne	94	Tokyo	382
Dusseldorf	264	Mexico City	416	Toronto	154
Edinburgh	639	Miami Area	736	Venice	364
Florence	341	Milan	345	Vienna	106
Fort Lauderdale	729	Monte Carlo	421	Waikiki	773
Fort Myers Area	730	Montreal	156	Washington D.C.	720
Frankfurt am Main	266	Munich	278	Zurich	558

GEOGRAPHICAL INDEX 939

KEY TO SYMBOLS .... BACK COVER GATEFOLD

The publishers and compilers of ABC Worldwide Hotel Guide cannot accept responsibility for any mistakes or omissions although every effort has been made to achieve absolute accuracy. The information shown is subject to change at very short notice and confirmation of the accuracy of the information should be sought whenever possible. Inclusion of an hotel in ABC Worldwide Hotel Guide is not intended to be an endorsement of the quality of that hotel.

Informing clients

Unfortunately there is no international agreement on the grading of hotels. Often the star system is used, but a three-star award can mean very different standards in different countries. Many countries do not employ hotel inspectors to enforce any standards, and the service and facilities offered may consequently be poor. It will always be difficult for the travel consultant to actually *recommend* a particular hotel, as the industry is constantly changing. Perhaps a very reliable chef has left, making the quality of meals in a restaurant disappointing. Perhaps management has changed, leading to a decline in discipline of staff and comfort for the guests.

We rely on hotel manuals to provide factual information. We must listen to clients who have just returned, and keep our own record on the feedback received from those clients. Many travel consultants have the opportunity to make educational visits to hotels, and this can help to build product knowledge. Many clients prefer to stay at hotels belonging to large chains or organizations; although the service offered is not particularly personal, standards are high and stability is usually guaranteed.

Exercise 1

Please study the extracts from the *ABC Worldwide Hotel Guide*. First study the contents page. You will see that in addition to all the information required about hotels, there are also 9 area maps and 97 location maps, and these will prove to be very useful. Details on how to obtain the ABC Worldwide Hotel Guide and other ABC Guides are given in Chapter 10.

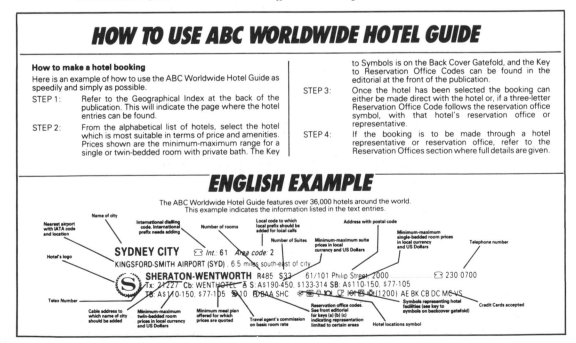

KEY TO SYMBOLS

The Key to Reservation Office Codes is to be found in the editorial at the front of the publication.

Hotel Information

R	No. of Rooms
E	No. of Executive Rooms
S	No. of Suites
U	No. of Units
☎	Telephone
Tx	Telex
Cb	Cables
⊗	Closed certain months of year
℞	Representatives

Minimum Meal Plan with Prices

A	Accommodation Only (EP)
B	Continental Breakfast
C	Full Breakfast
D	Half Board (MAP)
E	Full Board (AP)
S	Suite
E	Executive Room
SB	Single bed with bath

TB	Twin beds with bath
⑤	Commission Rate
(w)	Weekly Rates

Location of Hotel

✵	City Centre
🏘	City Suburbs
⚓	On Beach
♀	In Country
✈	Near Airport
⛰	In Mountains
⚓	By Lake

Hotel Facilities

❄	Air Conditioned Rooms
♀	Bar
⼱	Restaurant
⊡	Coffee Shop
🚗	Car Hire Desk
Ⓟ	Parking
⎛⎞	Lift

Leisure/Conferences

| ⊠ | Swimming Pool |

⚲	Tennis Court
♨	Health & Fitness Centre
🏢	Business Centre
🖳	Conferences (Capacity)

Credit Cards Accepted

AB	Australian Bankcard
AP	Airplus
AX	American Express
CB	Carte Blanche
DC	Diners Club
EC	Eurocard
JC	JCB Card
MC	MasterCard (Access)
VI	Visa (Barclaycard)

Travel Vouchers

UTV	Universal Travel Voucher (Mastercard)
VTV	Visa Travel Voucher
WTP	World Travel Payment (Citicorp)

| Adv | Advertisement Reference |

Canada
New Brunswick

Area: 28,353 sq. miles, 73,434 Km²
Population: 684,000   *Capital:* Fredericton
Largest City: Saint John   *Climate:* Cold Continental
Electric Current/Voltage: 110
Local Time: GMT minus 3 hrs. until 30 Oct., then GMT minus 4 hrs.
Monetary Unit: Dollar/Cents   *Exchange Rate:* C$1.27 to US$1

BATHURST ☎ *Int.:* 1   *Area code:* 506

KEDDY'S MOTOR INN S2 R88   80 Main Street, E2A 1A3 .... ☎ 546-6691
Tx: 01424513 Ⓐ SB: C$38, $30 TB: C$46, $37 ⑤10 ❄ 🖳 ⼱ ⎛⎞ Ⓟ 🖳 AX MC VI

CAMPBELLTON ☎ *Int.:* 1   *Area code:* 506

HOWARD JOHNSON LODGE R66   P.O. Box 800, E3N 3H2 (on Riverfront Drive) .... ☎ 753-5063
Res. (800) 268-4940 Tx: 01443170 Cb: HOJO Ⓐ SB: C$55-60, $44-48 TB: C$60-65, $48-52 ℞HOJ UIN
ASP(b) EXP(a) STR(a) TMI(a) TPS(a) ❄ 🖳 ♀ ⼱ ⊡ 🚗 ⎛⎞ Ⓟ 🖳 (max. 175) AX MC VI UTV VTV WTP

EDMUNDSTON ☎ *Int.:* 1   *Area code:* 506

HOWARD JOHNSON S4 R06   100 Rice Street, E3V 1T4 .... ☎ 739-7321 Res. (800)654-2000
Tx: 01445517 Ⓐ S: C$90-100, $71-79 SB: C$58-64, $46-51 TB: C$68-75, $54-59 ⑤10 ℞HOJ UIN ASP(b)
EXP(a) STR(a) TMI(a) TPS(a) ❄ 🖳 ♀ ⼱ ⊡ 🚗 (max. 500) AX CB DC MC VI
WANDLYN INN R134   P.O. Box 68, E3V 3K5 (on Trans-Canada Highway) .... ☎ 735-5525
Tx: 01445521 Ⓐ SB: C$49-65, $39-52 TB: C$55-85, $44-67 ⑤10 ❄ 🖳 ♀ ⼱ ⼱ 🖳 🖳 AX MC VI

FREDERICTON ☎ *Int.:* 1   *Area code:* 506
FREDERICTON AIRPORT (YFC) , 8.5 miles/13.5 Km from city

DIPLOMAT MOTOR R78   P.O. Box 634, E3B 5A6 (at 225 Woodstock Road) .... ☎ 454-5584 Tx: 01446179
SB: C$56-58, $44-46 TB: C$58-64, $46-51 ⑤10 ❄ 🖳 ♀ ⼱ Ⓟ 🖳 (max. 45) AX CB DC MC
VI UTV VTV
HOWARD JOHNSON LODGE S2 R118   P.O. Box 1414, E3B 5E3 (at 2 Princess Margaret Bridge)
☎ 472-0480 Res. (800) 268-4940 (in E. Canada) Tx: 01446232 Cb: HOJO Ⓐ S: C$125, $99
SB: C$58-69, $46-55 TB: C$66-78, $52-62 ⑤10 ℞HOJ UIN ASP(b) EXP(a) STR(a) TMI(a) TPS(a) 🏘 🖳 ♀ ⼱
⼱ Ⓟ 🚗 🖳 (max. 175) AX CB MC VI
KEDDY'S MOTOR INN S2 R120   P.O. Box 1510, E3B 5G2 (on Forest Hill Road) .... ☎ 454-4461
Tx: 01446110 Ⓐ SB: C$36-38, $29-30 TB: C$42-48, $33-38 ⑤10 🏘 🖳 ♀ ⼱ Ⓟ 🖳 (max. 600) AX MC VI
LORD BEAVERBROOK S7 R165   P.O. Box 545, E3B 5A6 (at 659 Queen Street) .... ☎ 455-3371
Res. (800) 561-0040 Tx: 01446134 Ⓐ SB: C$58, $46 TB: C$64, $51 ⑤10 ℞KCA(c) ❄ 🖳 ♀ ⼱ Ⓟ 🖳
⎛⎞ Ⓟ 🖳 🖳 (max. 350) AX CB DC MC VI
WANDLYN INN S1 R116   P.O. Box 214, E3B 4Y9 (at 58 Prospect Street West) .... ☎ 452-8937
Tx: 01446124 Ⓐ SB: C$49-65, $39-52 TB: C$55-85, $44-67 ⑤10 * ❄ 🖳 ♀ ⼱ ⼱ 🖳 🖳 (max. 200)
AX MC VI

GRAND FALLS ☎ *Int.:* 1   *Area code:* 506

BEST WESTERN PRES-DU-LAC MOTEL U100   P.O. Box 1170, E0J 1M0 .... ☎ 473-1300
Ⓐ SB: C$50, $40 TB: C$54-60, $43-48 ⑤10 ℞BWH   ❄ 🖳 ♀ ⼱ Ⓟ 🖳 ♨ (max. 120) AX CB DC MC VI

The second step is to read the extract 'How to use *ABC Worldwide Hotel Guide*'. Study the example, which is for Sydney City and the hotel Sheraton-Wentworth.

Thirdly, please study the 'Key to symbols' page. The best way to become familiar with the symbols is to practise reading the information provided. Let's look at the extract for accommodation in Canada, in particular the New

Brunswick area. There is a map to help us get our bearings, and some information on the size of the area, the population, the largest city, the local time, and the rate of exchange between Canadian dollars and American dollars.

Try finding the answers to the following questions:

(a) In which city is the Lord Beaverbrook hotel?
(b) Your client will be arriving by air. What is the distance from the airport to the city centre?
(c) How many rooms does the Lord Beaverbrook hotel have?
(d) Does the room rate include breakfast? Explain your answer.
(e) The reason for your client's visit to New Brunswick is to hold an international business women's convention for an estimated 800 delegates. Could this be held at the Lord Beaverbrook hotel? Explain your answer.
(f) Your client would like a hotel that offers half board. Which symbol would you look for?
(g) Does Keddy's Motor Inn at Bathurst accept the Airplus credit card?
(h) Where is the Wandlyn Inn at Edmundston situated?
(i) Give the tariff range in Canadian dollars for a single room with bath at the Howard Johnson Lodge in Fredericton.
(j) Give the rate of commission paid to travel agents by the Diplomat Motor hotel.

Making hotel reservations

Reservation outlets

There are many outlets for the travel agent to make hotel reservations:

Direct with the hotel   By telephone, fax, telex or letter, depending on the situation. When reservations are made by fax, telex or letter the requests are in writing; this is safer than relying on a telephone conversation.

Central reservation office   Large hotel chains such as Hilton Hotels and Penta Hotels have a central booking office. By making one telephone call the travel consultant can book more than one hotel in the chain, often in several different countries. The travel agency receives commission on the booking and can often obtain instant confirmation of the reservation.

Hotel representatives   A hotel representative or agent will represent many hotels in many different countries. Again, by making just one telephone call (or by calling up the information on the computer) the consultant can make reservations throughout the world with many different hotel companies. The travel agency receives commission for the reservations made.

Hotel consortium   This is when many individual hotels come together to form a consortium or association and provide a central reservation office. Once again the travel consultant can make just one contact with a hotel consortium to obtain confirmation of many different types of hotel in many different countries. Perhaps a beach hotel in Spain has decided to be part of a consortium with a mountain hotel in Switzerland, each promoting the other's business.

Airlines   Hotel reservations can be made through the airline taking your clients on the first main flight of the itinerary. All this can be tied in with the flight reservations made on the computer. In the event of flights being changed or cancelled, the accommodation can be easily amended to coincide with the flights.

Central Reservation Systems (CRS)   Many agencies can access hotel information and make reservations through their computers. This is particularly convenient when dealing with business travel.

Reservation details

When you make a reservation you need to be crystal clear with requests and with the information passed to the client. The points you need to be particularly wary of are as follows:

Time of arrival and time of departure   This is important. Guests can need a room at any time of day. Should the client expect to arrive in the early hours of the morning, say at 2 a.m., the room will have to be booked for the night, which will have the preceding day's date. Is the usual check-in time 12 noon or later? Unless the accommodation has been secured by paying a deposit (this can be done by using a credit card, which is especially useful if it is a last-minute booking) the accommodation will be released by say 6 p.m. and resold. So we will need to advise the hotel if our client is planning to be a late arrival.

Type of room and dates   We need to be sure we are reserving the type of room required. How many bedrooms are needed in the suite? Should the room have a balcony or a patio? Is a bath required by a client who will not accept a shower? Are we trying to squeeze four guests into a room that will accommodate only three? Is a view important to our clients? Must the room be located on a lower floor because our client is nervous of heights? There are hundreds of special requests that need attention. The correct dates are all-important too. Make sure the hotel reservations clerk is clear about the request. A clear way of stating the dates required is to say 24 June for three nights. Or 'in 24 June, out 27 June', leaving no doubt.

Tariff   This can change from the one given in the hotel guide, so we need to obtain the correct tariff. What does it include: meals, taxes, service charge? We need to ask these questions when making the booking.

Cancellation charges   We need to advise our clients *at the time of making the booking* about cancellation charges; waiting until the event is too late.

What would happen if you forgot to cancel the reservation, your client did not arrive, and the resevation had been guaranteed? The hotel will regard this as a no-show, and can charge the travel agency for the accommodation. This cost may be passed on to you by the manager; it cannot be passed on to the customer if you had been instructed to cancel the reservation. So, take time to double check the itinerary and reservations and follow them through; this is not easy to do if you are working under pressure, but it will be worth the peace of mind.

Hotel vouchers

So now you have made the reservation and you are happy about the details being correct. What happens next? Your travel agency may use a computerized system where vouchers,

Member of
THE GUILD OF
BUSINESS TRAVEL AGENTS

PLEASE SEND ACCOUNT TO

To

Your ref:

Our file ref:

As arranged please provide the following services for:

111537

METHOD OF PAYMENT

Charge our Account

Payment Herewith

Direct by Client

	Date			Date
ARRIVAL	Time		**DEPARTURE**	Time
	Flight			Flight

A. T. MAYS LTD.—Registered Head Office—Moffat House, Nineyard Street, Saltcoats, Scotland KA21 5HS

COPY FOR SUPPLIER

Note: 1. If prepayment is being effected by us—details are as shown opposite.
2. If credit is authorized forward invoice with original voucher as instructed above.

1 ....
2 ....
3 ....
Total ....
Less ....% Commission ....
Net amount due to you ....
Cheque enclosed/Currency transfer effected:

tickets, invoice and itinerary are issued by a press of the button. If not you may be using one of the standard hotel vouchers. Hotel vouchers can vary from agency to agency. We are using the Guild of British Travel Agents voucher as an example and this is typical of many of the points they cover.

The sample hotel voucher shown here has been preprinted. At the top left your agency can have printed its name, and on the right-hand side the name, address and registered number of the office to where the account must be sent. This may not be the same if you are working for a large travel company with many branches.

In the 'To' box you would write the name, address and telephone number of the hotel. You would make sure to write the telephone number because your client may have to amend the booking before arrival, and it will save time looking in the telephone directory.

'Your ref.' is the reference given to you by the hotel's reservation department. 'Our file ref.' is your file reference for this client. 'As arranged please provide the following services for' requires the name of the client and the reservation details. Under 'Arrival date, time, flight' and 'Departure date, time, flight' you would add those details; it is important that the hotel has this information in case of flight delays.

For 'Method of payment' a cross should be entered in the relevant box. 'Charge our account' would be used for business travellers whose company holds an account with your travel agency and will pay for the hotel accommodation at the end of the month. So in this case you are asking the hotel to send the bill to you, and you in turn pass it on to the business client. 'Payment herewith' is nice and straightforward: you are enclosing payment for the accommodation with the voucher. 'Direct by client' means that the customer will pay for the accommodation direct to the hotel, perhaps by credit card or travellers' cheques.

The voucher will have several copies:

1 Top copy to clients; they will present this to the hotel on arrival.
2,3 To hotel as confirmation: the hotel should return copy 3 to you with the commission cheque.

4 Your file copy.
5 Additional travel agency copy to chase up commission.

Commission

How does the travel agency receive the commission from the hotel?

Commission is paid *after* the client has completed the visit. Some hotels will automatically send a cheque paid in local currency, together with an itemized statement, at the end of each month. If the agency is prepaying or paying on behalf of the guest, the total amount less agency commission can be forwarded to the hotel. If the client has paid direct and the hotel has not sent the commission to the travel agent, the hotel will have to be asked to pay its dues. This is not always satisfactory; a lot of your time and company money can be wasted on telephone calls. For hotels that are reluctant to pay but have been specifically requested by clients, a prepayment rule could apply.

Summary of reservation procedure

Here is a reminder of the main points to note when making a hotel reservation:

1 Check the name, address and telephone number and all the information given in the hotel guide.
2 Check the tariff: is the rate quoted per room or per person?
3 What does the tariff include: tax, service charge?
4 Are there any supplements for sea view, balcony etc.?
5 Are there any cancellation charges?
6 Are the dates correct?
7 What meal basis is included: breakfast (English or continental), lunch or dinner?
8 Have there been any changes in the itinerary? If so, have you changed the hotel reservation?
9 How is payment to be made?
10 When and how much commission is to be paid to the travel agent?
11 Has the voucher been made out correctly? If a long itinerary is involved, has a separate voucher been issued for each hotel?
   Going through this checklist will become automatic after a while and will help to avoid the silly mistakes that can easily happen.

Theatre reservations

Why book with a travel agency? From the customer's point of view, the travel agent provides a very convenient service.

If a customer decides to book with a theatre direct, she has two choices. One is to visit the theatre box office during business hours, which could involve a long and expensive journey. The other is to telephone the theatre box office and give her credit card details. The theatre will then either post the tickets to the card holder or hold them until the client collects them on the day in question. If no credit card is owned then the customer can send a cheque with a covering note. Many theatres charge an agency fee for telephone and postal bookings, and a lot of patience is required by the customer trying to make contact by telephone to the theatre box office. If the show is fully booked for the date required, a quick decision needs to be made regarding an alternative date or theatre. If it is to be an alternative theatre, the process begins again, trying to get through to the next theatre box office on the list.

By contrast, when the customer books theatre tickets through a travel agent, she can sit in pleasant surroundings whilst the travel consultant does the job in a fraction of the time.

There are two types of theatre ticket agent:

Principal agent, who holds large allocations of theatre seats and may have direct reservation lines with many theatres.

Subagent (the travel agent), who holds an account with one or more principal agents and contacts them when required to make a booking.

The principal agent will keep the travel agent up to date with lists of shows, special events, posters to help advertise the theatres, prices of seats, theatre plans and books of theatre tickets. The reservations can be made by the travel agent either by telephoning the principal agent or by using the computer to view availability and to book.

When a client arrives at the travel agency and requests you to book some theatre tickets, take down the following details:

Name, address and telephone number of client   You may need to contact the client on the day in question. Anything could cancel the performance – a musicians' dispute, a freak storm!

Name of show and theatre   Be careful here. Occasionally clients will give the name of a theatre, but the show they would like to see is performing at a different venue.

Day and date wanted   Always look at the calendar and repeat the day as well as the date. Have alternative dates ready in case the show is fully booked on the day required.

Performance   Which performance would the client like to attend – matinée (afternoon) or evening?

Number of seats   How many seats are required?

Position of seats   Most theatres have seats called stalls on the ground floor, and a dress circle and an upper circle in tiers above. This is a matter of preference, but think of the type of performance. If most of the show takes place 'in the air' – a circus act perhaps – then circle seats might be the best choice. Many clients do not enjoy sitting in the front row of the stalls as this means looking up to the stage, which can be uncomfortable.

Cost of seats   The cost of the seats you quote to the client *includes* the agency fee. Ask the client for a price range in case you are unable to obtain the first choice.

When making the booking, remember to identify yourself to the principal agent by giving your agency account number; so have that information ready.

When you have contacted the principal agent and the seats are confirmed, show the position of the seats on the theatre plan to your client. Once they are accepted they cannot be cancelled or changed, so you have to be really sure this is exactly what the client wants. If the

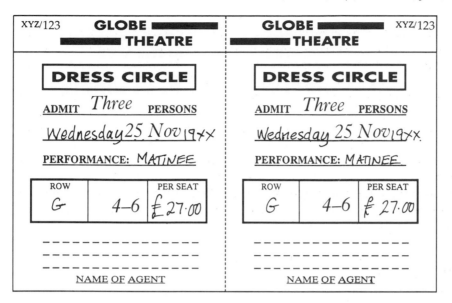

first choice was not available, you would not have to try contacting other theatres; the principal agent will be able to offer an alternative immediately because of the theatre seat allocations held by them.

You are now ready to issue the theatre voucher. The book of tickets will be clearly marked stalls, dress circle or upper circle. One book will be identified as miscellaneous vouchers to be used for special events not held at the theatre. Please study the example XYZ/123 for the Globe Theatre. You will see that the ticket is perforated in the middle; there is also a duplicate copy. On arrival at the theatre the client presents the top copy of the voucher to the usher, who tears it in half, keeps one part and returns the other half to the client. The duplicate copy is also in two halves; one half is sent to the principal agent as confirmation, and the other is retained at the travel agency as a file copy.

Each month the principal agent will send the travel agency a statement giving details of the number of tickets issued and the total amount that the travel agent must pay the principal agent, less commission for the work that has been done. The stubs in the ticket book will be checked against the statement to confirm the number of theatre bookings made during each month.

It is very easy to make a photocopy of the theatre plan and hand this to your client when handing over the tickets. It will help them to find their seats easily, and gives an extra touch of service.

Exercise 2

Try completing the theatre ticket numbered XYZ/456. The details are as follows:

The Globe Theatre, 4 seats commencing G8, cost £27.00 per person, afternoon performance on Wednesday 22 October 19XX.

Please study the seating plan of the Globe Theatre and mark the seats reserved by your clients.

Check your own completed theatre ticket with the example at the back of this book.

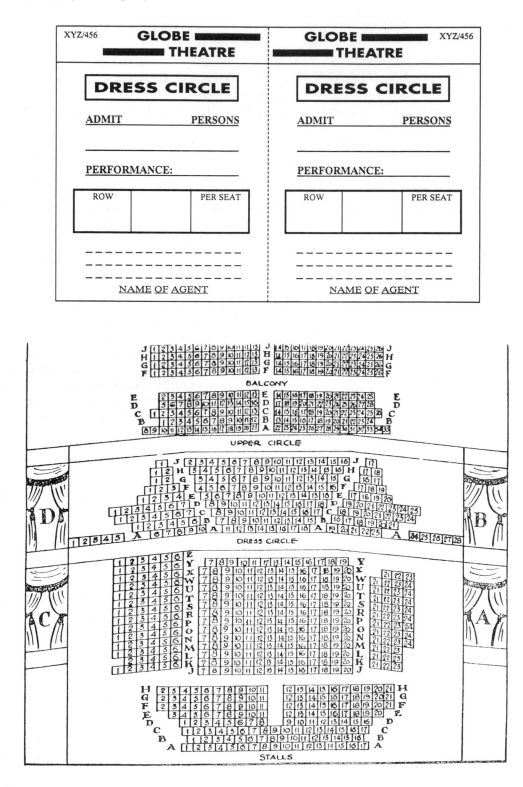

Stopover holidays

What is a Stopover Holiday? It is a mini package, rather like an inclusive tour except the passenger buys the flight ticket separately. They are given two sets of documents, one set for the flight and one set for the Stopover Holiday, and just like an inclusive holiday it has to be paid for, before travel begins.

These tailor-made packages are offered by airlines and each airline provides a brochure giving details of the booking conditions. Airlines usually stipulate that holidays are available only to passengers travelling on their own services. However, they are used as an incentive to travel on long distances with a specific airline. The type of fare paid for the journey should also be studied as many reduced fares carry conditions limiting the number of stopovers allowed. Almost every country in the world can offer a stopover scheme, making a long boring flight exciting with two or three days spent in interesting places along the way. Good hotels are used, and transport is provided between airport and hotel. Stopovers are ideal for business travellers and holiday-makers, and represent excellent value for money.

The first step in selling a stopover holiday is to consider the journey the clients are taking. Perhaps there is a specific choice of airline. Suggest making stopovers along the way, making the most use of the air fare from commencement of the journey to the final destination.

Study the brochures provided by the airlines, check the hotels used by reading the information and examining the city map in the *ABC Hotel Guide*, and consider the clients' interests. Are they making the stopover to do business, to sight-see, to shop, just to rest during a long flight – or perhaps for all these reasons? When you have investigated the clients' needs, then you are in a position to make recommendations regarding airline, locations for stopovers, and time to be spent at each place. The package will be limited by the flight schedule.

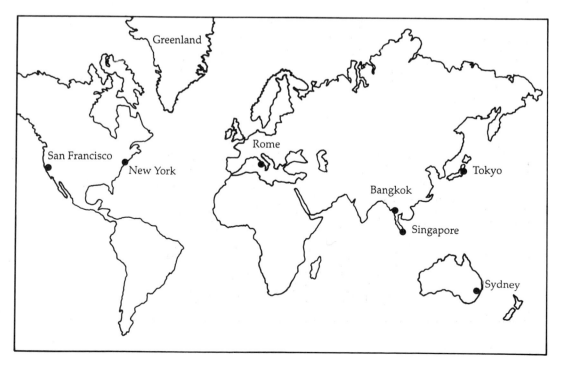

There are thousands of combinations; you can make each and every one exciting. Let's just look at one very simple journey with stopovers, starting at Sydney and finishing at San Francisco (see world map):

Sydney to Singapore (flying time approximately 8½ hours)   Shop for Thai silk, jewellery and made to measure dresses; visit the Tiger Balm Gardens.
Singapore to Bangkok (2½ hours)   Enjoy the floating market; travel along the waterways; visit the temples and shrines.
Bangkok to Rome (13 hours)   Visit the Vatican City, the independent state of just 44 hectares ruled by the Pope; marvel at the beautiful paintings by Michelangelo in the Sistine Chapel; see the Vatican Palace, guarded by Swiss in sixteenth-century uniforms.
Rome to New York (9 hours)   Visit the Empire State Building for the best views of New York; enjoy a ferry trip; see the Statue of Liberty; walk along Fifth Avenue.
New York to San Francisco (6 hours)   A charming compact city: visit Chinatown, Fisherman's Wharf, Alcatraz Island, the Golden Gate Bridge.

Apart from building your product knowledge on the attractions of possible stopover locations, you need to study the conditions attached to these offers, bearing in mind that the tariff contains great reductions. In many cases certain services are complimentary, such as car rental, extra night accommodation and city sight-seeing tours, so check with the airline in question.
    Here are a few questions you should be asking yourself in preparation for selling stopover holidays. The answers can be found in the airline stopover holiday brochures and the *ABC* information manuals.

Client   Interests; reasons for travelling; time available; maximum budget for the trip; nationality (to obtain visas).
Destinations   Flying time; climate; location of accommodation; map of city; places of interest; best time of year to visit.
Stopover programme   Conditions of booking. Which airline must be used, and on how many flights? What does the cost include: sight-seeing tours? Type of accommodation: single or double room? What is the cost for children? How much for an extra night's stay? What are the cancellation charges? What are the facilities of each chosen hotel? Any surcharges? Are the prices seasonal? Does the accommodation include breakfast or any other meals?

Having made the reservation with the airline, you will issue a miscellaneous charges order (MCO) in conjunction with the air ticket. An MCO is similar to an air ticket, and instructions on how it should be issued for a stopover holiday are given in the airline's instructions and also in the *Air Transport Ticketing Handbook*.

Bargain breaks

Holidays planned for a short period of time are very popular and provide an opportunity for the traveller to experience the flavour of a country at least when perhaps shortage of time or money would not permit a longer look. The choice of transport is excellent as bargain break holidays are packaged around travel by air, sea, coach, client's own car, and rail. Many of the holidays include a combination of these forms of transport. The packages are based usually on schedule flights allowing for flexibility with dates and number of days required. They can also be tailor-made 'go as you please' freedom.

Once again the advice is to study the *ABC Guide* for bargain break holidays and to collect the many brochures available and study the holidays offered. You will find a wonderful variety ranging from holidays close to home to far-off destinations.

Just one example is the Thomson Citybreaks brochure covering 30 cities, Paris, Nice, Amsterdam, Dutch Bulbfields, Rome, Florence, Venice, Madrid, Barcelona, Seville, Lisbon, Reykjavik, Brussels, Copenhagen, Dublin, Vienna, Salzburg, Cairo, Washington, Athens, Edinburgh, Stockholm, Bruges, Budapest, Istanbul, New York, Boston, Hong Kong, Leningrad, Moscow. There is a wide range of transport including the Venice Simplon-Orient-Express, and the packages usually include return travel by rail, sea, air, coach, transfers to the hotel on arrival, hotel accommodation of the grade chosen by the customer, including breakfast, guidebooks, street maps, and services of the Thomson Representative.

The ferry services offer excellent bargain break opportunities for travellers wishing to travel by car, with accommodation in cottages, chalets, farm houses, stately homes, camping sites and leisure parks to name but a few!

A bargain break holiday to London can be an enjoyable way of visiting the theatre and sight-seeing for people not living within easy reach of the capital. Many of the short break programmes operate throughout low seasons, for the United Kingdom – the winter months, November to March – and, apart from the benefit of perhaps having something cheerful to look forward to during what can be bleak months for some clients, they offer great value for money and the ability to enjoy the trip without excessive crowds.

The following exercises will help you check your knowledge of this chapter.

Exercise 3

   (a) Explain the following: (i) MAP (ii) AP (iii) efficiency.
   (b) The following categories of hotel are available: commercial/city, resort, motel. Which do you suggest to your clients in the following cases?
      (i) Business traveller visiting various clients in five different cities within the same week.
      (ii) Family of two adults and two children intending to spend two weeks enjoying the seaside.
      (iii) Couple visiting country and with rented car.
   (c) What does a Continental breakfast consist of?
   (d) Give the tariff range for a twin room at the Sheraton Wentworth Hotel in Sydney in local currency.
   (e) Give the location of the hotel in Sydney.
   (f) Give an example of a hotel consortium.

Exercise 4

Explain the difference between a theatre principal agent and a theatre subagent.

Exercise 5

Explain the benefits of stopover holidays.

Assignment for stopover holidays

Task 1

Contact three major airlines and obtain their brochure on stopover holidays.

Task 2

Study and write a report on the differences between the three airlines regarding the destinations offered, tariffs, what is included in the cost and conditions attached to the stopover programmes.

Task 3

You have a client travelling from London to Tokyo who has purchased an airline ticket that permits two stopovers.
  Write a report explaining:

(a) How you will identify the airlines offering a stopover programme.
(b) What information you will need from your client before suggesting where to make the break in journey.
(c) Choose two locations based on the information found from question (b) giving reasons for your choice, and details of the places to be visited.

5 Coaching and incoming tourism

Summary

In this chapter we are going to discuss:

- the benefits of travelling by coach;
- travelling by Greyhound coaches in the USA;
- European coach tours;
- incoming tourism;
- Greyhound map of the USA;
- exercises and assignments to complete.

Why sell coach travel? It can offer a versatile form of transport, providing the travel agent with convenient links between A and B, simple reservation procedures and excellent commission earnings. Let's think about the opportunities to sell coach travel: transfers between airports and hotels; half day or full day sight-seeing tours; group tours for local clubs and associations. Coach travel can be used for travelling from one city to another, providing a similar service to rail but at a lower cost. Coach tours can be enjoyed further when an escort is provided.

The coaches can be very luxurious, offering facilities such as reclining seats, toilets, air conditioning, entertainment and a buffet. Alternatively they can be very basic (uncomfortable for long journeys) or they might have a vintage charm! They come in all sizes; seating capacities range from 10 to 50, although the average is 40.

There are many interesting routes. Greyhound International offer a complete network across the United States of America and Canada. European railways have created Europabus to complete their already extensive rail network, providing luxury coaches for their 50,000 km of scenic routes across Europe. Where can you find the information? In the ABC directories, under the heading 'Coach tours'. Also study *Special Interest Overseas Touring Holidays*, which gives details of hundreds of touring holidays involving coach travel to almost every part of the world – with fascinating themes.

Why are coach tours so popular? For numerous reasons:

Fun together It is a fact that people enjoy doing things together. Friendships blossom, and an unaccompanied person can enjoy the companionship of a coach tour.

Convenience Many elderly clients benefit from a 'door-to-door' service; often the coach will pick up passengers from their home town or even at a central location near their home. Clients without their own transport find a coach tour an excellent way to sight-see.

Low cost   Students find a coach tour a cheap way of seeing a country. Travelling with a preplanned group is like buying merchandise wholesale; there is greater economy in the tour package which an individual traveller could not obtain. This applies to sight-seeing, entertainment, transfers, meals and hotel reservations.

Fixed outlay   As the coach tour is usually a completely packaged trip, the traveller is able to know the total cost in advance; there are no hidden or surprise expenses.

Worries gone   We sometimes overlook the importance of travel worries. Travellers are concerned about the many things that *could* go wrong. When the coach tour has a trained escort on board, the worries are removed! In the event of illness or other emergencies, travellers can be assured of their escort's personal interest in their welfare. There may be difficulties with a foreign language or currency. The presence of an experienced and congenial escort assures a carefree trip.

Please study the map of America with the Greyhound travelling times illustrated, the details of the AMERIPASS and the conditions of purchase.

Organizing a coach tour

Have you ever thought about the Greyhound coach network through the United States and Canada? If you are booking flights for your clients to travel to America, the chances are they intend to sightsee and will travel by coach or car. You can be confident when recommending Greyhound coaches that your clients will be comfortable as the vehicles are equipped with toilets, airconditioning and reclining seats. The Ameripass fare is good value for money. This entitles the purchaser to unlimited travel over Greyhounds' entire route system as well as many other routes of participating connecting services, with freedom to stopover as long as they wish providing travel is completed within the time limit shown on the pass. Ameripasses can be purchased with a validity of 4, 7, 15 and 30 days duration.

An Ameripass is a booklet of travel coupons and is left blank until the owner wishes to start the journey. The Greyhound agent will then punch the expiration date through the cover and all coupons, and the coupons remain in the book until detached by the driver. The Ameripass can be purchased long before arrival in the USA, but personal identification must be supplied (passport) when presenting the booklet for validation at the first boarding point.

You may need help with the following points.

Extensions: The Ameripass ticket may be extended – perhaps your client would like the ticket for 5 days or 17 days, for example. This can be done at an additional cost of £10.00 per day *at time of original purchase.*

Use by purchaser only: The Ameripass may not be transferred to another person and the purchaser may be requested to supply proof of their identity.

Baggage: Two pieces of baggage, weight not to exceed 100 lbs may be carried free of charge.

Lost or stolen tickets: Will not be replaced.

Refunds   No refund will be made on a partially used ticket. Only a totally unused Ameripass ticket will be redeemed to the original purchaser at the fare paid less an administration fee.

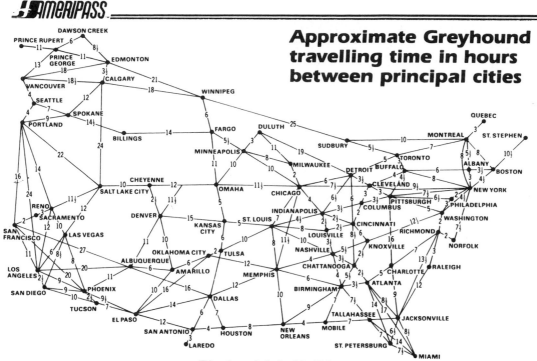

Approximate Greyhound travelling time in hours between principal cities

Ticket Validity

IMPORTANT CONDITIONS OF PURCHASE AND USE

TRAVEL PRIVILEGES: Greyhound AMERIPASS entitles purchaser to travel over Greyhound's entire route system and routes of participating connecting bus lines while pass is valid. See ticket agent for information about participating carriers. Pass purchaser has the privilege of stopping wherever desired for as long as desired and then continuing trip provided travel is completed within the time limit shown on the pass.

EXTENSIONS: The AMERIPASS ticket can be extended at £10 per day at the time of original purchase.

All travel must be completed by January 10, 1991 on the 7 day ticket; January 15, 1991 on the 15 day ticket; and January 30, 1991 for the 30 day ticket.

USE BY PURCHASER ONLY: The ticket coupons on the Greyhound AMERIPASS can only be used by the purchaser whose signature appears on the front page. Greyhound AMERIPASS and/or its ticket coupons may not be transferred. Upon request of any driver, agent or other authorised representative of Greyhound

Lines or participating carriers, the traveller must present acceptable identification properly identifying pass holder as the original purchaser.

BAGGAGE: You may check-free of charge up to two pieces of baggage. Total insured weight is not to exceed 100lbs. Liability is limited to $250.00 (U.S. dollars) for each pass bearer.

LIMITS OF LIABILITY: Greyhound will be responsible only for transportation over its routes. Greyhound assumes no responsibility for any acts or omissions of others occurring within or outside the U.S. except as imposed by laws regarding baggage.

Neither Greyhound Lines Inc. its Divisions or subsidiaries, nor the other participating carriers will be liable for delays or inconvenience caused by accidents, breakdowns, force majeure, acts of God, bad conditions of the road or failure to make connections. Seating aboard vehicles operated by Greyhound is without regard to race, colour, creed or national origin.

SUPPLEMENTAL CHARGES: Greyhound

AMERIPASS covers the intercity transportation of the bearer and his/her baggage. Any charges for supplemental services, if any, are not covered. This includes reserved seat and meal surcharges on certain services. In these cases, pass bearer has option of travelling aboard Greyhound's regular service between the points or paying the surcharges. Fares for sight-seeing tours and some side trips not served by Greyhound Lines are, of course, additional.

LOST OR STOLEN TICKETS: Safeguard your tickets as you would your money. Greyhound assumes no responsibility for lost or stolen tickets and they will not be replaced or redeemed.

REFUNDS: No refund will be made if any portion of the AMERIPASS has been used. A totally unused AMERIPASS will be redeemed to the original purchaser at the fare paid, less a refund handling charge. Application for such refund must be made to the selling agent. Refunds through office of sale only.

CHILDREN: Children 2-11 pay 50% of the adult fare. Children under 2 travel free but are not entitled to their own seat.

For complete conditions of sale, the tariff is available at all Greyhound offices.

All statements concerning fares, conditions and related facts are correct at time of going to press and are subject to change without notice.

GREYHOUND WORLD TRAVEL LTD.

Sussex House
London Road
East Grinstead
West Sussex RH19 1LD
Tel: 0342 317317
Telex: 95475
Fax: 0342 328519
Prestel: 54680

Your Greyhound Agent

In Chapter 2 we examined booking conditions in detail. At this stage, please think about a few general points to keep in mind for all coach travel.

1 Study the ABC directories to discover the names of the many companies offering coach travel and the destinations.
2 Contact local coach company or general sales agent (representing the coach operator) and obtain all information brochures, travel agent manuals and tickets where relevant.
3 Become familiar with conditions of booking and what the tour includes, i.e. full board, half board, single room supplements etc.
4 Get your facts straight about cancellation charges.
5 Dare we say it? Take the brochure home to read!
6 Follow the itinerary and check whether your client will require a visa.
7 Be aware of climatic changes and time zones (especially in the USA and Australia).
8 If the coach tour is just part of your clients' holiday, make sure the departure date and return date fit in with the remainder of your clients' itinerary.
9 Study the seating plan of the coach and the seat numbers. Does the coach operator work on a first come, first served system for seating, or will the passengers rotate during the coach tour?
10 Is the entire coach a no-smoking zone, or is the coach sectioned off into smoking and non-smoking areas?

European coach holidays

Because coach holidays are so popular there is a great variety of tour operators, routes and destinations. For the holidaymaker who does not own a car the coach holiday is a boon and many tours have local pick-up points or free or reduced rail travel to London enabling a trouble-free start to the holiday. Most of the coach companies operating tours to Europe have been in the business for many years and have a wealth of experience in planning the routes with care and a long success story of satisfied customers. Considerable cash savings are made by travelling through Europe by coach. It provides the opportunity of seeing the countryside. For clients who feel the travelling time is too long, there are a great selection of short holidays, centre holidays (coach to a centre and stay awhile) and a combination of transport such as coach cruising, air coach and rail coach, from which to choose.

Coach holiday brochures are usually well presented and easy to read. In the contents page the type of tour, destination and tour number is clearly listed, excellent photographs of the places to be visited, with maps, indicating the route chosen for each itinerary which are helpful. The cost of the holiday for each departure date again is usually clear and the many questions you will be asked by an interested customer can be answered quickly and confidently after a little practice, as most of the points are covered in the brochure.

Making a reservation

Once again we need to obtain all the necessary information from the client before going ahead with the reservation. Apart from personal details, we need to know where they intend to join the coach, any special requests, do they require visas, alternative dates at hand in case the tour is not available.

The reservation can be made by contacting the coach operator by telephone, fax, telex or by use of the office computer. Once the reservation has been made it will be secured by collecting a deposit from your client and you will then assist your client to complete the booking form. Usually within two weeks a written confirmation from the coach company will be received confirming the exact details which you must check against your original request and a date will be shown when balance of payment is due.

From the Greyhound extract please try the following quiz.

Exercise 1

When you have studied the extracts from the Greyhound brochure provided, try this exercise:

(a) What is the approximate travelling time between Los Angeles and San Francisco?

(b) Your client has purchased a Greyhound AMERIPASS valid for 15 days at the cost of £135.00. Now your client is in America and realizes 15 days is not allowing sufficient time. Can the ticket be extended? If so, what would be the cost?

(c) Can a lost Greyhound ticket be replaced?

(d) What is the approximate travelling time between Miami and Nashville?

Incoming tourism

Some travel agencies earn part of their income from providing services to incoming visitors. These services will include:

1 Meeting and greeting at airport or seaport
2 Transfers between airports/hotels and vice versa.
3 Sightseeing tours.
4 Courier services.
5 Secretarial services.
6 Interpreters.
7 Arranging conferences.
8 Obtaining tickets for special events, theatre bookings and concerts.
9 Special interest holidays.
10 Restaurant reservations.
11 Reconfirmation of flight reservations.
12 Any changes required to travel documents.

When thinking about our tour to America and the Netherlands in Chapter 2 the company arranging the transfers and sightseeing tours would be providing services for our incoming tourists. The agents receive commission on the various elements of the services provided, or by adding charges in the form of service fees.

There are companies dealing solely with this side of the industry and the job is, in fact, specialized. Whether or not you would be dealing with incoming tourists would depend mainly on the location of your office, and whether many overseas visitors were received.

When dealing with incoming tourists, whether on a large or small scale you will need detailed information on the area, historical knowledge, new venues, maps, brochures, organization and careful planning. Size of group and nationality will also be important and if involved in a sightseeing tour – an alternative route should an unexpected traffic diversion arise! You will develop a close working relationship with coach operators and understand the problems they try to avoid. The incoming tourism business is taking place throughout the world 24 hours per day, so there are many aspects to consider, with ships to meet at ports, an influx of tourists during peak seasons, and availability of transport, or length of sight-seeing tour.

Assignment: incoming tourism

Many towns, locations and countries have had to rethink their economies owing to industrial changes, and have turned to tourism. Choose a destination that has increased its appeal to tourists, and write a report covering the following topics:

1 Why the original industry has declined.
2 What attractions the destination has encouraged for tourists.
3 What facilities are suitable for incoming tourist and incentive travellers.
4 How accessible the destination has become.
5 Supply a brief history of the destination or country.

Second assignment

You have two clients who are planning to travel on a continental coach holiday and have a shopping list of questions to ask before making a booking. Choose any well-known, established coach holiday company, study their brochure and try to find the answers to the following queries:

(a) Can we be sure the couriers are experienced?
(b) Is the cost of the holiday subject to any surcharges?
(c) Are there any 'special offers' and if so, are we eligible?
(d) Can we join the coach in our home town? (Clients reside in same town as you, the reader).

(e) How can we be sure the route is scenic and not motorway travel?
(f) Can we be sure not to travel by coach during the night?
(g) What grade of hotels are used on the tour?

6 Car rental

Summary

In this chapter we discuss:

- the benefits of car rental for the customer and travel agent;
- understanding how to read a car rental manual;
- calculating journeys;
- important points to remember when selling car rental;
- how to issue a car rental voucher;
- central billing and direct billing;
- exercises and assignments to complete.

Let's think of some good reasons why a customer would wish to hire a car:

1 The rented car may be used during a business promotion.
2 It could be used to drive between the airport and the hotel.
3 It can be used to travel between cities, perhaps as a replacement during car maintenance or during rail/air cancellations.
4 It could be used for touring by holiday-makers.

Car rental provides *flexibility* – the freedom to go almost anywhere at any time, and to stop and stay as one pleases. It also provides *convenience* in a transfer between airport and hotel or in travel around a city, with all baggage safely in the boot of the car; it makes the journey comfortable. The 'rent it here, leave it there' system enables a customer to travel between two major points of his choice, and then to continue the trip using another form of transport if desired. Car rental is *cheap* compared with many other forms of transport, bearing in mind that four or five persons may be travelling in the vehicle. The accessibility of car rental stations is enormous. On this occasion we are using the reference material from Europcar Rental. They operate in 122 countries worldwide offering 266,700 vehicles at over 4,600 rental locations with more than 900 airport rental offices staffed by over 23,000 people.

There are many car rental operators, and most of them work along similar lines. Let's have a look now at general information on car rental.

Car rental information

Rates

Rates are usually calculated on a daily basis (24 hours) or a weekly basis (7 days). There is normally a time charge (this means the customer pays for the time he/she has the car – the number of days) and a distance (kilometre or mile) charge (the customer will be charged for the number of miles or kilometres he/she has travelled). So the cost of hiring a car would be quoted as so much per day plus so much per kilometre. Alternatively, there is the popular unlimited mileage rate. With this a greater time charge is made (number of days) and no mileage charges are made at all. For clients intending to travel long distances this could be very economical. We will have the opportunity of calculating the cost of car rental for different journeys later on and comparing the two systems.

In addition to these rates most car rental companies have special offers, and brochures are available explaining the great reductions. It is also well worth while contacting the car rental companies for any special rates that are unpublished but available. Car rental companies do not like to have cars standing idle over a weekend, and they will usually be pleased to negotiate competitive rates.

Car groups

Cars are divided into groups of similar models, normally ranging from A (the smallest cars) to H (the largest cars). It is important, when assisting your client to choose a car, to consider not only the number of passengers but also the amount of luggage to be carried. Although a small car will seat up to four people, the luggage capacity will be just one large suitcase, one small case and one overnight bag, which may not allow each passenger to take sufficient luggage perhaps. Car rental companies publish luggage capacity guides for each car type used in their fleet and this is very useful information to have.

There are other points to consider. One is the choice between manual and automatic transmission; your client may only be able to drive a car that has automatic transmission. Does your client require a two-door or a four-door car? A two-door car may mean difficulty for a passenger to reach the back seat.

Fuel consumption

A small car will travel approximately 10–12 kilometres per litre (28–31 miles per gallon), a medium car approximately 8–10 km/l (22–28 mile/gal) and a large car approximately 6–8 km/l (18–20 mile/gal). This information, and the price of petrol in countries to be visited, is important to know, as you can then advise your clients, enabling them to budget for their holidays.

Petrol

The rates quoted do not include petol. The client will normally rent a car with a full tank and return it also with a full tank. Oil and maintenance will usually be included in the cost; there is no charge for water!

Age restrictions

Both a minimum and a maximum age restriction can apply depending on the company, the country and the car group. The minimum age is often between 23 and 25 years and the maximum age between 65 and 70 years. A large car will often carry the condition that the drivers minimum age should be higher. For example, car groups A to G minimum age of 21 years: car groups H–W minimum age of 25 years. The reason behind this condition is that a 25 year old driver may have a greater sense of responsibility and more driving experience.

Driving licence

A valid and unendorsed driving licence is required. Does this mean that someone with an endorsed licence would be unable to rent a car? Not necessarily; this could be acceptable at the discretion of the rental company. Many countries require the driver to have an international driving permit. This can be obtained at the nearest office of the Automobile Association in the United Kingdom – but check where this can be obtained in your own area, in readiness to advise a client!

Deposits

Most car rental companies will require a deposit as security. The amount will vary, but is usually between £100 and £150. This is a very small amount when you consider that your client will be driving away with an article worth £10,000 or more! The payment of a cash deposit can be waived by using an acceptable credit card or car rental voucher. The travel agent would be able to issue a car rental voucher if the client had paid a deposit or even full payment to the travel company, or if the client had an account with the travel agency and paid at the end of each month.

We now come to a very important part of selling car rental which must be fully understood.

Insurance

Third party insurance

All reputable car rental companies include third party insurance within their rates. You should check the amount of cover provided to ensure that it is adequate and that it includes cover in the event of death or injury to third parties or damage to cars and other property belonging to third parties caused in an accident. This can be particularly important in the USA where the basic cover provided may not always be sufficient to meet the amounts awarded in any legal action arising from an accident. In this case extended cover is sometimes available as an 'optional extra' to clients.

Collision Damage Waiver (abbreviated as CDW)

The cost of the insurance will include damage to the car in the event of an accident. However, the renter could be liable to pay towards the costs of repairs which could be as much as £1,000. To waive this payment, the customer can pay an additional insurance called Collision Damage Waiver and should the car be involved in a collision, the renter will have nothing at all to pay.

Personal Accident Insurance

This insurance covers death or injury to the driver and passengers in the event of an accident in the rented car. Some companies include the premium within their all-inclusive rates, but because some customers choose not to take out Personal Accident Cover, it is generally available as an optional extra for a modest premium.

Good personal accident insurance will also include cover for personal belongings which may be damaged in an accident or stolen from the rented car.

Taxes

Taxes are imposed over and above the rental charges, and vary with the country.

Model

Car rental companies will try to provide a specified model when confirming the reservation, but they will usually only guarantee a particular group. If none of the vehicles from the specified group is available when the hirer collects the car, a larger model is normally available at no extra cost to the client.

Rates of exchange

The rates of exchange shown in the directories are meant purely as a guide. Always check the rate of exchange at the time of making the reservation with the car rental company.

How to read this Directory

COUNTRY-EUROPCAR COUNTRY CODE

RESERVATIONS OFFICE

Phone number, Postal address,
Telex number, Opening hours.

KENYA-38

[R] GDE Phone: **(254) 2/334722-3-4-5**
P.O. Box 40433, Nairobi
Telex: 22274 Mon-Fri 0800-1700, Sat 0800-1200

Your Europcar contact in Kenya, at your disposal free of charge for rental enquiries and domestic and/or international reservations.

RENTAL LOCATIONS

- addresses
- phone numbers
- telex numbers
- opening hours
- station codes

RENTAL LOCATIONS

Mombasa
Nkurumah Rd (312461) Tlx: 21285 **KDB**
Mon-Fri 0800-1700, Sat 0800-1200
Nairobi
Bruce House, Standard Str. (334722) **KDC**
Tlx: 22274 Mon-Fri 0800-1700, Sat 0800-1200
Nairobi Airport
Jomo Kenyatta Intl. Airport **NBO**
(822348) Daily 24 Hours

CAR GROUPS

CAR GROUPS

A	Toyota Starlet, Fiat Uno
B	Toyota Corolla 70 STW
C	Toyota Corolla 90 DLX
D	Toyota Corona A/C, Peugeot 405
E	Suzuki 4WD (2)
F	Isuzu Trooper 4WD A/C
G	Toyota Hiace Minibus (9 Seats)

All Cars Equipped With Radio.

RATES

- Daily Time and Mileage rates
- Weekly Time and Mileage rates
- Kilometre (or Mile) rates
- Weekly Unlimited Mileage rates
- Additional Days rates (to the Weekly Unltd.) or other special rates

Group		Daily	Weekly Ltd*	Km	Weekly Unltd	Add Days
A	KSH	380.	5200.	4.90	6400.	914.29
	US$	22.35	305.88	29	376.47	53.78
B	KSH	500.	6500.	5.90	7990.	1141.43
	US$	24.41	382.35	35	4.70	67.14
C	KSH	590.	7100.	610	8700.	1242.86
	US$	34.71	417.65	36	511.76	73.11
D	KSH	650.	7900.	6.80	9600.	1371.43
	US$	38.24	464.71	40	564.71	80.67
E	KSH	460.	6250.	5.90	7750.	1107.15
	US$	27.06	367.65	35	455.88	65.13
F	KSH	950.	11300.	9.50	13700.	1957.15
	US$	55.88	664.71	56	805.88	115.13
G	KSH	810.	10200.	9.00	12500.	1785.72
	US$	47.65	600.00	53	735.29	105.04

* Weekly Limited includes 700 KM
Local Currency Rates Valid, Gas Not Included,
Rates Subject To Charge Without Notice.

For rentals of 7 days or more, the lower rates, either Time and Mileage or Weekly Unlimited, will be charged automatically.

RENTAL CONDITIONS

- Driver's qualification
- Accepted means of payment
- Insurance
- Miscellaneous
- Chauffeur Driven Service and other services

Currency: Kenyan Shilling. Exchange Rate Used Above (For Guidance Only): KSH 17 To US$1
Tax: None
Age: 23 - 70
Drivers License: Held For At Least, Two Years
Cash Rental Deposit: Estimated Rental Charges Plus KSH 10000
Credit Cards Accepted: Amex, Diners, Eurocard, Visa
Deductible Collision Damage: KSH 10000
C.D.W.: Groups A-C: KSH 200 Per Day, Groups D-E: KSH 250 Per Day, Groups F-G: KSH 300 Per Day.
P.A.I.: KSH 30 Per Day Per Person
Delivery/Collection: Free Within City Limits
One-Way Rentals:
Domestic: Between Nairobi-Mombasa
Rental Less Than 7 Days KSH 1500,
Rental 7 Days Or More No Drop Charge.
Restriction Of Use: Cars Not Allowed To Leave Kenya
Car Availability:
Nairobi: Groups A-E On Freesell,
Mombasa: All Groups On Request.
Chauffeur Driven Service: Available On Freesell, KSH 600 Extra Per Day.

TAX *is additional*

ABBREVIATIONS USED

(A)	automatic transmission	**Km**	kilometre	**Stw**	station wagon
A/C	air conditioned	**Mnthly**	Monthly	**Sun.**	Sunday
Add.	additional	**Mon.**	Monday	**Thu.**	Thursday
APT	airport	**N/A**	not available	**Tlx.**	telex number
C.D.W.	Collision Damage Waiver	**OWR**	one-way rental	**Tue.**	Tuesday
DT	down-town	**P.A.I.**	Personal Accident Insurance	**Unltd.**	Unlimited
Fri.	Friday	[R]	Reservations Office	**Wed.**	Wednesday
I.K.C.	International Key City	**Sat.**	Saturday	**4WD**	4-wheel drive
				( )	*x* doors

Using a directory: Europcar

Please examine the extract from the Europcar Directory titled 'How to read this directory'. The country is Kenya. Study the explanation and the abbreviations used.

Reservation office   We have been given the address, telephone number, telex number and hours of business at the reservation office in Nairobi. We have been given the same information for other rental locations in Kenya.

Car groups   We have been given a description of the car model that applies to each alphabetical group.

Rates   We have been given the rates in two currencies, the Kenyan shilling and the US dollar. So, group A (Toyota Starlet or Fiat Uno) would cost KSH380 per day and KSH4.90 per kilometre. (Note that the US$ kilometre rates are in cents.) We have a choice of weekly tariffs. There is a weekly rate (7 days) with limited mileage; the note indicated by the * sign states that the rate of KSH5200 includes 700 km. There is an unlimited weekly mileage rate at KSH6400; additional days would be charged at KSH914.29. To the right of the rates columns there is a note advising that, for rentals of 7 days or more, the lower rates (either time and mileage or weekly unlimited) will be charged automatically.

Currency   We are advised that the rates are for guidance only, based on KSH17 to US$1.

Tax   There is no tax to be charged on the car rental rate in Kenya.

Age   The minimum age to rent a car is 23 years and the maximum age is 70 years.

Driver's licence   The driver's licence must have been held for at least 2 years.

Cash rental deposit   If the cost of the car rental is going to be paid by cash, then before driving away in the car the driver must pay the estimated cost of hiring the car plus a deposit of KSH10,000 (approximately US$588. This is returnable or deductible.

Credit cards   Europcar will accept Amex, Diners, Eurocard and Visa credit cards.

Deductible collision damage   If there is a collision which involves damage to the vehicle, the driver will have to pay up to KSH10,000 towards the cost of repair.

Collision damage waiver (CDW)   By paying an additional insurance, the collision damage amount of KSH10,000 can be waived. We are advised that on car groups A to C the cost of this extra insurance is KSH200 per day.

Personal accident insurance (PAI)   The cost of insuring against the renter (and passengers in the car) being injured is KSH30 per person per day.

Delivery/collection charges   Delivering the car to the client or collecting the car from the client incurs no charge if within the city.

One-way rentals   Between Nairobi and Mombasa for rentals of less than 7 days, a charge of KSH1500 is made. For rentals of 7 days or more, no charge is made. Please read the restriction note: cars are not allowed to leave Kenya, so the driver would not be allowed to collect a car in Nairobi and drop it off in, say, Kampala, Uganda. The distances between the two cities, the infrastructure conditions and the formalities involved would make this difficult; between countries in Europe the one-way system works well.

Car availability   We are advised that car groups A–E in Nairobi are on Freesell. This means that confirmation is automatic. You would still have to contact Europcar to make the booking, but you know the reservation will be confirmed. For car rental reservations in Mombasa, the reservation will be requested and not immediately guaranteed.

Chauffeur driven service   This is available.

Costing a car rental transaction

Mr R. Cloe collected a Peugeot 405 from his hotel in Nairobi on Wednesday 3 May at 1100 hours and returned the car to the Nairobi reservation office on Saturday morning at 0900 hours. Mr Cloe travelled 270 km and required CDW and PA insurance. His costs were as follows:

Group D KSH650 per day for 3 days	KSH1950
KSH6.80 per km × 270 km	1836
CDW group D KSH250 per day × 3 days	750
PAI KSH30 per person per day × 3 days	90
	KSH4626

To find the approximate cost in US dollars, divide KSH4626 by 17 (KSH17 = $1) to give $272.

Exercise 1: Let's try another one

Mr Mulenga collects a Suzuki 4WD(2) car from Nairobi Airport on 17 February at 1400 hours and returns the car to Nairobi Airport on 25 February at 1300 hours. He intends to travel extensively during that time and we will calculate the Weekly Unlimited mileage tariff. Mr Mulenga requires PAI and CDW insurance.

How many days will the client have the car? (8 days). So we will charge the weekly rate = 7 days plus one extra day, total 8 days.

We need to know the car group before we begin our calculations. The Suzuki is group E. Please study the details provided on Kenya first.

Group E weekly unlimited mileage	KSH 7750.00
Add one extra day	1107.15
CDW for group E KSH250 per day × 8 days	2000.00
PAI KSH30 per day × 8 days	240.00
	KSH 11097.15

And one more

Mr Kabemba collects a Toyota Corrola 70 STW from a hotel in Mombassa on 11 May at 1000 hours and returns the car on 12 May at 0900 hours and has driven 241 kilometres. He has personal accident and collision damage waiver insurance. What did this car rental cost? First of all name the car group (group B). For how long did Mr Kabemba rent the car? (one day). *Please check this calculation by following the information given under KENYA.*

Group B daily rate KSH500	KSH 500.00
Group B kilometre rate KSH5.90 per km × 240	
(our client drove 240 kilometres)	1416.00
PAI KSH30 per day × one day	30.00
CDW group B (A–C) KSH200 per day × one day	200.00
	KSH2146.00

EUROPEAN ONE-WAY RENTAL PLAN

International One-Way rentals can start from any of the following 66 **International Key Cities (I.K.C.'s)**
AUSTRIA : Innsbruck, Salzburg, Vienna. **BELGIUM :** Antwerp, Brussels, Charleroi, Gent, Liège, Mons, Ostend.
DENMARK : Aalborg, Aarhus, Copenhagen, Odense. **FRANCE :** Bordeaux, Cannes, Geneva Airport, Lille, Lyon, Marseille,
Montpellier, Nice, Paris, Rennes, Strasbourg, Toulouse. **GERMANY :** Berlin, Bonn, Bremen, Cologne, Düsseldorf, Frankfurt,
Hamburg, Hannover, Munich, Nuremberg, Stuttgart. **HOLLAND :** Amsterdam, Eindhoven, Rotterdam, The Hague.
ITALY : Bologna, Florence, Genoa, Milan, Naples, Pisa, Rome, Turin, Venice. **LUXEMBOURG :** Luxembourg city.
NORWAY : Oslo. **PORTUGAL :** Lisbon, Porto. **SPAIN :** Barcelona, Madrid. **SWEDEN :** Gothenburg, Malmoe, Stockholm.
SWITZERLAND : Basle, Berne, Geneva, Lausanne, Lucerne, Lugano, Zurich. **YUGOSLAVIA :** Belgrade, Ljubljana, Zagreb.

DROP-OFF CHARGES (in US $)	Zone 1	Zone 2	Zone 3	Zone 4	Zone 5
Small-Medium cars	NIL	100	200	300	400
Large-Luxury-Special Equipment cars	100	200	300	400	500

Above drop-off charges are in US Dollars. However, they are charged in local currency. See in each renting country section of this directory under
One-Way Rental: Eur. OWR Plan *what car groups are considered Small-Medium or Large-Luxury-S.E., and the equivalence of US Dollars 100.*

RENTING COUNTRY	ZONES OF RETURN				
	ZONE I	ZONE II	ZONE III	ZONE IV	ZONE V
AUSTRIA	Munich.	IKC's Switzerland, Yugoslavia. All cities Germany.	IKC's France, Italy. All cities Belgium, Holland, Luxembourg. Other cities Switzerland.	Other cities France, Italy, Yugoslavia.	All cities Denmark, Norway, Portugal, Spain, Sweden.
BELGIUM	Amsterdam, Bonn, Cologne, Düsseldorf, Eindhoven, Frankfurt, Lille, Luxembourg, Rotterdam, The Hague.	Paris, Strasbourg.	All IKC's not listed under Zone I or II.	Other cities France, Germany, Holland, Italy, Switzerland.	Other cities Austria, Denmark, Norway, Portugal, Spain, Sweden.
DENMARK	Gothenburg, Hamburg, Malmoe, Oslo, Stockholm.	Other cities Germany, Sth. Sweden All cities Belgium, Holland, Luxbg. Bergen.	All cities Austria, France, Switzerland.	IKC's Italy, Spain	Other cities Italy, Portugal, Spain. Helsinki
FRANCE	Brussels, Frankfurt, Geneva, Luxembourg, Stuttgart, Turin.	Other IKC's Belgium, Germany, Holland, Italy Spain, Switzerland.	Other cities Belgium, Germany, Holland, Italy, Spain, Switzerland.	IKC's Austria, Denmark, Portugal, Sweden.	Other cities Austria, Denmark, Portugal, Sweden. All cities Norway.
GERMANY	All cities Austria, Belgium, Holland, Luxembourg, Switzerland. Odense, Milan, Paris, Strasbourg.	Other IKC's France, Italy. Other cities Denmark. Ljubljana, Malmo, Zagreb.	Other cities France Other IKC's Sweden.	IKC's Norway, Portugal, Spain. Other cities Italy, Sweden. Belgrade	Other cities Norway, Portugal, Spain, Yugoslavia.
HOLLAND	All cities Belgium, Luxembourg, Bonn, Bremen, Cologne, Düsseldorf, Frankfurt, Hamburg, Hannover.	Other cities Germany. Calais, Copenhagen, Lille, Paris.	IKC's Sweden. All cities Switzerland.	All cities Austria.	Other cities Denmark, France, Sweden. All cities Italy, Norway, Portugal, Spain.
ITALY		IKC's Switzerland. Cannes, Innsbruck, Lyon, Monte-Carlo, Munich, Nice, Salzburg.	Other IKC's France. Other cities Austria, Switzerland. Cologne, Düsseldorf, Frankfurt, Ljubljana, Luxembourg, Nuremberg, Rjeka, Stuttgart.	All cities Belgium, Holland. Other cities France, Germany, Madrid, Barcelona.	Other cities Spain, Yugoslavia. All cities Denmark, Norway, Portugal, Sweden.
LUXEM-BOURG	IKC's Belgium, Holland, Bonn, Cologne, Düsseldorf, Frankfurt, Metz, Saarbruecken, Thionville, Trier.	Other cities Belgium. Epinal, Paris, Strasbourg.	Other IKC's France, Germany. IKC's Switzerland.	All IKC's Austria, Denmark, Italy, Norway, Sweden. Other cities France, Switzerland.	Other cities Austria, Denmark, Italy, Norway, Sweden. Alicante, Barcelona, Bilbao, Cascais, Faro, Lisbon, Madrid, Porto, San Sebastian, Valencia.
NORWAY			All cities Sweden.	All cities Denmark.	All cities Austria, Belgium, France, Germany, Holland, Switzerland.
PORTUGAL	Madrid.	Barcelona.	Other cities Spain. IKC's France.	Other cities France. IKC's other countries.	Other cities all countries.
SPAIN		Lisbon, Porto.	Other cities Portugal.	IKC's Austria, Belgium, France, Germany, Holland, Italy, Luxembourg, Switzerland.	IKC's Denmark, Norway, Sweden, Yugoslavia. Other cities all countries.
SWEDEN	Copenhagen, Oslo.	Other cities Denmark. Hamburg.	IKC's Belgium, Germany, Holland. Bergen, Kristiansand, Stavanger, Trondheim	IKC's Austria. France, Luxembourg, Switzerland. Other cities Germany.	Other cities Austria, Belgium, France, Holland, Luxembourg, Switzerland, Barcelona, Milan.
SWITZER-LAND	Munich, Stuttgart.	IKC's Austria, Luxembourg. Other IKC's Germany. Amsterdam, Brussels, Cannes, Lyon, Marseille, Milan, Nice, Paris, Strasbourg.	Other IKC's Belgium, France, Holland, Italy. Other cities Germany.	IKC's Spain. Other cities Belgium, France, Holland, Italy, Copenhagen.	IKC's Norway, Portugal, Sweden. Other cities Denmark, Spain.
YUGOSLAVIA	Klagenfurt, Trieste.	Graz, Salzburg, Venice, Vienna.	Other cities Austria, Bologna, Milan, Munich, Padova, Stuttgart, Verona, Zurich.	Basle, Berne, Florence, Frankfurt, Genova, Lucerne, Nuremberg, Turin.	Others cities Germany, Italy, Switzerland.

If Mr Kabemba had not paid the CDW insurance and had an accident incurring damage to the vehicle, how much could he expect to pay towards repair of the car? Please see Deductible Collision Damage = KSH10.000.

If Mr Kabemba does not guarantee payment by a credit card (it has to be Amex, Diners, Eurocard or Visa) and the travel agency has not guaranteed payment what is the total amount he has to pay before driving away with the Toyota Carolla?

See *Cash Rental Deposit* estimated rental charges plus KSH10000. So!

Estimated rental charges are	KSH 2146.00
Deposit	10000.00
Total	KSH 12146.00

Please study the extract from the Europcar Directory titled 'European one-way rental plan' (collecting the car in one city and leaving it in another). It is explained that one-way rentals can start from any of 66 International key cities (IKCs). So, Austria's international key cities are Innsbruck, Salzburg and Vienna. A client can collect a small or medium car in Vienna and leave it in Munich at no extra charge. If a client collected a small or medium car in Rotterdam and delivered it to Paris (find Holland in the column 'Renting country', then follow across to Paris, which is in zone 2), the charge would be US$100. How do you know which type of car is small, medium or large? We find this information under the heading One Way Rental. Examine the details on Luxembourg and we can read small/medium are groups A–D and large/special are groups E–S.

Next study carefully the extracts from the Europcar Directory for Luxembourg.

If your client collects a BMW 525 from Luxembourg Airport, and leaves the car at Odense, what is the cost for this convenience?

Find the car group under *Luxembourg* BMW 525 (Group M). Under *One Way Rental* we can see large cars are groups E–S. Where will we find Odense? Odense is an IKC (International Key City) in Denmark. Follow the column along FROM LUXEMBOURG to zone one, is Denmark mentioned? No. In zone two, can you see Denmark listed? No. Zone three? No. Zone four? YES. So, for a *large* car zone four (US$ 400). If your client had been leaving the car at another city in Denmark that was *NOT* listed as an International Key City, then we would move to zone five 'other cities' in Austria, Denmark, etc. that are not IKC.

Study again the *Abbreviations Used* section at the foot of 'How to read this directory' and use the guide to understand the abbreviations used in the Kenya and Luxembourg panel. When you have completed that task try to write the explanation of the following abbreviations using your own words.

DT	4WD
R	N/A
STW	

Now try to answer the following questions:

Europcar

APRIL - AUGUST

Group		Daily	Weekly	Km	Weekly Unltd	Add Days
D	LF	1160.	6960.	11.60	13630.	1947.14
	US$	33.27	199.60	.33	390.88	55.84
E	LF	1350.	8100.	13.50	17270.	2467.14
	US$	38.72	232.29	.39	495.27	70.75
F	LF	1555.	9330.	15.20	19520.	2788.57
	US$	44.59	267.57	.44	559.79	79.97
G	LF	1300.	7800.	10.30	13370.	1910.00
	US$	37.28	223.69	.30	383.42	54.77
H	LF	1770.	10620.	15.30	20810.	2972.86
	US$	50.76	304.56	.44	596.79	85.26
J	LF	2100.	12600.	17.80	24300.	3471.43
	US$	60.22	361.34	.51	696.87	99.55
L	LF	1230.	7380.	11.00	16750.	2392.86
	US$	35.27	211.64	.32	480.36	68.62
M	LF	3440.	20640.	32.40	29150.	4164.29
	US$	98.65	591.91	.93	835.96	119.42
N	LF	1670.	10020.	16.30	20810.	2972.86
	US$	47.89	287.35	.47	596.79	85.26
P	LF	1470.	8820.	13.90	19570.	2795.71
	US$	42.16	252.94	.40	561.23	80.18
R	LF	1370.	8220.	13.70	17440.	2491.43
	US$	39.29	235.73	.39	500.14	71.45
S	LF	1740.	10440.	15.60	20720.	2960.00
	US$	49.90	299.40	.45	594.21	84.89
T	LF	1980.	11880.	17.60	23630.	3375.71
	US$	56.78	340.69	.50	677.66	96.81
V	LF	2930.	17580.	18.40	26940.	3848.57
	US$	84.03	504.16	.53	772.58	110.37
W	LF	3430.	20580.	32.40	29150.	4164.29
	US$	98.37	590.19	.93	835.96	119.42

Local Currency Rates Valid, Gas Not Included,
Rates Subject To Change Without Notice.

Currency: Lux. Franc. Exchange Rate Used
bove (For Guidance Only): LF 34.87 To US$ 1
Tax:12%
Age: Groups A-E,G:21, Groups F,H-W:25
Drivers License: Held For At Least One Year
Cash Rental Deposit: Estimated Rental Charges
With Minimum LF 10000.
(No Cash Rental Possible For Groups
F,H,J,L,M,P,T)
Credit Cards Accepted: Air Plus, Amex,
Diners, Eurocard, Visa
Deductible Collision Damage:
Groups A-D,G : LF 25000,
Groups E,F,H,J,L,N-T : LF 35000,
Group M,V,W : LF 50000
C.D.W.: Per Day: Groups A-D,G: LF 375,
Groups E,F,H,J,L,N-T : LF 425,
Groups M,V,W: LF 800
P.A.I.: LF 150 Per Day
One-Way Rentals: Eur. OWN plan: (See
Explanation Page E3): Small/Medium: A-D,
Large/Special: E-S US$ 100.00: LF 3500
Other Services: Vans, Snow Tyres
Car Availability:
Luxembourg : Groups A-D,F,R,S On Freesell,
Dudelange: Group A-B,D On Freesell,
Other Cities : Groups A-D On Freesell

LUXEMBOURG-65

Ⓡ QQX Phone: **(352) 404228**
84 Route De Thionville2610 Luxembourg Telex: 3488
Mon-Fri 0800-1200/1330-1700

RENTAL LOCATIONS:

Dudelange
73 Route De Luxembourg (352/520252) **HCF**
Mon-Fri 0800-1200/1330-1730
Esch/Alzette
75 Boulevard Prince Henri (555312) **DBK**
Mon-Fri 0800-1200/1400-1800
Luxembourg (I.K.C.)
84 Route De Thionville (487684-404228) **RAA**
Tlx:3488 Mon-Fri 0800-1200/1315-1800,
Sat 1000-1200
Luxembourg Airport (I.K.C.)
Findel (434588) Mon-Sat 0900-2000, **LUX**
Sun 0900-1700
Redange/Attert
5 Rue Fraesbich (62199) **DRQ**
Mon-Fri 0800-1200/1400-1800
Rollingen/Mersch
Route De Luxembourg (329235-329254) **DBL**
Mon-Fri 0800-1200/1400-1800

CAR GROUPS
A VW Polo 1.1 (3), Seat Ibiza 1.2 (3)
B VW Golf 1.3 (3), Peugeot 205 GL 1.1 (5)
C VW Golf 1.6 Turbo Diesel (4)
D VW Jetta GL 1.8 (4), Peugeot 405 GL 1.6 (4)
E VW Passat CL 1.8 (4)
F Audi 80 S 1.8 (4)
G VW Golf 1.6 (A) (3)
H Audi 80 S 1.8 (A) (4)
J Audi 100 E 2.2 ABS (4), Audi 90 E 2.2 ABS (4)
L VW Minibus Caravelle C (9 Seats)
(Trailer Coupling)
M BMW 525 I 2.5 (A) A/C ABS (4)
N VW Jetta 1.8 Syncro (4)
P VW Minibus Caravelle C Turbo Diesel (9 Seats)
R VW Passat Variant 1.8 CL STW (5 seats)
S VW Minibus Caravelle GLI (7 Seats)
T VW Minibus Caravelle GL Syncro Turbo Diesel
(4WD) (9 Seats)
V Audi 90 E Quattro 2.2 ABS (4WD) (4)
W Audi 100 E Quattro 2.2 ABS (4WD) A/C (4)
All Cars Equipped With Radio

Group		Daily	Weekly	Km	Weekly Unltd	Add Days
A	LF	815.	4890.	8.15	8700.	1242.86
	US$	23.37	140.24	.23	249.50	35.64
B	LF	1080.	6480.	9.95	12070.	1724.29
	US$	30.97	185.83	.29	346.14	49.45
C	LF	1160.	6960.	11.60	13630.	1947.14
	US$	33.27	199.60	.33	390.88	55.84

Group		Daily	Weekly	Km	Weekly Unltd	Add Days
S	ESC	10000	66500	Free	66500	9500
	US$	67.92	451.67		451.67	64.52

Local Currency Rates Valid, Gas Not Included.
Rates Subject To Change Without Notice.

Currency: Escudo Exchange Rate Used Above (For
Guidance Only): ESC 147.23 To US$1
Tax:12%
Age:23
Drivers License: Held For At Least One Year
Cash Rental Deposit: Estimated Rental Charges
With Minimum ESC 30000
Credit Cards Accepted: Access, Amex, C. Blanche,
Diners, Eurocard, Master Card, Unibanco, Visa
Deductible Collision Damage:
Groups A-D : ESC 450000,
Groups E-G : ESC 800000,
Groups H,I,S : ESC 1200000.
C.D.W.: Per Day Groups A-D : ESC 1200,
Groups E-G : ESC 1600,
Groups H,I,S : ESC 2000
P.A.I.: ESC 300 Per Day
Delivery/Collection: Free To Airport
Other Services: Luggage Rack : ESC 300
Per Day, Baby Seat : ESC 500 Per Day.
Car Availability: Groups A-E On Freesell

MALTA-48

Ⓡ RRZ Phone: **(356)** 605038-228745-228580
38 Villambrosa Street,Hamrun, Telex: 989
Mon-Fri 0900-1800, Sat-Sun 0900-1300

RENTAL LOCATIONS:

Hamrun
38 Villambrosa Street (605038/228745) **RRX**
Mon-Fri 0900-1800, Sat-Sun 0900-1300
Luqa Airport
Counter On First Floor (605038/228745) **MLA**
Meets Reservations
Mellieha
Maritim Selmun Palace Hotel **FDV**
(605038/228745) Mon-Fri 0900-1100
Gawra
Suncrest Hotel, (605038-228745) **FIY**
Mon-Sun 0830-1245/1500-1800
Sliema
Holiday Inn Hotel Tigne (228745/605038) **FGC**
Daily 0830-1200/1430-1800

CAR GROUPS
A Ford Fiesta, Vauxhall Nova
B Mazda 323 (3), Fiat Uno (3)
C Ford Escort, Hyundai Pony, VW Golf, Mazda 323
D Mazda 323 STW Ford Escort STW
E Hyundai Pony (A), Mazda 323 (A)
F Hyundai Stellar A/C
G Mercedes 200 (A) A/C
H Minibus (9 Seats)
I Maruti Jeep

APRIL 1, 1990 - JUNE 30, 1990
DECEMBER 16, 1990 - JANUARY 3, 1991

Group		Daily	Weekly	Mile	Weekly Unltd	Add Days
A	ML	0.75	40.75	Free	43.75	6.25
	US$	26.52	132.58		132.58	18.94
B	ML	9.00	45.50	Free	45.50	6.50
	US$	27.27	137.88		137.88	19.70
C	ML	9.75	49.00	Free	49.00	7.00
	US$	29.55	148.48		148.48	21.21
D	ML	10.00	52.50	Free	52.50	7.50
	US$	30.30	159.09		159.09	22.73
E	ML	10.25	54.25	Free	54.25	7.75
	US$	31.06	164.39		164.39	23.48
F	ML	12.00	66.50	Free	66.50	9.50
	US$	36.36	201.52		201.52	28.79
G	ML	23.00	126.00	Free	126.00	18.00
	US$	69.70	381.82		381.82	54.55
H	ML	15.50	80.50	Free	80.50	11.50
	US$	46.97	243.94		243.94	34.85
I	ML	12.50	70.00	Free	70.00	10.00
	US$	37.88	212.12		212.12	30.30

Additional Driver ML 1.00 Extra Per Day
Local Currency Rates Valid, Gas Not Included,
Rates Subject To Change Without Notice.

JULY 1 - OCTOBER 31, 1990

Group		Daily	Weekly	Mile	Weekly Unltd	Add Days
A	ML	10.00	50.75	Free	50.75	7.25
	US$	30.30	153.79		153.79	21.97
B	ML	10.25	52.50	Free	52.50	7.50
	US$	31.06	159.09		159.09	22.73
C	ML	10.75	56.00	Free	56.00	8.00
	US$	32.58	169.70		169.70	24.24
D	ML	11.00	59.50	Free	59.50	8.50
	US$	33.33	180.30		180.30	25.76
E	ML	11.25	61.25	Free	61.25	8.75
	US$	34.09	185.61		185.61	26.52
F	ML	14.00	71.75	Free	71.75	10.25
	US$	42.42	217.42		217.42	31.06
G	ML	25.00	140.00	Free	140.00	20.00
	US$	75.76	424.24		424.24	60.61
H	ML	18.25	103.25	Free	103.25	14.75
	US$	55.30	312.88		312.88	44.70
I	ML	16.50	98.00	Free	98.00	14.00
	US$	50.00	296.97		296.97	42.42

MADEIRA-71/90

Ⓡ QRR Phone: Lisbon (351) 524558-524771
Avda A.A De Aguiar 24 C/D Telex: 12799

RENTAL LOCATIONS:

Funchal
Estrada Monumental 306 (28116/28176) **REA**
Tlx:72315 Daily 0830-1930

CAR GROUPS
A Seat Marbella (3)
B Opel Corsa (3)
C Ford Fiesta (3), Toyota Starlet
D Renault 5 GL, Peugeot 205 Junior,
Ford Escort CL
E Toyota Corolla, Opel Kadett 1.3 LS
F Renault 19
G Ford Sierra 1.6 GL (4) Sunroof
H Volvo 240 GLE (4) A/C Sunroof
I Minibus Diesel (9 Seats) (3)
S Opel Corsa Spider Convertible (2) (3 Seats)
Groups G And I Equipped With Radio,
Groups H Equipped With Radio Cassette
And Leather Inside

APRIL 1, 1990 - MARCH 31, 1991

Group		Daily	Weekly	Km	Weekly Unltd	Add Days
A	ESC	7200	44800	Free	44800	6400
	US$	48.90	304.29		304.29	43.47
B	ESC	8000	50400	Free	50400	7200
	US$	54.34	342.32		342.32	48.90
C	ESC	8400	47600	Free	47600	6800
	US$	57.05	323.30		323.30	46.19
D	ESC	10000	63000	Free	63000	9000
	US$	67.92	427.90		427.90	61.13
E	ESC	12900	81200	Free	81200	11600
	US$	87.62	551.52		551.52	78.79
F	ESC	13900	94500	Free	94500	13500
	US$	101.88	641.85		641.85	91.69
G	ESC	21200	135100	Free	135100	19300
	US$	143.99	917.61		917.61	131.09
H	ESC	26300	165200	Free	165200	23600
	US$	178.63	1122.05		1122.05	160.29
I	ESC	23300	148400	Free	148400	21200
	US$	158.26	1007.95		1007.95	143.99

Local Currency Rates Valid, Gas Not Included,
Rates Subject To Change Without Notice.

Additional Driver ML 1.00 Extra Per Day
Local Currency Rates Valid, Gas Not Included,
Rates Subject To Change Without Notice.

Currency: Maltese Pounds. Exchange Rate Used
Above (For Guidance Only) ML 0.33 To US$ 1
Tax: None
Age:25-70
Drivers License: Held For At Least Two Years
Cash Rental Deposit: Estimated Rental Charges
Credit Cards Accepted: Access, Airplus, Amex,
Diners, Eurocard, Mastercard, Visa
Deductible Collision Damage:
Groups A-G : ML 100, Groups H,I : ML 200
C.D.W.: Per Day, Groups A-E : ML 1.50,
Groups F-I : ML 2.00 (Minimum Charge 3 Days)
P.A.I.: ML 1 Per Day (Minimum Charge 3 Days)
Delivery/Collection: ML 3 Each Way In Vicinity
Of Europcar Stations (Free In Hamrun).
Other Services: Luggage Rack (ML 0.50 Per
Day) Available On Request. Infant Seat.
(ML 0.50 Per Day) Available On Freesell.
Car Availability: All Groups On Freesell
Chauffeur Driven Service: Available On
Request

European quiz

    (a) Give the hours of business for the Luxembourg Airport location.

    (b) Your client collects a VW Golf 1.6 (A) (3) car in Luxembourg City and leaves the car in Florence. What will be the drop-off charge?

    (c) Mr and Mrs A. Pavlosky collect an Audi 80 S 1.8 (4) at Luxembourg Airport on Wednesday 7 June at 1400 hours and return the car to the same airport on Wednesday 14 June at 1100 hours. During that time they travel 1050 km. They require CDW and PA insurance. Please advise the cost of both the unlimited mileage rate and the time and mileage rate. This time add tax to your calculations. Tax (in this case for Luxembourg, 12%), is always added to the final total.

    (d) Can the clients pay by cash? Explain your answer.

    (e) What is the minimum age required for Mr and Mrs Pavlosky?

    (f) If Mr Pavlosky had decided against the CDW insurance, what would he pay in the event of an accident?

    (g) Would you receive automatic confirmation of this reservation?

    (h) If Mr and Mrs Pavlosky decided to drive to Madrid and leave the car there, what would be the charge for this service?

Organizing car rental

So far we have looked at how to calculate different types of car hire and how to spot conditions quickly. Working in a travel agency, you would be responsible for actually making the reservation. The larger companies have a central reservation office; one telephone call and you will be able to reserve a car for your client in several countries. However, small firms are also easily located in the *ABC Guide* or the *Travel Trade Directory* under the appropriate separate towns.

    Car rental can also be reserved by using your office computer or by telex or fax machine. It is important to obtain all the necessary information *before* making that call.

    Here is the information you need to obtain:

1 City and country of rental and airport where applicable. Remember that many cities have more than one airport.
2 Date and time of rental and flight number where applicable.
3 Group of car required.
4 City where car will be returned.
5 Date and time of return.
6 Name, address and telephone number of customer.
7 Tariff name: unlimited mileage, business rate, holiday special etc.
8 Your company name and address.
9 Your company IATA code or car rental assigned number where applicable. This is for easy identification for the rental company to pay your agency the commission for the business!
10 Any additional equipment required, such as roof rack or baby seat.
11 Age of driver, licence details, insurance required.
12 How payment will be made: cash, credit card, deposit or full payment.

TO THE TRAVEL AGENT
HOW TO COMPLETE THE EUROPCAR EXCHANGE ORDER

A   GUARANTEED STERLING RATES IN EUROPE/REST OF THE WORLD
Featuring Unlimited Mileage, Collision Damage Waiver and Tax.

Europcar	Europcar≋ National	Exchange Order	40/
Customer's Name J. SMITH			Validation Stamp of Issuer as below
Rental Location Address MALAGA AIRPORT	Rental Location Telephone No. 327 469		
Rental Date 01·08·90 Time 10·00 AM	Flight BA 327		
Airport ✓ Down Town ○ Rail Station ○ Hotel ○ Other ○		Date 01·04·90	
Check-in-Location MALAGA AIRPORT	Check-in Date & Time 08·08·90 10·00 AM		
Car Group A	Model of Car Preferred RENAULT 5		
Remarks SUPERDRIVE STERLING INCLUSIVE RATE			
Payment Maximum Value US $1500	Tick if Applicable	Specified amount to be billed to Issuer £189·00	

Vouchers must be validated with Issuer's Stamp and dated.

- To qualify for the Super Drive rate and for the voucher to be valid, the remarks box MUST read EXACTLY as shown.
- A validation stamp MUST appear on ALL copies of the Exchange Order and the date shown.
- Do not tick this box.
- Enter the fully all inclusive rate for the entire rental as quoted by the Europcar reservations office or shown in the brochure.

B   GUARANTEED STERLING RATES IN THE USA
Featuring Unlimited Mileage and Collision Damage Waiver.

Europcar	Europcar≋ National	Exchange Order	40/
Customer's Name J. SMITH			Validation Stamp of Issuer as below
Rental Location Address CHICAGO O'HARE	Rental Location Telephone No.		
Rental Date 01·08·90 Time 10·00 AM	Flight BA 767		
Airport ✓ Down Town ○ Rail Station ○ Hotel ○ Other ○		Date 01·04·90	
Check-in-Location CHICAGO O'HARE	Check-in Date & Time 08·08·90 10·00 AM		
Car Group F	Model of Car Preferred CHEVY LUMINA		
Remarks PASSPORT RATE RECAP NO...			
Payment Maximum Value US $1500	Tick if Applicable	Specified amount to be billed to Issuer $249.95 (£160·00)	

Vouchers must be validated with Issuer's Stamp and dated.

- To qualify for the Super Drive rate and for the voucher to be valid, the comment which MUST be written in the remarks box is PASSPORT RATE.
- A Recap number MUST be written after the words PASSPORT RATE. There are different Recap numbers depending on the renting location. The proper Recap number MUST be shown for the correct rate to be applied. Details of Recap numbers are available from Europcar Central Reservations.
- Do not tick this box.
- The rate put in the specified amount box MUST be expressed firstly in DOLLARS with the guaranteed Sterling equivalent put alongside it in brackets.

C   GUARANTEED STERLING RATES IN CANADA
Rates include 1,050kms free per week and Loss Damage Waiver.

Europcar	Europcar≋ National	Exchange Order	40/
Customer's Name J. SMITH			Validation Stamp of Issuer as below
Rental Location Address EDMONTON AIRPORT	Rental Location Telephone No.		
Rental Date 01·08·90 Time 10·00 AM	Flight BA 464		
Airport ✓ Down Town ○ Rail Station ○ Hotel ○ Other ○		Date 01·04·90	
Check-in-Location EDMONTON AIRPORT	Check-in Date & Time 08·08·90 10·00 AM		
Car Group E	Model of Car Preferred CHEVROLET SPRINT		
Remarks SUPERDRIVE RATE			
Payment Maximum Value US $1500	Tick if Applicable	Specified amount to be billed to Issuer $283.60 (£148·95)	

Vouchers must be validated with Issuer's Stamp and dated.

- To qualify for the Super Drive rate the remarks box MUST read EXACTLY as shown.
- Do not tick this box.
- The rate put in the specified amount box MUST be expressed firstly in DOLLARS with the guaranteed Sterling equivalent put alongside it in brackets.

Ensure that these sections highlighted in red are ALWAYS completed as shown.

Vouchers

The method of payment is important. Your agency may hold the car hire vouchers of the principal companies. A voucher will be numbered and completed by you, and then presented by the client to the car rental company. Europcar have Travelmax, a commission tracking system which guarantees that travel agents receive commission on all rentals from their customers. By issuing the Preferred Customer Card, it ensures that the commission entitlement is tracked on any reservation made subsequently by that customer.

Your client may have already paid for the hire through your travel agency, or he may wish to pay a deposit to your agency and the balance to the rental office. Perhaps your client would find it more convenient to pay the whole amount direct to the car rental company using his credit card. Either way, the commission earned by you for making that booking is passed to your travel agency.

Completing the car rental voucher is simple. The format for all car rental vouchers is very similar, and you would be relaying the information obtained before making the reservation on to the voucher. Please study the example provided by Europcar, which is self-explanatory. The voucher will have several copies, so remember to press hard when writing! The copies are usually different colours for easy distribution; there will be copies for the customer, the car rental company and the travel agency. So! How do we all get paid eventually?

Direct billing and central billing

Direct billing is when the local car rental company receives the travel voucher from your customer. After use of the car, the car rental company will invoice your travel agency for the amount stated on the billing copy of the travel voucher. In turn, the travel agency will have an agreement to pay the car rental company for all the car rental customers at, say, the end of each month. At this point you can understand how important it is to complete the information required for form of payment and total correctly on the travel voucher. You may only collect a deposit and wish the balance to be paid directly to the car rental company by the client. Alternatively you may wish the full amount to be invoiced to your agency.

Central billing is when the local car rental company sends the invoice to the car rental head office. The head office collects all invoices on that travel agent's behalf, and at the end of each month sends that agent one statement for the reservations that have been made throughout the world, advising the amount due to the car rental company.

Whether your travel agency use direct or central billing system depends largely on the number of car rental reservations made each month. The direct billing system would be used when only a few reservations are made and the central billing system for a larger number.

How and why should we be good at selling car rental? Here are a few key points to keep in mind.

First of all we must think of the benefits for the customer.

Mobility, flexibility, convenience, cost, speed, suitability, 24 hour emergency service

You may be able to think of other benefits.

Secondly, get to know many of the car rental companies and their services. Fully understand the car rental directory, become familiar with the booking conditions, practise costing car rental so that you will be quick and accurate when faced with a real customer!

Always write clearly on the car rental travel voucher – double check the information given.

Thirdly, keep up to date with all the many special offers. Remember airlines, hotels and tour operators world-wide work with car rental companies, offering excellent competitive rates, so we need to be aware of these in order to assist our clients to have the best deal available for his/ her needs. We are very fortunate in the travel business to have a wealth of information at our finger tips – if we only knew where to look!

And why do we wish to promote car rental? The travel agent can enjoy one of the highest commissions earned – does that seem very mercenary to you? We wish to offer a full and professional service to our customers and we are assisting the car rental companies to keep their vehicles on the road – so everyone is pleased!

The following exercises will help you check your knowledge of this chapter.

Exercise 2

    (a) What is the cost to collect a small or medium car in Paris and leave it in Salzburg?
    (b) What is the cost to collect a large luxury car in Oslo and leave it in Berne?
    (c) Give the maximum age to rent a car on Malta.

Exercise 3

    (a) Mrs Grimley decides to rent a Toyota Starlet whilst on holiday on the island of Madeira. She will have the car for 3 days and drive 150 km. The cost is to include CDW, PAI and tax. Calculate the cost in local currency.
    (b) Advise the minimum age condition.
    (c) If our client had not paid the CDW insurance, what might she pay in the event of an accident?

Exercise 4

    (a) Mr D. Hume will be visiting Malta on 24 August, and needs a car for 7 days. He will collect and deliver the car at Luqa Airport. Calculate in local currency the cost on an unlimited mileage rate for a Mercedes 200 to include CDW and PAI.
    (b) Can Mr Hume pay with the Diners credit card?

Exercise 5

    (a) Why do you think there are no 'one way rental' details for Madeira?
    (b) Mr and Mrs Bolton have collected a VW Golf 1.6 turbo diesel (3) at Luxembourg Airport on 10 July at 1500 hours and have returned the car to Bologna on 19 July at 1000 hours. They will use the weekly unlimited mileage rate and have PAI and CDW. Calculation should include tax.
    (c) Advise the one way rental charge.
    (d) Advise the approximate cost of the car rental in US dollars.
    (e) If Mr and Mrs Bolton had not paid the CDW insurance, what is the total amount they could expect to pay towards the repairs to the vehicle in the event of a collision?
    (f) Mrs Bolton passed her driving test eighteen months ago, will she be qualified to drive the car?

Assignment

Try the following assignment based on the IATA/UFTAA examination paper.

(a) Describe six services offered by car rental companies.

(b) Explain four advantages of car rental for the customer.

(c) Collect a selection of brochures giving details of car rental packages then write a report on each company explaining:

    (i)   the type of package

    (ii) the country destinations

    (iii) calculate the cost of three different types of car rental package holidays based on two adults travelling together in June.

(d) Discover how many car rental companies are operating within your own country.

7 Car ferries

Summary

In this chapter we discuss:

- the benefits of car ferry services;
- information required before making a car ferry reservation;
- making the reservation;
- car insurance;
- how to calculate fares from the Sealink brochure;
- how to read the *ABC Shipping Guide;*
- exercises and assignments to complete.

What are the advantages of ferry services?

The service is frequent, the cost is economical, and one can take one's own car on board; all this makes travelling by car ferry attractive. The English Channel is one of the busiest waterways in the world, and there is a great choice of shipping companies, sailing schedules, routes, fares and ships. Many of the ships provide entertainment, sleeping facilities, bars, restaurants, and shops where duty-free goods may be purchased.

Many ferry companies offer package holidays. These include the ferry crossing with passengers and car, and hotel, camping, farmhouse or caravan site accommodation.

Ferry services operate throughout the world. Have a look at a world map; study the waterways dividing countries and ports, especially in the Mediterranean and Scandinavian seas.

Once again there are many manuals to help us find the information required for ferry services throughout the world: *ABC Shipping Guide, ABC Car Ferry Guide, Thomas Cook European Railway and Shipping Timetable, Thomas Cook Overseas Railway and Shipping Services Timetable,* and the car ferry companies' brochures.

What information would we need?

Ships

We need to know the name, the size, the capacity for cars and passengers, the facilities on board, and whether the ship is air conditioned and stabilized. There are different types of craft; for example, a hovercraft is part ship, part aircraft that rides on a cushion of air just above the surface of the sea, and ferries passengers and cars over short distances at a speed of 110 km/hour.

Routings

We need to study maps and discuss the best routings. Some clients prefer a longer car journey and a shorter sea journey, when given the choice. Other clients enjoy the ferry crossing as part of the holiday, and are happy to travel the shorter part of the journey by road. It all depends on how good a sailor the client is. So we will need information on mileages and sailing times.

Car lengths

We need to know this because it affects the fare. The tariffs are published by length of vehicle. Details of the length of each car model can be found in the *ABC Guide*.

Motorists' information

Once disembarked from the ferry, the motorist will continue the journey by car. Regulations vary from country to country. The sort of requirements we would check are as follows:

Passports   Validity, and whether visas are required.
Driving licence   Whether an international licence is required.
Insurance   For the car, against breakdowns, loss or damage, etc.
Green card cover   Within Western Europe motor vehicle insurance is compulsory for minimum Third Party risks. Most UK motor insurance policies provide this for all EEC countries and certain other Western European countries. If your client has comprehensive insurance they may find the overseas cover will automatically reduce to minimum Third Party cover unless the insurer is notified travel is to the Continent. In some cases the insurer will charge an additional premium and will issue an International Green Card of insurance which is the usual evidence of motor insurance recognized in most Western European countries. Although not a legal requirement, drivers are strongly recommended to carry the Green Card because it may prove more effective than a UK insurance certificate in establishing to the overseas authorities that the driver has adequate motor insurance.
Personal travel insurance   Against medical expenses, cancellation, loss of baggage, etc.
Bail bond insurance   Is required by some countries should the driving offence warrant legal detention.
Identification plate   These are stickers to be placed on the rear of the car or caravan and are supplied by the ferry companies.
Vehicle registration documents   Essential when travelling abroad with a car.
First aid kit   Compulsory in Austria.

Fire extinguisher   Sensible to take one on the journey even if not compulsory.
Spare headlamp bulbs   Compulsory in Spain.
Headlights   Often have to be dipped. Sometimes have to be amber coloured.
Seatbelts   Often compulsory in front and back seats.
Warning triangle   In the event of a breakdown, a red warning triangle may have to be displayed behind the vehicle.

Using a car ferry guide: ABC

Please study the extracts from the *ABC Car Ferry Guide.* First examine the Contents.
   Now look at 'Motorists' information', and compare the difference in regulations between Andorra and Belgium. For each country there is a map and useful facts. We are given the address of the tourist office in the United Kingdom. You will see that the insurance Green Card is compulsory in Andorra, and advisable but not compulsory in Belgium. An

ABC CAR FERRY GUIDE

SINGLE COPY: £15.00   PUBLISHED ANNUALLY

CONTENTS

INTRODUCTION and USE OF PUBLICATION.. 3
MOTORISTS' INFORMATION.. 5
EUROPEAN MILEAGES... 11

FERRIES (including Hovercraft & Hydrofoil)
UK PORT INFORMATION... 12
FERRY OPERATORS 16
UK & OVERSEAS FERRY SERVICES CONTENTS' LIST...................... 20
(including PORTS OF CALL. Also see back cover flap)
FERRY SERVICES ROUTE MAPS 23
(including reference numbers to Ferry Services)
UK FERRY SERVICES 29
OVERSEAS FERRY SERVICES 45

MOTORAIL
UK STATION INFORMATION 67
MOTORAIL OPERATORS.. 68
UK & OVERSEAS MOTORAIL SERVICES CONTENTS' LIST 69
(including CITY STATIONS. Also see back cover flap)
MOTORAIL SERVICES ROUTE MAP.. 70
(including reference numbers to Motorail Services)
UK MOTORAIL SERVICES 71
OVERSEAS MOTORAIL SERVICES 72

CAR LENGTHS... 80

FOR A COMBINED BASIC INDEX
TO FERRY AND MOTORAIL ROUTES
PLEASE TURN TO BACK COVER FLAP

The publishers and compilers of ABC Car Ferry Guide cannot accept responsibility for any mistakes or omissions although every effort has been made to achieve absolute accuracy. The information shown is subject to change at very short notice and confirmation of the accuracy of the information should be sought whenever possible.

international driving licence is required in Andorra but not in Belgium. Full medical costs must be paid in Andorra; in Belgium full medical costs are paid at the time, but a refund of 75 per cent is available on application. Seat belts are not compulsory in Andorra but they are in Belgium.

Let's look at some overseas ferry services. Please study the further extracts from the *ABC Car Ferry Guide*. The first example is a ferry service between Barcelona and Minorca (Mahon), and

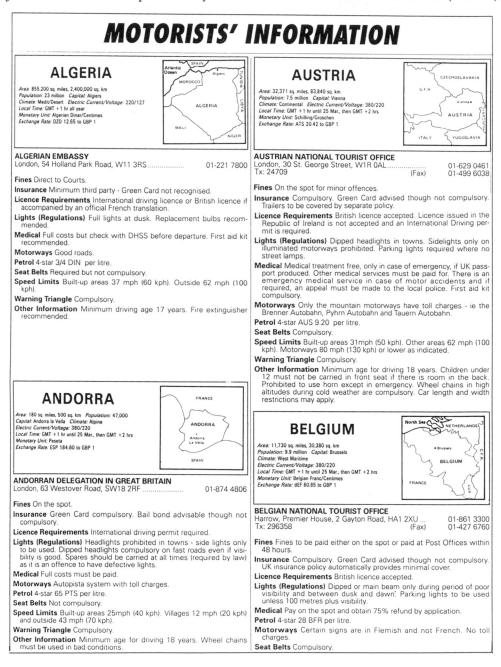

MOTORISTS' INFORMATION

ALGERIA

Area: 855,200 sq. miles, 2,400,000 sq. km
Population: 23 million *Capital:* Algiers
Climate: Medit/Desert *Electric Current/Voltage:* 220/127
Local Time: GMT +1 hr all year
Monetary Unit: Algerian Dinar/Centimes
Exchange Rate: DZD 12.65 to GBP 1

ALGERIAN EMBASSY
London, 54 Holland Park Road, W11 3RS................. 01-221 7800

Fines Direct to Courts.
Insurance Minimum third party - Green Card not recognised.
Licence Requirements International driving licence or British licence if accompanied by an official French translation.
Lights (Regulations) Full lights at dusk. Replacement bulbs recommended.
Medical Full costs but check with DHSS before departure. First aid kit recommended.
Motorways Good roads.
Petrol 4-star 3/4 DIN per litre.
Seat Belts Required but not compulsory.
Speed Limits Built-up areas 37 mph (60 kph). Outside 62 mph (100 kph).
Warning Triangle Compulsory.
Other Information Minimum driving age 17 years. Fire extinguisher recommended.

ANDORRA

Area: 180 sq. miles, 500 sq. km *Population:* 47,000
Capital: Andorra la Vella *Climate:* Alpine
Electric Current/Voltage: 380/220
Local Time: GMT +1 hr until 25 Mar., then GMT +2 hrs
Monetary Unit: Peseta
Exchange Rate: ESP 184.60 to GBP 1

ANDORRAN DELEGATION IN GREAT BRITAIN
London, 63 Westover Road, SW18 2RF 01-874 4806

Fines On the spot.
Insurance Green Card compulsory. Bail bond advisable though not compulsory.
Licence Requirements International driving permit required.
Lights (Regulations) Headlights prohibited in towns - side lights only to be used. Dipped headlights compulsory on fast roads even if visibility is good. Spares should be carried at all times (required by law) as it is an offence to have defective lights.
Medical Full costs must be paid.
Motorways Autopista system with toll charges.
Petrol 4-star 65 PTS per litre.
Seat Belts Not compulsory.
Speed Limits Built-up areas 25mph (40 kph). Villages 12 mph (20 kph) and outside 43 mph (70 kph).
Warning Triangle Compulsory.
Other Information Minimum age for driving 18 years. Wheel chains must be used in bad conditions.

AUSTRIA

Area: 32,371 sq. miles, 83,840 sq. km
Population: 7.5 million *Capital:* Vienna
Climate: Continental *Electric Current/Voltage:* 380/220
Local Time: GMT +1 hr until 25 Mar., then GMT +2 hrs
Monetary Unit: Schilling/Groschen
Exchange Rate: ATS 20.42 to GBP 1

AUSTRIAN NATIONAL TOURIST OFFICE
London, 30 St. George Street, W1R 0AL................... 01-629 0461
Tx: 24709   (Fax) 01-499 6038

Fines On the spot for minor offences.
Insurance Compulsory. Green Card advised though not compulsory. Trailers to be covered by separate policy.
Licence Requirements British licence accepted. Licence issued in the Republic of Ireland is not accepted and an International Driving permit is required.
Lights (Regulations) Dipped headlights in towns. Sidelights only on illuminated motorways prohibited. Parking lights required where no street lamps.
Medical Medical treatment free, only in case of emergency, if UK passport produced. Other medical services must be paid for. There is an emergency medical service in case of motor accidents and if required, an appeal must be made to the local police. First aid kit compulsory.
Motorways Only the mountain motorways have toll charges - ie the Brenner Autobahn, Pyhrn Autobahn and Tauern Autobahn.
Petrol 4-star AUS 9.20 per litre.
Seat Belts Compulsory.
Speed Limits Built-up areas 31mph (50 kph). Other areas 62 mph (100 kph). Motorways 80 mph (130 kph) or lower as indicated.
Warning Triangle Compulsory.
Other Information Minimum age for driving 18 years. Children under 12 must not be carried in front seat if there is room in the back. Prohibited to use horn except in emergency. Wheel chains in high altitudes during cold weather are compulsory. Car length and width restrictions may apply.

BELGIUM

Area: 11,730 sq. miles, 30,380 sq. km
Population: 9.9 million *Capital:* Brussels
Climate: West Maritime
Electric Current/Voltage: 380/220
Local Time: GMT +1 hr until 25 Mar., then GMT +2 hrs
Monetary Unit: Belgian Franc/Centimes
Exchange Rate: BEF 60.85 to GBP 1

BELGIAN NATIONAL TOURIST OFFICE
Harrow, Premier House, 2 Gayton Road, HA1 2XU ... 01-861 3300
Tx: 296358   (Fax) 01-427 6760

Fines Fines to be paid either on the spot or paid at Post Offices within 48 hours.
Insurance Compulsory. Green Card advised though not compulsory. UK insurance policy automatically provides minimal cover.
Licence Requirements British licence accepted.
Lights (Regulations) Dipped or main beam only during period of poor visibility and between dusk and dawn'. Parking lights to be used unless 100 metres plus visibility.
Medical Pay on the spot and obtain 75% refund by application.
Petrol 4-star 28 BFR per litre.
Motorways Certain signs are in Flemish and not French. No toll charges.
Seat Belts Compulsory.

OVERSEAS FERRY SERVICES

Barcelona/Minorca (Mahon)
Map G, Rte: 229

TRASMEDITERRANEA

Agent: Melia Travel   01-409 1884

CANGURO SERIES 8700t ST AC 250 cars 200 cabins 982 pax

DETAILS OF SERVICE:
Frequency: Five sailings per week during summer, two per week in winter
Duration at sea: 9 hours

PRICE RANGES:
Car: Min: £58.10, Max: £108.50
Motor Cycle: Min: £14.40, Max: £22.50
Passengers: With seat: £22.80; With berth: Min: £36.30, Max: £56.60
Cabins: Min: £36.60; Max: £57.40
Children's Reductions: Under 2 free. 2-11 half fare
Deposit Requirements: £20 or full fare, plus £6.50 telex fee
Cancellation Charges: 10%-20%, depending on notice given

Valencia/Ibiza
Map G, Rte: 235

TRASMEDITERRANEA

Agent: Melia Travel   01-409 1884

ALBATROS SERIES 7360t ST AC 120 cars 1000 pax
CANGURO SERIES 8700t ST AC 250 cars 200 cabins 982 pax

DETAILS OF SERVICE:
Frequency: Two sailings per week all year
Duration at sea: 9 hours

PRICE RANGES:
Car: Min: £58.10; Max: £108.50
Motor Cycle: Min: £14.40; Max: £22.50
Passengers: With seat: £22.80; With berth: Min: £36.30, Max: £56.60
Cabins: Min: £36.60; Max: £57.40
Children's Reductions: Under 2 free. 2-11 half fare
Deposit Requirements: £20 or full fare, plus £6.50 telex fee
Cancellation Charges: 10%-20%, depending on

MEDITERRANEAN (WEST)

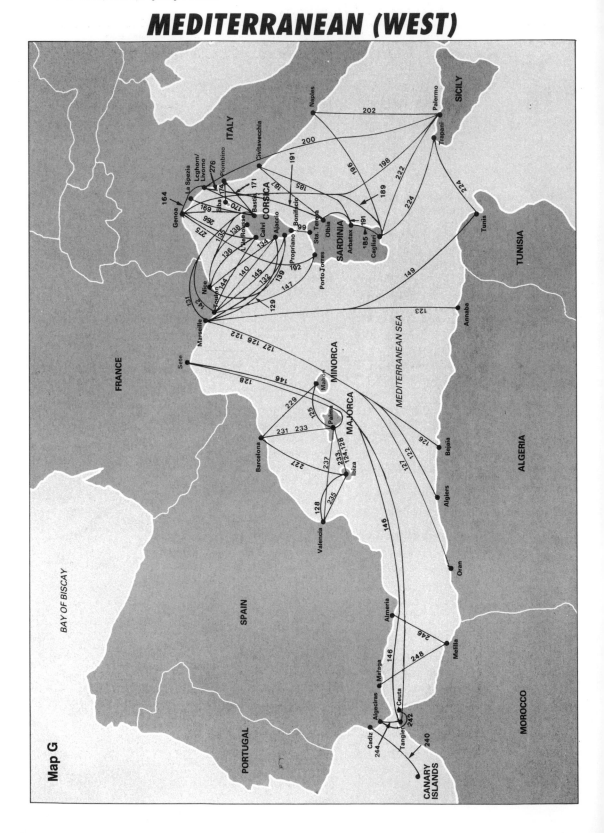

Map G

HARWICH - HOOK OF HOLLAND

Ships: Stena Normandy (until June) Stena Brittanica (from June) and Koningin Beatrix Check-in time 1 hour

PRICES

ALL CAR PRICES NOW INCLUDE DRIVER

	STANDARD SINGLE FARE				FARESAVER 2 DAY (53 HOUR) RETURN [2]			
	D	C	B	A	D	C	B	A
	DAY	NIGHT Compulsory Cabin Berth Reservation	DAY	NIGHT Compulsory Cabin Berth Reservation	DAY	NIGHT Compulsory Cabin Berth Reservation	DAY	NIGHT Compulsory Cabin Berth Reservation
CAR / MOTORISED CARAVAN / MINIBUS INCLUDING DRIVER	£	£	£	£	£	£	£	£
Up to 6.00 metres in length and up to 2.20 metres in height	60.00	87.00	76.00	100.00	60.00	87.00	76.00	100.00
Over 6.00 metres in length and / or over 2.20 metres in height	90.00	144.00	122.00	170.00	150.00	258.00	198.00	310.00
TOWED TRAILER / CARAVAN								
Up to 6.00 metres in length and up to 2.20 metres in height	30.00	57.00	46.00	70.00	60.00	114.00	92.00	140.00
Over 6.00 metres in length and / or over 2.20 metres in height	60.00	114.00	92.00	140.00	120.00	228.00	184.00	280.00
ADDITIONAL MOTORIST PASSENGERS / FOOT PASSENGERS								
Adult	30.00	30.00	30.00	30.00	30.00	30.00	30.00	30.00
Child (4 but under 14 years)	FREE	15.00	15.00	15.00	FREE	15.00	15.00	15.00
Infant (under 4 years)	FREE 1	FREE	FREE	FREE	FREE1	FREE	FREE	FREE
MOTORCYCLE / SCOOTER AND RIDER	45.00	51.00	51.00	54.00	45.00	51.00	51.00	54.00
BICYCLE / TANDEM (rider charged as foot passenger)	3.00	5.00	3.00	6.00	3.00	5.00	3.00	6.00

FARESAVERS

FARESAVER SPECIAL SINGLE	1 Jan - 24 June & 9 Sept - 30 Dec			25 June - 8 September*			
	DAY	NIGHT		DAY	NIGHT		
		Sun-Thurs	Fri-Sat	Sun-Thurs	Fri-Sat	Sun-Thurs	Fri-Sat
Car (up to 6.00 metres in length and up to 2.20m height) & up to 6 passengers	£70	£90	£120	£80	£105	£120	£150

A RETURN CROSSING MUST BE BOOKED but there are no restrictions on the length of stay.
For the return fare add together the two appropriate single fares.

FARESAVER CAMPERS SPECIAL SINGLE	1 Jan - 24 June & 9 Sept - 30 Dec			25 June - 8 September			
	DAY	NIGHT		DAY	NIGHT		
		Sun-Thurs	Fri-Sat	Sun-Thurs	Fri-Sat	Sun-Thurs	Fri-Sat
Both car and trailer / caravan (each up to 2.20 metres in height and up to 6.00 metres in length) Driver and up to 5 passengers.	£90	£120	£150	£105	£125	£150	£175
Car and trailer / caravan (either over 2.20 metres in height and / or over 6.00 metres in length) Driver and up to 5 passengers.	£105	£145	£175	£125	£145	£180	----

A RETURN CROSSING MUST BE BOOKED but there are no restrictions on the length of stay.
For the return fare add together the two appropriate single fares.

CABINS

NIGHT SAILINGS PRICE	£		NIGHT CROSSINGS -
Royal Stateroom - 4 Berth	85	per cabin	**COMPULSORY CABIN**
Captain's Class Cabin - 4 Berth	60	per cabin	**OR BERTH**
Business Class Cabin - 2 Berth	55 *	per cabin	**RESERVATIONS**
2 - Berth Outside Deluxe Cabin	50 *	per cabin	ON NIGHT CROSSINGS
Single Outside Cabin	40	per cabin	ALL PASSENGERS
Single Inside Cabin	35	per cabin	MUST HAVE A CABIN
2 - Berth Outside Cabin	20	per berth	OR BERTH
2 - Berth Inside Cabin	18	per berth	RESERVATION.
4 - Berth Outside Cabin	12 *	per berth	**50%** Reduction on Day
4 - Berth Inside Cabin	10	per berth	Sailings

All Cabins have shower and toilet facilities.   *Not available on Stena Normandy

NOTES

1. CHILDREN Up to two children per adult travel free on these sailings. Additional children pay £15.00

2. FARESAVER 2 DAY (53 HOUR) RETURN The price is determined by the date and the time of the outward sailing. The return journey may be made on any sailing departing upto a maximum of 53 hours after arrival at the Hook of Holland.

3. VEHICLES INTENDED FOR SALE ; vehicles over 6.00 metres in length and/or over 2.20 metres in height carrying commercial goods, horse or cattleboxes/trailers conveying livestock are excluded from these tariffs. Please contact Harwich (0255) 243434.

4. VEHICLES under 6.00 metres in length and under 2.20 metres in height carrying goods, that require entry on the ship's manifest will be carried at these tariffs subject to a manifest fee of £17.00 (Dfl. 60) payable at the port of departure.

TIMETABLE — HARWICH - HOOK OF HOLLAND

JAN 1130 2130	FEB 1130 2130	MAR 1130 2130	APR 1130 2130	MAY 1130 2130	JUN 1130 2130
1-31 D C	1-28 D C	1-31 D C	1-30 D C	1-31 D C	1-24 D C / 25-30 B A

JUL 1130 2130	AUG 1130 2130	SEP 1130 2130	OCT 1130 2130	NOV 1130 2130	DEC a1130 a2130
1-31 B A	1-31 B A	1-8 B A / 9-30 D C	1-31 D C	1-30 D C	1-24 D C / 25-26 NO SERVICE / 27-30 D C / 31 NO SERVICE

TIMETABLE — HOOK OF HOLLAND - HARWICH

JAN 1200 2230	FEB 1200 2230	MAR 1200 2230	APR 1200 2230	MAY 1200 2230	JUN 1200 2230
1-31 D C	1-28 D C	1-31 D C	1-30 D C	1-31 D C	1-24 D C / 25-30 B A

JUL 1200 2230	AUG 1200 2230	SEP 1200 2230	OCT 1200 2230	NOV 1200 2230	DEC a1200 a2230
1-31 B A	1-31 B A	1-8 B A / 9-30 D C	1-31 D C	1-30 D C	1-24 D C / 25-26 NO SERVICE / 27-30 C C / 31 NO SERVICE

IMPORTANT
Please be sure you make a reservation for your journeys to avoid the disappointment of arriving at the port to find the ship full.

STANDARD RETURN FARE
Just add the two Standard Single Fares together for the Standard Return Fare.

CHOICE OF RETURN CROSSING
To travel out one route and return another - add the respective fares for each route to arrive at the return fare.

SAILING TIMES
HARWICH TO HOOK OF HOLLAND

Depart	Arrive
11.30	19.00
21.30	07.00

HOOK OF HOLLAND TO HARWICH

Depart	Arrive
12.00	17.45 *
22.30	06.45

*ON THE FOLLOWING DATES arrival time at Harwich will be 16.45.
17-30 March inclusive
29 Sept to 26 Oct inclusive.

we are given a reference to map G route 229. Please study map G, find Barcelona and follow the line numbered 229 to Minorca (the port is Mahon). Returning to the ferry services details, we can see that the shipping company is called Trasmediterranea. They have an agent in London called Melia Travel, and the telephone number has been given.

The shipping company has a ship called *Canguro Series*. Its size is 8700 gross registered tonnes (8700 t) and it is stabilized and air conditioned (ST and AC). It can accommodate 250 cars, has 200 cabins and can take 982 passengers (pax). We are given the frequency of the service and the duration at sea (9 hours).

There is a range of prices for cars, motor cycles and passengers, a choice of accommodation in seats, berths and cabins, and children's reductions. There are charges for reservations and for cancellations by the customer. You will notice that we have been given a range of prices; for detailed information we would refer to the shipping company's brochure.

Using a brochure: Sealink

We are going to use extracts from the Sealink brochure. All brochures vary in layout and presentation, but the basic information provided is very similar. There are a lot of brochures to read, and it is essential to become familiar with the most used routes from your country in order to speed the reservation. Dare we say it again? Take the brochures home to read! A brochure will contain photographs of the interiors of the ships; helpful information and maps for planning the route; any savings on fares that can be achieved; sailing times; names of ships; tariffs; onward travel arrangements; package tour arrangements; insurance; instructions for making reservations; and, most important, the booking conditions.

Let's find out how much it costs to travel by sea, taking a car from Harwich to the Hook of Holland. Please study the extracts from the Sealink brochure giving details of sailings and tariffs.

The actual brochure page uses colour coding (blue, yellow, pink and grey) to assist agents and customers in establishing the correct fare, but without colour we can still calculate the fare by reading carefully the date: the times: the tariff code = A B C or D.

Many factors influence the chargeable fare: the season (time of year); the sailing date; the time of sailing (on the Harwich to Hook of Holland route there are two sailings per day); the length of the vehicle; the number of people travelling; the length of time spent on the European continent; whether a caravan or trailer is being towed onboard; and the grade of accommodation.

Take a little time to study this page now, before we go through it together.

We are given the name of the ships operating on this route and the check-in times (1 hour before sailing).

Let's look at the standard single fare and the timetable information. You will see that all car prices now include driver, this means if 3 adults are travelling in a car from Harwich to Hook of Holland we would charge the appropriate rate for the car which *includes* the driver and add the cost for the two additional passengers.

We will begin to calculate the fare for the following customers: 2 adults and one car 5.50 metres in length and below 2.20 metres in height travelling Harwich to Hook of Holland on 21 January on the 1130 hours sailing would be calculated this way.

PLEASE READ THE TIMETABLE.

January: between 1–31 and day sailing 1130 hours (our client is sailing on 21 January) the tariff is letter 'D'. The cost up to 6.00 metres in length (our customers' car is 5.50 metres) and below 2.20 metres in height, the charge is £60.00 and this *includes* the driver's fare. We therefore have one additional passenger – look at the passengers' fare for tariff 'D' and you will see £30.00.

Returning Hook of Holland to Harwich on a day sailing on 16 August at 1200 hours, same clients, same car, the tariff is 'B'. So look at the Standard Single Fare for tariff 'B'. Day sailing £76.00 for car and driver, £30.00 remains the same for the additional passenger. When calculating fares always get into the habit of setting out your calculations as illustrated because it is the same format as the sea ticket and will speed up the task of issuing the travel document.

OUTWARD JOURNEY		RETURN JOURNEY		
Harwich to Hook of Holland		Hook of Holland to Harwich		
21 January day sailing tariff D		16 August day sailing tariff C		
Car length 5.40 m/driver	£60.00	£76.00		
1 adult	£30.00	£30.00		
	£90.00	£106.00	Total £196.00	

Let's try another one using the standard single fare.

Two adults, one child aged 8 years travelling Harwich to Hook of Holland 26 June day sailing (tariff B) returning Hook of Holland to Harwich 7 July day sailing (tariff B) the car is over 6.00 metres in length.

OUTWARD JOURNEY		RETURN JOURNEY		
Harwich to Hook of Holland		Hook of Holland to Harwich		
26 June day sailing tariff B		7 July day sailing tariff B		
Car & driver over 6.00 m	£92.00	£92.00		
1 adult	30.00	30.00		
1 child	15.00	15.00		
	£137.00	£137.00	Total £274.00	

We are given details of a faresaver special single (one way) fare. Let's calculate this type of fare for our first customer. The details were car 5.50 metres in length, 21 January for 2 adults. Using the Faresaver Special single fare day sailing between 1 January–24 June and 9 September–30 December the fare for a car up to 6.00 metres in length *and* up to six passengers (six passengers maximum, can be less) outward fare £70.00.

Our customer was returning on 16 August, we will say, for this example, the 16 August is a Wednesday. Between 25 June–8 September for day travel on a Wednesday (Sun.–Thurs.) the fare for the car and up to six passengers is £80.00 making a total of £150.00. As the standard fare total is £196.00 the special fare should be used.

We are also given the details of a *RETURN* Faresaver when the customer is staying *no longer than 2 days (53 hours)* on the European continent. Please read the notes *(2) Faresaver 2 days.* You will see the 53 hours time limit begins after arrival at the Hook of Holland, please follow the next calculation.

Two adults, two children ages 10 and 7 years travelling with a car 5.20 metres in length,

Harwich to Hook of Holland, day sailing on 9 October, returning Hook of Holland to Harwich on 11 October, day sailing.

Check the sailing times. Departure from Harwich 1130 arrival Hook of Holland 1900 hours (on 9 October). For the return journey depart Hook of Holland 1200 hours and arrive Harwich at 1845 hours on 11 October. See the note * between 29 Sept.–26 Oct. arrival time in Harwich is one hour later i.e. 1845 hours. Count up the number of hours from arrival to departure at Hook of Holland. From 1900 hours on 9 October until 1200 hours on 11 October is 41 hours.

Please read the Faresaver 2 DAY notes again, the price is determined by the date and time of outward sailing, our client is travelling 9 October = tariff 'D' (October 1–31). Remember these are return fares, but still show the breakdown for outward and return fares as before.

OUTWARD		RETURN	
Harwich/Hook of Holland		Hook of Holland/Harwich	
Car/driver £60.00	£30.00	£30.00	
Adult £30	15.00	15.00	
Children free			
	£45.00	£45.00	Total £90.00

So far we have calculated day time sailing only, please read the notes on night sailings. On night crossings it is compulsory to reserve sleeping accommodation, a cabin or a berth (bunks one above the other). The cabins are described for us Royal Staterooms, Captain's Class, Business Class, providing details of the number of people to be accommodated in each unit.

If a customer would like the use of a cabin on a day sailing they can reserve one and pay half the nightsailing tariff for the cabin. Often a family with a very young baby to care for, or a traveller needing some sleep after a long drive will need the use of a cabin during the daytime crossing. When calculating the cost of sleeping accommodation be careful to know when the rate is for the *cabin* and when it is *per berth*. Let's say we have a passenger travelling alone and wishes to have a single outside cabin, the route is Harwich to Hook of Holland on 12 June departing 2130 hours and returning Hook of Holland to Harwich on 26 June at 2230 hours.

TARIFF C		TARIFF A	
Harwich/Hook of Holland		Hook of Holland/Harwich	
Car/driver	£87.00	£100.00	
Single cabin	40.00	40.00	
	£127.00	£140.00	Total £267.00

Read the information provided on the Harwich to Hook of Holland page again making special note of the following.

1   All car prices include driver.
2   Additional charges when taking caravan or trailer.
3   Charge for additional passengers.
4   Children *under* 4 years are infants and travel free.
5   See the note referring to number of children per adult permitted to travel free of charge.
6   Not taking a car but taking a motor-cycle? Check fare.
7   Taking a bicycle? (Hard work!) Charge for the bicycle and the rider is charged the same as a foot passenger. A foot passenger is someone travelling without a vehicle.
8   Read notes for vehicles intended for sale.
9   Read notes for vehicles carrying certain goods. (Mainly you will be booking holiday-makers.)
10   Check sailing times.

11 Be clear on standard fares (single one-way fares charge for travel in each direction) faresavers special single fares (charge for travel in each direction). Faresavers 2 day return fares. Date and time of outward journey determines the return fare.

Try the following calculations without looking at the back of the book for the answers. Use the Standard Single Fare.

Exercise 1

Three adults, one child 7 years old, travelling Harwich to Hook of Holland on 12 August on the 2130 hours sailing with a car under 6.00 metres plus a caravan under 6.00 metres. Returning on 27 August at 2230 hours from Hook of Holland to Harwich, 3 adults, one child, same car. A 4 berth inside cabin is required on both sailings.

Compare this fare with the Faresaver. We will say this family will travel out on a Monday 12 August and back on a Saturday 27 August.

Please try one more.

Exercise 2

Three adults departing Harwich for the Hook of Holland on 25 April 11.30 hours sailing and returning on the Hook of Holland to Harwich crossing on 27 April at 1200 hours. They are taking one car over 6.00 metres. No accommodation is required. Please calculate the *cheapest* fare.

We are unable to publish the timetables for all the different routes for the many ferry companies, and have just reproduced one from which to work. Sealink operate many other routes, Southampton to Cherbourg, New-haven to Dieppe, Folkestone to Boulogne, Dover to Calais, and like the many other ferry companies they have many package holidays for travellers using the ferry services that include accommodation and special rates for onward travel by other ferry services. A ferry company offers many services in addition to the sea crossing.

How can we find out about the different ferry companies? From the *ABC Shipping Guide.*

ABC *Shipping Guide*

We are now going to read a few extracts from the *ABC Shipping Guide*. It has approximately 300 pages, and provides a wealth of information at your fingertips:

1 Explanations on how to use the guide.
2 Shipping companies worldwide, listed in alphabetical order with the addresses of their

How to use

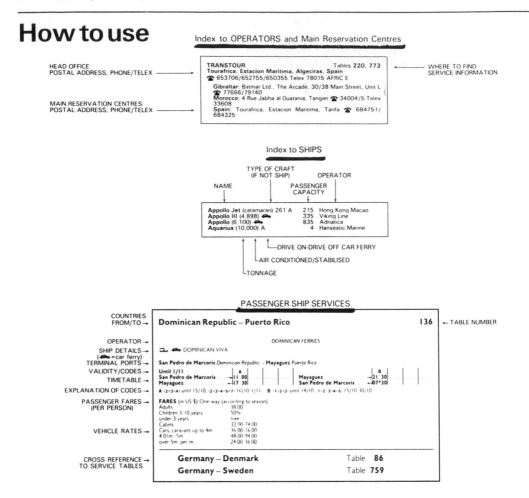

Index to OPERATORS and Main Reservation Centres

HEAD OFFICE:
POSTAL ADDRESS, PHONE/TELEX ⟶

TRANSTOUR   Tables **220, 773**
Tourafrica, Estacion Maritima, Algeciras, Spain
☎ 653706/652755/650355 Telex 78015 AFRIC E
Gibraltar: Batmar Ltd., The Arcade, 30/38 Main Street, Unit L
☎ 77666/79140
Morocco: 4 Rue Jabha al Ouatania, Tangier ☎ 34004/5 Telex 33608
Spain: Tourafrica, Estacion Maritima, Tarifa ☎ 684751/684325

MAIN RESERVATION CENTRES:
POSTAL ADDRESS, PHONE/TELEX ⟶

⟵ WHERE TO FIND SERVICE INFORMATION

Index to SHIPS

NAME   TYPE OF CRAFT (IF NOT SHIP)   OPERATOR
PASSENGER CAPACITY

Appollo Jet (catamaran) 261 A   215   Hong Kong Macao
Appollo III (4.898) 🚗   335   Viking Line
Appollo (6.100) 🚗   835   Adriatica
Aquarius (10,000) A   4   Hanseatic Marine

DRIVE ON-DRIVE OFF CAR FERRY
AIR CONDITIONED/STABILISED
TONNAGE

PASSENGER SHIP SERVICES

COUNTRIES FROM/TO ⟶   **Dominican Republic – Puerto Rico**   **136**   ⟵ TABLE NUMBER

OPERATOR ⟶   *DOMINICAN FERRIES*
SHIP DETAILS ⟶   🚗 DOMINICAN VIVA
(🚗 =car ferry)
TERMINAL PORTS ⟶   **San Pedro de Marcoris** *Dominican Republic* – **Mayaguez** *Puerto Rico*
VALIDITY/CODES ⟶   Until 1/11   A   B
TIMETABLE ⟶   San Pedro de Marcoris   →11 00   Mayaguez   →21 30
                Mayaguez   →17 30   San Pedro de Marcoris   →07*30
EXPLANATION OF CODES ⟶   A (2×3)(4) until 15/10, (2-3-4-5)(7) 16/10-1/11   B 1-2-3 until 14/10, 1-2 3-4-5 15/10-30/10
PASSENGER FARES ⟶   **FARES** (in US $) One-way (according to season)
(PER PERSON)   Adults   38.00
             Children 3-10 years   50%
             under 3 years   free
             Cabins   32.00-74.00
VEHICLE RATES ⟶   Cars, caravans up to 4m   36.00-76.00
             4.01m -5m   48.00-94.00
             over 5m per m.   24.00-36.00

CROSS REFERENCE ⟶   **Germany – Denmark**   Table **86**
TO SERVICE TABLES   **Germany – Sweden**   Table **759**

SERVICES
Passenger Ship Services start at Page 101 and are in alphabetical order of countries. There is a separate section on passenger-carrying cargo ships (freighters)

CRUISES
Monthly updated lists of worldwide cruises and fly-cruises, river, waterway and coastal cruises, yacht and schooner cruisers. Sections are divided in geographical areas of departure which are listed on page 201. The principal cruises are listed in date order, with geographical headings at the top of each page. Embarkation and disembarkation ports are shown in bold type.

head offices and reservation centres throughout the world.

3 Names and details of ships operating, again in alphabetical order.

4 Maps of international car ferry routes, plus distances between main European cities.

5 List of international ports.

6 Timetable of ship services, including cargo-passenger services.

7 Calendar, useful to have at hand.

8 Details of all cruises from all ports of the world.

Please study the 'How to use' extract from the *ABC Shipping Guide*. All ABC Guides have an editorial page giving details of any changes that have taken place after the book was printed. It is a Stop Press update so should be read first. This has three sections as follows:

Great Britain: P & O European Ferries, Channel House, Channel View Road, Dover, Kent CT17 9TJ ☎ (0304) 203388 Telex 965104
Greece: Minoan Lines, 4 Astingos Street, Piraeus ☎ 4136103 Telex 213265 MINO GR
Netherlands: World Wide Reis-en Passagebureau B.V., Meent 62, NL-3011 JM Rotterdam ☎ (010) 4139293 Telex 23639 WWAIR NL
Switzerland: Astor Reisen, Shaffhauserstrasse 89, CH-8152 Glattbrugge. Telex 825427
USA: P & O European Ferries, Main Street, P.O. Box A, Saltillo, PA17253-0400 ☎ (814) 4483945 Telex 825196
West Germany: Seetours International, Seilerstrasse 23, D-6000 Frankfurt-am-Main 1 ☎ (069) 13330 Telex 413836

MISR EDCO SHIPPING CO. S.A.E. Tables **140, 145**
1 El Central Street, El Manshia, Alexandria, Egypt
☎ 4824797, 4832397, 4837632 Telex 54786 MEDCO UN
Egypt: Menatours, 28 Chambre de Commerce St., Alexandria ☎ 808407/806909 Telex 54097-54044
Menatours, 7 El Bostane el Saidi and Sabri Abou Allam St., Cairo ☎ 750775/767022 Telex 20431 MENAT UN
Jordan: Telstar Travel & Tourism, Jabal Amman-3rd Circle, Riyadh Centre, Saadah Street, Al Jazirah Bldg., Amman ☎ 640213/640214/624104 Telex 21604 Tlstar JO Telefax 640168 P.O. Box 194
Telstar Travel & Tourism, Near Jordan-Kuwait Bank (behind Post Office), P.O. Box 1077, Aqaba ☎ 314724/314734/315123 Telex 62294 Tlstar JO
Saudi Arabia: Yusuf Bin Ahmed Kanoo, P.O. Box 812, Kilo 4, Mekka Road, Jeddah ☎ 6823759/6475251/6475524 Telex 401039 KANOO SJ

MK LINE Table **758**
Skeppsbron 6, S-21120 Malmö, Sweden
☎ 040 104880 Telex 33575 MK LINES
Denmark: MK Line, Havnegade 44, DK-1058 Copenhagen ☎ 01 156875

MOLS LINIEN A/S Table **111**
DK-8400 Ebeltoft, Denmark
☎ (06) 34 16 00 Telex 60777
Great Britain: DFDS Seaways, Parkeston Quay, Harwich CO12 4QG ☎ (0255) 240240 Telex 987542

MORE OG ROMSDAL FYLKESBÅTAR Table **640**
Fylkeshuset, N-6400 Molde, Norway
☎ (072) 52411 Telex 40287 Telefax (072) 51913

MUROTO KISEN K. K. Table **540**
Toyo Cho Kannoura, Aki Gun Kochi Pref. 781-74, Japan
☎ 08872.9.2206

MURRAY RIVER CRUISES Cruises **C475, C476**
151 Franklin Street, Adelaide, S.A. 5000, Australia
☎ 211.8333 Telex 88164 Telefax 212 5782
Australia: Westrail Travel Centre, City Railway Station, Wellington Street, Perth, W.A. 6000 ☎ 326 2811
South Australian Government Travel Centre, King William Street, Adelaide, S.A. 5000 ☎ 212 1644
25 Elizabeth Street, Melbourne, Vic. 3000 ☎ 614 2431
143 King Street, Sydney, NSW 2000 ☎ 232 8388
Victorian Tourism Commission 221, Queen Street, Brisbane, Queensland 4000 ☎ 221 4300
Captain Stuart Marine Pty. Ltd., P.O. Box 2796, Brisbane, Queensland 4001 (Brisbane Explorer only) ☎ 888 524
New Zealand: Australian International Marketing, P.O. Box 22-733, Otahuhu, Auckland ☎ 39 2698/39 2699

NAGGAR TOURS OF EGYPT Cruises **C213**
32 Sabri Abu Alam Street, Cairo, Egypt
☎ 742946 Telex 92351/93907
France: Naggar Travel, 15/17 Rue des Mathurins, F-75009 Paris ☎ 268113 Telex 215523
Italy: Naggar Travel Agency, Corso di Porta Romana 74, I-20122 Milan ☎ 573865/592109
Spain: Viajes de Naggar, Princesa Numero 2, Of.3, Piso 8°, 28008 Madrid
USA: Naggar Travel, 6363 Wilshire Boulevard, Suite 411, Los Angeles, CA 90048 ☎ 655.1616 Telex 215462
Naggar Travel Agency & Nile Cruises, 2125 Center Avenue, Suite 108, Fort Lee, NJ 07024 ☎ 585.2180 Telex 237987
Naggar Tours, 323 Geary Street, Suite 510, San Francisco, CA 94102 ☎ 392.0393 Telex 470600
West Germany: Naggar Tours, Am Hauptbahnhof 10, 5 Stk. Room 519, D-6000 Frankfurt-am-Main 1 ☎ 69.746792 Telex 4170604

NAIAS STEAMSHIP COMPANY Table **374**
3 Akti Tzelepi, Piraeus, Greece
☎ 4120224/4120469 Telex 212959 NAN GR

NAUTICAL TRADING (ST. KITTS) LTD. Table **684**
Caribbean Hydrofoil Inc., P.O. Box 6092, San Juan, Puerto Rico
☎ (809) 721.5322

NAUTILUS LINE Table 1034
Keller Shipping S.A., Holbeinstrasse 68, CH-Basle 2, Switzerland
☎ (061) 237940 Telex 962 135 SHIP CH/963 751 KSRO CH Telefax 61 224 897
France: La Franco Suisse de Consignations Maritimes S.A., 25 Blvd. des Dames, F-13002 Marseilles ☎ 91.90.77.60 Telex 440352 FRASUMA F Telefax 91.91.50.98
Great Britain: Walford Lines Ltd., Maritime House, 1 Linton Road, Barking, Essex IG11 8HW ☎ (01) 591 8899 Telex 897411 WALBRO Telefax 594 05 85

NAVARMA SpA. Tables **431, 492, 688**
Viale Elba 4, I-57037 Portoferraio, Italy
☎ (0565) 916 743/916 758 Telex 590590 NAVARM I
Austria: Cosmos Travel Agency Ltd., Kärntnerring 15, A-1010 Vienna ☎ (0222) 5226610 Telex 131223 COSA
Corsica: Colonna d'Istria, Rue Commandant Luce de Casablanca 4, 20200 Bastia, Corsica ☎ 314629/316247 Telex 460987
France: see Corsica
Great Britain: Serena Holidays, 40/42 Kenway Road, London SW5 0RA ☎ (01) 373 6548/49 Telex 918526 SMSGRP G
Italy: L. V. Ghianda, Via Vittorio Veneto 24, I-57100 Leghorn ☎ (0586) 28 314 Telex 500190 GHIALI I
Luxembourg: Keiser Tours, Centre Commercial Louvigny, 34 Rue Philippe II, L-2340 Luxembourg ☎ 47.27.17 Telex 3131 KEISER LU
Sardinia: AMAR, Corso V. Emanuele 19, Porto Torres ☎ (079) 516154 Telex 790009 AMAR I
Switzerland: Ouboter Reisen AG, Pelikanplatz 15, CH-8022 Zurich ☎ (01) 211 3611 Telex 812424 OUB CH
West Germany: Seetours International, Seilerstrasse 23, D-6000 Frankfurt-am-Main 1 ☎ (069) 1333-0 Telex 4 189723 SFS

NAVIERA MAGALLANES S.A. Table **76**
Av. Suiza 248, Cerrillos, Santiago, Chile
☎ 5572650/5579842/5573419 Telex 340885 MAGSA CK
Chile: Terminal Angelmò s/n., Puerto Montt ☎ 3318/3754 Telex 370055 NAMAG CK
Ave. Independencia 830, 2° Piso, Punta Arenas ☎ 22593/26600 Telex 380060 NAVIN CK
Pedro Montt s/n, Terminal Maritimo, Puerto Natales ☎ 287 Telex 380018 NATAL CK

NAVIGATION LAVOIE INC. Table **63**
Iles aux Grues, Québec, Canada
☎ 248.2968
See Société des Traversiers du Québec

NAVIGAZIONE LAGO DI COMO Table **488**
Via Rubini 22, I-22100 Como, Italy
☎ 27.33.24/26.02.34

NAVIGAZIONE LAGO MAGGIORE Table **490**
Viale F. Baracca, I-28041 Arona, Italy
☎ (0322) 46651

NAVIGAZIONE LIBERA DEL GOLFO Table **498**
Molo Beverello, Naples, Italy
☎ 320763

NAVIGAZIONE SUL LAGO DI GARDA Table **489**
Piazza Matteotti 2, I-25015 Desenzano del Garda, Italy
☎ (030) 914 1321/914 1323 Telex 303114 NAVIGA I

NCL = NORWEGIAN CRUISE LINES

NEGROS NAVIGATION COMPANY INC. Table **667**
Negros Navigation Building, 849 Pasay Road, Makati, Philippines D-3116
☎ 816.34.81/2/3/4/5/6/7/8 Telex 772 2307 NNC PH

NEW BRUNSWICK DEPARTMENT OF TRANSPORTATION Tables **41, 45**
P.O. Box 6000, Fredericton, N.B. E3B 5H1, Canada

NEW ENGLAND STEAMBOAT LINES INC. Table **821**
One Marine Park, Haddam, Connecticut 06438, USA
☎ (203) 345.4507

NEW SOUTH WALES URBAN TRANSIT AUTHORITY Table **17**
6th Level, Alliance Building, 19-31 Pitt Street, Sydney, NSW 2000, Australia
☎ 241.3734 Telex AA 177609 Telefax 2514149
Australia: Manly Wharf, Manly ☎ 977.3028

NEW YORK CITY DEPARTMENT OF TRANSPORTATION Table **834**
Bureau of Transit Operations, Battery Maritime Building, Foot of Whitehall, New York, NY 10004, USA
☎ (212) 806.6900/6940

NEW ZEALAND RAILWAYS CORPORATION Table **608**
Searail, Railways Private Bag, Wellington, New Zealand
☎ 725599 Telex NZ 31046

NIBBE Table 1184
West Germany: Navis Travel Agency, Billhorner Kanalstrasse 69, D-2000 Hamburg 28 ☎ (040) 78948.234/235 Telex 2162265/2162268/2162574 NAVI D Telefax (040) 7899762

NIGERIAN NATIONAL SHIPPING LINE LTD. Table 1058
Development House, P.O. Box No 326, 21 Wharf Road, Apapa, Lagos, Nigeria
Great Britain: Nigerian National Shipping Line Ltd., Ibex House, 42/47 Minories, London EC3N 1DY ☎ (01) 480 5694/5639 Telex 884581
Nigerian National Shipping Line Ltd., West Africa House, 25 Water Street, Liverpool L2 0TY ☎ (051) 236 5444
West Germany: Nigerian National Shipping Line Ltd., Mattentwiete No 1, D-2000 Hamburg 1 ☎ 362227 Telex 2164891

NILE VALLEY RIVER TRANSPORT CORPORATION Table **147**
P.O. Box 122, Aswan, Egypt Arab Republic
☎ 3348 Wadnil

NIPPON CAR FERRY K.K. Table **526**
8-7 Kyobashi 2-chome, Chuo-ku, Tokyo, Japan
☎ (03) 563 5351

NIPPON ENKAI FERRY K.K. Table **522**
10-7 Shinbashi 1-chome, Minato-ku, Tokyo, Japan
☎ (03) 573 1911; Reservations (03) 574 9561

NIPPON KOSOKU FERRY K.K. Table **535**
4-14 Yaesu 1-chome, Chuo-ku, Tokyo, Japan
☎ (03) 274 1801

NOORDZEE VEERDIENSTEN = NORTH SEA FERRIES

NORFOLK LINE BV Table 1055
Kranenburgweg 211, 2583 ER Scheveningen, Netherlands
☎ (070) 527400 Telex 31515
Great Britain: Norfolk Line Ltd., Atlas House, Southgates Road, Great Yarmouth, Norfolk ☎ (0493) 856133 Telex 975741 Telefax (0493) 856133 ext. 276

NOR-SVE LINJEN Table **764**
Phønixbryggen 1, N-1600 Fredrikstad, Norway
☎ (0532) 15035

NORTH AGEAN LINES = LOUCAS NOMICOS SONS FERRY SERVICES

NORTH FERRY CO. INC. Table **827**
Box 589, Shelter Island Heights, NY 11965, USA
☎ (516) 749 0139

NORTH SEA FERRIES/NOORDZEE VEERDIENSTEN Tables **228, 269**
Beneluxhaven, Europoort, P.O. Box 1123, 3180 AC Rozenburg Z.H., Netherlands
☎ (01819) 55500 Telex 26571

—continued

Belgium: North Sea Ferries (Belgium), Leopold II Dam (Havendam), B-8380 Zeebrugge ☎ (050) 543430 Telex 81469
Great Britain: North Sea Ferries, King George Dock, Hedon Road, Hull HU9 5QA ☎ (0482) 795141 Telex 592349
Northern Ireland: Belfast Car Ferries, 47 Donegall Quay, Belfast BT1 3ED ☎ (0232) 220364/226800 Telex 74268 BELFER
USA: P & O European Ferries, Main Street, P.O. Box A, Saltillo, PA 17253-0400 ☎ (800) 458 3606 Telex 825196

NORTH SPORADES SHIPPING CO. LTD. = LOUCAS NOMICOS SONS FERRY SERVICES

NORTHUMBERLAND FERRIES LTD. Table **56**
94 Water Street, P.O. Box 634, Charlottetown, Prince Edward Island C1A 7L3, Canada
☎ (902) 566.3838 Telex 014.44186 Telefax (902) 566.1550
Canada: Ferry Terminal, Wood Islands, P.E.I. ☎ (902) 962.2016; (Traffic Information: 1.800.565.0201 for N.S., N.B. and P.E.I.); Ferry Terminal, Caribou, N.S. ☎ 485.6580

NORWAY LINE Table **623**
Postboks 4004, N-5023 Bergen-Dreggen, Norway
☎ 05-322780 Telex 40425 NLINE
Great Britain: Norway Line, Tyne Commission Quay, North Shields, Tyne & Wear NE29 6EA ☎ (091) 2961313 Telex 537275

NORWEGIAN CRUISE LINES Cruises **C5, C40, C50**
One Biscayne Tower, Miami, Florida 33131, USA
☎ (305) 358 6680
Australia: MacDonald International Pty. Ltd., 16 Spit Junction, Mossman, NSW 2088 ☎ 960.2011 Telex 25824
Austria: Transnautic, Freudenauer Hafenstrasse 8-10, A-1020 Vienna ☎ (0222) 240 555 Telex 132 849/132 873
Meridian Holidays, Kårntnerring 17/2, A-1010 Vienna ☎ (0222) 53 25 480 Telex 131434
Belgium: Wirtz Travel Agency, 44 de Keyeeriel, Antwerp ☎ (03) 31 78 00 Telex 31 484
Wirtz Travel Agency, Shell Building, Rue Ravenstein 66, B-1000 Brussels ☎ (02) 137630 Telex 21393
Pasteels S.A., Rue Ravenstein 20, B-1000 Brussels ☎ (02) 5136270 Telex 23471
Denmark: Dane Tours, Bredgade 27, DK-1260 Copenhagen ☎ 01 11 41 42 Telex 25270
France: Comitour, 161 Rue St. Honore, F-75001 Paris ☎ 260.38.55 Telex 680 008
Loisirs S.A., 7 Rue Rouget de Lisle, F-75001 Paris ☎ 296.20.61 Wingate Travel, 19 bis Rue du Mont Thabor, F-75001 Paris
☎ 260.39.85 Telex 68229
Zenith Tour Operator, 14 Rue Therese, F-75001 Paris ☎ 742.65.80 Telex 210376
Great Britain: Norwegian Cruise Lines, 3 Vere Street, London WIM 9HQ
☎ (01) 408 0046 Telex 261827
Luxembourg: Keiser Tours, Centre Commercial Louvigny, 34 Rue Philippe II, L-2340 Luxembourg ☎ 47 27 17 Telex 3131 KEISER LU
Netherlands: VCK-Zeereisen, De Ruyterkade 139, P.O. Box 1418, NL-1011 AC Amsterdam ☎ (020) 262216 Telex 14561
Norway: Kloster Cruise Travel, Soerkedalsveien 31, P.O. Box 100, Smestad, N-0309 Oslo 3 ☎ (010) 47.2.46.64.70 Telex 77521
A/S Saga Tours, Ruselokkvn 18, P.O. Box 1481-Vika, Oslo 1
South Africa: Travel Vision, P.O. Box 4779, Johannesburg 2000, Transvaal ☎ 33.73633 Telex 483701
Sweden: Respecialisterna Resebureau A.B., 32 Birger Jarlsgatan, Box 5112, 10243 Stockholm S ☎ (0823) 3430 Telex 10869
Switzerland: American Express IBC, Kreuzstrasse 26, CH-8034 Zurich ☎ 327051 Telex 58404
Cosulich, Beckenhofstrasse 26, CH-8035 Zurich ☎ 363 5255 Telex 816 114
Kreuzfahrten-Zentrale, Koenizstrasse 74, Postfach 1806, CH-3001 Berne ☎ (010) 41.31.46.14.44 Telex 911566
West Germany: Deutsches Reiseburo GmbH. (ABC Department), Escherheimer Landstrasse 25/27, D-6000 Frankfurt-am-Main 1 ☎ (069)-15660 Telex 4 152 920
Neckerman und Reisen, Abteilung Abwicklung, Postfach 11 90 92, D-6000 Frankfurt-am-Main ☎ (0611) 26901 Telex 41529750
Trans Atlantik Reisen, Kurfürstenanlage 3, D-6900 Heidelberg ☎ 06221-27181-86 Telex 461 715
Norwegian Cruise Lines, Rossmarkt 10, 4th floor, D-6000 Frankfurt-am-Main ☎ 069.280659 Telex 4170463

NORWEGIAN COASTAL CRUISES = DFDS SEAWAYS

NURMES-MARINA Table **172**
Kirkkokatu 12, SF-75500 Nurmes, Finland
☎ 976 21244

NUR TOURISTIC GmbH. Cruises **C10**
Postfach 111343, D-6000 Frankfurt-am-Main 11, West Germany
☎ (069) 26900 Telex 415 2970 NT D

OCEAN CRUISE LINES (UK) LTD. Cruises **C5, C10, C30, C35, C40, C45, C50, C55**
10 Frederick Close, Stanhope Place, London W2 2HD, Great Britain
☎ Administration: (01) 723 5557; Reservations: (01) 724 7555 Telex 264088 OCL G Telefax (01) 402 0490
Argentina: Orangfur S.A., Cangallo 725, 10° Piso, CP 1038 Buenos Aires ☎ (46) 1193 Telex 17557
Austria: Caravelle Seereisen & Touristic Guide, Bayerngasse 3/3, A-1030 Vienna ☎ (0222) 732270 Telex 133286 CHACRA
Belgium: Transcruise, Rue de Facqz 115, B-1050 Brussels ☎ (02) 537 45 88/538 6027 Telex 62968 CRUISE B
Brazil: Ocean Cruise Lines, c/o Dickenson S.A., Ave. Pedroso de Morais 433, 10° Andar, CEP 05419 São Paulo ☎ 11.8150688 Telex 1180044
France: Compagnie Générale de Croisières, 22 Rue Royale, F-75008 Paris ☎ (1) 42.60.36.63 Telex 215 755 F
Greece: Horizon Travel, 14 Nikis Street, 105 57 Athens ☎ 323 3144 Telex 215359
Hong Kong: Swire Travel Ltd., Swire House, 9 Connaught Road, Central ☎ 5 8448448 Telex 73206
Israel: Ophir Tours, 32 Ben Yehuda Street, P.O. Box 3378, Tel Aviv ☎ (010) 03 209745/209777 Telex 361406/33624/341343

—continued

Index to operators and main reservation centres

The first address in bold type is the shipping company's head office. Other addresses listed are the main reservation centres. The table numbers tell us where to find the service information.

Index to ships

We have the name of the ship, the type of craft, and the size of the ship (gross registered tonnes). We can see at a glance whether the ship is air conditioned (A) or stabilized (S). (A stabilizer is a retractable fin extending into the water on either side of the ship to ensure a smooth sailing in rough seas.) The drawing of a car indicates that the vessel is a car ferry. We are given the number of passengers allowed to sail on the vessel, and the name of the operator.

Passenger ship services

We are looking at the service between the Dominican Republic and Puerto Rico; the table number is 136. The operator is Dominican Ferries, and the ship is a car ferry called *Dominican Viva*. The name of the port in the Dominican Republic is San Pedro de Marcoris, and the name of the port in Puerto Rico is Mayaguez. The sailings are valid until 1 November (1/11).

The service coded A departs San Pedro de Marcoris at 1100 hours and arrives Mayaguez at 1730 hours. The explanation for code A show that until 15 October (15/10) the ship sails on Tuesdays (2), Wednesdays (3) and Thursdays (4); between 16 October and 1 November the ship sails on Tuesdays, Wednesdays, Thursdays, Fridays and Sundays. Service B departs Mayaguez at 2130 hours and arrives San Pedro de Marcoris at 0730 hours; the * sign means the next day. The code B days are also explained.

Passenger fares are per person, and one-way fares are published in US dollars. Some fares vary according to season; it would be impossible to publish all the various fare combinations for every shipping company, so fare ranges are used. On this car ferry, the passenger fares are fixed and the other fares vary with season. The adult fare is $38.00. Children of 3–10 years pay 50 per cent of the adult fare; infants under 3 years travel free. Cabins are available at between $32.00 and $74.00. We have also been given the costs of taking cars and caravans on the ferry; these depend on the size of the vehicle.

Occasionally services are cross-referenced to others. In this example there are references to services from Germany to Denmark and Sweden.

Exercise 3

Using the extracts provided from the *ABC Shipping Guide*, please find the following information:

(a) Give the address of the head office of the Norwegian Cruise Lines.
(b) Which table number would you refer to for the MK line?

Ships

SHIP	PAX	OPERATOR
Nile Legend (2,035) A	140	Presidential Nile
Nile President (2,035) A	140	Presidential Nile
Nile Princess (640) A	66	Presidential Nile
Nile Star A	68	Swan Nile
Nile Symphony (2,035) A	140	Presidential Nile
Nils Holgersson (22,000) 🚗	1,600	TT Line
Nimpkish (266) 🚗	138	British Col. Ferry Corp.
Ninfea (130) S	255	Nav. Lago di Como
Nisqually (1,368) 🚗	665	Washington S.F.
Nissos Chios (3,159) AS 🚗	1,070	Hellenic Coastal Lines
Nivanga (353) S	56	Tuvalu Govt.
Nomentana (10,500) 🚗	1,300	Tirrenia
Noordam (33,930) AS	1,340	Holland America
Noord Nederland (1,064) 🚗	700	Terschellinger
Nordenham (774) 🚗	500	Weserfähre
Nordfjord I (870) 🚗	350	Fylkesbaatane
Nordfriesland (950) 🚗	780	Wyker Ds.
Nordhordland (799) S 🚗	480	A.S. Bergen Nord.
Nordic Ferry (6,455) AS 🚗	650	P & O European Ferries
Nordic Prince (23,200) AS	1,040	Royal Caribbean
Nordnorge (2,611)	410	Ofotens Ds.
Nordstjernen (2,194)	450	Troms Fylkes
Norland (12,988) AS 🚗	900	North Sea Ferries
Norris Castle (922) A 🚗	850	Red Funnel
Norrona (7,457) 🚗	250	Smyril Line
Norsea (31,000) AS 🚗	1,250	North Sea Ferries
Norstar (12,988) AS 🚗	900	North Sea Ferries
Norsun (31,000) AS 🚗	1,250	North Sea Ferries
Northern Ranger (2,561) A	131	Marine Atlantic
Northern Star (164)	566	Star Ferry
North Island Princess (841) 🚗	186	British Col. Ferry Corp.
North Star (299) 🚗	300	Cross Sound Ferry
North Star (3,095) AS	158	Exploration Cruises
Nørvøy (275) 🚗	230	More og Romsdal
Norway (70,202) AS	1,896	NCL
Oarai (15,139) AS 🚗	656	Nippon Enkai Ferry K.K.
Oberoi Shehrayar A	150	Bales Tours
Ocean Islander (5,000) AS	260	Ocean Cruise Lines
Ocean Pearl (12,456) AS	485	Pearl Cruises
Ocean Princess (12,218) AS	460	Ocean Cruise Lines
Oceanic (27,645) AS	1,035	Premier Cruise Lines
Ocean Traveller (40,966)	10	Egon Oldendorff
Oceanus (7,554) AS	540	Epirotiki
Odessa (13,758) AS	512	Black Sea
Odin Sydfyen (498) 🚗	338	Sydfyenske Ds.
Øen (99) 🚗	125	Søby-Mommark
Oerd (1,105) A 🚗	1,000	Wagenborg
Ofelia (2,089) 🚗	800	Scandinavian F.L.
Ogasawara Maru (3,550) AS 🚗	1,041	Ogasawara Kaiun
Oglasa (1,833) 🚗	1,180	Toremar
Oikaze (129)		Kyodo Kisen Kaisha
Okayama Maru (1,138) 🚗	600	Utaka-Kokudo
Okesa (296) (jetfoil)	282	Sado K.K.
Oki (2,100) 🚗	928	Okikisen K.K.
Okiji (2,584) 🚗	928	Okikisen K.K.
Olau Britannia (14,996) 🚗	1,600	Olau
Olau Hollandia (13,500) AS 🚗	1,600	Olau
Olavsbussen (199) (westamaran) A	140	Fosen Trafikklag
Oldenburg (288)	250	Lundy Company
Oleanda (291) A	40	Blue Lagoon
Ølen (487) 🚗	350	Hardanger
Olovaha (707)	340	Shipping Corp. of Polynesia
Oltenita (818) A	120	Lüftner
Olympia (9,955) 🚗	502	Kuk Gae
Olympia A	107	Scylla Tours
Olympia (37,583) AS 🚗	2,500	Viking Line
Olympic (773) 🚗	605	Washington S.F.
Omineca Princess (765) 🚗	200	British Col. Ministry
Omo (66) 🚗	100	Omo Faergefart
Omogo (685) 🚗	475	Setonaikai
Omonia (302) 🚗	234	Stefanos Ioannides
Opal (654)	429	Copenhagen Line
Orcadia (619)	296	Orkney Islands
Orient Express (12,343) AS 🚗	800	British Ferries Orient-Express
Orient Princess (11,000) AS	318	SA Tours
Ormoc (568)	560	Aboitiz
Ørnen (281) (catamaran)	234	Flyvebådene
Orpheus (4,075) A	285	Swan Hellenic
Ørsta (220) 🚗	133	More og Romsdal
Os (592) 🚗	350	Hardanger
Osiris	141	Hilton International
Oster (318) S 🚗	250	A.S. Bergen Nord.
Ostfriesland (942) A 🚗	1,200	AG Ems/Borkumlijn
Otagawa (698) AS 🚗	400	Setonaikai
Otohime (154)	400	Fukuoka City
Otoki III (36) A 🚗	97	Meitetsu Kaijyo
Otoki V (37) A 🚗	97	Meitetsu Kaijyo
Otome Maru (3,313) A 🚗	1,380	Sado K.K.
Ouranos (3,777) 🚗	460	Fragline
Our Lady of Guadalupe (938) A	842	Carlos A. Gothong
Our Lady Pamela (313) (catamaran)	470	Sealink
Our Lady Patricia (312) (catamaran)	470	Sealink
Ourø (99) 🚗	148	I/S Faergefarten Orø-Holbaek
Overchurch (468)	1,200	Merseyside P.T.E.
Ozamis City (2,740)	1,214	William Lines
Pace (1,450) 🚗	250	Italian State Rlys.
Pacific Northwest Explorer (97) A	80	Expl. Cruise Lines
Pacific Princess (20,636) AS	650	Princess Cruises
Palmelense (304)	500	Transportes Tejo E.P.
Paloma (5,625) 🚗	396	Afroessa Lines S.A.
Panagia Tinou (4,951) AS 🚗	1,849	Ventouris Ferries
Panorama		Trinidad & Tobago
Paolo Veronese (4,520) 🚗		Siremar
Para (1,982) (catamaran) A	140	ENASA
Park City (1,129) A 🚗	1,000	Bridgeport & Port Jefferson
Park Liner (267) AS	560	Fukuoka City
Pascoli (6,909) AS 🚗	1,000	Tirrenia
Patra Express (7,356) AS 🚗	1,400	Ventouris Ferries
Patria (277) S	900	Nav. Lago di Como
Patria (330) A	50	Feenstra Rijn Lijn
Patty (11,293)	7	Mineral Shipping Co.
Peconic Queen (97)	182	Service Maritime Carteret–Jersey
Peder Paars (19,763) AS 🚗	2,000	Danish State Rlys.
Pegasus (12,576)	700	Epirotiki
Pegasus (249) A (westamaran)	181	Service Maritime Carteret–Jersey
Pegasus (300)	40	Seetours
Pelee Islander (334) 🚗	285	Pelee Island
Peng Lai Hu (299) A	291	Jiangmen
Pentland Venture (40)	184	Thomas & Bews
Peruana	80	Conerj
Peter (70)	150	Christiansøfarten
Peter Pan (22,000) 🚗	1,600	TT Line

SHIP	PAX	OPERATOR
Peter Wessel (6,800) 🚗	1,500	Larvik Line
Petite-France	140	Alsace Croisieres
Petrarca (6,909) AS 🚗	1,000	Tirrenia
Pico (332) (jetfoil) A	260	Far East Hydrofoil
Pidder Lyng (999)	800	Wyker Ds.
Pielinen (371) 🚗	300	Nurmes-Marina
Piemonte (302)	525	Nav. Lago Maggiore
Piero della Francesca (2,080) 🚗	686	Siremar
Pietro Novelli (1,580) 🚗		Siremar
Pinhal Novo (893)	1,608	Cam. de Ferro Portugueses
Pinturicchio 🚗		Siremar
Pioneer (1,071) 🚗	356	Cal. MacBrayne
Pisanello (131) (hydrofoil)	125	Siremar
Placido de Castro (337)	300	ENASA
Planasia Island (984) 🚗	1,000	Toremar
Point Gammon (99)	500	Hy-Line
Polarlys (2,163)	450	Troms Fylkes Ds.
Polynesia (1,400) A	126	Windjammer
Pomerania (7,414) 🚗	983	Polska Z. Baltycka
Ponta Delgada (332) (jetfoil)	260	Far East Hydrofoil
Porsangerfjord (746) 🚗	399	Finnmark
Portelet (3,987) AS 🚗	1,000	British Channel Island
Porto Brandäo (196)	377	Transportes Tejo E.P.
Portoferraio (498) 🚗	644	Navarma
Porto Novo (300)	175	Agencia Nacional
Poseidon	400	Collée-Hölzenbein
Poseidon	108	Feenstra Rijn Lijn
Povl Anker (8,200) AS	1,500	Bornholmstrafikken
Powell River Queen (1,486) 🚗	400	British Col. Ferry Corp.
Pride (209)	225	Strandfaraskip
Prince Edward (1,772) 🚗	300	Northumberland
Prince Laurent (4,909) 🚗	1,302	P & O European Ferries/ RTM
Prince Nova (1,765) A 🚗	300	Northumberland
Prince of Brittany (5,465) AS 🚗	1,000	Brittany Ferries
Prince of Wales (458) S 🚗 (hovercraft)	280	Hoverspeed
Princesa Guacimara (210) (jetfoil)	212	Cia. Trasmed.
Princesa Guayarmina (210) (jetfoil)	212	Cia. Trasmed.
Princesse Clementine (289) (jetfoil)	316	P & O European Ferries/ RTM
Princesse Marie Christine (5,543) 🚗	1,200	P & O European Ferries/ RTM
Princess M (8,000) 🚗	1,200	Marlines
Priness Marguerite (5,911) 🚗	1,300	British Col. Steamship
Princess of Acadia (10,070) A 🚗	650	Marine Atlantic
Princess of Saimaa	84	Saimaan Matkailu
Princess Okinawa (5,000) 🚗	500	Ryukyu Kaiun
Prins Albert (6,019) AS 🚗	1,400	P & O European Ferries/ RTM
Prinseca Marissa 🚗		Louis Cruise Lines Ltd.
Prinses Beatrix (2,332) 🚗	1,000	Provinciale Stoombtn.
Prinses Christina (3,088) 🚗	1,000	Provinciale Stoombtn.
Prinses Christina	114	Rijn Moezel Kompas
Prinses Juliana (6,682) 🚗	1,200	Provinciale Stoombtn.
Prinses Margriet (2,295) 🚗	1,000	Provinciale Stoombtn.
Prinses Maria-Esmeralda (5,543) 🚗	1,200	P & O European Ferries/ RTM
Prinsesse Anne Marie (3,487) 🚗	785	Danish State Rlys.
Prinsesse Benedikte (3,668)	1,500	Danish State Rlys.
Prinsesse Elisabeth (3,572) 🚗	785	Danish State Rlys.
Prinsesse Ragnhild (16,631) AS 🚗	896	Jahre Line
Prinses Stephanie (287) (jetfoil) A	316	P & O European Ferries/ RTM
Prins Henrik (6,211) 🚗	1,500	Danish State Rlys.
Prins Joachim (10,607)	2,000	Danish State Rlys.
Prins Willem-Alexander (3,472) 🚗	1,000	Provinciale Stoombtn.
Pristina (11,750) A	12	Yugoslav Gt. Lakes
Proteus (999) 🚗	900	Kinopraxis Pleion
Provence (7,824) AS 🚗	1,280	SNCM
Provence	10	Rhein-Flotel
Psara (500)	214	Miniotis
Puijo		Saimaan Matkailu
Pyramids (200) A	44	Pyramids Nile Cruises
Pyynikki (29,000) AS	61	Runoilijan Tie
Quadra Queen II (771) 🚗	200	British Col. Ferry Corp.
Queen Cleopatra (90) A	40	Pyramids Nile Cruises
Queen Coral 7 (4,973) AS 🚗	500	Terukuni Yusen
Queen Diamond (8,822) A 🚗	597	K.K. Diamond Ferry
Queen Elizabeth 2 (67,139) AS	1,815	Cunard Line
Queen Flower 2 (7,000) AS 🚗	1,505	Kansai Kisen K.K.
Queenfoil (hydrofoil) (127)	108	Transtour
Queen Nabila	104	Naggar Tours
Queen Nabila II	104	Naggar Tours
Queen Nefertiti (200) A	44	Pyramids Nile Cruises
Queen of Alberni (5,872) 🚗	1,415	British Col. Ferry Corp.
Queen of Burnaby (4,902) 🚗	987	British Col. Ferry Corp.
Queen of Coquitlam (6,551) 🚗	1,442	British Col. Ferry Corp.
Queen of Cowichan (6,551) 🚗	1,466	British Col. Ferry Corp.
Queen of Esquimalt (9,304) 🚗	1,394	British Col. Ferry Corp.
Queen of Nanaimo (4,938) 🚗	987	British Col. Ferry Corp.
Queen of New Westminster (4,903) 🚗	791	British Col. Ferry Corp.
Queen of Oak Bay (6,968) 🚗	1,466	British Col. Ferry Corp.
Queen of Prince Rupert (5,864) 🚗	458	British Col. Ferry Corp.
Queen of Saanich (9,302) 🚗	1,394	British Col. Ferry Corp.
Queen of Sidney (3,127) A 🚗	989	British Col. Ferry Corp.
Queen of Surrey (6,968) 🚗	1,466	British Col. Ferry Corp.
Queen of the Islands (1,717) 🚗	483	British Col. Ferry Corp.
Queen of the North (8,889) 🚗	750	British Col. Ferry Corp.
Queen of Tsawwassen (3,127) 🚗	989	British Col. Ferry Corp.
Queen Vergina (6,240) AS 🚗	1,200	Stability Line
Queen of Vancouver (9,357) 🚗	1,360	British Col. Ferry Corp.
Queen of Victoria (9,294) 🚗	1,360	British Col. Ferry Corp.
Queen Salamasina (714) 🚗	216	Western Samoa

SHIP	PAX	OPERATOR
Queenscliff (1,184)	1,100	New S. Wales
Quiberon (7,920) 🚗	1,140	Brittany Ferries
Quinalt (1,368) 🚗	665	Washington S.F.
Quinitsa (1,107) 🚗	300	British Col. Ferry Corp.
Quinsam (1,457) 🚗	400	British Col. Ferry Corp.
Quirino (985) 🚗	1,000	Caremar
Raasay (69) 🚗	50	Cal. MacBrayne
Radisson 🚗	250	Soc. des Traversiers du Québec
Ragnvald Jarl (2,196)	585	Nordenfjeldske
Raketa (hydrofoil)		Ceskoslovenska
Ramon Aboitiz (1,705)	641	Aboitiz
Ramses (90) A	40	Pyramids Nile Cruises
Ramses of Egypt	78	Naggar Tours
Ramtind (475) 🚗	250	Torghatten
Rana (421) 🚗	200	Helgeland Trafik.
Raromatai Ferry (450) 🚗		Cie Maritime des Iles Sous-le-Vent
Rauma (674) 🚗	325	More og Romsdal
Regent Sea (17,234)	708	Regency Cruises
Regent Star (24,500) AS	960	Regency Cruises
Reggio (3,713) 🚗	2,000	Italian State Rlys.
Regina del Garda (192) 🚗	185	Nav. Sul Lago di Garda
Reg-Rat Milatz	230	Bingen-Rüdesheimer
Regula (2,472) A 🚗	900	Scandinavian F.L.
Reichenau (80)	250	Bodensee
Reine Astrid (5,429) 🚗	1,200	P & O European Ferries/ RTM
Reis (46) 🚗	80	Venus Travel
Reli (160)	136	Kenya Railways
Remacum	150	Gebruder Kolb
Renzo (76)	300	Nav. Lago di Como
Republica di Pisa	60	Grimaldi Medferry
Republica di Venezia (37,000) 🚗	60	Grimaldi Medferry
Resolution (hovercraft)	80	Hovertravel
Rethimnon (7,291) AS 🚗	1,444	ANEK
Rex (47)	160	Koster Trafik
Rex Rheni (245) A	150	Rederij Rijnvakantie
Rex Rhenus	280	Bingen-Rüdesheimer
Rhein	1,190	KD German Rhine
Rheinfelden (163)	405	Basler Personen
Rheinland (942) A 🚗	1,200	AG Ems/Borkumlijn
Rheinpfeil (64) (hydrofoil)	64	KD German Rhine
Rhododendron (937) 🚗	546	Washington S.F.
Rhone (364) S	1,000	Cie. Gen. Lac Leman
Rhum (69) 🚗	50	Cal. MacBrayne
Rhy-Blitz (97)	235	Basler Personen
Riace (2,377) 🚗	500	Italian State Rlys.
Ribatejense (304)	506	Transportes Tejo E.P.
Richard Robbins	18	Classic Sail Windjammer
Rijnhaven (176) A	142	Rederij Rijnvakantie
Rinjani (13,860) A	1,596	Pel. Nas. Indonesia
Rio Amazonas (350) A	54	SAR
Rio Grande (94) A	200	Biwako Kisen K.K.
Ritan (81) 🚗	140	Stranfaraskip
Ritsurin (2,800) 🚗	758	Kansai Kisen/ Kato Kisen
River Aboine (10,985)	12	Nigerian National
River Adada (13,164)	6	Nigerian National
River Asab (10,986)	12	Nigerian National
River Guma (10,985)	12	Nigerian National
River Gurara (13,194)	6	Nigerian National
River Ikpan (13,363)	6	Nigerian National
River Jiminl (10,985)	12	Nigerian National
River Kerawa (10,985)	12	Nigerian National
River Maje (13,197)	6	Nigerian National
River Majidun (13,161)	6	Nigerian National
River Ngada (13,364)	6	Nigerian National
River Ogbese (13,197)	6	Nigerian National
River Oli (13,165)	6	Nigerian National
River Oshun (13,197)	6	Nigerian National
River Osse (10,985)	12	Nigerian National
River Rima (10,986)	12	Nigerian National
Roana (1,400) 🚗	500	R Line
Robert J. Irwin (200) 🚗	12	New Brunswick
Robin Hood (12,600) A 🚗	1,600	TT Line
Roine (71) AS	121	Suomen Hopealinja
Rokko (3,000) A 🚗	742	Kansai Kisen/Kato Kisen
Roland of England III (1,000)	150	European Yacht
Roma (23) 🚗	90	Nav. Sul Lago di Garda
Roma (328)	600	Nav. Lago Maggiore
Romanza (7,538) A	600	Chandris
Romso (5,603) 🚗	1,500	Danish State Rlys.
Rondine (20) S	105	Nav. Lago di Como
Rondonia (2,657) (catamaran)	500	ENASA
Roraima (2,657) (catamaran)	500	ENASA
Rosalia (5,768) 🚗	2,000	Italian State Rlys.
Rosella (10,500) 🚗	1,700	Viking Line
Roseway	36	Yankee Schooner Cruises
Roslagen (1,612) AS 🚗	600	Eckerö Linjen
Rostand (21,653) AS	2	Cie. Gen. Maritime
Rotterdam (38,644) AS	1,114	Holland America
Rottum (92) 🚗	1000	Wagenborg Passag.
Røusse (1,234)	750	Luftner/Donau
Rousseau (14,000)	2	Cie. Gen. Maritime
Royale (15,483) AS	700	Premier Cruise Line
Royal Iris (1,234)	750	Merseyside P.T.E.
Royal Odessey (17,884) AS	806	Royal Cruise Line
Royal Princess (44,348) AS	1,200	Princess Cruises
Royal Viking Sea (28,018) AS	500	Royal Viking Line
Royal Viking Sky (28,078) AS	500	Royal Viking Line
Royal Viking Star (28,221) AS	700	Royal Viking Line
Roylen Sunbird A (catamaran)	250	Roylen Cruises
Rugen (6,465) S 🚗	1,468	Deutsche Reichsbahn
Rum Hart (373)	512	Wyker Ds.
Runden (149) 🚗	175	Sejerofargen
Ruzizi		SNCZ
Ryokufu		Kyodo Kisen Kaisha
Sachikaze (130)		Kyodo Kisen Kaisha
Sado Maru (572) 🚗	573	Sado K.K.
Safina-e-Abid (5,578)	1,218	Pan-Islamic Steamship
Safina-e-Arab (8,477)	1,294	Pan-Islamic Steamship
Sagafjord (24,109) AS	505	Cunard
Sagittarius (10,000) A	4	Hanseatic Marine
St. Anselm (7,003) 🚗	1,400	Sealink
St. Brendan (5,426) 🚗	1,400	B+I Line/Sealink
St. Caspar (395)	80	Compass Tours
St. Catherine (2,036) S 🚗	1,000	Sealink
St. Cecelia 🚗		Sealink
St. Christopher (6,996) 🚗	1,400	Sealink
St. Clair (4,468) AS 🚗	735	P & O Ferries
St. Columba (7,836) 🚗	2,241	Sealink
St. David (7,196) 🚗	1,200	Sealink
St. Eugene IV	44	Armement Borotra
St. Georges XII (141) S	118	Armement Borotra
St. Helen (2,983) 🚗	680	Sealink
St. Helena (3,150)	76	St. Helena Shipping
St. Killian II (10,256) AS 🚗	1,500	Irish Ferries
St. Magnus (1,206) 🚗	12	P & O Ferries
St. Nicholas (14,368) 🚗	2,100	Sealink

Great Britain – Northern Ireland 274

BELFAST CAR FERRIES

SAINT PATRICK II

Liverpool *Great Britain* – **Belfast** *Northern Ireland*

	X			
Liverpool →	11 00			
Belfast ←	20 00			

	X			
Belfast →	22 00			
Liverpool ←	07*15			

FARES (in UK £) (according to season)	One-way	Round trip
Foot passengers	25.00-28.00	42.00-48.00
Cars	42.00-73.00	70.00-124.00
– passengers	16.00-19.80	28.00-36.40
Motorcycles	15.00-17.00	26.00-27.00
Motorcycle combinations	26.00-29.00	44.00-47.00
Bicycles	free	free

Children 5-15 years 50%; under 5 years free
Cabins extra
Reductions – please apply to operator

Great Britain: Northern Ireland – Isle of Man

Table **612**

Great Britain – Norway

Tables **150, 620, 622, 623**

Great Britain – Spain 280

BRITTANY FERRIES

QUIBERON

Plymouth *Great Britain* – **Santander** *Spain* Journey time 24 hours

Until 15/5 & 18/9-15/12
Plymouth → 10 00③⑦
Santander → 18 30①④

16/5-15/9
Plymouth → 08 00①; 11 30③
Santander → 11 00④; 14 00②

FARES (in UK £)	One-way
Foot passengers	55.00
Motorists/passengers	52.00
Cars up to 4m. long	48.00-103.00
4.01m.-4.50m. long	56.00-114.00
4.51m.-5.50m. long	63.00-131.00
Motorcaravans, minibuses, trailers per m.	13.50-26.00
Motorcycles	16.00-30.00
Bicycles	free- 6.00 (according to season)

Cabins available at extra charge

Great Britain – Sweden 283

DFDS SEAWAYS

TOR BRITANNIA; TOR SCANDINAVIA

Harwich *Great Britain* – **Gothenburg** *Sweden*

	Until 10/2		11/2-4/6		5/6-14/8			15/8-30/9		
	⑤	⑦	⑤	②⑦	B	C	A	⑤	②⑦	
Harwich →	13 30	19 30	11 30	16 30	11 30	16 30	16 30	11 30	16 30	
Gothenburg ←	14*30	20*30	12*00	20*00	12*00	17*00	20*00	12*00	20*00	

	④	⑧	②④	⑧	D	E	②④	⑥	
Gothenburg →	12 00	17 30	12 00	15 00	15 00	19 30	12 00	15 00	
Harwich ←	10*30	16*30	13*30	14*00	13*30	18*00	13*00	14*00	

A-14/8 only.

B-Harwich →
6/1988 5, 7, 9, 13, 15, 17, 21, 23, 27, 29
7/1988 1, 5, 7, 11, 13, 15, 19, 21, 25, 27, 29
8/1988 2, 4, 8, 10, 12

C-Harwich →
'/1988 9, 11, 17, 19, 23, 25
1988 1, 3, 7, 9, 15, 17, 21, 23, 29, 31
$/1988 4, 6, 12

D-Gothenburg →
6/1988 6, 8, 10, 14, 16, 18, 20, 24, 28, 30
7/1988 2, 6, 8, 12, 14, 16, 20, 22, 26, 28, 30
8/1988 3, 5, 9, 11, 13

E-Gothenburg →
6/1988 10, 12, 18, 22, 24, 26
7/1988 2, 4, 8, 10, 16, 18, 22, 24, 30
8/1988 1, 5, 7, 13

IO SAILINGS: from Harwich 31/5

FARES One-way	UK£	S.Kr.
Adults		
– 2, 3, & 4 berth cabins	60.00-154.00	630-1,300
– single cabins	118.00-175.00	1,230-3,000
Cars, motorcaravans up to 6m. long		
up to 1.85m. high	free-40.00	free-400
over 1.85m. high	11.00-60.00	600-650
Caravans etc.	18.00-20.00	200-250
Motorcycles, scooters	15.00-18.00	150-200
Mopeds, bicycles	4.00-5.00	50

NOTE: Round trip discounts are available for passengers whose journey originates in Gothenburg.

Great Britain – Sweden 284

DFDS SEAWAYS

Newcastle *Great Britain* – **Gothenburg** *Sweden* **and v.v.**

Summer service only

FARES (in UK £)	One-way
Adults	
– couchettes/reclining chairs	85.00-94.00
– 2, 3, & 4 berth cabins	97.00-169.00
– single cabins	136.00-190.00

Reduced rates for children – please apply to operator

Cars, motorcaravans up to 6m. long	One-way 1-3 paying pax	One-way 4 or more paying pax
up to 1.85m. high	36.00	free
over 1.85m. high	54.00	18.00
Motorcycles, scooters	15.00	
Mopeds, bicycles	4.00	

For details of special 'Super Savers' please apply to operator

Great Britain – United States 286

CUNARD

QUEEN ELIZABETH 2

Southampton *Great Britain* – **New York** *New York, USA* – **Baltimore** *Maryland, USA* – **Newport News** *Virginia, USA* – **Fort Lauderdale** *Florida, USA*

Southampton →	16 00		11/5	5/6	20/6	1/7A	22/7	1/8B	16/8B	29/8	11/9B	26/9B	15/10C
New York ←	08 00		16/5	10/6	25/6	6/7	27/7	6/8	21/8	3/9	16/9	1/10	20/10
Baltimore ←	14 30												21/10
Newport News ←	08 00												
Fort Lauderdale ←	09 00												

continued →

Table 286—continued

Fort Lauderdale →	19 00	27/4											30/10
Baltimore →	12 00												
Newport News →	19 00												
New York →	15 00	29/4	22/5	12/6	25/6	10/7	27/7	11/8	21/8	6/9	21/9	1/10	31/10
Southampton ←	17 00	4/5	27/5	17/6	30/6	15/7D	1/8D	16/8D	26/8D	11/9D	26/9D	6/10D	5/11

A-Departs 11 30 and calls at **Cherbourg** *France* 1/7 at 20 00. B-Departs 20 00. C-Departs 19 00. D-Arrives 13 00.

FARES (in UK £) Rooms/Cabins	Low Season	Mid Season	High Season
– single	875-2,685	1,005-2,950	1,060-3,110
– double	700-3,720	800-4,075	850-4,300

Great Britain – West Germany 287

DFDS SEAWAYS

HAMBURG

Harwich *Great Britain* – **Hamburg** *West Germany*

	Until 29/2		1/3-30/9	
	②④	⑥	B	C
Harwich →	15 30	19 30	15 30	16 30
Hamburg ←	13*00	16*45	13*00	13*00

	Until 29/2		1/3-30/9	
	①③⑤		E	F
Hamburg →	16 30		16 30	16 30
Harwich ←	12*00		12*00	13*00

B-Harwich →
3/1988 1 and alternate dates until 31
4/1988 2 and alternate dates until 30
5/1988 2 and alternate dates until 30
6/1988 1 and alternate dates until 29
7/1988 1 and alternate dates until 31
8/1988 2 and alternate dates until 30
9/1988 1 and alternate dates until 23
C-Harwich →
9/1988 25, 27, 29

E-Hamburg →
3/1988 2 and alternate dates until 30
4/1988 1 and alternate dates until 29
5/1988 1 and alternate dates until 31
6/1988 2 and alternate dates until 30
7/1988 2 and alternate dates until 30
8/1988 1 and alternate dates until 31
9/1988 2 and alternate dates until 22
F-Hamburg →
9/1988 24, 26, 28, 30

FARES One-way	UK£	DM
Adults		
– couchettes	35.00-54.00	98-188
– economy cabin	35.00-54.00	–
– 2, 3, & 4 berth cabins	46.00-84.00	210-334
– single cabins	91.00-113.00	298-392
Cars, motor caravans up to 6m. long		
up to 1.85m. high	free-40.00	free-98
over 1.85m. high	18.00-60.00	155-158
Caravans etc.	17.00-20.00	60-62
Motorcycles, scooters	15.00-18.00	55-56
Mopeds, bicycles	4.00-5.00	15-16

Great Britain: Mainland – Channel Islands 290

BRITISH CHANNEL ISLAND FERRIES

CORBIÈRE; PORTELET

Portsmouth – St. Peter Port *Guernsey C. I.* – **St. Helier** *Jersey C. I.*

Until 25/3	②③④	⑤⑦			
Portsmouth →	22 00	22 00			
St. Peter Port ←		06*30			
St. Peter Port →		07*30			
St. Helier ←	06*30	09*30			
St. Helier →	08*30				
St. Peter Port ←	10*30				

	③④⑥	①⑥		
St. Helier →	08 30	19 30		
St. Peter Port ←	10 30	21 30		
St. Peter Port →	12 00	22 45		
Portsmouth ←	19 00	07*00		

FARES (in UK £) (according to season)	One-way	Round trip 5 days
Adults	26.00-32.00	38.00-46.00
Children 5-15 years	13.00-16.00	19.00-23.00
under 5 years	free	free
Cars	33.00-46.00	46.00-60.00
Trailers up to 1.82m. high		
up to 2.50m. long	19.00	–
2.51m.-5m. long	38.00	–
Motorcycles	9.00	–
Bicycles	free	free

Mid-week Round trip saver ①②③④: 2 Adults + 2 Children OR 3 Adults without car 106.00-142.00; with car 160.00-224.00

On Board Accommodation	From Portsmouth Day	From Portsmouth Night	From Weymouth Day	From Weymouth Night
Pullman seats	–	2.00	–	2.00
Couchettes	–	–	2.00	4.00
Cabins				
– 2 berth	10.00	18.00	–	–
– 4 berth	3.00-4.00	6.00-8.00	–	–

For special reductions please apply to operator

Great Britain: Mainland – Channel Islands 291

CONDOR LTD.

Hydrofoils: to be advised

Weymouth – St. Peter Port *Guernsey C. I.* – **St. Helier** *Jersey C. I.* **and v.v.**

Service resumes operating 25/3. Schedules to be advised

FARES (in UK £)	One-way	Round trip
Adults	26.00	52.00
Children 2-14 years	13.00	26.00
under 2 years (not occupying a seat)	free	free

Great Britain: Mainland – Channel Islands 292

TORBAY SEAWAYS

Torquay – Alderney *C. I.*

January to March: Irregular cargo service—Limited accommodation for 12 passengers. Please apply to operator for details

DEVONIUN II

Torquay – Alderney *C. I.* – **St. Peter Port** *Guernsey C. I.* – **St. Helier** *Jersey C. I.* **and v.v.**

Service resumes operating in April

FARES (in UK £) Passengers Torquay	One-way	Round trip
– Jersey	30.00	48.00
– Guernsey	26.00	42.00
– Alderney	26.00	42.00

Cars Torquay	One-way	Round trip
– Jersey	30.00	50.00
– Guernsey	30.00	45.00
– Alderney	30.00	45.00

Cabins from 5.00 to 30.00 per pax one way
Reductions for children – please apply to operator
Mid-week family savers – car with 4 fare paying pax 40.00 return

(c) (i) Does the Navarma SpA shipping company have a reservation office in Switzerland?
    (ii) Where is the company's head office?

(d) (i) Name the operator for the ship *Royal Odessey*.
    (ii) What is the GRT of that ship?
    (iii) How many passengers may travel?
    (iv) What does AS mean?

(e) (i) What type of ship is the *St Clair*?
    (ii) Name the shipping company.
    (iii) How many passengers may travel?
    (iv) What is the size of this ship?

(f) (i) Name the service for table 283.
    (ii) Name the shipping company.
    (iii) From which port in Britain do the ships sail?
    (iv) Can your client sail from Harwich to Gothenburg on 16 June?
    (v) The ship sails from Harwich at 1130 hours. Give the time of arrival in Gothenburg.

(g) Explain the following: ②,⑥,①.

Making the reservation

We follow the same format of investigating our clients' needs and obtaining all the relevant information regarding the clients' personal details and requests. We have a choice when making the reservation: either we contact the shipping company direct if they have an office in our country: or we contact the general sales agent acting for the shipping company; or we may be working in an office that is using the computerized reservation system. Once the reservation is confirmed, we would assist the client to complete the booking form, making sure that the booking conditions are understood. Deposit or full payment is collected.

The ticket may be issued by the shipping company or by yourself. If you will be issuing the ticket, follow the designated boxes. The kind of detail you will enter on the ticket will be as follows: passenger's name; how many people travelling; ages of children; travel dates for outward and return journeys; class of travel; length of car; type of accommodation confirmed; name of ship; outward and return charges; details of any special tariff; and booking reference.

Let's make a checklist of the sort of questions we may be asked by the customer, and the sort of information we should certainly supply to the customer. All the answers can be found in the *ABC* guides and the ferry companies' brochures.

1 Has the travel insurance been fully explained?
2 Is the length of the vehicle correct for the fare charged?
3 Should the client take a warning triangle?
4 What are the speed limits for countries to be visited?
5 Is the motorist entitled to a reduced fare or excursion?
6 Are motorway toll taxes payable?
7 Have reporting times been entered on the ticket?
8 Is the passenger's driving licence valid for all the countries to be visited?
9 Has the passenger been correctly briefed regarding his passport, visa and health requirements?

10 Does the car require rear seat belts?
11 Have you placed the travel ticket and useful information leaflets, maps etc. in a travel wallet to provide a good presentation?
12 Finally, have you reminded your clients of the duty-free shop on board, where many goods such as perfumes, cigarettes and alcohol can be purchased at tax-free prices?

It just remains to wish your clients *bon voyage* – and 'cheers'!

The following exercises will help you check your knowledge of this chapter.

Exercise 4

(a) Name the capital of Algeria.
(b) Is a charge made for motorway travel in Austria?
(c) Are seat belts compulsory in Algeria?
(d) Give the minimum age to drive a car in Austria.
(e) Name the countries that border Austria.
(f) Give the speed limit within the city of Salzburg.
(g) (i) Give the sailing frequency between Valencia and Ibiza.
     (ii) How long does the journey take?
     (iii) How many passengers does the *Albatros Series* hold?
(h) (i) Give the map route number between Almería and Melilla.
     (ii) In which country is Melilla?
(i) (i) Give the map route number between Sète and Tangier.
     (ii) In which country is Sète?

Exercise 5

(a) Find the cheapest fare for the following reservation: Mr and Mrs K. Banda, and daughter aged 7 years, travelling Harwich to Hook of Holland Friday 3 July, returning Hook of Holland to Harwich Tuesday 7 July; day sailings in each direction; no cabins required; car 5.50 metres in length and 1.70 metres in height.
(b) What time does it sail from the Hook of Holland?
(c) Give the check-in time.
(d) How long does the sailing take?

Exercise 6

(a) What part does the editorial play in guide books and manuals?
(b) In which country does the Norfolk Line BV have a head office?
(c) Which table number would you use for information on the New Zealand Railways Corporation?

(d) (i) You are working in San Francisco and have clients wishing to take a cruise in Egypt. You have suggested a cruise operated by Naggar Tours of Egypt. How will you make the reservation?
(ii) They will be travelling on the ship *Queen Nabila*. Is it air conditioned?
(iii) How many passengers does it carry?

(e) (i) Give the tonnage of the *Robin Hood* car ferry.
(ii) How many passengers does it carry?
(iii) Name the operator.

(f) (i) Which shipping company operates a service between Great Britain and Spain?
(ii) Name the ports.
(iii) How long does the sailing take?
(iv) What would be the return fare for a foot passenger?

(g) (i) Name the ship that sails between Great Britain and the USA.
(ii) Give the table number to find the information.
(iii) If your client departed Southampton 11 May, when would he/she arrive New York?
(iv) Give the date the ship departs New York to return to Southampton.

Assignment: car ferries

You are employed by the largest car ferry company in your country. Prepare a talk to trainees about the benefits of car ferries. Your talk is to include the following points: routings; fares; accommodation; facilities on board; package holiday by car/ship.

8 British and continental rail and motor rail

Summary

In this chapter we discuss:

- various rail services worldwide;
- benefits of rail travel;
- Eurotunnel;
- British rail timetables and reservations;
- maps and timetables to study;
- how to read Thomas Cook continental rail timetable;
- explanation of signs;
- practical exercises and assignment to complete.

Understanding rail travel, the calculation of fares and issuing of tickets, like air travel, is a specialized job and most travel agencies either obtain their tickets from a representative of the railways or if they wish to develop direct links, they employ fully qualified staff. However, it is necessary to be able to read timetables, understand the maps and services available in order to give a complete service.

Why travel by train? Some people have always been fascinated by train travel, and still today, others like to travel on steam trains. Many people use trains for holidays (package holidays based on rail travel), independent travel (many specially reduced fares reflect the encouragement for travel during off-peak times for holiday makers, senior citizens, students, etc.). There is an endless choice available for routes, type of trains and fares.

Have you thought of travelling on the Orient Express with its 1920s theme and elegance, or through the magnificent Canadian Rockies by train? Perhaps the Glacier Express would appeal – a train taking you over the roof of Switzerland, the 'slowest' express in the world will take you between Zermatt and St Moritz or Davos through the most spectacular scenery passing through Alpine meadows and dramatic mountain peaks.

Speed is often a reason for rail travel, especially on short journeys when the difficulty and frustrations of congested roads and car parking can be very off-putting for motorists. With the development of high speed MAGLEV trains (Magnetic Levitation) rail travel across Europe will present strong competition to air travel. Although rail travel from, say, Brussels to Paris is approximately 2½ hours and the flight is approximately 50 minutes, the train service begins in the centre of Brussels and arrives in the centre of Paris. The time gained by air travel is soon lost in travelling to and from the airport in both countries, in the necessary pre-flight check-in times, and in customs and baggage clearance.

Travellers can also find rail travel relaxing. They can move around in the train, enjoy lunch with a view of picturesque scenery, or take advantage of the space to work on business.

The motor-rail services, also known as car sleepers, are excellent for travellers who wish to use both car and train, the car is boarded on to the train, and the driver and party, accommodate the passenger part of the train. They are able to collect their car on arrival at the destination, this takes away the long often boring part of a journey and leaves the driver with a shorter journey by car and the freedom of independent transport during the remainder of the holiday.

Worldwide travel

American railways are mainly used for the transportation of goods and the most popular form of transport is by coach or air. The railway companies offering transcontinental (Atlantic to Pacific coasts) passenger services are AMTRAK in the USA and Via Rail Canada (VIA) throughout Canada. They offer two classes of service, first and coach. First class offers superior accommodation with air conditioning, adjustable seats and on some trains meals served in the compartment. Coach class also offers comfortable reclining seats, air conditioning and the transcontinental trains also have sleeping cars. Between Los Angeles and Las Vegas a MAGLEV service is under consideration. Maglev or Magnetic Levitation trains, originally a British invention, are operated by magnets and are capable of speeds over 300 miles per hour.

USSR trains have 'Soft class' equivalent to first class providing upholstered seats and 'Hard class' equivalent to second class with plastic or leather seats which convert to sleeping accommodation for night travel. On the lines serving Western Europe, the trains have sleeping cars which conform to Western European standards. The Trans-Siberian route used by many tour operators packaging unusual rail holidays, is a popular route.

Japan are also developing MAGLEV trains. Travelling by their rapid-transit 'Bullet trains' at a speed of 130 miles per hour between Tokyo and Hakata is a good way of seeing the country.

India still has some steam trains for the enthusiast but a journey on the 'Palace on Wheels' a de luxe train made up of the original carriages used by Indian princes is an exotic way to see the many famous Indian sights.

Generally most countries around the world offer rail travel but the class of services varies considerably from country to country. Always check frequency of service, availability of accommodation, safety, and standards before recommending the service to your clients.

Eurotunnel

The Eurotunnel is due to open in June 1993 and is a tunnel between 25 and 45 metres below the sea bed operating between Folkestone in the United Kingdom and Sangatte in France. Passenger vehicles and their occupants will be transported through the Tunnel in enclosed wagons which will be brightly lit and air conditioned. The overall transit time for passenger vehicles through the System from entrance to exit of the terminals is expected to be generally between 50 and 80 minutes.

The Railways are planning a 24 hour service between London and Paris and London and Brussels. The service between London and Paris is expected to take just over 3 hours and between London and Brussels about 3 hours 10 minutes. With the introduction of the high-speed rail link between Lille and Brussels (planned for 1995) the travel time between London and Brussels is expected to be reduced to approximately 2 hours 40 minutes. Eventually by the year 2000 when a high-speed rail link between the Tunnel and London is in operation the travelling time between London and Paris would be 2 hours 30 minutes and between London and Brussels 2 hours 10 minutes.

The growth of cross Channel market has increased considerably over the years with the increase of car ownership and will continue to do so as the single European Community plans progress.

Speed and reliability (the service will not be affected by adverse weather conditions) will appeal to many travellers. Will the public still use the ferry services? In Chapter 7 we discussed the benefits of car ferries such as, a great choice of routes (Eurotunnel has only one) for many people the sea crossing is part of the holiday, entertainment and many enjoyable facilities are on board, and very competititve fares apply. Eurotunnel and the ferry companies are offering different services to the travelling public and the travellers will make their choice.

British Rail

Let's plan a journey by British Rail. Start by studying the British Isles map. You will notice that all the railway lines have numbers and these refer to the table numbers giving details of the service. We have a client who would like to travel to Dover from London – which table number would you choose? You could choose both 500 and 501. Please study table number 501. The first column provides the distance from London to stations listed. From London to Dover the distance is 126 kilometres. The next column lists the stations from London Victoria and the small d. means depart and a. means arrive. Please read the codes at the foot of the table a = Sundays only (7); b = 5–7 minutes later on Saturdays (6); f = weekdays only (A) stands for weekdays; g = not on Sundays. When a knife and fork is shown above the train times this means refreshments are available on the train. If no code is shown the service operates every day. Are you ready?

You have a client who must be at Dover by 1130 hours on a Tuesday. Which train would you suggest? There is a train leaving London Victoria at 0920 hours arriving Dover Western Docks at 1105 hours.

Another wishes to arrive at Sheerness-on-Sea after 1900 hours on a Sunday. Which train would you suggest? The 1750 hours from London Victoria arrives Sheerness-on-Sea at 1908 hours.

Your client must be in Ramsgate around 12 noon and will board the train at Chatham. Which train would you suggest? 1051 hours arrival Ramsgate 1211 hours. Are refreshments available on the train? Yes, see knife and fork.

To make a reservation requiring a seat or sleeping accommodation you would either use your computer, checking availability and making the reservation or telephone British Rail reservation office.

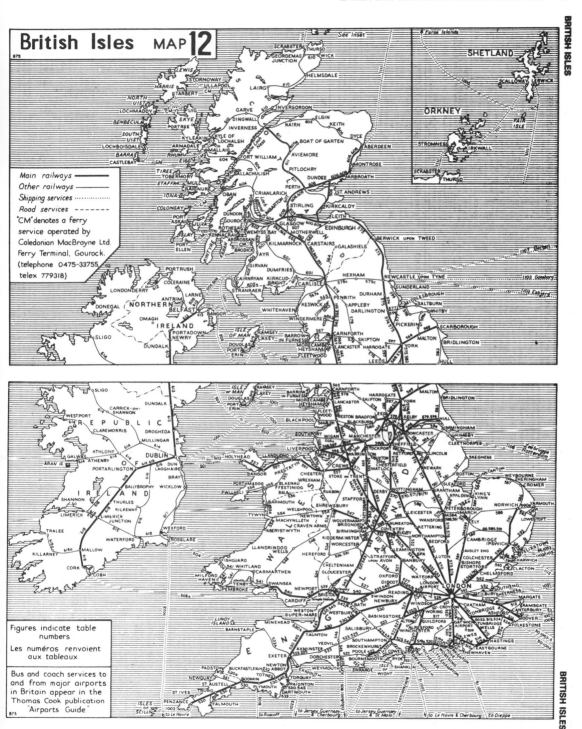

British Isles MAP **12**

Main railways ————
Other railways ————
Shipping services ············
Road services − − − − − −
"CM" denotes a ferry
service operated by
Caledonian MacBrayne Ltd.
Ferry Terminal, Gourock.
(telephone 0475-33755
telex 779318)

Figures indicate table
numbers

Les numéros renvoient
aux tableaux

Bus and coach services to
and from major airports
in Britain appear in the
Thomas Cook publication
"Airports Guide"

BRITISH ISLES

Often a reservation is not required but a rail ticket is necessary. Your travel agency will have a book of rail tickets pre-printed and you will be required to complete each information section of the ticket. The information you will provide will be: the name of the station of departure and arrival, date of travel, validity of ticket, class of travel, description of fare, for example, ordinary single, city saver, ordinary return, number of adults and children, total of fare charged and your travel agency code number confirming place of issue.

Like all accountable documents details of the tickets and fare charged will be sent to British Rail each month.

Table 501		LONDON—SHEERNESS/RAMSGATE/DOVER																						All 1, 2 class		BR (212, 213)	
km		ⒶⒶ	ⒶⒶ	✗		✗	✗										✗						✗	✗		
0	London Victoria .... d.	0523	0523	0653	0723	0750	0820	0823	0850	0920	0923	0950	0953	1020		....	1023	1050	1053	1120	1123	1150	1153	1220		
54	Rochester .... d.	0618	0618	0748	0817				0917				1018		1048		....	1118		1148		1218		1248		....
55	Chatham .... d.	0622	0621	0751	0820	0833	0903	0920	0933	1003	1021	1033	1051	1103		....	1121	1133	1151	1203	1221	1233	1251	1303		....
58	Gillingham .... d.	0626	0625	0755	0825	0836	0906	0924	0936	1006	1025	1036	1055	1106		....	1125	1136	1155	1206	1225	1236	1255	1306		....
72	Sittingbourne .... d.	0640	0639	0809	0841	0848	0918	0939	0948	1018	1039	1048	1109	1118		....	1139	1148	1209	1218	1239	1248	1309	1318		....
85	Sheerness-on-Sea .... a.	0714	0708	0840f	0908	0903		1008			1108					....		1208			1308					
84	Faversham .... {a.	0650	0649	0820	0851	0857	0927	0949	0957	1027	1049	1057	1119	1127		....	1149	1157	1219	1227	1249	1257	1319	1327		
	.... {d.	0652	0659	0822b	0859	0857	0927	0959	0957	1027	1059	1057	1129	1127		....	1159	1157	1229	1227	1259	1257	1329	1327		
101	Herne Bay .... d.	0707		0838b		0911			1011				1111	1144			....		1211	1244			1311	1344		
119	Margate 500 .... a.	0723		0855b		0930			1029				1126	1201			....		1226	1301			1326	1401		
127	Ramsgate 500 .... a.	0733		0905b		0940			1039				1139	1211			....		1239	1311			1339	1411		
99	Canterbury East .... d.		0713		0913		0940	1013		1040	1113				1140		1213			1240	1313			1340		
124	Dover Priory 500 .... a.		0741		0941		1000	1042		1100	1141				1200		1241			1300	1341			1400		
126	Dover Western Docks .... a.		0750		0947a		1006	1047a		1105	1147a				1205		1247a			1305	1347a			1405		

		✗	✗						ⒶⒶ	ⒶⒶ	ⒶⒶ	✗	ⒶⒶ	ⒶⒶ	ⒶⒶ	ⒶⒶ		ⒶⒶ	ⒶⒶ				✗	✗	✗
London Victoria .... d.		1223	1250	1253	1320	1323	1350	1353		1720	1723	1750	1750	1815	1823	1853	1920		1923	1950				2250	2323	2350
Rochester .... d.		1318		1348		1418		1448			1818	1848			1918	1946			2018						0018	
Chatham .... d.		1321	1333	1351	1403	1421	1433	1451		1805	1821	1851	1833	1857	1921	1949	2003		2021	2033				2333	0021	0033
Gillingham .... d.		1325	1336	1355	1406	1425	1436	1455	approx	1806	1825	1855	1836	1902	1925	1953	2006		2025	2036				2336	0025	0036
Sittingbourne .... d.		1339	1348	1409	1418	1439	1448	1509	the	1818	1839	1918	1848	1915	1939	2007	2018		2039	2048				2348	0039	0048
Sheerness-on-Sea .... a.			1408				1508		same				1908	1935			2039			2110				0010g		
Faversham .... {a.		1349	1357	1419	1427	1449	1457	1519	minutes	1827	1849	1928	1857	1924	1949	2017	2027		2049	2057				2357	0049	0059
.... {d.		1359	1357	1429	1427	1459	1457	1529	past	1827	1859	1929	1857	1925	1959	2029	2027		2059	2057				2357	0100	0059
Herne Bay .... d.		1411	1444			1511	1544		each				1911	1941			2041			2113				0012		0114
Margate 500 .... a.		1426	1501			1526	1601		hour				1926	1957			2056			2129				0029		0130
Ramsgate 500 .... a.		1436	1511			1536	1611		until				1939	2008			2106			2141				0041		0140
Canterbury East .... d.		1413		....	1440	1513	....	....		1840	1913	1943			2013	2043	....		2115	....				....	0116	....
Dover Priory 500 .... a.		1441		....	1459	1541	....	....		1900	1941	2011			2042	2111	....		2142	....				....	....	....
Dover Western Docks .... a.		1447a		....	1504	1547a	....	....		1905	1947a	2016			2047	2116	....		2149	....				....	....	....

a—Ⓐ only.   b—5–7 minutes later on Ⓐ.   f—Ⓐ only.   g—Not Ⓐ.

Using rail guides, maps and timetables

There is a wonderful selection of guides maps and timetables giving worldwide travel information which can be obtained from:

Thomas Cook Publishing Office,
PO Box 227,
Peterborough, PE3 6SB,
United Kingdom.
Tel: (0733) 505821/268943
Fax: (0733) 505792

These Thomas Cook manuals are also available in Australia, Austria, Belgium, Denmark, Finland, France, Ireland, Italy, Japan, Netherlands, New Zealand, North America, Norway, South Africa, South America, Sweden, Switzerland and Germany.

Now study the *Thomas Cook European Timetable* contents page. You will see that we are given page numbers and table numbers (services numbers) to find the information quickly. This book gives general useful information, international rail details on car sleepers, airport links, holiday trains etc., international shipping details and train services listed in area order. The timetable is published monthly. From time to time the format is changed, and the information is constantly being updated. Therefore the extracts are for training purposes only, and the latest edition should be used for actual reservations.

Each edition has a section on how to read the timetables, and an explanation of the signs used in the book. Please study the 'Explanation of signs' page now (take your time!). Follow this by reading the 'Specimen table' (take even more time!).

The best way to learn how to use the timetable is to begin finding the information. From the extracts provided, please find answers to the following questions.

ISSN 0952-620X

MARCH, 1992
Published Monthly

THOMAS COOK

EUROPEAN
——TIMETABLE——

CONTENTS
INHALT   TABLE DES MATIERES   CONTENIDO

——INFORMATION——
Auskunft   Renseignements   Informacion

	page		page
Calendar	2	Travel Information	8-10
Newslines	3	Index	11-26
Explanation of Signs	4	Town Plans	30-36
How to use the Timetable	5-7	Books, Guides and Maps	525-528

——TIMETABLES——
Fahrpläne   Tableaux   Horarios

	tables		tables
Airport Links	5	International Services	12-89
Albania	949	Ireland	630-649
Austria	800-849	Irish Sea	620-626
Belgium	200-217	Italy	352-408
Bulgaria	960-965	Netherlands	220-239
Car Sleepers	1	Norway	481-491
Czechoslovakia	870-887	Poland	850-869
Denmark	450-464	Portugal	442-449
Finland	492-498	Romania	950-958
France	100-199	Shipping Services	1001-1550
Germany	650-788	Spain	410-441
Great Britain	500-611	Sweden	465-479
Greece	970-980	Switzerland	250-333
Holiday Trains	93-94	Yugoslavia/Croatia/Slovenia	930-945
Hungary	890-898	Former U. S. R.	900-926

INTERNATIONAL SERVICES SUPPLEMENT : Advance summer timings for major international routes appears on pages 505-536.

Publishing Manager : Jennifer Rigby MA MBA
Sales Manager : Richard Dearing

Editor : Brenden Fox BA
Assistant Editor : Bernard Horton
Compilers : David Gunning and Christopher Bane BA

☎(Sales) 0733 505821   (Editorial) 0733 267023   Fax 0733 505792

For rail tickets and reservations,
contact the THOMAS COOK RAIL CENTRE, Oxford.
☎ 0865 340441   Fax 0865 792721

Thomas Cook Logo

Thomas Cook Publishing,
P. O. Box 227,
Peterborough, England,
PE3 6SB.

Registered Office,
45 Berkeley Street,
London, W1A 1EB.
(Company Registration No. 198600 London)

EXPLANATION OF SIGNS

EXPLANATION OF SIGNS	ZEICHENERKLÄRUNG		EXPLICATION DES SIGNES	EXPLICACION DE LOS SIGNOS
TRANSPORT SERVICES	**BEFÖRDERUNGSDIENSTE**		**SERVICES**	**SERVICIOS DE TRANSPORTE**
Through carriage	Kurswagen		Voiture directe	Vagón directo
Sleeping Car	Schlafwagen		Voiture-lit	Coche-cama
Couchette Car	Liegewagen		Couchettes	Coche-litera
Restaurant Car	Speisewagen		Voiture-restaurant	Coche-restaurante
Buffet car or light refreshments available	Buffet-Wagen oder Verkauf von Erfrischungen		Buffet ou rafraichissements	Coche-comedor o refrigerios disponibles
Bus or coach service	Buslinien		Service autobus ou autocar	Servicio de autobuses o autocares
Shipping service	Schiffahrtslinie		Service maritime	Servicio de transportes
DAYS OF RUNNING	**VERKEHRSTAGE**		**JOURS DE CIRCULATION**	**DIAS DE SERVICIO**
Daily except Sundays and holidays	Täglich außer Sonntag und Feiertage		Chaque jour sauf les dimanches et fêtes	Diario excepto domingos y festivos
Mondays to Fridays only, except holidays	Montag bis Freitag außer Feiertage		Des lundis au vendredis, sauf les fêtes	De lunes a viernes, excepto festivos
Daily except Saturdays	Täglich außer Samstag		Tous les jours sauf les samedis	Diario excepto sábados
Saturdays, Sundays and holidays	Samstag, Sonntag und Feiertage		Les samedis, dimanches et fêtes	Sábados, domingos y festivos
Sundays and holidays	Sonntag und Feiertage		Les dimanches et fêtes	Domingos y festivos
Mondays, Tuesdays	Montags, Dienstag		Les lundis, mardis	Lunes, Martes
Wednesdays, Thursdays	Mittwoch, Donnerstag		Les mercredis, jeudis	Miércoles, Jueves
Fridays, Saturdays	Freitag, Samstag		Les vendredis, samedis	Viernes, Sábados
Sundays	Sonntag		Les dimanches	Domingos
Mondays to Thursdays	Montag bis Donnerstag		Des lundis aux jeudis	De lunes a jueves
Except on the day stated	Außer an dem angegebenen Tag		Sauf le jour indiqué	Excepto el día indicado
OTHER SYMBOLS	**WEITERE SYMBOLE**		**AUTRES SIGNES**	**OTROS SIMBOLOS**
Reservation obligatory	Reservierung erforderlich		Reservation obligatoire	Reserva obligatoria
Frontier station	Grenzbahnhof		Gare frontalière	Estación fronteriza
Train does not stop	Zug hält nicht		Pas d'arrêt du train	El tren no se detiene
Separates two trains in the same column where no connection is possible	Trennt zwei Züge in derselben Spalte wenn kein Anschluss möglich ist		Sépare deux trains dans la même colonne quand il n'y a pas de correspondance	Separa dos trenes en la misma columna donde no es posible la conexión
Train numbers (bold figures above train times)	Zug-nummer (fettgedruckte Nummer über den Fahrplanzeiten)		Numero du train (en chiffres gras au-dessus des tableaux horaires)	Número de tren (impreso en negrita sobre el horario de trenes)
Vice versa	Umgekehrt		Vice versa	Viceversa
Airport	Flughafen		Aéroport	Aeropuerto

Other symbols are explained in the footnotes to each table or in the introduction to each country.

For dates of public holidays, see page 2.

Sonstige Symbole sind in den Fussnoten zu den einzelnen Fahrplänen oder in der Einführung zu den einzelnen Ländern erklärt.

Die öffentlichen Feiertage sind auf Seite 2 ange führt.

Les explications des autres signes se trouvent dans les notes en bas de la page de chaque tableau ou dans l'introduction de chaque pays.

Pour les dates des jours fériés voir page 2.

Los demás simbolos se describen en las notas al pie de cada tabla o en la introducción a cada pais.

Para días festivos véase la página 2.

SPECIMEN TABLE

For each table we have selected the towns to be shown. The omission of a town does not mean that it has no railway station. The main towns are shown in **bold**.

These are train numbers (always shown in **bold**). Most European trains are referred to by train numbers and not by departure time.

This is an extra-fast (Rapide) train. Some countries charge extra for these. Please read the introduction above the first table for each country.

Seat reservation obligatory. If you have not reserved a seat in advance, you may not be allowed on.

This train has no ordinary seating accommodation. The minimum you must pay is for a couchette berth. If the train consisted solely of sleeping cars, the symbol would be ▬.

The black diamond ◆ means that there is more information about this train in the footnotes below the table.

This train runs on Fridays only. Railways (and airlines) number the days from ① Monday to ⑦ Sunday.

Where we have to show two different trains in the same column, they are separated by a thick black line if they do not connect with each other.

Train 22 either runs non-stop from Klausenburg to Hermannstadt, or goes by a different route.

Train 10 does not stop at Mühlbach (Süd).

This local train runs from Monday to Friday, except holidays. The sign ⓧ is one of the standard symbols explained on page 4.

Most times shown are departures (dep.). Trains usually arrive at main stations five or more minutes earlier, at other stations 1–2 minutes earlier.

This train has a name as well as a number. Only the most important trains have names.

Distances are rounded to the nearest kilometre and are actual measurements. Some railways use a different scale (tariff–km.) for calculating fares.

Towns in italics only have those services which connect with or run through to or from the main service shown. The full service will be found on the table indicated in bold (**824**).

The operator's name, followed by the corresponding table numbers in the operator's own timetable.

Changes are expected to this service after the expiry date shown.

Train 2017 has first and second class seats (12) and light refreshments (⚲).

Train 6213 runs daily except Sundays and holidays (X). This is one of the standard symbols explained on page 4.

Train 2712 runs every day of the year, so it does not need any head note.

There are other trains between these stations, shown in Table 820.

Weissenburg to Frankenstein is a branch line, so it is shown with the station names indented and placed between two horizontal rules. Through coaches to or from the main line are shown by a footnote.

This is the heading of another daily train, separate from the one shown above. Through passengers have to change at Frankenstein.

Mühlbach has more than one station, so we show the distinguishing station name.

Grossau is the junction for a branch line with its own Table (**825a**).

Times are shown in 24-hour time throughout the book (see the clock face on page 1) and are in local time (except USSR — see above Table 854).

These times refer to connecting trains, because the stations are in *italics*. Through passengers have to change at Hermannstadt, unless through coaches are indicated by a footnote, or a break in the horizontal rule. Additionally, connecting times are shown in *italics* where possible.

In tables with a central list of stations, the times should be read downwards on the left, but **upwards** on the right.

In addition to the main portion starting from Klausenburg, with 1, 2 class seats and a dining car (X), this train has first and second class seats coaches from Weissenburg (which is on a branch line). These join the main train at Frankenstein.

This train has second class couchettes (simple sleeping berths, four or six to a compartment, folded away by day).

This train begins at a station on another table (**820**).

Table 825   Transylvanian Rlys (200/201)
KLAUSENBURG – HERMANNSTADT

22 Exp	10 Rap	6012 12▣	2	km		Service to May 30.		2017 12 ⚲	6213 X	2713 12
0332	0600	1830		0	dep.	Klausenburg 820 ..... arr.		1240		2238
	0725	2055		131	arr.	Frankenstein 826 ..... dep.		1015		2005
	0635	....		44	dep.	Weissenburg ..... arr.		1136		
	0717	....		0	arr.	Frankenstein ..... dep.		1020	12	
	0732		2	131	dep.	Frankenstein ..... arr.		1005		1933
				160	dep.	Mühlbach (Süd) ..... dep.		0923		1857
	0819	0610		187	dep.	Stolzenburg ..... dep.		0845		1805
		0627		199	dep.	Grossau 825a ..... dep.		0824		1734
0720	0905	0705		211	arr.	Hermannstadt ..... dep.		0805		1653
	0910			211	dep.	Hermannstadt 824 ..... arr.	0742			1644
	0953			266	arr.	Rossmarkt 824 ..... dep.	0610			1520

◆ NOTES (LISTED BY TRAIN NUMBERS)
10—▭ and X Klausenburg-Rossmarkt; ▭ Weissenburg-Rossmarkt.
22—DRACULA ▬ 1, 2 cl and ▬ 2 cl. Grosswardein-Hermannstadt. Not Dec. 24, 25, 31.
†— From Grosswardein (Table 820).

FOOTNOTES explain non-standard symbols used in the table and give details of sleeping and dining accommodation, through cars to other lines, and dates of running of seasonal trains. Standard symbols such as ▭, ⊗, ⊞ and † are explained on page 4.

Sleeping cars in Western Europe

1–First class Single compartment.

2–Standard double compartment (second class in Britain and Norway, first class elsewhere).

3–Second class tourist compartment (upper, middle and lower berths).

4 and 5–Type T2 car with two-berth upper and lower compartments (first class in Spain, second class elsewhere). The lower compartments can also be used as first class (Special) singles.

Couchette cars have four or six berths per compartment, each with pillow and rug.

Exercise 1

(a) Your client wishes to travel from London to Guernsey via Portsmouth. What is the table number? Turn to the index page, find London in bold print, follow through to Guernsey and tables 507 and 508.

INDEX

Laxey, 619
Leamington Spa, 524, 527
Le Buisson, 137a, 138b
Lecce, 393, 396
Lecco, 357
Lech, 735
Le Châble, 286, 329
Le Châtelard, 285
Le Creusot, 150, 160
Le Croisic, 123, 128
Le Dramont, 1000

LEEDS
Birmingham, 545
Bradford, 575, 580
Bristol, 545
Cardiff, 545
Carlisle, 578
Doncaster, 575
Edinburgh, 575
Harrogate, 597
Hull, 579
Leicester, 570
Liverpool, 569
London, 570, 575
Manchester, 569, 580
Morecambe, 578
Newcastle, 574
Nottingham, 570
Plymouth, 545
Preston, 580
Scarborough, 569
Sheffield, 545, 570, 574a
Torquay, 545
York, 569, 574, 597

Leer, 629, 639, 644
Leeuwarden, 66, 227, 242
Le Fayet (see St. Gervais)
Leghorn (see Livorno)
Legnica, 793, 852
Legoland, 1000
Le Havre, 51, 120, 190, 1007, 1022
Lehrte, 620, 637
Leicester, 570, 588
Leiden, 10X, 66, 222, 223, 225, 236
Leigh on Sea, 592
Leikanger, 481a
Leipzig, 61, 67, 87, 637, 687, 766, 767, 768,
  768a, 769, 770a, 771, 772, 773, 775, 776, 816,
  852
Leiria, 449
Leixões, 1000
Leksand, 480
Le Lavandou, 195
Le Lioran, 145
Le Locle Ville, 157, 253
Lelystad, 226a
Le Mans, 118, 121, 123, 126
Lemberg, 1500
Lemgo, 1000
Le Monastier, 187
Le Mont Dore, 140, 149
Lenninakan, 874

Leningrad, 62, 495, 853, 855, 859, 863, 866,
  867, 868, 869
Lenk, 255
Lens, 109
Lenzerheide, 346
Leoben, 27, 41, 42, 745, 755, 762
Leon, 418, 421, 438a
Leonidas, 1467
Leopoldov, 811
Le Puy, 148, 187
Lequeitio, 1000
Lerici, 1000
Lerida, 412, 430
Lermoos, 756
Leros, 1468
Lerwick, 1111, 1200
Les Arcs (Var), 151
Les Arcs (Savoie), 1000
Les Aubrais, 136, 138, 141, 142
Les Avants, 255
Lesce Bled, 781
Les Diablerets, 279
Le Sepey, 279
Les Evzies, 138b
Lesine, 1000
Leskovac, 730
Les Marecottes, 285
Les Menuires, 5, 1000
Les Sables d'Olonne, 134
Les Salins à Hyeres, 193
Les Tines, 285
Letmathe, 635
Le Touquet, 1000
Le Treport, 112
Le Tretein, 235
Leucate, 1000
Leuchars, 606
Leuk, 251
Leukerbad, 1000
Leuven, 205, 1500

Levadia, 891
Le Val André, 1000
Levant (see Ile du Levant)
Levanto, 355, 360
Levanzo, 1430a
Leverkusen, 1000
Levisham, 598a
Levkas, 1464
Lewes, 51, 514, 515a
Leysin, 283
Lezignan, 138, 139
Le Zoute, 1000
L'Hospitalet, 147
Lianokladion, 891
Liáo, 1500
Liberec, 809a, 809b
Libourne, 136, 137a, 140, 144
Libramont, 218
Lichkov, 819
Lichtenfels, 669, 687
Lichtervelde, 219a
Lido di Jesolo (see Jesolo)
Liechtenstein (see Vaduz)
Liège, 5, 10B, 19, 20, 21, 23, 53, 62, 63, 64,
  206, 215, 216, 217, 219
Liegnitz, 1500
Lienz, 727
Lier, 213
Liestal, 260, 277
Lignano, 1000
Lila, 1500
Lille, 11A, 12, 12a, 14, 15, 57, 101, 104,
  105, 107, 116, 150, 201, 202
Lillehammer, 483, 491
Lillestrøm, 471, 483
Limassol, 1400, 1442, 1454, 1460, 1470
Limburg (Lahn), 650
Limerick, 504, 615, 618
Limerick Junction, 615, 618
Limmared, 467
Limoges, 12a, 59, 138, 138a, 138b, 144
Limone, 365
Limone sul Garda, 372
Linares-Baeza, 414, 416, 431, 434, 441
Lincoln, 571, 575b, 582, 584
Lindau, 10Q, 256, 667, 674, 675, 686, 697,
  753
Linec, 1500
Lingen (Ems), 639
Linköping, 465
Linosa, 1430a
Linthal, 268
Linz (Austria), 10F, 10G, 10U, 10V, 20, 26,
  29, 31, 32, 41, 42, 57, 61, 64, 69, 72, 663,
  725, 740, 750, 751, 755, 760, 810a
Linz (Germany), 626, 700
Lione, 1500
Liorne, 1500
Lipari, 1430, 1430a
Lippstadt, 654
Lipcse, 1500
Lipsia, 1500
LISBOA
Town plan, page 31
Bordeaux, 28, 58
Coimbra, 445, 446
Estoril, 443
Faro, 450
Figueira da Foz, 449
Irun, 28, 58, 446
Lagos, 450
London, 28, 58
Madrid, 44, 448
Paris, 28, 58, 446
Porto, 445
Salamanca, 28, 58, 446
Lisbon (see Lisboa)
Lisburn, 612, 613
Lisieux, 111, 122, 127
Lison, 117, 122
Lissabon, 1500
Lisse, 1000
Littlehampton, 519

LIVERPOOL
Town plan, page 31
Belfast, 503
Birmingham, 558
Bournemouth, 527
Brighton, 524
Bristol, 545
Cardiff, 545
Carlisle, 555
Chester, 557a
Coventry, 558
Douglas, 1001
Dover, 524
Dublin, 502
Edinburgh, 565
Folkestone, 524
Gatwick Airport, 524
Glasgow, 565
Grimsby, 596
Hull, 569

LIVERPOOL—continued
Leeds, 569
London, 553
Manchester, 569, 596
Oxford, 527
Newcastle, 569
Norwich, 588, 591
Plymouth, 545
Portsmouth, 527
Scarborough, 569
Sheffield, 591, 596
Southampton, 527
Southport, 553a
Torquay, 545
Wigan, 568
York, 569
Livigno, 349
Livorno (Leghorn), 24, 60, 354, 355, 355a,
  1416, 1418, 1419, 1420, 1424, 1427, 1500
Livração, 447
Ljubljana, 10Z, 13, 35, 38, 46, 64, 65, 72, 89,
  390, 762, 763, 781, 783, 784, 785
Llafranch, 1000
Llanberis, 1000
Llandovery, 548
Llandindod, 548
Llandudno, 555, 557
Llanelli, 541, 548
Llangollen, 556, 556a
Llanuwchlyn, 556
Lloret de Mar, 1000
Loano, 356
Locarno, 270, 271, 348, 369
Lockerbie, 565
Lod, 1500
Lodingen, 1223
Lódz, 850, 850a
Loèche (see Leuk)
Logrono, 415, 423, 439a
Lohne, 637, 620, 637, 637a
Lokeren, 202
Lokoshaza, 831
Lomnica (see Tatranska Lomnica)

LONDON
Town plan, page 32
Underground plan, page 34
Aberdeen, 575, 608
Algeciras, 58
Alicante, 59
Amsterdam via Hoek, 10X, 66, 220
Amsterdam via Oostende, 52, 53
Ancona, 55, 69
Antwerpen, 52, 53, 66
Arnhem, 66
Athinai, 55, 65
Avignon, 12, 12a, 54
Barcelona, 12a, 59
Basel via Calais, 14, 15, 57, 176
Basel via Hoek, 30, 68
Basel via Oostende, 16, 63, 176
Bastia, 1500
Beograd, 13, 64, 65
Berlin, 17, 18, 23, 62, 67
Bern, 14, 16, 55, 63, 68
Biarritz, 58
Bielefeld, 62, 67
Birmingham, 524, 527, 552
Blackpool, 565
Bologna, 15, 37, 55, 57, 63
Bolzano, 69
Bonn, 17, 30, 64, 68, 69
Bordeaux, 58
Boulogne, 33, 49, 50
Bourg St. Maurice, 56
Bournemouth, 527
Bradford, 575
Bremen, 19, 21, 22, 62, 67
Brno, 13, 16, 55, 63
Brighton, 518
Brindisi, 55
Bristol, 535
Brive, 12a, 59, 94
Brussels via Calais, 201
Brussels via Oostende, 16, 52, 53, 206
Brussels via Hoek, 66
Bucuresti, 20
Budapest, 20, 64
Calais, 50
Cambridge, 589
Cannes, 12, 54
Canterbury, 512
Cardiff, 540
Carlisle, 5t 5, 601
Chamonix, 56
Channel Islands, 507, 508
Cheltenham, 537
Chester, 547, 557
Chur, 14, 16, 26, 33, 57, 63, 68
Copenhagen (see Kobenhavn)
Cork, 504
Coventry, 526, 552
Darlington, 575
Davos, 33, 57, 63, 68
Den Haag, 10X, 66

LONDON—continued
Derby, 570
Dieppe, 51
Doncaster, 575
Dortmund, 23, 62, 70
Dover, 512, 513
Dresden, 67
Dublin, 501, 502, 504
Duisburg, 21, 62, 70
Dundee, 608
Düsseldorf, 21, 23, 62, 68, 70
Eastbourne, 516
Edinburgh, 575
Eindhoven, 27, 30, 66
Essen, 21, 23, 62, 70
Evian les Bains, 56
Exeter, 523, 530
Firenze via Basel, 15, 57
Firenze via Modane, 60
Firenze via Hook, 68
Firenze via Simplon, 55
Fishguard, 504
Folkestone, 512
Fort William, 604
Frankfurt/Main, 20, 64, 69
Gatwick Airport, 516
Gdynia, 1249
Genève, 55, 56
Genova, 15, 24, 54, 57, 60, 68
Glasgow, 565, 601
Gloucester, 537, 539
Göteborg, 62, 1103
Graz, 27, 64
Grimsby, 575b
Guernsey, 507, 508
Hagen, 62, 70
Hamburg, 19, 21, 22, 62, 67, 1103
Hannover, 17, 18, 23, 62, 67
Harrogate, 597
Harwich, 590, 1103, 1105
Hastings, 514, 515
Heidelberg, 21, 61, 64, 69
Hendaye, 58
Hereford, 536
Hilversum, 66
Hirtshals, 1105
Hoek van Holland, 10X, 66
Holyhead, 501, 557
Hull, 575
Innsbruck, 14, 33, 57, 63
Interlaken, 14, 63, 68
Inverness, 575, 607, 611
Ipswich, 591
Irun, 58
Istanbul, 65
Jersey, 507, 508
Karlsruhe, 30, 61, 68
Kassel, 70
Klagenfurt, 27, 64, 69
København, 19, 21, 22, 62, 67, 1103
Koblenz, 27, 30, 64, 68, 69
Köln via Hoek, 30, 68, 69
Köln via Oostende, 20, 21, 23, 53, 62,
  64, 206
Kristiansand, 1105
Lausanne, 13, 16, 55
Leeds, 570, 575
Le Havre, 51
Leicester, 570
Leipzig, 67
Leningrad, 62
Liège, 53, 206
Lille, 14, 15, 57, 101
Limerick, 504
Limoges, 12a, 59
Lincoln, 575b
Lisboa, 28, 58
Liverpool, 553
Ljubljana, 13, 64, 65
Llandudno, 557
Lourdes, 58
Lowestoft, 593
Lugano, 14, 15, 16, 30, 57, 63, 68
Luxembourg, 16, 63
Luzern, 14, 16, 26, 33, 57, 63, 68
Lyon, 54
Madrid, 58
Mainz, 20, 30, 61, 64, 68, 69
Malaga, 58
Manchester, 524, 527, 553
Margate, 512
Marseille, 12, 54
Merano, 64, 69
Middlesbrough, 577
Milano via Simplon, 13, 37, 55
Milano via Calais-Basel, 14, 15, 57
Milano via Hoek, 68
Milano via Oostende-Basel, 16, 63
Montpellier, 12a, 54
Montreux, 13, 55
Moskva, 17, 23, 62, 67
Munchen, 27, 61, 64, 65, 69
Napoli, 24, 60
Narbonne, 12a, 59, 94

LONDON—continued
Newcastle, 575
Nice, 12, 54
Nijmegen, 66
Norwich, 589, 590
Nottingham, 570
Nürnberg, 20, 64, 69
Oostende, 16, 52, 53
Oslo, 62, 1105
Osnabrück, 18, 21, 29, 62, 67
Oxford, 527, 538
Paderborn, 70
Paris via Boulogne, 33, 50, 102
Paris via Calais, 50, 102
Paris via Dieppe, 51, 113
Paris via Le Havre, 51
Paris by rail/hovercraft, 49
Perpignan, 12a, 53, 94
Perth, 565, 607
Peterborough, 575, 576
Pisa, 24, 60
Plymouth, 530
Port Bou, 12a, 53, 94
Porto, 28
Portsmouth, 520, 521
Praha, 64
Preston, 565
Ramsgate, 512
Rapallo, 60
Rijeka, 64
Rimini, 15, 55, 57, 63
Roma via Calais-Basel, 15, 57
Roma via Hoek, 68
Roma via Oostende-Basel, 63
Roma via Pans-Modane, 24, 60
Roosendaal, 52, 53, 66
Rosslare, 504
Rotterdam, 10X, 66, 220
Rouen, 51, 115
St. Moritz, 33, 57, 63, 68
St. Raphael, 12, 54
Salisbury, 523
Salzburg, 27, 57, 61, 64, 69
Sevilla, 58
Sheffield, 570
Shrewsbury, 547
Sicily, 60
Sofia, 65
Southampton, 522
Southend on Sea, 592
Stirling, 607
Stockholm, 22, 62, 67
Stranraer, 505
Strasbourg, 14, 15, 16, 57, 61, 63, 176
Stratford upon Avon, 526
Stuttgart, 21, 64, 69
Swansea, 540
Tarbes, 58
Thessaloniki, 65
Tilbury, 592
Torino, 24, 60
Torquay, 530
Toulon, 12, 54
Toulouse, 12a, 59, 94
Trieste, 13, 55
Utrecht, 66
Venezia, 13, 33, 37, 55
Ventimiglia, 12, 54
Vienna (see Wien)
Villach, 27, 64, 69
Wakefield, 575
Warszawa, 17, 23, 62, 67
Waterford, 504
Weymouth, 509, 522
Wien, 20, 57, 61, 64, 69
Wiesbaden, 64, 69
Windsor, 526
Worcester, 536, 537
Worthing, 520
Wuppertal, 62, 70
Wurzburg, 20, 64, 69
Yarmouth, 590
York, 575
Zagreb, 64, 65
Zürich, 14, 16, 33, 57, 63, 68

Londonderry, 612
Londra, 1500
Londres, 1500
Longford, 614
Longueau, 172, 127, 150
Longueville, 171
Longuyon, 134, 177, 181
Longwy, 177, 181
Lons-le-Saunier, 156
Lorient, 126
Lörrach (Basel)
Losanna, 1500
Los Rosales, 416
Loughborough, 573, 570a
Lourdes, 58, 77, 78, 94, 137
Louvain (see Leuven)
Louvain-la-Neuve, 1000
Lowen, 1500
Lowestoft, 593

Table 507 LONDON – PORTSMOUTH – CHANNEL ISLANDS

British Rail (156, 157) and British Channel Islands Ferries

m.v. *Corbière,* 4,250 tons (car ferry).

1st and 2nd class rail. One class only on ship. Sailing times liable to alterations, due to tidal variations. Passengers should report one hour before sailing time.

													877												
					12 ✕			12 Be 🍷														12 ⑥⑦	12 ✕	
....	....	....	....	....	0655	....	....	1855	....	....	dep.	London (Waterloo) 521	arr.	....	....	....	....	....	....	....	....	0926	0944	....
....	....	....	....	....	0825	....	....	2025	....	....	arr.	Portsmouth Harbour 521	dep.	....	....	....	....	....	....	....	....	0755	0755	....
												(bus) connection to/from quay.												
						⛴ C R	⛴ A R		⛴ B R					⛴ D R					⛴ A R	⛴ C R	⛴ D R			
....	....	....	....	....	....	1000	1000	....	2200	....	dep.	Portsmouth Cont. Ferry Port	arr.	....	....	....	....	....	0700	0700	0700	....	....	....
....	....	....	....	....	....	1800	1945x	....	0930x	....	arr.	Jersey	dep.	....	....	....	....	....	2200	1930x	1930x	....	....	....
....	....	....	....	....	....	1930	|	....	|	....	dep.	Jersey	arr.	0930	....	....	....	....	1945	|	|	....	....	....
....	....	....	....	....	....	2145	1630'	....	0630	....	arr.	Guernsey	dep.	0730	....	....	....	....	1800	2245	2300	....	....	....

A— Tues. to Sats. until Apr. 14 and Sept. 29–Dec. 30.
B— Suns. until Apr. 12 and Sept. 27–Dec. 27.
C— Weekdays Apr. 15–May 9 and Sept. 14–26, daily May 11–Sept. 12.
D— Mons. until Apr. 13 and Sept. 28–Dec. 28
x— Via Guernsey.

Table 508 LONDON – WEYMOUTH – CHANNEL ISLANDS

British Rail (157, 158), Condor Ltd. and British Channel Island Ferries

m.v. *Portelet,* 3,987 tons (car ferry) and Condor Ltd hydrofoils.

1st and 2nd class rail; One class only on ship. Sailing times liable to alterations, due to tidal variations. Passengers should report one hour before sailing time.

							Service until Sept. 27						
12 G 🍷	12 H ⊗	12 ✕ ⊗	12 ⑦ 🍷	12 ✕ ⊗	km					12 ✕ ⊗	12 ⑦ 🍷	12 ✕ ⊗	12 ⑦ 🍷
0944	1130	1132r	1830	1832	*0*	dep.	**London** Waterloo **522**	arr.	....	1618t	1714t	2210	2215
1117	1243	1242r	1945	1942	*115*	dep.	Southampton **522**	arr.	....	1507t	1544t	2039	2041
1205	1317	1316r	2018	2016	*172*	dep.	Bournemouth **522**	arr.	....	1433t	1452t	1950	1944
1304	1415	1415r	2132	2122	*228*	arr.	Weymouth Town **522**	dep.	....	1332t	1348t	|	|
b	b	b	2210	2207		arr.	Weymouth Quay	dep.	....	b	b	1855	1849
	A‡	C‡		⛴ E R	*230*				D‡	B‡		⛴ F R	
....	1500	1400	....	2245		dep.	Weymouth Quay	arr.	1130	1230	....	1800	....
....	1700	1600	....	0645	*346*	arr.	**Guernsey**	dep.	0930	1030	....	1300	....
....	1730	1630	....	0715		dep.	**Guernsey**	arr.	0900	1005	....	1230	....
....	1820	1720	....	0915	*387*	arr.	**Jersey**	dep.	0800	0905	....	1030	....

A— Daily Apr. 10–Sept. 12.
B— Daily Apr. 10–Sept. 26.
C— Daily Sept. 13–Oct. 19.
D— Daily Sept. 27–Oct. 24.
E— Daily Apr. 15–Sept. 26.
F— Daily Apr. 16–Sept. 27.
G— Suns. from Sept. 13.
H— Suns. to Sept. 6.
b— Passengers make their own way between Weymouth Town and Weymouth Quay.
r— One hour earlier from Sept. 13.
t— One hour earlier from Sept. 27.
‡— Condor Ltd. hydrofoil. Reservation advisable

ITALY

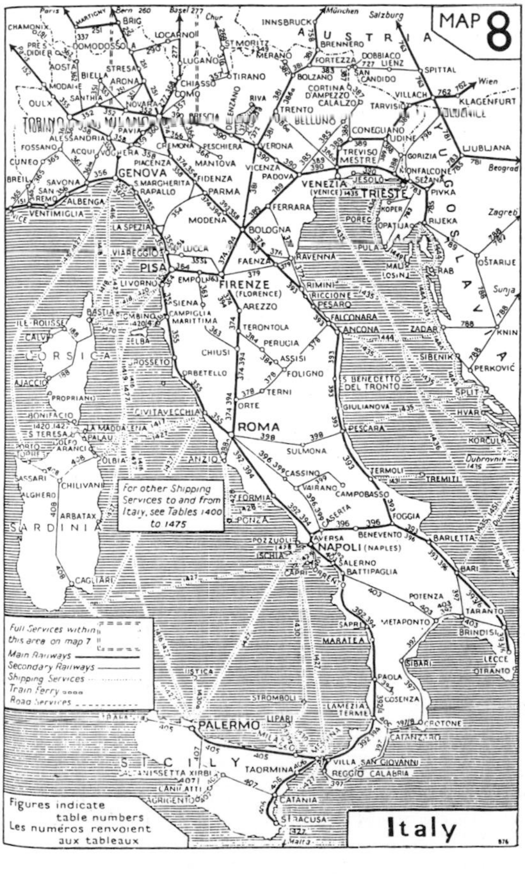

(b) From which station in London does the train depart? We need to look at the services page. Use table 507 (via Portsmouth) and Waterloo is the London station.

(c) Give details of departure and arrival times for train and ship.

Waterloo		0655	1855
Portsmouth		0825	2025
Portsmouth	1000	1000	2200
Guernsey	2100	1630	0630

Notes ABC explains the availability of these three sailings.

(d) Name the shipping company (British Channel Island Ferries).

(e) Name the car ferry (*M. V. Corbiere*).

Exercise 2: Try this one without help

(a) Your client wishes to follow the coast road by train from Pisa to Naples. Which table numbers would you use? Study the map of Italy and follow the railway line along the coast.

(b) If your client departed Pisa at 1432 hours, what time would he/she arrive at Naples Central Station?

(c) What is the train number?

ITALY—354a/355

Table 355 — (PARIS/LYON) – MODANE – TORINO – GENOVA – ROMA – (NAPOLI)

Table 1454
STABILITY LINE

m.v. *Vergina*, 6,128 tons   m.v. *Queen Vergina* .

			Service Apr. 2–Nov. 1			
....	1930④	dep.	Piræus	arr.	0700③	....
....	0700⑤	arr.	Heraklion.........................	dep.	1930②	....
....	1030⑤	dep.		arr.	1500②	....
....	1400⑥	arr.	Limassol	dep.	1200①	....
....	2100⑥	dep.		arr.	0700①	....
....	0600⑦	arr.	Haifa	dep.	2000②	....

		J				K		
....	A	2130	dep.	Ancona .... arr.		0500	F	....
....	B	1730	arr.	Corfu......................... arr.		0600	E	....
....	C	0600	arr.	Patras......................... arr.		2000	D	....
....	C	1500	arr.	Piræus......................... arr.		0630	D	....
....	D	0130	arr.	Mykonos......................... arr.		2030˚	C	....
....	D	1200	arr.	Rhodes......................... arr.		0600	C	....
....	E	1200	arr.	Limassol......................... arr.		0730	B	....
....	F	0700	arr.	Haifa......................... dep.		2100	A	....

A—1st day.   B—2nd Day.   C—3rd day.   D—4th day.   E—5th day.   F—6th day.   J—July 10, 20, 30, Aug. 7, 19, 29, Sept. 8, 18, 28.   K—July 5, 15, 25, Aug. 4, 14, 24, Sept. 3, 13, 23.

Exercise 3

Your client wishes to travel between Piraeus (Greece) and Limassol (Cyprus). You suggest the Stability Line.

(a) Give the times of departure and arrival.
(b) Give the date in August the ship leaves Piraeus and arrives Limassol. Your client would like the first sailing in August.

Making reservations

It takes time to learn how to use the Thomas Cook timetables, but it is well worth the effort. It is good to be able to complete the job in hand and follow the reservation through.

Obtain a copy of the timetable, and take time to read it properly. Try working out examples, and make sure you understand the signs.

Check the following:

1 Through carriages: just a certain number of carriages on the train go to the destination, *not* the entire train.
2 Type of accommodation available.
3 Class of travel.
4 Meals available.
5 Is a reservation on the train obligatory?
6 What happens at a frontier station?
7 Make sure you understand days of operation.
8 Make sure the train actually stops at the station required.
9 Check connecting trains.
10 Always give the client the train number.

CAR-SLEEPER TRAINS

Table 1   CAR-SLEEPER TRAINS   TRAINS AUTOS-COUCHETTES—AUTOREISEZÜGE   *07*

Car-Sleeper trains are composed of special wagons or vans for the conveyance of motor-cars, with sleeping cars and couchettes enabling the driver and passengers to travel overnight in comfort in the same train. Plain breakfast is served without charge on all car-sleeper services, except in Great Britain where sleeping car passengers are served with free morning tea and biscuits. The car-sleeper trains from Calais, Boulogne and Dieppe run in connection with the cross-Channel car ferries shown in Table 1003. At Paris and Roma, cars are loaded and unloaded at separate goods stations.

Aberdeen, T2
Algeciras, K1
Alicante, K1
Almeria, K1
Amiens
 Avignon, A2
 Biarritz, A9
 Bologna, A5
 Bordeaux, A9
 Brive, A7
 Narbonne, A7
 Toulouse, A11
Athinai, N4
Auray
 Lyon, F1
 Metz, F1
 Paris, E11
 Strasbourg, F1
Avignon
 Amiens, A2
 Boulogne, A2
 Brussels, G6
 Dieppe, A1
 Frankfurt, M1
 Hamburg, M1
 Hannover, M1
 's-Hertogenbosch, H6, H7
 Karlsruhe, L2
 Liège, H6, H7
 Karlsruhe, L2
 Liège, H6, H7
 Lille, A2, A12
 Metz, F1
 Mulhouse, F1
 Paris, E1, E2
 Rouen, A1
 Strasbourg, F1
Barcelona K1
Bari
 Bologna, J5
 Milano, J5
 Torino, J1
Basel
 Berlin, O4
 Bremen, M5
 Düsseldorf, L10
 Hamburg, M5
 Hannover, M5
 Köln, L10
Bayonne, G1
Beograd, R20
Berlin
 Basel, O4
 Innsbruck, O4
 Karlsruhe, O4
 München, O5
 Villach, O6
 Westerland, O1
Biarritz
 Amiens, A9
 Boulogne, A9
 Brussels, G1
 Düsseldorf, L1
 Frankfurt, L1
 Köln, L1
 Liège, H1
 Lille, A15
 Metz, F1
 Paris, E19
 Saarbrucken, L1
 's-Hertogenbosch, H1
 Strasbourg, F1
Biasca, H4, L5
Bilbao, K1
Bischofshofen, R5
Bologna, A5, J5, J13
Bolzano
 Düsseldorf, L15
 Frankfurt, L15, M10
 Hamburg, M10
 Hannover, M10
 Köln, L15
 Roma, J7
Bordeaux
 Amiens, A9
 Boulogne, A9
 Brussels, G1
 Frankfurt, L1
 's-Hertogenbosch, H1
 Liège, H1
 Lille, A15
 Lyon, F1
 Marseille, F1
 Metz, F1
 Paris, E20, F15
 St. Raphael, F1
 Strasbourg, F1
Boulogne
 Avignon, A2
 Biarritz, A9
 Bologna, A5
 Bordeaux, A9
 Brive, A7, A11
 Milano, A10

Boulogne *contd*
 Nantes, A8
 Narbonne, A7, A11
 St. Raphael, A3
 Toulouse, A11
Bremen, M5, M11
Briançon, E8
Brig, G4
Brindisi, J5
Bristol, T7
Brive, A7, E25, F1, G2, G3, H2
Brunico, J7
Brussels
 Avignon, G6
 Bayonne, G1
 Bordeaux, G1
 Biarritz, G1
 Brig, G4
 Brive, G2, G3
 Ljubljana, G5
 Milano, G4
 Narbonne, G2
 St. Raphael, G6
 Salzburg, G5
 Tarbes, G3
 Toulouse, G2, G3
 Villach, G5
Budapest, Q7, R15
Cadiz, K1
Calais, A4, A6, A16
Calalzo, J7
Carlisle, T4
Cartagena, K1
Catania, J4, J13, J14
Clermont-Ferrand, E13
Coruña, K1
Dieppe, A1
Dresden, Q7
Düsseldorf
 Basel, L10
 Biarritz, L1
 Bolzano, L15
 Innsbruck, L17
 Karlsruhe, L10
 Lindau, L14
 Ljubljana, L24
 Milano, L5
 München, L12, L20
 Narbonne, L3
 Salzburg, L18
 Villach, L23
Edinburgh, T1, T7
Évian les Bains, E4
Feldkirch, R2, R10
Fort William, T3
Frankfurt/Main
 Avignon, M1
 Biarritz, L1
 Biasca, L5
 Bolzano, L15, M10
 Bordeaux, L1
 Ljubljana, L24
 Milano, L5
 Narbonne, L3, N1
 Niebüll, O2
 Rimini, Q1
 Roma, Q4
 St. Raphael, L2
 Villach, L21, L23
 Westerland, O2
Gap, E9
Gdynia, R15
Genova, J3
Gijon, K1
Göteborg, R16
Graz, R9, R10
Grenoble, E7
Hagen, L21
Hamburg
 Avignon, M1
 Basel, M5
 Bolzano, M10
 Innsbruck, M9
 Karlsruhe, M5
 München, M11
 Narbonne, M2
 Rijeka, M12
 Sonthofen, M14
 Verona, M10
 Villach, M12
Hannover
 Avignon, M1
 Basel, M5
 Bolzano, M10
 Innsbruck, M9
 Karlsruhe, M5
 München, M11
 Narbonne, M2
 Poznan, Q5
 Siofok, Q6
 Sonthofen, M14
 Verona, M10

Hannover *contd*
 Villach, M12
Helsinki, R13, R14
's-Hertogenbosch
 Avignon, H6, H7
 Biarritz, H1
 Biasca, H4
 Bordeaux, H1
 Brive, H2
 Ljubljana, H5
 Milano, H4
 Narbonne, H2, H6
 St. Raphael, H7
 Salzburg, H5
 Toulouse, H2
 Villach, H5
Huelva, K1
Innsbruck
 Berlin, O6
 Düsseldorf, L17
 Hamburg, M9
 Hannover, M9
 Wien, R1
Inverness, T2
Karlsruhe
 Avignon, L2
 Berlin, O4
 Bremen, M5
 Düsseldorf, L10
 Hamburg, M5
 Hannover, M5
 Narbonne, M2, N1, Q2
 Köln, L10
 St. Raphael, L2
Kassel, N1
Kiruna, R16, R17
Köln
 Basel, L10
 Biarritz, L1
 Bolzano, L15
 Karlsruhe, L10
 Lindau, L14
 Ljubljana, L24
 Milano, L5
 München, L12
 Narbonne, L3
 Salzburg, L18
 Siofok, Q6
 St. Raphael, L2
 Verona, M10
 Villach, L23
 Wien, L22
Koper, R20
Lamezia Terme, J3
Liège
 Avignon, H6, H7
 Biarritz, H1
 Bordeaux, H1
 Brive, H2
 Narbonne, H2, H6
 St. Raphael, H7
 Toulouse, H2
Lienz, R4
Lille
 Avignon, A2, A12
 Biarritz, A15
 Bordeaux, A15
 Brive, F1
 Nantes, A14
 Narbonne, F1
 Nice, A4
 St. Gervais, A13
Lindau, L14
Linz, R2
Lisboa, E24, K1
Ljubljana
 Beograd, R20
 Brussels, G5
 Düsseldorf, L24
 Frankfurt, L24
 's-Hertogenbosch, H5
 Köln, L24
 Stuttgart, L24
London
 Aberdeen, T2
 Carlisle, T4
 Edinburgh, T1
 Fort William, T3
 Inverness, T2
 Penzance, T9
Lulea, R16, R17
Lyon
 Auray, F1
 Bordeaux, F1
 Nantes, F1
 Paris, E2
 Saintes, F1
Madrid
 Algeciras, K1
 Alicante, K1
 Almeria, K1
 Barcelona, K1
 Bilbao, K1

Madrid *contd*
 Cadiz, K1
 Cartagena, K1
 Coruña, K1
 Gijon, K1
 Huelva, K1
 Lisboa, K1
 Malaga, K1
 Paris, E23
 Pontevedra, K1
 San Sebastian, K1
 Santander, K1
 Sevilla, K1
 Valencia, K1
 Vigo, K1
Malaga, K1
Malmö, R17
Maribor, R20
Marseille
 Bordeaux, F1
 Nancy, F1
 Nantes, F1
 Paris, E2
 Strasbourg, F1
Metz
 Auray, F1
 Avignon, F1
 Biarritz, F1
 Bordeaux, F1
 Nantes, F1
 Narbonne, F1
 Nice, F1
 St. Raphael, F1
Milano
 Bari, J5
 Boulogne, A10
 Brindisi, J5
 Brussels, G4
 Catania, J4
 Düsseldorf, L5
 Frankfurt, L5
 's-Hertogenbosch, H4
 Köln, L5
 Lamezia Terme, J3
 Napoli, J3
 Palermo, J4
 Paris, E16
 Roma, J6
 Villa San Giovanni, J3
Moskva, R14
Moutiers-Salins, A16, E6
Mulhouse
 Avignon, F1
 Narbonne, F1
 St. Raphael, F1
München
 Athinai, N4
 Berlin, O5
 Bremen, M11
 Düsseldorf, L12, L20
 Hamburg, M11
 Hannover, M11
 Köln, L12
 Münster, L20
 Narbonne, Q2
 Paris, E22
 Rijeka, Q3
 Rimini, Q1
 Roma, Q4
 Split, N3
 Thessaloniki, N4
Münster, L20, L21
Nancy
 Marseille, F1
 Narbonne, F1
 Nice, F1
Nantes
 Boulogne, A8
 Lille, A14
 Lyon, F1
 Metz, F1
 Nice, F1
 Paris, E14
 St. Raphael, F1
 Strasbourg, F1
Napoli
 Milano, J3
 Torino, J3
 Zürich, Q9
Narbonne
 Amiens, A7
 Boulogne, A7
 Brussels, G2
 Calais, A6
 Düsseldorf, L3
 Frankfurt, L3, N1
 Hamburg, M2
 Hannover, M2
 's-Hertogenbosch, H2, H6
 Karlsruhe, M2, N1, Q2
 Kassel, N1
 Köln, L3
 Liège, H2, H6

Narbonne *contd*
 Lille, F1
 Metz, F1
 Mulhouse, F1
 München, Q2
 Nancy, F1
 Paris, E12
 Reims, F1
 Strasbourg, F1
 Stuttgart, Q2
 Zürich, Q8
Nice
 Calais, A4
 Lille, A4
 Metz, F1
 Nancy, F1
 Nantes, F1
 Paris, E3
 Strasbourg, F1
 Toulouse, F2
Niebüll, O2
Oulu, R13
Palermo, J4, J10
Paris
 Auray, E11
 Avignon, E1, E2
 Biarritz, E19
 Bordeaux, E20
 Briançon, E8
 Brive, E25
 Clermont, E13
 Evian les Bains, E4
 Gap, E9
 Grenoble, E7
 Lisboa, E24
 Lyon, E2
 Madrid, E23
 Marseille, E2
 Milano, E16
 Moutiers-Salins, E6
 München, E22
 Nantes, E14
 Narbonne, E12
 Nice, E3
 Quimper, E11
 Rimini, E15
 St. Brieuc, E10
 St. Gervais, E5
 St. Raphael, E3
 Saintes, E21
 Tarbes, E18
 Toulon, E3
 Toulouse, E17
Penzance, T9
Pontevedra, K1
Poznan, Q5
Pula, R10
Quimper, E11
Reims, F1
Rijeka
 Beograd, R20
 Hamburg, M12
 München, Q3
 Salzburg, Q3
 Stuttgart, Q3
 Wien, R8
Rimini
 Frankfurt, Q1
 Hamburg, M12
 München, Q1
 Paris, E15
 Stuttgart, Q1
 Wien, R7
Roma
 Bolzano, J7
 Brunico, J7
 Calalzo, J7
 Catania, J14
 Frankfurt, Q4
 Milano, J6
 München, Q4
 Palermo, J10
 Torino, J2
 Villa S. Giovanni, J9
Rouen, A1
Rovaniemi, R13
St. Brieuc, E10
St. Gervais, A13, E5
St. Raphael
 Bordeaux, F1
 Boulogne, A3
 Brussels, G6
 Dieppe, A1
 Düsseldorf, L2
 Frankfurt, L2
 's-Hertogenbosch, H7
 Karlsruhe, L2
 Köln, L2
 Liège, H7
 Metz, F1
 Mulhouse, F1
 Nantes, F1
 Paris, E3
 Rouen, A1

St. Raphael *contd*
 Strasbourg, F1
Saintes, E21, F1
Salzburg
 Brussels, G5
 Düsseldorf, L18
 's-Hertogenbosch, H5
 Köln, L18
 Rijeka, Q3
 Split, N3
 Stuttgart, L18
 Thessaloniki, N4
 Wien, R1
San Sebastian, K1
Santander, K1
Sevilla, K1
's-Hertogenbosch
 Listed under 'H'
Siofok, Q6
Sonthofen, M14
Split, N3, R9, R20
Strasbourg
 Auray, F1
 Avignon, F1
 Biarritz, F1
 Bordeaux, F1
 Marseille, F1
 Nantes, F1
 Narbonne, F1
 Nice, F1
 St. Raphael, F1
Stuttgart
 Ljubljana, L24
 Narbonne, Q2
 Niebüll, O2
 Rijeka, Q3
 Rimini, Q1
 Siofok, Q6
 Villach, L21, L23
 Westerland, O2
Tampere, R13
Tarbes, E18, G3
Thessaloniki, N4
Torino
 Bari, J1
 Catania, J4
 Lamezia Terme, J3
 Napoli, J3
 Palermo, J4
 Roma, J2
 Villa San Giovanni, J3
Toulon, E3
Toulouse
 Auray, F1
 Boulogne, A11
 Brussels, G2, G3
 's-Hertogenbosch, H2
 Liège, H2
 Nice, F2
 Paris, E17
Turku, R13
Valencia, K1
Vasterås, R17
Venezia, R6
Verona, M10
Vigo, K1
Villach
 Berlin, O6
 Brussels, G5
 Düsseldorf, L23
 Feldkirch, R10
 Frankfurt, L21, L23
 Hagen, L21
 Hamburg, M12
 Hannover, M12
 's-Hertogenbosch, H5
 Kassel, M12
 Köln, L23
 Münster, L21
 Nürnberg, M12
 Stuttgart, L21, L23
 Wien, R3
Villa San Giovanni
 Bologna, J13
 Genova, J3
 Milano, J3
 Roma, J9
 Torino, J3
Westerland, O1, O2
Wien
 Bischofshofen, R5
 Feldkirch, R2
 Innsbruck, R1
 Lienz, R4
 Köln, L22
 Rijeka, R8
 Rimini, R7
 Salzburg, R1
 Split, R9
 Venezia, R6
 Villach, R3
Zagreb, R20
Zürich, Q8, Q9

11 What type of train is it?
12 Make sure you are reading the timetable in the correct direction – up, down or across.
13 Are there connections by bus or ship?
14 Study the airport maps provided, and give connecting services by train or bus to the city centre.
15 Study the network of car sleeper trains, and local car carrier routes through Alpine tunnels.

This chapter just scratches the surface of worldwide rail routes. It would be impossible to dig deeper in a book covering all aspects of travel agency work, but I hope it has got you interested and keen to learn more.

Exercise 4

We mentioned car sleeper trains earlier. Please study Table 1 of the Thomas Cook timetable, giving details of the routes. The 'from' city is in bold type and the 'to' city is in light type. The code next to the city (H5, J4 etc.) is the service reference and links up with the map provided. Please study the map and consider the great choice of routes.
(a) Your client, Herr Pingel, wishes to travel by motor-rail from Hamburg to Innsbruck. What service reference would you use?
(b) Could your client stop over at Munich on that service?
(c) From Innsbruck he would like to travel to Vienna. What is the service number?

Exercise 5

This exercise uses information given earlier in this chapter.
(a) Your client departs Genova at 0452 hours for Rome. Which table number will you use?
(b) Can your client book sleeping accommodation?
(c) At what time does the train arrive in Rome?
(d) Which route does this take?

Exercise 6

This exercise uses information given earlier in this chapter.
(a) Your client is travelling from London to Belfast. Name the station of departure in London.
(b) Name the port of departure in the United Kingdom.
(c) Name the port of arrival in Ireland.
(d) If your client departed from London at 1000 hours, what time would he/she arrive in Belfast?

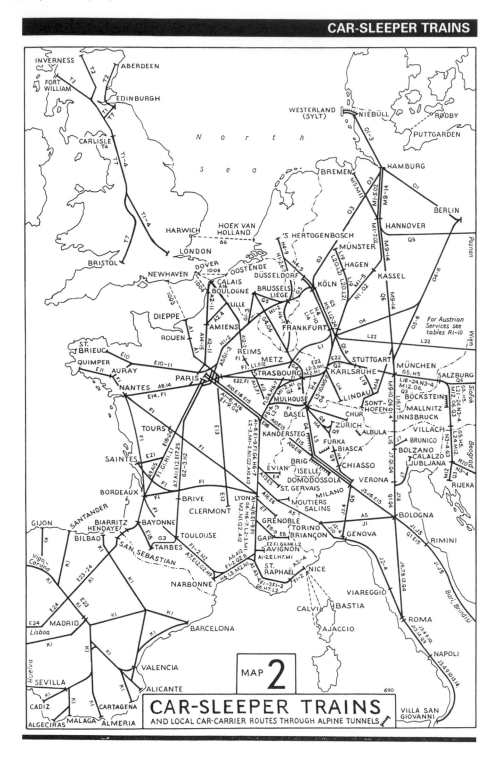

CAR-SLEEPER TRAINS

Assignment: international rail travel

Using a complete copy of the *Thomas Cook European Timetable*, plan the most logical journey by rail and ship for a three-week holiday in Scandinavia, i.e. Denmark, Sweden, Norway and Finland. Begin by studying the contents page and referring to the maps and table pages.

9 Cruising

Summary

In this chapter we discuss:

- life on board ship;
- passenger density;
- helping the clients;
- cruise areas;
- using a cruise brochure;
- general travel information;
- making the reservation;
- exercises and assignments to complete.

What is a cruise? It is a specially planned return voyage, with entertainment on board and organized shore excursions. Travellers normally return to their port of origin on the same vessel. Whilst the cruise may call at several ports and islands, giving the passenger an opportunity to see a variety of new places of interest, the ship is the traveller's home during the entire trip. Many cruises leave from UK ports but there is also a good choice for clients wishing to take a Flycruise – a flight to a large cruising area – the Mediterranean or Florida and begin the cruising holiday from that foreign port.

What is life like on board?

It is *wonderful*! There is something to please everyone!

There is a wide choice of cabins (sleeping accommodation). The ship will have many decks (the floors of the ship), and the lower the deck the cheaper the cabin. Cabins range in size from small single cabins, through cabins able to sleep 2–6 passengers, to cabins with separate sitting-rooms. Cruise ships are all one class; each passenger has the full run of the ship. The food will be excellent, equal to a very good class hotel ashore; there could be complaints about eating too much!

The entertainment will be varied. When the ship is not in port, there will be deck games, swimming pools, keep fit classes, navigational bridge visits, lectures on interesting subjects, film shows and talks on places to be visited.

For clients wishing to have a restful holiday there are quiet lounges, sheltered decks, and a library in which to find peace and quiet. There will be plenty of facilities for children, with trained staff on duty to care for them. The morning may begin with some keen passengers walking several times around the ship. Each morning a programme of the day's events will be slipped under your cabin door, so you will be well informed.

The evening will bring the difficult decision of which entertainment to choose. There will be dancing to a choice of music – disco, ballroom, Scottish or old tyme. Bingo, theatre, films, cabaret and casino will be available. Many cruises have a special interest theme – cricket, astronomy, bridge, sequence dancing, classical music and many more – in addition to the planned programme.

Perhaps your client would like to spend more than a couple of days in a picturesque resort; then the 'stay-a-while' cruise programme would be ideal. Perhaps a two-week cruise could be combined with a week in a hotel. There are many combinations from which to choose.

Passengers and passenger density

People on cruises come from all walks of life, and represent a complete cross-section of the population. Because of the wide variety of cruises available it is very important for you, the travel agent, to find the right cruise for your client.

An elderly passenger would not be happy aboard a ship that caters for young and very lively passengers. Are your clients seeking the sunshine? Will they waste two days of their holiday by travelling through wintry weather before enjoying the warm climate? If so, perhaps a fly-cruise is what they would really enjoy. Fly perhaps from London to Athens and then begin the cruise holiday from Piraeus, a port in Greece.

The size of the ship and the number of passengers on board are important points to consider. Ships come in all sizes – and we assess the size in gross registered tonnes (GRT). A ship could be 2000 GRT or 80,000 GRT. In order to keep the cost of a cruise down, it is necessary for a ship to carry as many passengers as is comfortably possible. This is known as a high density ship. There is less space but cheaper fares, and the ratio of crew members to passengers is lower. A low density ship has few passengers for its size, and therefore higher fares. There is more space and better cabins, and the ratio of crew to passengers is higher. There might be just one crew member to look after only two passengers.

The way to establish the density of a ship is to divide the GRT by the number of passengers. The higher the figure, the more facilities and crew there are per passenger, and thus the lower the density of passengers. A ship that is 67,140 GRT and has 1600 passengers is low density: 67,140/1600 = 41.96. A ship that is 67,140 GRT and has 3400 passengers is high density: 67,140/3400 = 19.74.

There is not an official 'cut-off' line between high and low density. The majoriy of cruises are high density but the crew:passenger ratio must always be considered plus the fact that a high density ship may sail with only 75% occupancy. Should you have a query from a client wanting this information, check with the shipping company concerned for up-to-date advice on the number of reservations confirmed.

Factors in cruise costs

As we can see so far, the range of choice is tremendous; so the range of fares will also be very wide. The following facts will affect the fare:

1   Length of cruise.
2   Type of cabin and size.
3   Position of cabin.
4   Date (season) of travel.
5   Number of persons in cabin.
6   Density of ship.

We will have the opportunity of costing a cruise holiday in a moment. At first glance it may seem an expensive holiday, but we must bear in mind that the fare represents not only the transportation costs, but also hotel accommodation, meals and entertainment together with opportunities to visit foreign ports. Most of the cruise business is repeat business, and 99 per cent of cruise passengers will tell you it was worth every penny. For many, no other holiday is ever quite the same as a cruise!

Nautical terms

At this stage we should learn some nautical terms; they will be needed when making the reservation.

Aft   Towards the rear of the vessel.
Amidships   In the middle of the vessel.
Berth   Nautical term for bed: means where the ship docks in port, as well as a bed in a cabin.
Bow   The foremost part of the ship.
Cabin   The bedroom on board ship: also called a stateroom.
Course   The ship's route during the voyage.
Deck   Each floor of a ship.
Disembark   To leave the ship.
Drill   Any exercise ordered by the captain: a lifeboat drill is usually held on the first day at sea.
Embark   To board a ship.
Free port   A port not included in customs territory.
Funnel   The chimney of a ship.
Hold   The area below deck where cargo is stored.
Lifeboat   A small launch designed to carry passengers, crew and cargo.
Manifest   List of ship's passengers, crew and cargo.
Port   Left side of ship looking forward: indicated by red navigational lights.
Starboard   Right side of ship looking forward: indicated by green navigational lights.

In dead of night when two ships are passing, think of the following rule: 'Green to green, red to red, perfect safety, go ahead'!

Helping the clients

How can we become really good at selling cruises?
  Become familiar with the itineraries, the cost, the conditions of booking. Always put

yourself in your clients' shoes: what would be a wonderful cruise for *them*? Be aware of the different type of cruises, fly-cruises, special interest and special offers available. You may feel there are so many jobs to do in one day at the travel agency that there is little time to build up this information: then take the brochures home to study!

Be ready to answer your clients' questions. The answers can be found in the shipping companies' manuals (copies should be at your travel agency) and often in the cruise lines brochures. Although your clients can read the information in the brochures for themselves, it is good to be able to be helpful and volunteer information and useful hints.

A few of the topics your clients will wish to know about will be as follows:

Shore excursions　Need I book in advance? Yes, the popular ones can become fully booked. However, they can also be booked on board.

What happens if I am ill?　Most cruise ships have a well-equipped hospital in the charge of registered doctors and qualified nursing staff.

What about my laundry?　The ships will have laundry and pressing services on board, available through the cabin steward at extra charge. However, there are also laundry rooms fitted with sinks, drying cupboards, ironing boards and irons, for passengers wishing to do their own laundry.

Health and beauty facilities　Most cruise ships have fitness centres, with exercise equipment and saunas and massage facilities. Some passengers may feel a visit to the fitness centre is a *MUST* with all the fine food in which to indulge! There will be hair salons offering beauty treatments, and facilities for passengers to use their own hair dryers if they prefer.

Outside contact　Will your clients be cut off from the rest of the world whilst aboard? No, the ships are fitted with modern worldwide telecommunications systems including telephone, telex and fax equipment.

What should I wear?　This depends on the cruise. Some cruises are more up-market than others. Check with the shipping company: you do not want your clients to feel uncomfortable. By day the dress is casual; sports or leisure wear is appropriate. In the evenings most passengers like to dress up a little (especially the ladies!) and there could be two or three formal evenings on the cruise. Generally, dark lounge suits and ties for the men and smart cocktail dresses for the ladies should be taken. If an evening suit is necessary, and your client does not want to buy one, it can be hired for the duration of the cruise from a dress hire shop.

Tipping　This can be a worry to some passengers, so put their minds at rest! It is a very personal way of expressing satisfaction for the way you have been looked after during the cruise. The shipping company sends each passenger a leaflet for guidance as to whom, how much and when you might tip. Generally the restaurant and cabin personnel will receive a gratuity and, at your clients' discretion, the *maître d'hôtel* and bar staff.

Cruise guides

So, to learn the details of a particular cruise we would study the brochure and the shipping company's manual: but how can we find out which cruises go where?

The two main guides are the *ABC Shipping Guide* and the *OAG Worldwide Cruise and Shipline Guide*. We have studied the *ABC Shipping Guide* in Chapter 7. It has approximately 300 pages and provides a wealth of information at your finger tips, for example:

1 Explanation on how to use the guide.
2 Details of the operators throughout the world and main reservation centres.
3 Details of liners, cruise ships, car ferries, hovercraft, hydrofoils, jetfoils, cargo-passenger ships and river craft.
4 Maps of international car ferry routes.
5 International ports.
6 Passenger ship services.
7 Cruises throughout the world in area order.
8 Unusual river, waterway and coastal cruises around the world.
9 Yacht and schooner cruises.

CRUISES

Cruises on the following pages are published in two sections, including details of operators, ships, fare range and full itineraries. Principal Cruises and Fly-cruises are shown in date order; River, Waterway and Coastal Cruises/Yacht and Schooner Cruises are listed geographically according to itinerary. Ports of embarkation and disembarkation are shown in bold type.

Cruises are arranged in the following sections:

Principal Cruises
from
C5	Great Britain
C10	Europe
	North America:
C30	West Coast
C35	East Coast
C40	Florida & The Gulf
C45	Mexico & Central America
C48	Hawaii
C50	The Caribbean
C55	South America
C60	East & West Africa
C65	South Africa & Indian Ocean Ports
C70	The Far East & Papua New Guinea
C75	Australia & New Zealand
C80	Pacific Islands

River, Waterway and Coastal Cruises
from
C120–C199	Europe
C200–C239	North Africa
	North America:
C240–C249	West Coast
C250–C299	East Coast
C300–C339	Florida & The Gulf
C340–C341	Mexico & Central America
C342–C344	The Caribbean
C345–C399	Virgin Islands
C400–C410	South America
C411–C419	China
C420–C459	The Far East & Papua New Guinea
C460–C479	Australia & New Zealand
C480–C489	Pacific Islands

Yacht and Schooner Cruises
from
C500–C510	Europe/Great Britain
C511–C529	Mediterranean/North Africa
C530–C619	North America: East Coast
C620–C649	The Caribbean
C650–C689	Pacific Islands

There is a special section for cruising in the *ABC Shipping Guide*, please examine the extract. You will read the index is arranged in cruise areas and this means it is easy to find the information. For cruises from Great Britain we would turn to section C5 of the *ABC Shipping Guide*, for cruises from Mexico and Central America we would turn to section C45, for cruises from Australia and New Zealand we would turn to section C75. By studying this page you will realize cruising areas are worldwide.

C5 Cruises from Great Britain

Dates From	To	Ship	Operator	Fare Range	Itinerary
1988					
28/7	7/8	GALILEO	Chandris	UK£707-1028	London ✈, New York (3 nights hotel), Hamilton, New York, London ✈
28/7	8/8	AMERIKANIS	Chandris	UK£756-1050	London ✈, New York (4 nights hotel), St George's, New York, London ✈
29/7	5/8	HOLIDAY	Carnival	from UK£765	London ✈, Miami, Cozumel, Playa del Carmen, Grand Cayman, Ocho Rios, Miami, London ✈
29/7	7/8	COSTA RIVIERA	Costa Line	UK£945-1235	London ✈, Port Everglades, Charlotte Amalie, Christiansted, Nassau, Port Everglades, London ✈
29/7	7/8	ISLAND PRINCESS	Princess Voyages	from UK£1498	London ✈, Whittier (1 night hotel), Columbia Glacier, College Fjord, Glacier bay, Skagway, Juneau, Ketchikan, Vancouver, London ✈
29/7	7/8	NORWAY	NCL	UK£995-3380	London ✈, Miami, Philipsburg, St John, Charlotte Amalie, Great Stirrup Cay, Miami, London ✈
29/7	7/8	SOVEREIGN OF THE SEAS	Royal Caribbean	UK£885-1470	London ✈, Miami (1 night hotel), Labadee, San Juan, Charlotte Amalie, Miami, London ✈
29/7	7/8	SUN PRINCESS	Princess Voyages	from UK£1548	London ✈, Vancouver (1 night hotel), Juneau, Skagway, Glacier Bay, Ketchikan, Misty Fjords, Vancouver, London ✈
29/7	8/8	CUNARD COUNTESS	Cunard	from UK£895	London ✈, San Juan (1 night hotel), La Guaira, St George's, Bridgetown, Fort de France, Charlotte Amalie, London ✈
29/7	8/8	SUN VIKING	Royal Caribbean	UK£885-1275	London ✈, Miami (1 night hotel), Cozumel, Georgetown, Ocho Rios, Labadee, Miami, London ✈
29/7	10/8	BRITANIS	Chandris	UK£740-999	London ✈, Miami (3 nights hotel), Key West, Playa del Carmen, Cozumel, Miami (3 nights hotel), London ✈
29/7	10/8	ROYAL PRINCESS	Princess Voyages	from UK£1475	London ✈, Vancouver (1 night hotel), Juneau, Valdez, Columbia Glacier, Glacier Bay, Ketchikan, Vancouver, London ✈
29/7	11/8	ROYAL ODYSSEY	Royal Cruise	US$3248-5698	Tilbury, Amsterdam, Zeebrugge, Le Havre, Lisbon, Palma, Barcelona, Ajaccio, Civitavecchia, Villefranche
29/7	15/8	CUNARD COUNTESS	Cunard	from UK£1295	London ✈, San Juan (1 night hotel), La Guaira, St George's, Bridgetown, Fort de France, Charlotte Amalie, San Juan, Tortola, Philipsburg, Pointe à Pitre, St Lucia, St John's, Charlotte Amalie, San Juan, London ✈
30/7	6/8	AUSONIA	Siosa Crociere	UK£505-985	London ✈, Genoa, Barcelona, Majorca, Tunis, Valletta, Catania, Capri, Genoa, London ✈
30/7	6/8	CELEBRATION	Carnival	from UK£765	London ✈, Miami, San Juan, Charlotte Amalie, Philipsburg, Miami, London ✈
30/7	6/8	FESTIVALE	Carnival	from UK£940	London ✈, San Juan, Charlotte Amalie, Philipsburg, Bridgetown, Fort de France, San Juan, London ✈
30/7	6/8	JUBILEE	Carnival	from UK£765	London ✈, Miami, Nassau, San Juan, Charlotte Amalie, Miami, London ✈
30/7	6/8	LA PALMA	Intercruise	UK£495-1405	London ✈, Venice, Piraeus, Rhodes, Heraklion, Corfu, Dubrovnik, Venice, London ✈
30/7	6/8	OCEAN ISLANDER	Ocean Cruise	UK£895-1450	London ✈, Nice, Costa Smeralda, Naples, Lipari Is, Taormina, Olympia, Corfu, Kotor Bay, Dubrovnik, Venice, London ✈
30/7	6/8	ROMANZA	Chandris	UK£499-850	London ✈, Venice, Dubrovnik, Corfu, Heraklion, Kusadasi, Mykonos, Piraeus, Venice, London ✈
30/7	6/8	TROPICALE	Carnival	from UK£650	London ✈, Los Angeles, Puerto Vallarta, Mazatlan, Cabo San Lucas, Los Angeles, London ✈
30/7	8/8	SEA PRINCESS	Princess Voyages	from UK£1498	London ✈, Vancouver (1 night hotel), Ketchikan, Juneau, Skagway, Glacier Bay, College Fjord, Whittier, London ✈
30/7	8/8	SEAWARD	NCL	UK£840-1565	London ✈, Miami, Great Stirrup Cay, Ocho Rios, Grand Cayman, Playa del Carmen, Cozumel, Miami, London ✈
30/7	8/8	SKYWARD	NCL	UK£840-1520	London ✈, Miami, Cancun, Cozumel, Grand Cayman, Great Stirrup Cay, Miami, London ✈
30/7	8/8	SONG OF AMERICA	Royal Caribbean	UK£885-1370	London ✈, Miami (1 night hotel), Cozumel, Georgetown, Ocho Rios, Labadee, Miami, London ✈
30/7	8/8	STARWARD	NCL	UK£930-1555	London ✈, Miami ✈, San Juan, Bridgetown, Fort de France, Philipsburg, St John, Charlotte Amalie, San Juan, Miami ✈, London ✈
30/7	12/8	CROWN ODYSSEY	Royal Cruise	US$2898-6668	Tilbury, Kiel Canal, Travemunde, Helsinki, Leningrad, Stockholm, Copenhagen, Oslo, Amsterdam, Tilbury
30/7	13/8	CANBERRA	Canberra Crs	UK£1008-3626	Southampton, Ponta Delgada, Tenerife, Lanzarote, Funchal, Praia da Rocha, Lisbon, Southampton
30/7	14/8	CUNARD PRINCESS	Cunard	from UK£1655	London ✈, Vancouver (1 night hotel), Ketchikan, Tracy Arm, Juneau, Skagway, Yukatat Sound, Hubbard Glacier, Columbia Glacier, College Fjord, Whittier, Prince William Sound, Skagway, Juneau, Ketchikan, Vancouver, London ✈
31/7	7/8	ENRICO COSTA	Costa Line	—	London ✈, Genoa, Villefranche, Barcelona, Palma, Port Mahon, Tunis, Palermo, Naples, Genoa, London ✈
31/7	7/8	OCEAN PRINCESS	Ocean Cruise	UK£750-1375	London ✈, Copenhagen, Flam, Gudvangen, Hellesylt, Geiranger, Bergen, Oslo, Fredericia, Copenhagen, London ✈
1/8	16/8	QUEEN ELIZABETH 2	Cunard	from UK£1340	Southampton, New York (5 nights hotel), Southampton
1/8	16/8	QUEEN ELIZABETH 2	Cunard	from UK£1635	Southampton, New York, Hamilton, Martha's Vineyard, New York, Southampton
1/8	16/8	THE VICTORIA	Chandris	UK£940-1231	London ✈, San Juan, Charlotte Amalie, Fort de France, St George's, La Guaira, Willemstad, San Juan (6 nights hotel), London ✈
2/8	11/8	NORDIC PRINCE	Royal Caribbean	UK£910-1280	London ✈, New York (1 night hotel), St George's, Hamilton, New York, London ✈
2/8	11/8	SONG OF NORWAY	Royal Caribbean	UK£915-1280	London ✈, New York (1 night hotel), St George's, Hamilton, New York, London ✈
3/8	13/8	THE AZUR	Chandris	UK£655-1225	London ✈, Venice, Bari, Katakolon, Heraklion, Thera, Kusadasi, Istanbul, Istanbul, Piraeus, Corfu, Dubrovnik, Venice, London ✈
3/8	15/8	SAGAFJORD	Cunard	from UK£1745	London ✈, Anchorage, Cook Inlet, Homer, Kenai Fjord, Seward, Prince William Sound, Hubbard Glacier, Sitka, Skagway, Juneau, Endicott Arm, Ketchikan, Albert Bay, Vancouver, London ✈

In the next extract we have chosen C5 (cruises from Great Britain). The information has been given in date order, the date the cruise begins and ends. The name of the ship, the operator, a fare range (the lowest and highest fare), (the shipping companies brochure would be consulted for the complete range and up-to-date fare), and finally a brief outline of the itinerary. A fly cruise is indicated by an aircraft.

Let's look at a cruise in more detail.

Find a departure for 30 July (30/7) you will see several cruises for that date study the cruise for the ship *Jubilee*, the itinerary ends in London on 6 August (6/8), the tour operator is called Carnival and the fare range begins at £765.00. This is a fly cruise, passengers travel by air from London to Miami then cruise to Nassau, San Juan, Charlotte Amalie, and return to Miami, then travel by air from Miami to London.

Again on 30 July there is a cruise on the ship *Canberra* departing from Southampton, no flight involved.

Incidentally when the *Canberra* sails from Southampton the Royal Marines Band stands on the quayside and provides the passengers with a musical send-off and colourful streamers are thrown between friends and relations standing on the quayside and the passengers on the ship, creating a sparkling atmosphere.

This particular cruise sails to the Canary Islands and Portugal returning to Southampton on 13 August (13/8). The tariff ranges from £1008 to £3626 depending on size of the accommodation, the level of deck, (accommodation is cheaper on the lower decks of a ship).

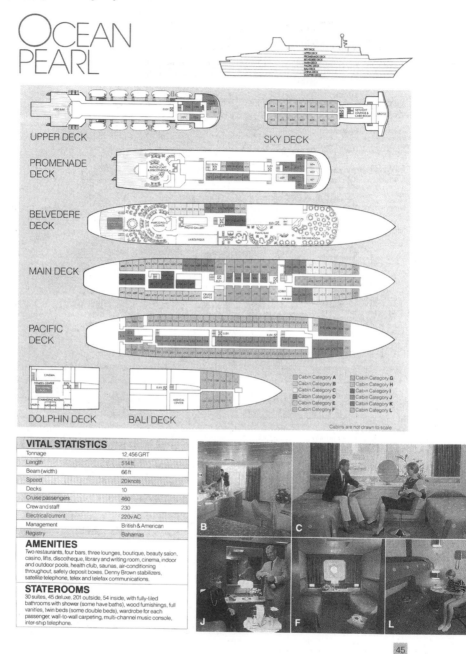

Using a brochure: Thomas Cook

Each shipping company has its own style of setting out information in its cruising brochure. The brochures are usually nice and clear to read and have beautiful photographs. For travel consultants, reading travel brochures can be an interesting and enjoyable way of building up travel geography and knowledge.

VACATION STRETCHERS

FAR EAST OPTIONAL EXCURSIONS & CRUISE TARIFF

Pearl's Vacation Stretcher tours give you the opportunity to enhance your Far East experience by visiting fascinating inland destinations not usually featured on cruise itineraries.

Each of these excursions is an optional package, separate from the land programmes included in your holiday. Some are offered pre- or post-cruise, extending your stay abroad. Others are offered within the time-frame of the cruise itself. As space is limited, Vacation Stretchers should be reserved when you book your cruise.

Xi'an & Guilin: 5 nights

Available on China Dynasty itineraries. All meals in China are included.

The ancient city of Xi'an contains the treasures of 11 dynasties. Most famous of these is the amazing army of over 6,000 terracotta statues. Guilin is known for a different beauty: its magnificent Li River scenery and unusual limestone peaks and spectacular caves created by centuries of erosion.

Rates: £435 per person double; £595 single.

Chiang Mai & Chiang Rai: 4 nights

Available on Great Cities of Asia and Bangkok, Bali & Beyond sailings. All meals are included except in Bangkok.

Located in the northern hills of Thailand, the walled city of Chiang Mai is the country's second largest. From here, visit fascinating Hill Tribe villages and stay in the mountain resort of Chiang Rai.

Rates: £375 per person double; £465 single.

TERRACOTTA SOLDIERS OF XI'AN

Lake Toba: 3 nights

Available on all Spice Islands sailings; passengers leave ship in Penang and rejoin in Sibolga. All meals are included.

A 3-day excursion to the beautiful mountain resort of Lake Toba in North Sumatra, a volcanic paradise set amidst the tribal lands of the Batak people.

Rates: £175 per person double; £210 single.

Jogjakarta & the temples of Borobudur: 2 nights

Available on all Spice Islands sailings; passengers leave ship in Jakarta and rejoin in Bali. All meals are included.

This air excursion to the heart of Central Java gives you the chance to visit the charming sultanate of Jogjakarta, the magnificent temples of Borobudur and, in Bali, a performance of the legendary barong dance.

Rates: £215 per person double; £265 single.

Bangkok: 3 nights

Available on Spice Islands and China Dynasty sailings. Meals are not included.

An air excursion to the Far East's most exotic city, to enjoy its great sightseeing, shopping and nightlife.

Rates: £245 per person double; £375 single.

Hotel Accommodation for pre- or post-cruise stays

City	First Class Hotels	Deluxe Hotels
Agra	Sheraton	Sheraton (deluxe rooms)
Bangkok	Dusit Thani, Novotel, Siam Intercontinental	Shangri-La, Hilton
Beijing	Shangri-La	Shangri-La (deluxe rooms)
Delhi	Holiday Inn, Meridien	Holiday Inn (deluxe rooms)
Hong Kong	Marco Polo, Prince, Hong Kong	Shangri-La
Jaipur	Mansingh	Rambagh Palace, Jai Mahal
Singapore	Westin Stamford, Hilton, Marco Polo, Carlton	Westin Plaza, Meridien, Royal Holiday Inn Crowne Plaza

Passengers in cabin categories A,B & C will, wherever possible, be accommodated in Deluxe hotels. Passengers in cabin categories D-L will be accommodated in First Class hotels. You can upgrade from First Class to Deluxe hotels subject to availability, supplements available on request.

TARIFF Including return flights from London

Cabin Category	Type of Cabin	Deck season	China Dynasty		Great Cities of Asia		Bangkok, Bali & Beyond		The Spice Islands		Jewels of India
			Value season	High season	Value season	High season	Value season	High season	Value season	High season	All sailings
L	2-berth (u/l) inside	Main	£2195	£2295	£1995	£2195	£2150	£2250	£1895	£1995	£2450
K	Single inside	Main	2975	3125	2825	2925	3095	3250	2695	2895	3450
J	2-bed inside	Pacific	2295	2395	2150	2350	2275	2375	1995	2150	2575
I	2-bed sup inside	Belvedere Main	2450	2550	2250	2450	2425	2525	2150	2295	2725
H	2-bed outside	Ball	2625	2725	2375	2595	2575	2695	2295	2450	2895
G	Single outside	Various	3395	3595	3050	3295	3650	3795	3250	3495	3095
F	2-bed outside	Pacific	2750	2895	2595	2695	2795	2950	2475	2650	3150
E	2-bed sup outside	Various	2895	3050	2695	2895	3050	3195	2595	2795	3395
D	2-bed dlx outside	Various	3050	3250	2850	3050	3250	3395	2795	2995	3595
C	Sup-deluxe outside	Various	3295	3495	3050	3250	3550	3695	3050	3250	3950
B	Deluxe Suite	Sky, Upper Main	3550	3695	3195	3395	3795	3950	3150	3395	4195
A	Explorer Suite	Main	3750	3895	3350	3575	3950	4095	3295	3550	4350

Prices are per person based on double occupancy in all categories except G & K. Single occupancy of double cabins, 75% supplement. Third and fourth person in cabin charged at L rate. All rates are in £ sterling. All cabins have bath or shower. See page 45 for deck plans. Prices for the Pearl Suite available on request.

For this book we are using the Thomas Cook *World of Cruising* brochure as an example. Please begin by studying the plan of the ship named the *Ocean Pearl*. Nine decks are listed, and eight of those decks contain cruise facilities and accommodation (China deck is not used by the passengers).

This page provides us with a lot of information. We can see where the cabins are located. Make a note of where the bars, restaurants, lounges, swimming pools and lifts (elevators) are situated. When making a reservation you will be able to show your client the cabin (stateroom) in exact relation to all the amenities. Elderly clients may wish to be near a lift; young clients may wish to be near a pool. As we have stressed before, it is important to consider your clients' needs.

This page of the brochure also gives us the vital statistics of the *Ocean Pearl*: tonnage, length, width (beam), speed, decks, cruise passengers, crew and staff, electrical current (useful information for use of hair dryers and shavers), management and registry.

Is the *Ocean Pearl* a high density or a low density ship? Divide the tonnage of the ship by the number of passengers: 12,456/460 = 27.07. Thus there is lots of room to move about; this is a low density ship. What is the crew/passenger ratio? Divide the number of passengers by the number of crew and staff: 460/230 = 2. Thus there is one member of staff to look after two passengers; that is very low, and the passengers should receive an excellent service.

This page of the brochure also gives details of the amenities on board and describes the staterooms (cabins). The actual brochure page uses colour coding to assist agents and customers in establishing the correct fare.

Please study the 'Vacation stretchers' example page; it explains the Far East optional excursions and cruise tariff. We will begin with the tariff. There is a choice of five cruises on the *Ocean Pearl*: China Dynasty, Great Cities of Asia, Bangkok, Bali and Beyond, Spice Isands and Jewels of India. You will see that the tariff includes the return flight from London.

The first row is cabin category L. In the brochure, its colour (pink) corresponds with the colour of the cabins shown on the deck plan on main deck. In the tariff we are given a description of the cabin: 2-berth (u/l) inside. This means upper (u) and lower (l) berths, one bed above the other; inside cabin means no porthole (window). You can see a photograph of this type of cabin in the picture marked L on the ship's plan page.

We continue to look along the tariff rows to find the price details. For all except the Jewels of India cruise, there are value season and high season prices. You will notice that cabin category L has the cheapest tariff, and cabin category A the most expensive.

Please read the descriptions of the staterooms, look at the photographs, and compare the tariff and cabin category colour codes with the deck plan. Immediately beneath the tariff there is an explanation. The prices shown are per person, based on two persons sharing a cabin, except for categories G and K which are for single cabins. Should your client require a double cabin for single occupancy, then there will be a 75 per cent supplement on the per person charge. Can four passenger share a cabin? Yes! Please read the note below the tariff: third and fourth persons in a cabin will be charged at the L rate.

An Explorer Suite on the main deck is the most superior accommodation. It will have a lounge in addition to the bedroom, and will offer elegance and comfort. The cost of this accommodation on the Jewels of India cruise is £4350.00. On the upper deck there is a very special suite called the Pearl Suite, and the tariff for this must be requested from Thomas Cook.

As an example, your clients have chosen a 2-bedded, outside cabin (has porthole) on Bali deck. The cabin category is therefore H, and the cost for the value season on the Spice Islands cruise would be £2295.00 per person.

Let's try some more.

Exercise 1

(a) Name the cost of cabin category J, 2-bed inside cabin on Pacific deck, for the China Dynasty cruise in high season.
(b) On which decks will you find super-de luxe outside cabins in category C?
(c) Which cabin number is the closest to the Marco Polo Lounge? Name the cabin category, and the cost of the cruise in value season for the Great Cities of Asia itinerary.
(d) On which decks are the swimming pools?
(e) Your client will be travelling alone, and would like cabin category B, de luxe suite on Sky deck, with sole use of the cabin. You can offer cabin 801 near the elevator. Your client will be travelling on the Jewels of India cruise. How much will it cost?

Please read the optional excursions details on the tariff page. Each cruise offers exciting and interesting ports of call. Shore excursions are available for passengers who wish to have their sightseeing tours organized for them. On the Far Eastern tours the excursions involve leaving the ship for several nights, giving the passengers an opportunity of discovering a country in closer detail.

Please study the itinerary for the Spice Islands cruise. This holiday is for 20 days, and begins with a flight from London to Singapore. Three days are spent in Singapore. On the fifth day the ship sails from Singapore, calling at Malaysia, Thailand, Indonesia and Bali. There are opportunities to make additional trips; the details of those are on the itinerary and tariff page we have just been studying. The map is a great asset, bringing the cruise to life. The sailing dates are also given; for this cruise the value season sailings are 21 February and 26 November, and the high season sailings are 22 April and 3 September.

Exercise 2

Using the extracts from the Thomas Cook *World of Cruising* brochure, please deal with the following details for the Spice Islands tour:

(a) Your clients would like to see Lake Toba.
   (i) At which stage of the itinerary would this take place?
   (ii) Where would the passengers rejoin the cruise?
   (iii) How much would this excursion cost in addition to the cost of the cruise?
(b) Give the amount of time spent at Bali.
(c) When would your clients take the Temples of Borobudur tour?
(d) Please advise the cost for the following: two clients sharing a cabin category F for the Spice Island cruise, departing 26 November, and taking the excursion to Lake Toba.

Singapore to Singapore 19 days

Day	Location	Arrive	Depart
Pre-Cruise Singapore			
1	Depart London		
2	Arrive Singapore. Transfer to hotel.		
3	Singapore (sightseeing)		
4	Singapore		
Ship Schedule			
5	Singapore	–	1.00pm
6	Penang, Malaysia	1.00pm	7.00pm
7	Phuket, Thailand	9.00am	midnight
8	Cruise Andaman Sea & Indian Ocean	–	–
9	Sibolga, Indonesia	2.00pm	6.00pm
10	Nias, Indonesia	8.00am	5.00pm
11	Padang, Indonesia	8.00am	4.00pm
12	Cruise Indian Ocean	–	–
13	Jakarta, Indonesia	8.00am	5.00pm
14	Cruise Java Sea	–	–
15	Bali, Indonesia	8.00am	–
16	Bali	–	6.00pm
17	Cruise Java Sea	–	–
18	Cruise Java Sea/ cross Equator	–	–
19	Singapore. Morning arrival. Transfer to airport for return flight.		
20	Arrive London		

SPICE ISLANDS

Now study the extracts concerning cruise information. These pages give general travel information, booking conditions, and details of the booking agreement. When you have examined these extracts, try to help the clients in the following exercise.

Exercise 3

(a) Client A has booked the cruise Great Cities of Asia, departing 31 March. The cruise is for 21 days and our client's passport expires on 28 July. Is the passport valid for this cruise?

(b) Client B holds a UK passport, and is taking the Jewels of India cruise. Is a visa required?

(c) What is the baggage allowance for client C, travelling on the fly-cruise to the Rio carnival?

(d) Client D would like to know who is operating these cruises, Thomas Cook or Ocean Cruise Lines.

(e) Clients E would like to know why Ocean Cruise Lines cannot guarantee that the ship will call at every port advertised, because they do not want to book the cruise Great Cities of Asia and miss visiting Brunei.

CRUISE INFORMATION

Things to know before you go

Passports With the exception of some of the Mediterranean cruises where a UK visitor's passport is acceptable, a full passport is required. Passports should be valid for a minimum of six months after date of entry into most countries in the Far East.

Visas Each passenger is responsible for obtaining the required travel documents. UK passport holders require individual visas for Turkey, India and Argentina. For China, Burma, Poland, Bulgaria and Russia, group visas are obtained on your behalf; if you wish to go ashore independently in these countries, you must obtain individual visas.

Health requirements Vaccinations against illnesses such as Cholera, Typhoid and Polio are often required for some of the countries featured in this brochure. You are advised to consult your Doctor for advice.

Baggage There is no limit for cruise passengers, but we recommend that baggage be limited to two pieces per person. Free airline baggage allowance is usually 20 kg per person. Porterage is included at the pier on embarkation and disembarkation. Carry valuables, breakable items and hand luggage separately.

Booking Conditions

This brochure has been prepared with the co-operation of Thomas Cook Ltd. However, the holidays in this brochure have been organised solely by Ocean Cruise Lines UK Ltd., and your contract will be with them. Thomas Cook does not arrange or in any way control these holidays and, accordingly, has no liability, contractual or otherwise, to you in respect of them.

When you book your cruise with Thomas Cook we want you to be so satisfied that you'll book with us again next year. We also want you to know where you stand with Ocean Cruise Lines. So please read the following paragraphs.

This is a binding holiday agreement between both you and OCL UK Ltd. It is important that you read these pages and indeed all of the relevant parts of this brochure since they form the basis of your agreement with OCL UK Ltd so that you are fully informed of your rights and obligations and can relax knowing that your holiday is covered by OCL's guarantee.

If there is anything else you need to know, ask your local Thomas Cook Travel Shop before booking.

OCL's responsibility
General The information given in this brochure has been compiled in good faith by OCL, and to the best of our knowledge all details were accurate at the date of printing. OCL will use its best endeavours to provide the arrangements and facilities set out in this brochure, but it is important to note that OCL neither has, nor accepts, any liability for the acts or omissions, whether through the negligence or otherwise, of airlines, coach operators, hoteliers or any other person providing services in connection with your holiday, unless the person is either employed by OCL or is an agent under their direct control. No carrier, whether airline, cruise line, coach company or other, can be held responsible for any act, omission or event during the time passengers are not aboard the aircraft, ship, coach etc.

Optional excursions Optional excursions are described in the brochure for the purpose of information only and do not form any part of the reservation. OCL cannot guarantee that optional excursions will be available at a given time.

Third-party conditions All arrangements for the provision of transport, accommodation and other services are made by OCL as agent only. All arrangements are subject to the conditions of business of the person, firm or company providing such arrangements. A copy of relevant conditions are available on request.

The cruise The cruise portion of the holiday is operated by Ocean Cruise Lines S.A. Panama (Ocean Princess and Ocean Islander) or Pearl Cruises of Scandinavia Ltd Cayman Islands (Ocean Pearl), and is subject to conditions contained in the Passenger Travel Contract sent with your confirmation.

Delay/loss of baggage OCL does not accept responsibility for loss or expense due to delay, sickness, weather, strikes, force majeure, war, quarantine or negligence of anyone not employed by OCL.

Temporary or permanent loss of baggage is the responsibility of the passenger unless the loss occurs due to OCL's negligence. Baggage, is carried at the owner's risk.

Holiday alterations As arrangements for these holidays are planned many months in advance, very occasionally it may become necessary to make alterations. Where a change is made OCL will inform you or your Thomas Cook Travel Shop as soon as is reasonably possible.
You may either:
a) accept the change, OR **b)** book any other available holiday from the brochure, OR **c)** cancel your booking and receive a full refund

OCL is not able to guarantee that the ship will call at every advertised port or follow every part of an advertised route. Alterations will only be made if necessary due to adverse conditions, and in this event OCL will be under no obligation or liability to the Passenger.

Passenger safety OCL reserves the right, without incurring any liability whatsoever, to terminate the travel arrangements, before or after the commencement of travel, for any passenger who in their opinion appears likely to endanger the health or safety or impair the comfort of other passengers. Should this occur, full cancellation charges will apply and OCL will be under no obligation whatsoever for any additional costs incurred.

Disabled passengers Passengers with physical disabilities, other handicaps or illnesses requiring special treatment or assistance, including persons confined to wheelchairs, must advise OCL in writing of the nature of their condition at the time of requesting reservations.

OCL reserves the right to refuse passage to passengers who have failed to notify them of such disabilities or who, in their opinion, are unfit for travel or are considered to constitute a danger to themselves or others on board.

Unfortunately, due to operational difficulties beyond OCL's control, passengers confined to wheelchairs, even when accompanied by a helper, CANNOT participate in the three-day Beijing visit. In addition, because of the amount of strenuous walking and climbing of stairs involved on sightseeing tours throughout China, those with physical disabilities will encounter difficulties almost everywhere. For these reasons, and due to the regrettable lack of proper facilities in this part of the world, China cruises are not recommended for handicapped passengers

Air flights The cost of air travel for fly/cruise holidays is included in the fare. OCL reserves the right to select the carrier and the routing for all holidays in this brochure. Prices are based on promotional air fares for which OCL holds allocations. If you choose to travel on dates other than those published, or request a particular carrier or routing, a higher fare may apply. In the event that OCL's allocation is full, or has been released back to the airline (usually 45 days prior to departure) air fares at the promotional rate may not be available and a supplement to the normal fare may be payable. Flight availability may necessitate departure from Heathrow and return to Gatwick or vice versa.

Regional domestic flights and upgrades on scheduled flights can be arranged.

Flights booked by OCL comply with the boarding requirements of the Civil Aviation Authority and are

We strongly recommend that you and all members of your party be properly insured as soon as you book at your local Thomas Cook Travel Shop. Please ask our staff for full details of the cover available. To ensure that you will benefit from the most advantageous premiums, these will be advised to you at the time you make your booking. Do ask our staff or an insurance broker if you are in any doubt as to whether this special insurance is sufficient for your needs.

Holiday Care Assistance
To underline Thomas Cook's special approach to our customers, we are offering you our additional Holiday Care Assistance benefits giving greater protection for your party.

Holiday Care Assistance gives you cover if your transport to and from the airports fails; if when you're abroad you need special advice, medical information or if your tickets are stolen; if, unfortunately you have an accident your legal advice and costs are covered up to £25,000. Even if when you get home your house needs emergency repairs, Holiday Care Assistance will ensure they're carried out quickly.

Remember to ask for details at your Thomas Cook Travel Shop when you are booking.

The all inclusive car rental service to and from your UK airport

When you're off on your Thomas Cook holiday with Ocean Cruise Lines, Skydrive will see that you get away to a flying start – and that you have an easy road home.

Skydrive prices start at just £70.00 for rental to and from the airport and all prices include Unlimited Mileage, Collision Damage Waiver and VAT. That means a family of four can pay as little as £8.75 per person each way. With no worries about mileage charges or airport parking costs you will be assured of a smooth take-off with Skydrive – and, of course, the more passengers there are, the more economical your rental will be!

Skydrive offers:–
■ return journey
■ all inclusive low prices
■ a selection of cars
■ no limit on distance
Ask your local Thomas Cook Travel Shop for more details on the trouble-free way to start – and end – your holiday.

© Ocean Cruise Lines 1989 Printed in England 11/89

(f) Client F is disabled and travels with the help of a wheelchair. Would this client be able to travel on the cruise to Scandinavia?

(g) This is a very special occasion for clients G. They would like to commence their fly-cruise to South America by flying first class to Miami before boarding the ship for the cruise. Could this be arranged?

(h) Client H would like to know where the ship was registered.

(i)   Client I believes the port charges for each cruise are an expensive addition to the cost of the cruise. True or false?

(j)   Client J is concerned that the sudden increase in oil prices will affect the cost of the cruise, even though the reservation has been confirmed and the deposit has been paid. Can you help?

(k)   Client K is going on the Amazon Adventure cruise, departing 21 March. Assuming there are 28 days in February, by which date must the client pay the balance?

(l)   Client L is booked to travel on the Baltic Capitals cruise, departing 12 July. He would now like to change to the Scandinavia and Russia cruise, departing 10 June. Today is 10 March. What charges will be made to the client for making these alterations?

(m) Client M is very disappointed because, owing to unforeseen circumstances, he must cancel his place on the cruise departing 3 June. Today is 15 May. What will the cancellation charges be?

Making a reservation

Making the booking is simple; all you need to do is telephone the applicable cruise company and request the accommodation. You need to know:

1   Name of ship.
2   Cruise number.
3   Departure date.
4   Number of passengers.
5   Passengers' names and nationalities.
6   Cabin preference: outside, double, single etc.
7   Your agency ABTA number: to ensure your agency receives the commission from the shipping company.

Your client will need to complete the booking form, in the brochure. Help your client with all the important queries:

Passports   Validity, endorsements, entry permits.
Visas   Double check each country on the itinerary.
Vaccinations   Again, double check each port of call for health regulations.
On board reservations   Dining room, and excursions.
Insurance   Essential: explain fully to client.
Contact addresses   Friends and relations may wish to keep in touch.
Port taxes   Are they included in the cost of the cruise? This depends on the cruise company, so read the conditions in each cruise brochure.
Currency   Advise which currency is used on board, and the best way to take money on board.
Travellers' cheques   Explain the procedure.
Credit cards   Are they acceptable on board? If so, which ones?
Letter of credit   Your clients may prefer to arrange a letter of credit. This is a certain amount deposited with the purser. Withdrawals are made by the passenger when needed. Any money not used by the passenger during the voyage is returned. There is no charge for this service.

Make sure you understand and can advise on the conditions of booking. What are the penalties in the event of cancellation? When is the balance of payment due? What is the amount of the deposit required to secure the booking? Are there any special reductions that apply to our clients' circumstances? The answers to all these questions can be found by *reading the cruise brochure.*

The cruise ticket is normally issued by the cruise company. When received, compare the information on the ticket with the details on your passenger's file.

It is customary, and a nice thing to do, to send flowers to your client on board ship, wishing them *bon voyage.* When checking passports, make a note if a birthday is to be celebrated on board, and arrange with the shipping company for a birthday cake or a bottle of champagne. The commission earned on a cruise booking is good, enabling your agency to afford this gesture. Your client will not forget the thrill of receiving flowers in the cabin, and will no doubt bring more business to you.

First assignment

Answer the following examination questions taken from a past ICM examination paper.

You are an expert on selling cruises and have been asked to train a newcomer to the office. Prepare your training programme to cover the following points.

(a) why are people attracted to cruising?
(b) food and entertainment;
(c) the cost;
(d) the ship;
(e) ports of call;
(f) anticipate the questions your clients will ask about cruising.

Second assignment

Using a complete edition of the *ABC Passenger Shipping Guide* study cruise area C30 and choose three different dates, ships, operators and itineraries and follow the course of each cruise on a map.

Third assignment

Collect brochures from three different cruise companies and compare their cruises making notes on:

(a) the costs;
(b) the itineraries;
(c) amenities onboard;
(d) brochure presentation

Write a report on your findings.

10 Airline reservations

In this chapter we are going to discuss:

- the functions of IATA;
- IATA subareas;
- logical routings;
- IATA three-letter codes;
- reading the air ABC;
- time differences;
- elapsed flying time;
- minimum connecting times;
- passport, visa and health regulations;
- special services for passengers;
- airport information;
- fares and conditions and how to understand them
- the mileage system
- ticketing and reservations
- exercises to complete

A book of this size can only be a brief overview of the subject and will require supplementary training, guidance and practical experience to enable the student to become proficient. Here are details of a few courses operating throughout the world.

1 Your own national airline.
2 ABTA National Training Board,
   Waterloo House,
   11/17 Chertsey Road, Woking, Surrey, GU21 5AL, England.
3 IATA, International Air Transport Association,
   Agency Training Unit,
   P.O. Box 160, CH-1216 Cointrin – Geneva, Switzerland.
4 Institute of Commercial Management,
   P.O. Box 125, Bournemouth, Dorset, BH2 6JH, England.
5 Peyton Training Services,
   3, Wallasey Crescent,
   Ickenham, Uxbridge, Middlesex, UB10 8SA, England.

You may be thinking 'What does IATA do?'. It is an association, created in 1919, when six airlines agreed to set up the Air Traffic Association aiming to foster collaboration between air transport operators. It has now grown to approximately 188 airlines throughout the world which are either active or associate members of, what is now, the International Air Transport Assocation.

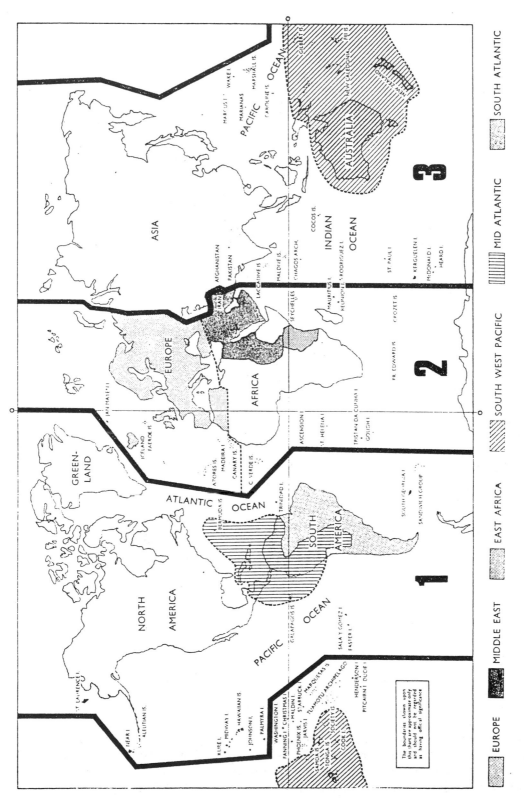

Can you imagine airline personnel from 188 different airlines using different languages, different safety regulations, different methods of documentation? It would be chaotic! As you can now imagine there is a great need for standardization within the air industry. The international language is English and all pilots and traffic controllers give and receive instructions using the English language. We now have standardization with documentation, rules governing fare calculations and ticketing followed by travel personnel whether based in Tokyo, Sydney or London, in fact everywhere throughout the world. We have controls with air space, regulations governing the flight to fly over another country, to land in another country, to collect and deliver passengers from/to another country. Noise pollution is controlled and monitored and IATA has been instrumental in getting airlines to work together in many areas, for example:

Safety	Finding joint solutions to problems beyond the resources of any single company.
Environment	Noise and smoke emission.
Security	Protection for passengers.
Medical	Physiological and psychological factors effecting safety, comfort and efficiency of aircrews and passengers.
Legal	Concern for the liability of air carriers and their legal relationship with their customers.
Finance and accounting	Simplifying accounting, includes matters related to currency and exchange, taxation and insurance.
Standardization	Of fares, documentation and code of ethics.

Countries and cities

IATA has three main offices. The Geneva office deals with matters concerning Europe, Africa and the Middle East, the Montreal office with the Americas, and the Singapore office with the Far East and Australasia.

Please study the IATA world map with traffic conference areas. The areas are as follows:

1 North, South and Central America; the Hawaiian Islands; the Bahamas; Bermuda; Greenland; the Caribbean.
2 Europe, including Russia to the west of the Ural Mountains; islands adjacent to Europe, such as the Azores and the Canary Islands; the Middle East, including Iran; Iceland; Africa and the adjacent islands.
3 Asia, including Russia to the East of the Ural Mountains; the islands of the Pacific Ocean west of the International Date Line; Australasia.

Area 1 is often referred to as the Western hemisphere, and areas 2 and 3 as the Eastern hemisphere. The International Date Line separates area 1 and area 3.

The three IATA areas have been divided into smaller subareas; please study the extract from the ABC air tariff.

You will see we have countries divided into the following areas.

Central Africa   Malawi, Zambia, Zimbabwe.

IATA SUB-AREA DEFINITIONS

CENTRAL AFRICA:
Malawi, Zambia, Zimbabwe

EASTERN AFRICA:
Burundi, Djibouti, Ethiopia, Kenya, Rwanda, Somalia, Tanzania and Uganda.

MID ATLANTIC AREA: Bahamas, Bermuda, Bolivia, Belize, Canal Zone, Colombia, Costa Rica, Ecuador, El Salvador, French Guiana, Guatemala, Guyana, Honduras, the islands of the Caribbean Sea (including Puerto Rico and the Virgin Islands), Nicaragua, Panama, Peru, Surinam, Venezuela.

MIDDLE EAST:

Aden, People's Republic of Southern Yemen	Lebanon
	Qatar
Bahrain	Saudi Arabia
Cyprus	Sudan
Egypt (Arab Republic) of Egypt)	Sultanate of Oman
	Syria
Iran	United Arab Emirates (comprised
Iraq	of Abu Dhabi, Ajman, Dubai,
Israel	Fujairah, Ras Al Khaimah,
Jordan	Sharjah, Umm Al Qaiwain)
Kuwait State	Yemen

NORTH ATLANTIC AREA: Canada, Mexico, USA, (including Hawaii and Alaska but excluding Canal Zone, Puerto Rico and the Virgin Islands; American Samoa; Canton, Guam, Midway and Wake Island).

SOUTH ASIAN SUBCONTINENT:

Afghanistan	Nepal
Bangladesh	Pakistan
Bhutan	Republic of Maldives
India	Sri Lanka

SOUTH ATLANTIC AREA: Argentina, Brazil, Chile, Paraguay, Uruguay

SOUTH EAST ASIA:

Brunei	Micronesia
Burma	Mongolian Republic
China (People's Republic)	Phillippines
Hong Kong	Singapore
Indonesia	Taiwan
Kampochea	Thailand
Laos	USSR (East of URALS)
Malaysia	Vietnam

SOUTHERN AFRICA
Botswana, Lesotho, Mozambique, South Africa, South West Africa (Namibia) and Swaziland.

SOUTH WEST PACIFIC:

Australia	Papua New Guinea
Cook Islands	Samoan Islands
Fiji Islands	Society Islands
Kiribati	Solomon Islands
New Caledonia	Tonga
Loyalty Islands	Tuvalu
New Zealand	Vanuatu
	All intermediate Islands

WESTERN AFRICA:

Angola	Guinea Bissau
Benin	Ivory Coast
Burkina Faso	Liberia
Cameroon	Mali
Cape Verde	Mauritania
Central African Republic	Niger
Chad	Nigeria
Congo	Sao Tome and Principe
Equatorial Guinea	Senegal
Gabon	Sierra Leone
Gambia	Togo
Ghana	Zaire
Guinea	

Eastern Africa	Burundi, Djibouti, Ethiopia and so on.
Mid Atlantic	Bahamas, Bermuda, Bolivia and so on.
Middle East	Aden, Bahrain, Cyprus and so on.
North Atlantic	Canada, Mexico, USA and so on.
South Asian Sub-Continent	Afghanistan, Bangladesh, Bhutan and so on.
South Atlantic	Argentina, Brazil, Chile and so on.
South East Asia	Brunei, Burma, China and so on.
Southern Africa	Botswana, Lesotho, Mozambique and so on.
South West Pacific	Australia, Cook Islands, Fiji Islands and so on.
Western Africa	Angola, Congo, Ghana, Sierra Leone and so on.

At this point please study a world atlas and locate all the countries listed in the IATA sub-areas, paying particular attention to those countries that are un-familiar to you.

Exercise 1

So! Looking at the world map for IATA areas and the extract from the ABC tariff for subarea definitions, try to complete the following table:

City	Country	IATA area	Subarea
Bogota	Colombia	1	Mid Atlantic
Bangkok			
Vancouver			
Nairobi			
Nicosia			
Los Angeles			
Wellington			

Exercise 2

How is your geography? Geography is very important in a travel and tourism career. (*The Geography of Travel and Tourism* by Brian Boniface and Chris Cooper is a useful reference book.) We can learn by studying maps, reading travel articles, watching travel programmes on TV and generally being up to date with what is going on in the world. Listen to your clients: they often have up-to-the-minute information.

To test your geography knowledge, try to write down the countries in which the following cities are located:

City	Country
Madras	
Istanbul	

Beirut
Damascus
Kuala Lumpur
Monte Carlo
Manila
Colombo
Osaka
Blantyre
Chittagong

City codes

All cities have been given a three-letter code by IATA. Where more than one airport serves a city, each *airport* has a three-letter code. For example, London is LON but there are several airports: London City Airport is LCY; London Gatwick Airport is LGW; London Heathrow Airport is LHR; London Luton Airport is LTN; and London Stansted Airport is STN. The complete list is published in the *ABC Airways Guide*.

The three-letter code is not always the first three letters of the city because so many cities begin with the same spelling (e.g. Madras/Madrid). So it really is essential to learn the codes and look them up in the ABC guide; do not guess! Cities with the same name can turn up in several countries. For example, Hamilton can be found in Canada, New Zealand and Scotland: which one did our client want?

There are many factors that influence an itinerary: the customer's choice; the regulations surrounding the fare construction; the availability and accessibility of flights and acceptable departure and arrival times.

We also have to develop a sense of direction! We would want to route our clients in the most direct and logical way, without back-tracking. The following exercise tests this.

For a one-way journey beginning in Greece decide on the most logical route for the following cities.
BRU   ATH   HEL   PAR
Study a map of Europe and you should have the answer of ATH PAR BRU HEL.

Let's try another one. A return journey beginning in Bulgaria.
BUD   LON   SOF   AMS   CPH
Study the atlas and find the furthest country from Bulgaria, all the stops are to be made on the outward journey.
BUD = Budapest. LON = London. SOF = Sofia. AMS = Amsterdam. CPH = Copenhagen.
SOF BUD AMS LON CPH SOF
Now, try exercise 3.

Exercise 3

From the list of European cities with the three-letter codes supplied by the

8.3.4   Europe

COUNTRY

City, Province	Code	Airport	Code
ALBANIA			
Tirana	TIA		
AUSTRIA			
Vienna	VIE		
BELGIUM			
Brussels	BRU		
BULGARIA			
Sofia	SOF		
CYPRUS			
Nicosia	NIC	Larnaca	LCA
CZECHOSLOVAKIA			
Prague	PRG		
DENMARK			
Copenhagen	CPH		
FINLAND			
Helsinki	HEL		
FRANCE			
Bordeaux	BOD		
Lyon	LYS		
Marseille	MRS		
Nice	NCE		
Paris	PAR	Charles de Gaulle	CDG
		Le Bourget	LBG
		Orly	ORY

8.3.4   Europe (cont'd)

COUNTRY

City, Province	Code	Airport	Code
ITALY			
Milan	MIL		
Naples	NAP		
Rome	ROM	Ciampino	CIA
		Leonardo da Vinci	FCO
		(Fiumicino)	
Turin	TRN		
Venice	VCE		
LUXEMBOURG			
Luxembourg	LUX		
MALTA			
Valletta	MLA		
NETHERLANDS			
Amsterdam	AMS		
Rotterdam	RTM		
NORWAY			
Bergen	BGO		
Oslo	OSL		
POLAND			
Warsaw	WAW		
PORTUGAL			
Lisbon	LIS		
Funchal (Madeira)	FNC		
ROMANIA			
Bucharest	BUH		

8.3.4   Europe (cont'd)

COUNTRY

City, Province	Code	Airport	Code
GERMANY, Democratic Republic			
Berlin, East	SXF	Schoenefeld	SXF
GERMANY, Federal Republic			
Berlin, West	BER	Tegel	TXL
Cologne	CGN		
Dusseldorf	DUS		
Frankfurt	FRA		
Hamburg	HAM		
Munich	MUC		
Stuttgart	STR		
GIBRALTAR			
Gibraltar	GIB		
GREECE			
Athens	ATH		
HUNGARY			
Budapest	BUD		
ICELAND			
Reykjavik	REK		
IRELAND			
Dublin	DUB		
Shannon	SNN		

8.3.4   Europe (cont'd)

COUNTRY

City, Province	Code	Airport	Code
SPAIN			
Barcelona	BCN		
Las Palmas, Canary Islands	LPA		
Madrid	MAD		
Malaga	AGP		
Palma de Mallorca	PMI		
Tenerife, Canary Islands	TCI		
SWEDEN			
Gothenburg	GOT		
Stockholm	STO		
SWITZERLAND			
Geneva	GVA		
Zurich	ZRH		
TURKEY			
Ankara	ANK		
Istanbul	IST		
UNITED KINGDOM			
Belfast	BFS		
Birmingham	BHX		
Edinburgh	EDI		
Glasgow	GLA		
London	LON	Gatwick	LGW
		Heathrow	LHR
Manchester	MAN		
U.S.S.R. (West of Urals)			
Leningrad	LED		
Moscow	MOW	Sheremetyvo	SVO
YUGOSLAVIA			
Belgrade	BEG		
Zagreb	ZAG		

WORLDWIDE REPRESENTATION

If you need additional copies of any ABC publication, we have offices and agents worldwide to assist you. If you are not resident in any of the countries listed below, please contact ABC International at the address at the bottom of this page; subscribers to Algeria, Tunisia, and Morocco should apply to Reed Travel Group, France.

ARGENTINA
C.A.S.A. de Representacoes Ltda
Av. Santa Fe, 951-4 Piso
1059 Buenos Aires
Tel: (1) 3258073/3258101
Fax: (1) 3258264
Telex: 25580 Setiel Ar.

AUSTRALIA
Reed Travel Group, Suite 201
229 Pacific Highway
North Sydney, N.S.W. 2060
Tel: (2) 959 3800
Fax: (2) 929 4989

**BELGIUM &
LUXEMBOURG**
Schuyt en Co. N.V., Hansa-Huis
Suikerrui 5 (Bus nr. 3)
2000 Antwerpen
Tel: (3) 231 45 54
Telex: 33860 SDL-ANT B
Fax: (3) 232 58 91

BRAZIL
C.A.S.A. de Representacoes Ltda
A Company of Panrotas Group
Av. Jabaquara 1761
04045 Sao Paulo-SP
Tel: (11) 2750211
Telex: 56693 PANR BR
Fax: (11) 2761602

CHILE
Interrep Ltda
Huerfanos 1160, Of 1110
PO Box 300- V
Santiago 1
Tel: (2) 6984371,6960281
Fax: (2) 715408
Telex: 340322 TRAVEL CK

COLOMBIA
Travelrep Ltda
Carrera 13 A 89-53 of 301
Bogota
Fax: (1) 2269388
Tel: (1) 2268088/2575997/2576014
Telex: 42611 GRKCO

CYPRUS
Cyprus Trade & Tours
101 Makarios 111 Avenue
PO Box 1386
Commercial Union Building
Nicosia
Tel: (2) 450181
Fax: (2) 450874
Telex: 2055 JAMES CY

EGYPT
Universal Travel Co
55 Al Gomhouria Street
Cairo
Tel: (2) 906444/900002
Fax: 919199
Telex: 92329 UNIFUN

FRANCE
Reed Travel Group
ABC France Ltd.
14 Rue des Parisiens
92600 Asnières
Tel: (1) 47 90 39 00
Telex: 612096F
Fax: (1) 47 90 06 43

GREECE
Falcon Ltd.
14 Nikoloudi & Papada Str.
Athens 115 26
Tel: (1) 692 5168
Fax: (1) 691 4055
Telex: 223 854 HLDS

HONG KONG
Reed Travel Group
10/F Toppan Building
22a Westlands Road, Quarry Bay
Tel: 8115525
Telex: 74166 FEST HX
Fax: 565 9215

INDIA & NEPAL
Strand Book Stall, "Dhannur"
Sir P.M. Road, Bombay 400 001
Tel: (22) 2861994, 291719
Telex: 011-3020 SBS IN
Fax: 1183020

ITALY
Reed Travel Group
ABC Italy Ltd
Via Torino 47
20123 Milano
Tel: (2) 862917
Fax: (2) 805 7771
Telex: 340055

JAPAN
Tozaisha Limited, Orikomi Building
6th Floor, 6-11-7 Ginza, Chuo-Ku
Tokyo 104
Tel: (3) 573-3191/6
Telex: 29133 TOZAITYO J
Fax: (3) 573-3199

KENYA
Kenpub Distributors
P.O. Box 48439, Nairobi.
Tel: (2) 333376/721185
Fax: (2) 721185

KOREA REPUBLIC
Buyeon Company Ltd
Room 302 Daedong Bldg
601-31, Yoksam-Dong, Kangnam-ku
Seoul, CPO Box 8648
Tel: 546-1726, 557-7101/2
Fax: 554-8601

KUWAIT
Alghanim Travel, Head Office
Algho Shuwaikh, P.O. Box 81
Kuwait 13001
Tel: (965) 4842988/4843988
Telex: 44900 GANIM KTATA
Fax: (965) 4847244

MALAYSIA
Reed Travel Group, c/o Intermag
18-14 Jalan 14/22
46100 Petaling Jaya, Selangor
Tel: (3) 755 2735/757 4718
Fax: (3) 757 1891

MALTA
Sapienzas, 26 Republic Street
Valletta
Tel: (356) 633621

**MIDDLE EAST & NORTH
AFRICA (Other than
Kuwait, Saudi Arabia &
UAE)**
WTS Travel Ltd., PO Box 425
Paphos, Cyprus
Tel: (6) 237967
Telex: 5566WTS CY
Fax: (6) 237518

NETHERLANDS
Schuyt & Co. International b.v.
Gedempte Oude Gracht 35
Haarlem
Tel: (23) 325440
Telex: 41532 SCO NL
Fax: (23) 327017

NEW ZEALAND
Reed Travel Group
Travel House, 6 Walls Road
P.O. Box 12-540, Penrose
Auckland
Tel: (09) 5252360
Telex: NZ 60139
Fax: (09) 5252227

PAKISTAN
Aviation Services Limited
Hotel Metropole Building
Club Road, Karachi 17
Tel: (21) 512051, 516525, 510011
Telex: 24329 METRO PK
Fax: (21) 514301

PHILIPPINES
AD Strategists Inc
308 Dona Narcisa Building
Paseo de Roxas, Makati
Metro Manila
Tel: (3) 817-58-86, 86-73-54
Telex: 23312 RHPA PH

SAUDI ARABIA
Saudi Tourist & Travel Bureau Ltd
P.O. Box 863, Al Johara Building
Medina Road South, Jeddah 21421
Tel: (2) 665 4272
Fax: (2) 665 4609
Telex: 603894 STTB SJ

SINGAPORE
Reed Travel Group
19-07 International Plaza
10 Anson Road
Singapore 0207
Tel: (65) 227-7100
Fax: (65) 227-7122
Telex: RS 35923 AIRABC

SOUTH AFRICA
Houston Travel Marketing
Services, P.O. Box 75262
Gardenview 2047, Transvaal
Tel: (11) 614-7213/4
Telex: 4-83195
Fax: (11) 614-3927

SPAIN
Ian Dornan International
Calle Arenal, 21
28013 Madrid
Tel: (1) 247 2930
Fax: (1) 542 4005
Telex: 45522 CCBE E

SWITZERLAND
ABC International
Reed Telepublishing AG
Rue du Cornavin 11
1211 Geneva
Tel: 022 7382929
Fax: 022 7282924

TAIWAN
Taiwan Travel Inc.
9 Nanking East Road
Section 3, 11th Floor, Taipei 10410
Tel: (02) 506 2311
Telex: 20335
Fax: (02) 5072472

THAILAND
Reed Travel Group
c/o Prestige Travel Consultants
5/12 Santi Townhouse
Wireless Road (Opp. Hilton Hotel)
Bangkok 10330
Tel: (2) 252 4620
Telex: 84001 SCORPIO TH

UNITED ARAB EMIRATES
DNATA, PO Box 1515, Dubai
Tel: (4) 228151
Telex: 45728 DNATA EM
Fax: (4) 277847

URUGUAY
Pan Tours, Oddal Ltda
Convencion 1177
Montevideo
Tel: (2) 921131/32
Fax: (2) 921172
Telex: 26906

U.S.A. & CANADA
Reed Travel Group,
131 Clarendon Street, Boston
MA 02116
Tel: (617) 262-5000
Telex: 4951813
Fax: (617) 262-0960

VENEZUELA
Morgan Tours
Ed. Roraima Of. 9-C
Av. F de Miranda
Campo Alegre
Caracas
Tel: (2) 261 7217
Fax: (2) 261 9265
Telex: 23516 MORGNVC

**WEST GERMANY &
AUSTRIA**
Reed Travel Group
Reed Telepublishing GmbH
Heerdter Landstrasse 193
Postfach 270164
D-4000 Düsseldorf 11
Tel: (211) 50 30 62
Fax: (211) 50 40 10

ABC International, Church Street, Dunstable, Bedfordshire, LU5 4HB, England.
Tel: 0582 600111, Telex: 82168 AIRABC G, Fax: 0582 695230

ABC INTERNATIONAL
REED TRAVEL GROUP
PART OF REED INTERNATIONAL P.L.C.

CONTENTS—BLUE BOOK

HOW TO USE QUICK REFERENCE SECTION—see pages 71-75 in this book

General Information

Important Notes-refer before using Guide	2
Advertisement and Subscription Enquiries	3
Airlines of the World (Head Offices)	4-11
Airline Designators (encoding)	4-11
Airline Code Numbers (decoding)	12,13
Airline Designators (decoding)	14,15
Bank and Public Holidays	16,17
International Time Calculator	18,19
IATA	20
Aircraft Types	21
Minimum Connecting Times	22-35
Two Letter State Codes (decoding)	36
Schedule Texts (Explanation of Abbreviations)	36
City/Airport Codes	37-43
Shared Airline Designator Codes	56
Flight Routings	45-69

Quick Reference A-M

How to use	72-75
Worldwide city to city timetables A-M in alphabetical order	77-3000

VALIDITY OF INFORMATION THIS MONTH

THROUGH FLIGHTS-published if operating or commencing operation at any time during the period 1 August-27 October

At the request of individual airlines, certain through flights commencing operations beyond this period are also published

TRANSFER CONNECTIONS-published if operating or commencing operation at any time during the period 1 August-29 September
During Bank and Public Holidays flights are often subject to cancellation and change. Individual airlines should be contacted for exact details.

Refer to RED BOOK for

QUICK REFERENCE N—Z
FARES SECTION
NORTH AMERICAN PROMOTIONAL FARES
ADVANCE SCHEDULES SECTION
AIRLINE FEATURE SECTION
INTERNATIONAL CAR HIRE DIRECTORY

For air cargo rates and flight schedules refer to monthly ABC AIR CARGO GUIDE

CONTENTS—RED BOOK

HOW TO USE QUICK REFERENCE SECTION—see pages 71-75 in Blue Book

Quick Reference N-Z

Worldwide City Timetables N-Z in alphabetical order	3002-4000

VALIDITY OF INFORMATION THIS MONTH

THROUGH FLIGHTS-published if operating or commencing operation at any time during the period 1 August-27 October

At the request of individual airlines, certain through flights commencing operations beyond this period are also published

TRANSFER CONNECTIONS-published if operating or commencing operation at any time during the period 1 August-29 September
During Bank and Public Holidays flights are often subject to cancellation and change. Individual airlines should be contacted for exact details.

Fares Section

Contents	F1
IATA Traffic Conference Areas	F2
Important/Stop Press	F3
World Currency Conversion & Exchange Rates	F4,F5
Fares Construction	F6-F5
Ticket & Sales Taxes	F7
Airport Taxes	F8
Free Baggage Allowances	F9-F10
Excess Baggage Charges	F11-F13
Ticketed Point Mileages	F14-F40
Excess Mileage Percentage Tables	F41
Validity Indicator For Special Fares	F42,F43
Fare Notes	F44-F108
Normal & Excursion Fares (Display Explanation)	F109-F112
Normal & Excursion Fares (Including Visit U.S.A Fares)	F113-F298

North American Promotional Fares

Alaska Airlines	AS1
Northwest Airlines	NW1-NW10
TWA-Trans World Airlines	TW1-TW5

Advance Schedules Section (Winter 1990/91)	OR1-OR24

Airline Feature Section

The timetable network of individual airlines in alphabetical order	AF1-AF76

International Car Hire Section

See end of Airline Feature Section	CH1-CH4

Refer to BLUE BOOK for

GENERAL INFORMATION
and
QUICK REFERENCE A-M

For air cargo rates and flight schedules refer to monthly ABC AIR CARGO GUIDE

IATA-UFTAA Travel Agents' Diploma Course, study a map of Europe and decide upon a logical travel order for the following cities (you will need to look up the codes to find the cities):

VIE, STO, ATH, BEG, MAD, OSL, LON, GVA

Check your answer only when you feel happy about the direction of travel.

ABC World Airways Guide

A general word is necessary about the *ABC World Airways Guide*. Details are published in two books, the Blue Book and the Red Book. Each book contains approximately 1120 pages, and we can only reproduce extracts. Should you require the complete volumes or any of the other excellent reference books published by Reed Travel Group, please contact either ABC International in Dunstable, UK, or your nearest worldwide representative: see the details provided.

Please study the contents pages for the Blue Book and the Red Book. You will realize that there is a wealth of information at your fingertips; everything is very quick and easy to find. The secret is to take time in the beginning to read the explanations of codes throughout; you will then be able to find so much useful information and give the correct advice to your clients.

Aircraft Types

IN SERVICE ON REGULAR SCHEDULE AIRLINE ROUTES

CODING OF ABBREVIATIONS

J—Pure Jet, T—Prop-Jet, P—Propeller, H—Helicopter, A—Amphibian/Seaplane

Aerospatiale AS 350/355 Ecureuill Helicopter	H	NDE
Aerospatiale Caravelle (All series)	J	CRV
Aerospatiale N 262/Frakes Mohawk 298	T	ND2
Aerospatiale SA365 Dauphin-2 Helicopter	H	NDH
Aerospatiale-British Aerospace (BAC) Concorde	J	SSC
Aerospatiale/Aeritalia ATR-42/72	T	ATR
Agusta 109 Helicopter	H	AGH
Airbus Industrie A300-600C Freighter	J	ABF
Airbus Industrie A300C4 (Mixed Configuration)	J	ABM
Airbus Industrie A300 (All series passenger)	J	AB3
Airbus Industrie A310 Freighter	J	31F
Airbus Industrie A310 (All series) Passenger	J	310
Airbus Industrie A320 (All series)	J	320
Antonov AN-12 Freighter	T	ANF
Antonov AN-24	T	AN4
Antonov AN-26 Freighter	T	AN6
Beechcraft (All series prop and turboprop)		BEC
Beechcraft C99	T	BE9
Beechcraft 1900	T	BE1
Boeing Canada DHC-7 Freighter	T	DHF
Boeing Canada DHC-7 (Mixed Configuration)	T	DHM
Boeing Canada DHC-3 Otter	P	DHO
Boeing Canada DHC-2 Beaver	P	DHP
Boeing Canada DHC-6 Twin Otter	T	DHT
Boeing Canada DHC-4 Caribou	P	DH4
Boeing Canada DHC-7 Passenger	T	DH7
Boeing Canada DHC-8 (All series)	T	DH8
Boeing Canada Turbo Beaver	T	DHB
Boeing 377 Stratocruiser Freighter	P	37F
Boeing 707 (Mixed Configuration)	J	70M
Boeing 707 Freighter (All series)	J	70F
Boeing 707 Passenger (All series)	J	707
Boeing 727 (Mixed Configuration)	J	72M
Boeing 727 Freighter (All series)	J	72F
Boeing 727 Passenger (All series)	J	727
Boeing 727-200 Passenger	J	72S
Boeing 737 Passenger(All series)	J	737
Boeing 737-200 Freighter	J	73F
Boeing 737-200 (Mixed Configuration)	J	73M
Boeing 737-200 Passenger	J	73S
Boeing 737-300 Passenger	J	733
Boeing 737-400 Passenger	J	734
Boeing 737-500 Passenger	J	735
Boeing 747 (Mixed Configuration)	J	74M
Boeing 747 Freighter	J	74F
Boeing 747 Passenger (All series)	J	747
Boeing 747 SP	J	74L
Boeing 747-300 (Mixed Configuration)	J	74D
Boeing 747-300 Passenger	J	743
Boeing 747-400 (Mixed Configuration)	J	74E
Boeing 747-400 Passenger	J	744
Boeing 757 Freighter	J	75F
Boeing 757-200 Passenger	J	757
Boeing 767 (All series)	J	767
Boeing 767 Freighter	J	76F
Boeing 767-300/300ER	J	763
British Aerospace ATP	T	BAT
British Aerospace (BAC) 111 (All series)	J	B11
British Aerospace(Hawker Siddeley) Heron	P	DHH
British Aerospace (Handley Page) Herald	T	HPH
British Aerospace (Hawker Siddeley) Argosy Freighter	T	HSF
British Aerospace (Hawker Siddeley) Argosy (Mixed Configuration)	T	HSM
British Aerospace (Hawker Siddeley) 748 Passenger	T	HS7
British Aerospace (Hawker Siddeley) 125	J	H25
British Aerospace (Hawker Siddeley) 748 (Mixed Configuration)	T	H7M
British Aerospace Jetstream 31	T	J31
British Aerospace (Hawker Siddeley) Trident (All series)	J	TRD
British Aerospace (BAC-Vickers) Viscount (All series)	T	VCV
British Aerospace (BAC-Vickers) Merchantman Freighter	T	VGF
British Aerospace 146 Freighter	J	14F
British Aerospace 146 (All series) passenger	J	146
Canadair CL-44	T	CL4
Canadair Regional Jet	J	CRJ
Casa 212/Nusantara 212 Aviocar	T	CS2
Casa/Nusantara 235	T	CS5
Cessna (All series prop and turboprop)		CNA
Cessna Citation	J	CNJ
Convair (All series prop and turboprop) Freighter		CVF
Convair (All series prop and turboprop)		CVR
Curtiss C-46 Commando	P	CWC
Dassault-Breguet Mercure	J	DAM
Dassault-Breguet Mystere-Falcon(All series)	J	DFL
Dornier DO28	P	DOS
Dornier 228 (All series)	T	DO8
Douglas DC-3 Freighter	P	D3F
Douglas DC-3 Passenger	P	DC3
Douglas DC-3(Mixed Configuration)	P	D3M
Douglas DC-4 Freighter	P	D4F
Douglas DC-6A Freighter	P	D6F
Embraer EMB 110 Bandeirante	T	EMB
Embraer EMB 120 Brasilia	T	EM2
Fairchild (Swearingen) Metro/Merlin	T	SWM
Fairchild Industries FH227	T	FK7
Fokker F27 Friendship (All series)	T	F27
Fokker F28 Fellowship (All series)	J	F28
Fokker F50	T	F50
Fokker 100	J	100
GAF N22/N24 Nomad	T	CD2
Gates Learjet	J	LRJ
Grumman Albatross	A	GRA
Grumman Goose	A	GRG
Grumman Mallard	A	GRM
Gulfstream Aerospace Gulfstream 11/111/1V	J	GRJ
Gulfstream Aerospace(Grumman) Gulfstream 1/1-C	T	GRS
Ilyushin IL-14	P	IL4
Ilyushin IL-18	T	IL8
Ilyushin IL-62	J	IL6
Ilyushin IL-76 Freighter	J	IL7
Ilyushin IL-86	J	ILW
Israel Aircraft Ind. Arava 101B/102	T	RV1
Israel Aircraft Ind 1124 Westwind Freighter	J	WWF
Israel Aircraft Industries Westwind Passenger	J	WWP
LET L-410UVP Turboprop	T	L4T
Lockheed L100 Hercules Freighter	T	LOH
Lockheed L1011 TriStar (All series)	J	L10
Lockheed L1011 TriStar (500 series)	J	L15
Lockheed L188 Electra Passenger	T	LOE
Lockheed L188 Electra Freighter	T	LOF
Lockheed L188 Electra (Mixed Configuration)	T	LOM
Martin 404	P	MR4
McDonnell Douglas DC-8 (All series passenger)	J	DC8
McDonnell Douglas DC-9 (All series passenger)	J	DC9
McDonnell Douglas DC-10 Freighter	J	D1F
McDonnell Douglas DC-10(Mixed Configuration	J	D1M
McDonnell Douglas DC-10 Passenger(All series)	J	D10
McDonnell Douglas DC-8 Freighter(All series)	J	D8F
McDonnell Douglas DC-8 (Mixed Configuration)	J	D8M
McDonnell Douglas DC-8 (All 60 and 70 series passenger)	J	D8S
McDonnell Douglas DC-9 Freighter	J	D9F
McDonnell Douglas DC-9 (All 30,40,50 and 80 series passenger)	J	D9S
McDonnell Douglas MD-11	J	M11
McDonnell Douglas MD-80 (All series passenger)	J	M80
McDonnell Douglas MD-87	J	M87
Mil Mi-8 Helicopter	H	MIH
Mitsubishi MU-2	T	MU2
NAMC YS-11	T	YS1
Partenavia P68 Victor	P	PN6
Pilatus Britten Norman Trislander	P	BNT
Pilatus Britten Norman Islander	P	BN1
Pilatus PC6 Turbo-Porter	T	PL6
Piper (All series prop and turboprop)		PAG
Rockwell Commander	P	ACD
Saab SF 340	T	SF3
Saunders ST-27	T	SA2
Shorts Skyvan	T	SHS
Shorts 330 Passenger	T	SH3
Shorts 360	T	SH6
Sikorsky S-58 Helicopter	H	S58
Sikorsky S-61 Helicopter	H	S61
Sikorsky S-76 Helicopter	H	S76
Tupolev TU-134	J	TU3
Tupolev TU-154	J	TU5
Westland 30 Helicopter	H	WLH
Yakovlev YAK 40	J	YK4
Yakovlev YAK 42	J	YK2
Yunshuji 5	P	YN5
Yunshuji 7	T	YN7
Bus		BUS
Equipment Varies		EQV
Hovercraft		HOV
Launch/Boat		LCH
Limousine		LMO
Road Feeder Service (Truck)		RFS
Train		‡‡‡

DECODING OF ABBREVIATIONS

J—Pure Jet, T—Prop-Jet, P—Propeller, H—Helicopter, A—Amphibian/Seaplane

ABF	J	Airbus Industrie A300-600C Freighter
ABM	J	Airbus Industrie A300C4 (Mixed Configuration)
AB3	J	Airbus Industrie A300 (All series passenger)
ACD	P	Rockwell Commander
AGH	H	Agusta 109 Helicopter
ANF	T	Antonov AN-12 Freighter
AN4	T	Antonov AN-24
AN6	T	Antonov AN-26 Freighter
ATR	T	Aerospatiale/Aeritalia ATR-42/72
BAT	T	British Aerospace ATP
BEC		Beechcraft (All series prop and turboprop)
BE1	T	Beechcraft 1900
BE9	T	Beechcraft C99
BN1	P	Pilatus Britten Norman Islander
BNT	P	Pilatus Britten Norman Trislander
B11	J	British Aerospace (BAC) 111 (All series)
CD2	T	GAF N22/N24 Nomad
CL4	T	Canadair CL-44
CNA		Cessna (All series prop and turboprop)
CNJ	J	Cessna Citation
CRJ	J	Canadair Regional Jet
CRV	J	Aerospatiale Caravelle (All series)
CS2	T	Casa 212/Nusantara 212 Aviocar
CS5	T	Casa/Nusantara 235
CVF		Convair (All series prop and turboprop) Freighter
CVR		Convair (All series prop and turboprop)
CWC	P	Curtiss C-46 Commando
DAM	J	Dassault-Breguet Mercure
DC3	P	Douglas DC-3 Passenger
DC8	J	McDonnell Douglas DC-8 (All series passenger)
DC9	J	McDonnell Douglas DC-9 (All series passenger)
DFL	J	Dassault-Breguet Mystere-Falcon(All series)
DHB	T	Boeing Canada Turbo Beaver
DHF	T	Boeing Canada DHC-7 Freighter
DHH	P	British Aerospace(Hawker Siddeley) Heron
DHM	T	Boeing Canada DHC-7 (Mixed Configuration)
DHO	P	Boeing Canada DHC-3 Otter
DHP	P	Boeing Canada DHC-2 Beaver
DHT	T	Boeing Canada DHC-6 Twin Otter
DH4	P	Boeing Canada DHC-4 Caribou
DH7	T	Boeing Canada DHC-7 Passenger
DH8	T	Boeing Canada DHC-8 (All series)
DOS	P	Dornier DO28
DO8	T	Dornier 228 (All series)
D1F	J	McDonnell Douglas DC-10 Freighter
D1M	J	McDonnell Douglas DC-10(Mixed Configuration
D10	J	McDonnell Douglas DC-10 Passenger(All series)
D3F	P	Douglas DC-3 Freighter
D3M	P	Douglas DC-3(Mixed Configuration)
D4F	P	Douglas DC-4 Freighter
D6F	P	Douglas DC-6A Freighter
D8F	J	McDonnell Douglas DC-8 Freighter(All series)
D8M	J	McDonnell Douglas DC-8 (Mixed Configuration)
D8S	J	McDonnell Douglas DC-8 (All 60 and 70 series passenger)
D9F	J	McDonnell Douglas DC-9 Freighter
D9S	J	McDonnell Douglas DC-9 (All 30,40,50 and 80 series passenger)
EMB	T	Embraer EMB 110 Bandeirante
EM2	T	Embraer EMB 120 Brasilia
FK7	T	Fairchild Industries FH227
F27	T	Fokker F27 Friendship (All series)
F28	J	Fokker F28 Fellowship (All series)
F50	T	Fokker F50
GRA	A	Grumman Albatross
GRG	A	Grumman Goose
GRJ	J	Gulfstream Aerospace Gulfstream 11/111/1V
GRM	A	Grumman Mallard
GRS	T	Gulfstream Aerospace(Grumman) Gulfstream 1/1-C
H25	J	British Aerospace (Hawker Siddeley) 125
H7M	T	British Aerospace (Hawker Siddeley) 748 (Mixed Configuration)
HPH	T	British Aerospace (Handley Page) Herald
HSF	T	British Aerospace (Hawker Siddeley) Argosy Freighter
HSM	T	British Aerospace (Hawker Siddeley) Argosy (Mixed Configuration)
HS7	T	British Aerospace (Hawker Siddeley) 748 Passenger
ILW	J	Ilyushin IL-86
IL4	P	Ilyushin IL-14
IL6	J	Ilyushin IL-62
IL7	J	Ilyushin IL-76 Freighter
IL8	T	Ilyushin IL-18
J31	T	British Aerospace Jetstream 31
LOE	T	Lockheed L188 Electra Passenger
LOF	T	Lockheed L188 Electra Freighter
LOH	T	Lockheed L100 Hercules Freighter
LOM	T	Lockheed L188 Electra (Mixed Configuration)
LRJ	J	Gates Learjet
L4T	T	LET L-410UVP Turboprop
L10	J	Lockheed L1011 TriStar (All series)
L15	J	Lockheed L1011 TriStar (500 series)
MIH	H	Mil Mi-8 Helicopter
MR4	P	Martin 404
MU2	T	Mitsubishi MU-2
M11	J	McDonnell Douglas MD-11
M80	J	McDonnell Douglas MD-80 (All series passenger)
M87	J	McDonnell Douglas MD-87
NDE	H	Aerospatiale AS 350/355 Ecureuill Helicopter
NDH	H	Aerospatiale SA365 Dauphin-2 Helicopter
ND2	T	Aerospatiale N 262/Frakes Mohawk 298
PAG		Piper (All series prop and turboprop)
PL6	T	Pilatus PC6 Turbo-Porter
PN6	P	Partenavia P68 Victor
RV1	T	Israel Aircraft Ind. Arava 101B/102
SA2	T	Saunders ST-27
SF3	T	Saab SF 340
SHS	T	Shorts Skyvan
SH3	T	Shorts 330 Passenger
SH6	T	Shorts 360
SSC	J	Aerospatiale-British Aerospace (BAC) Concorde
SWM	T	Fairchild (Swearingen) Metro/Merlin
S58	H	Sikorsky S-58 Helicopter
S61	H	Sikorsky S-61 Helicopter
S76	H	Sikorsky S-76 Helicopter
TRD	J	British Aerospace (Hawker Siddeley) Trident (All series)
TU3	J	Tupolev TU-134
TU5	J	Tupolev TU-154
VCV	T	British Aerospace (BAC-Vickers) Viscount (All series)
VGF	T	British Aerospace (BAC-Vickers) Merchantman Freighter
WLH	H	Westland 30 Helicopter
WWF	J	Israel Aircraft Ind 1124 Westwind Freighter
WWP	J	Israel Aircraft Industries Westwind Passenger
YK2	J	Yakovlev YAK 42
YK4	J	Yakovlev YAK 40
YN5	P	Yunshuji 5
YN7	T	Yunshuji 7
YS1	T	NAMC YS-11
100	J	Fokker 100
14F	J	British Aerospace 146 Freighter
146	J	British Aerospace 146 (All series) passenger
31F	J	Airbus Industrie A310 Freighter
310	J	Airbus Industrie A310 (All series) Passenger
320	J	Airbus Industrie A320 (All series)
37F	P	Boeing 377 Stratocruiser Freighter
70F	J	Boeing 707 Freighter (All series)
70M	J	Boeing 707 (Mixed Configuration)
707	J	Boeing 707 Passenger (All series)
72F	J	Boeing 727 Freighter (All series)
72M	J	Boeing 727 (Mixed Configuration)
72S	J	Boeing 727-200 Passenger
727	J	Boeing 727 Passenger (All series)
73F	J	Boeing 737-200 Freighter
73M	J	Boeing 737-200 (Mixed Configuration)
73S	J	Boeing 737-200 Passenger
733	J	Boeing 737-300 Passenger
734	J	Boeing 737-400 Passenger
735	J	Boeing 737-500 Passenger
737	J	Boeing 737 Passenger(All series)
74D	J	Boeing 747-300 (Mixed Configuration)
74E	J	Boeing 747-400 (Mixed Configuration)
74F	J	Boeing 747 Freighter
74L	J	Boeing 747 SP
74M	J	Boeing 747 (Mixed Configuration)
743	J	Boeing 747-300 Passenger
744	J	Boeing 747-400 Passenger
747	J	Boeing 747 Passenger (All series)
75F	J	Boeing 757 Freighter
757	J	Boeing 757-200 Passenger
763	J	Boeing 767-300/300ER
767	J	Boeing 767 (All series)
76F	J	Boeing 767 Freighter
BUS		Bus
EQV		Equipment Varies
HOV		Hovercraft
LCH		Launch/Boat
LMO		Limousine
RFS		Road Feeder Service (Truck)
‡‡‡		Train

The codes used in this publication are Aircraft General Designators as specified in Appendix A Standard Schedule Information Manual issued by IATA.

Aircraft types

The *ABC World Airways Guide* publishes details of aircraft types. Please study the extract. A code is used to describe the aircraft: pure jet (J), prop-jet (T), propeller (P), helicopter (H) or amphibian/seaplane (A) (can touch down on land or sea). Some of the descriptions give the number of passengers allowed on board. If you know the aircraft code but not the description (the code only is given in the timetable), the lower half of the page very kindly *decodes* the abbreviations!

It is often very important to clients to know the aircraft type before making the journey, and it is part of giving a good service to supply *all* the information.

For example, the aircraft coded 747 is a Boeing 747 jet, and it accommodates 400 passengers. Incidentally, the 747 is often referred to as a jumbo because of its size. The 747 cruises at 30,000 ft at 575 mph and has four engines, all mounted on the wings.

As another example, the aircraft coded SSC is a British Aerospace Concorde (BAC). This is a supersonic aircraft. It flies at a height of 50,000 ft, approximately 20,000 ft higher than subsonic jets; this means it can avoid any bad weather conditions. It reduces flying times by half, carries up to 100 passengers (the body of the aircraft is long and narrow) and cruises at speeds in excess of 1450 mph – twice the speed of sound. It is used on long journeys, but is also used extensively on charter flights: tour operators charter the Concorde for special short flights, such as anniversaries, birthdays and fun days.

Flight information

We now need to know our air industry codes, or at least where to find the information. The red and blue books of the *ABC World Airways Guide* will provide all the information and your travel agency will have several copies from which to work. The ABC Guide is published monthly and it is important to refer to the current guide for up-to-date information.

Please study the extract titled 'Quick reference section – how to use'. We are given, as an example of how to read the timetable, the flights between Oslo and Paris. Oslo is in Norway. The three-letter code is OSL. The city is +0200, which means two hours ahead of Greenwich Mean Time (GMT).

We are advised that there are two airports (APT): Fornebu, with three-letter code FBE; and Gardermoen, with three-letter code GEN. Fornebu Airport is 5 miles (8 km) south-west of Oslo (SW of Oslo), and Gardermoen is 32 miles (51 km) north-east of Oslo (NE of Oslo).

Every airline is also given a two-letter code and identification number. We are advised of the number of minutes before departure to check in for that particular airline's domestic (Dom) and international (Int) flights.

The ABC World Airways guide publish the two-letter and identification number for every airline and can be found easily in the ABC. For the purpose of reading the check-in times at Fornebu and Gardermoen airports, just the airlines used in this explanation will be decoded.

BU   Braathans (Norway)
CO   Continental Airline (USA)
DA   Danair Services (UK)
EO   Air Nordic (Sweden)

Quick Reference Section—How to use

The ABC Quick Reference Section gives a world-wide coverage of flight information. Nearly 4,000 cities arranged alphabetically combine to give more than 83,000 city to city entries. The information you require is easy to find. FROM each Departure City TO each Arrival City; which airlines fly the route and when they go. The *specially prepared example* below shows how clearly and concisely this and other information is presented.

OSLO TO PARIS

FROM **OSLO** NORWAY **(OSL)** +0200

APT ●FORNEBU (FBU) 5mls/8kms SW of Oslo. Check-in Dom 30mins, Int 35 except BU 20, CO, DA, EO 30, FI 60, ID, KL 45, SU 60, VB 30, WF 20.
●GARDERMOEN (GEN) 32mls/51kms NE of Oslo. Check-in Int 45mins except LY 2hrs 15, First/Business Class 75, NC Dom 20, Int 30, NW 60, TW Int 60.

STR To FORNEBU AIRPORT
BUS
Service, from City Centre (Central Station, Vestbanen Station, Braathen SAFE Terminal). Journey Time 20mins. Enquiry, Tel: 02-596814.
To GARDERMOEN AIRPORT
BUS
Service, from City Centre (Hotel Scandinavia, Holbergs Gate). Report 1hr 45mins prior to departure.

DEPARTURE CITY INFORMATION

Clock Time (e.g. +0200) variation from GMT applicable during the period of validity of this guide.

Three letter codes (e.g. OSL, FBU) identify Cities and Airports - see page 37.

APT — Airport (and code where more than one airport serves the departure city) with distance from City centre.
● highlights each airport at multi-airport cities.

STR — Surface Transport City to Airport.

PARIS FRANCE (PAR)

ORY-ORLY CDG-CH DE GAULLE

ARRIVAL CITY INFORMATION

City name and code plus code and name of each airport served at multi-airport arrival cities.

Validity From	To	Days Of Service	Dep	Arr	Flight No	Acft	Class	Stops

KEY TO FLIGHT INFORMATION

Shown at the top of the first column on each page.
Acft — refers to the type of aircraft (see page 21).
Class — refers to inflight Class of Service (see decode below).
Stops — refers to the number of stops en-route for through flights and transfer connections. For en-route stops see Flight Routings page 45.

Validity From	To	Days Of Service	Dep	Arr	Flight No	Acft	Class	Stops
25 Mar	-	12345 7	0755FBU	1005CDG	SK 561	D9S	CMBGK	0
-	-	1234567	1410FBU	1625CDG	AF 1135	737	CM	0
31 Mar	-	1234567	1600FBU	1820ORY	SK 571	D9S	CMBGK	0
					SK 571 - Op subj to confirmation			
-	-	1234567	1640FBU	1855CDG	SK 569	D9S	CMB	0

THROUGH FLIGHT INFORMATION

Flights are shown in chronological order of departure.
Through flight notes apply to the flight immediately above the note.
Departure and arrival times are shown in **bold type**.
For explanation of abbreviated Schedule Texts see page 36.

TRANSFER CONNECTIONS

Ⓐ	-	1234567	0730FBU	0835CPH	SK 683	M80	CMBG	0
			0940CPH	1135CDG	SK 563	M80	CMBGK	0
Ⓑ	23 Mar	12345	0750FBU	0915LGW	AE 040	737	CYMBL	0
			1200LHR	1400CDG	AF 813	AB3	CM	0
Ⓒ	26 Mar	-	12345	1415FBU	1525CDG	SK 411	D9S	FY	0
			1615CPH	1830AMS	SK 555	D9S	Y	0
			1920AMS	2020CDG	KL 333	DC9	CMBG	0
Ⓓ	26 Mar	-	12345	1540FBU	1850BRU	SN 774	73S	CYBK	1
			2000BRU	2050CDG	SN 211 /AF 211	73S	CYBK	0

TRANSFER CONNECTION FLIGHT INFORMATION

Flights are shown in chronological order of departure.

SINGLE CONNECTIONS involving one change of flight en-route are shown on two lines. The first line is from departure city to the transfer point and the second line from the transfer point to the arrival city.

DOUBLE CONNECTIONS involving two changes of flight en-route are shown on three lines. The first line is from departure city to the first transfer point, the second line is from the first to the second transfer point, and the third line is from the second transfer point to the arrival city.

Airport codes (e.g. CPH) are used to indicate transfer points.

Change of airport at a transfer point is indicated by the relevent codes (e.g. LHR, LGW) against the arr. and dep. times at the transfer point. Times at point of origin and final destination are shown in **bold type**. A minority of transfer connections are via a higher fare routing. If in doubt, check with the initial carrier to verify if the standard fare applies.

Ⓐ Single transfer via Copenhagen
Ⓑ Single transfer with change of airports at London
Ⓒ Double transfer via Copenhagen and Amsterdam
Ⓓ Single transfer via Brussels

ALL TIMES ARE LOCAL CLOCK TIMES

EXPLANATION OF CODES AND SYMBOLS

DAYS OF SERVICE
1 = Monday, 2 = Tuesday, etc.
(e.g. 1 3 567 = Monday, Wednesday, Friday, Saturday, Sunday)

STOPS
0 = Non stop, 1 = One stop, 2 = Two stops, etc.
M = Multi-stop (more than 8 stops)

DAY INDICATOR
* Following day ‡ Third day
§ Fourth day ¶ Arrival previous day

CLASSES OF SERVICE/RESERVATIONS BOOKING DESIGNATORS
When the Class of Service/Reservations Booking Designators decoded below are displayed as small letters (eg fy) this indicates the availability of an OFF PEAK TARIFF
R Supersonic Class
P First Class Premium/Luxury First Class
F First Class
A First Class Discounted
J Business Class Premium
C Business Class/Coach/Economy Class on some flights/Sky Coach Class/Thrift Class (Brazil)
D Controlled Inventory or Business Class Discounted
S Standard Class
W Coach/Economy Premium Class
Y Coach/Economy Class/Business Class on some international flights
B Coach/Economy Discounted Class
H Coach/Economy Discounted Class
Q Coach/Economy Discounted Class
M Coach/Economy Discounted Class
T Coach/Economy Discounted Class
K Thrift Class

L Thrift Discounted Class
V Thrift Discounted Class
G Conditional Reservation
U Air Shuttle (no reservations needed, seat guaranteed)
E Air Shuttle (no reservations allowed)

◆ 'Shared Designator' flight—see page 44

Aircraft Types (e.g. D9S) - see page 21
Airline Prefixes (e.g. SK) - see page 14
City/Airport codes (e.g. OSL) - see page 37

FOR TARIFF INFORMATION AND MILEAGES REFER TO FARES SECTION.

FI   Icelandair (Iceland)
KL   KLM Royal Dutch Airlines (The Netherlands)
SU   Aeroflot (USSR)
VB   Birmingham European Airways (UK)
WF   Wideroe's Flyveselskap (Norway)

In the ABC extract we can read the latest check-in time at Fornebu airport for domestic flights is 30 minutes and for international flights 35 minutes *except* for the following airlines on international flights.

BU the latest check-in time is 20 minutes
CO, DA, EO check-in time 30 minutes
FI 60 minutes
ID, KL 45 minutes
SU 60 minutes
VB 30 minutes
WF 20 minutes

We are given the same information for Gardermoen airport.
    STR means surface transport between the city centre and the airport. Here we are advised that a bus can be used from Central Station to Fornebu Airport, and that the journey takes 20 minutes.
    From Hotel Scandinavia (city centre) to Gardermoen Airport there is also a bus service and passengers are advised to report for the bus 1¾ hours before flight departure.
    On arrival at Paris we have two airports, Orly (ORY) and Charles de Gaulle (CDG).
    The next table gives us the flight details. The validity is from certain dates and to (until) certain dates. The first flight operates from 25 March as no (until) date is shown the flight operates until further notice. The days of service are coded from Monday (1) through to Sunday (7). The departure time is given on the 24-hour clock. The city of departure or airport of departure is indicated: in this example the first flight leaves Fornebu Airport at 0755 hours. The arrival is at 1005 hours at Charles de Gaulle airport in Paris. Flight number is SK 561 (Scandinavian airlines). The aircraft (Acft) is a D9S (we would look at the aircraft types page for the decoding). Letter codes are used to indicate the McDonnell Douglas. Did you check? Class of travel available on the aircraft: see the explanation of codes and symbols. Notice that there is no first class (F) on this short flight. The last column tells us how many stops the aircraft makes en route. In this example we see a circle meaning no stops are made, i.e. it is a direct non-stop flight.
    Now study the transfer connections flight information box.

Single transfer

In the first example the passenger will travel from Oslo (FBU airport) to Paris (CDG airport) via Copenhagen (CPH). The flight departs FBU at 0730 hours, arrives CPH at 0835 hours, departs CPH at 0940 hours and arrives CDG at 1135 hours.

Validity From	To	Days of Service	Dep	Arr	Flight No.	Acft	Class	Stops

FROM GDANSK POLAND (GDN) CONTINUED

From	To	Days	Dep	Arr	Flight No.	Acft	Class	Stops
-	-	123456	1505	1610	LO516	AN4	Y	0
-	-	123456	1640	1745	LO520	AN4	Y	0

GDYNIA POLAND

See GDANSK

FROM GEBE INDONESIA (GEB) +0900

From	To	Days	Dep	Arr	Flight No.	Acft	Class	Stops
TERNATE (TTE)								
-	-	2 4 6	0830	0835	MZ7943	CS2	Y	0

FROM GEELONG VI AUSTRALIA (GEX) +1000

APT GEELONG General check-in 15mins.

From	To	Days	Dep	Arr	Flight No.	Acft	Class	Stops
LAUNCESTON (LST)								
-	-	2 4 6	1400	1530	FB306	PAG	S	0
FB 306 -Op subj to confirmation								

FROM GELADI ETHIOPIA (GLC) +0300

APT GELADI Check-in ET Dom 45mins.

From	To	Days	Dep	Arr	Flight No.	Acft	Class	Stops
DIRE DAWA (DIR)								
-	-	2	1225	1440	ET426	DHT	SML	1
-	-	6	1225	1440	ET466	DHT	SML	1
WARDER (WRA)								
-	-	2	1225	1255	ET426	DHT	SML	0
-	-	6	1225	1255	ET466	DHT	SML	0

FROM GEMENA ZAIRE (GMA) +0100

APT GEMENA Check-in 60mins except ZM 2hrs.

From	To	Days	Dep	Arr	Flight No.	Acft	Class	Stops
GBADOLITE (BDT)								
-	-	2	1055	1125	QC224	73S	FY	0
KINSHASA (FIH)								
-	-	2	0900	1020	ZM[illegible]	[illegible]	Y	0
-	-	5	1200	1425	Q[illegible]	73S	FY	1
-	-	6	1650	1810	ZM537	727	Y	0
MBANDAKA (MDK)								
-	-	5	1200	1250	QC723	73S	FY	0

FROM GENDA WUHA ETHIOPIA (ETE) +0300

APT GENDA WUHA General check-in 45mins.

From	To	Days	Dep	Arr	Flight No.	Acft	Class	Stops
BAHAR DAR (BJR)								
-	-	1 34 6	1205	1325	ET303	DHT	SML	1
GONDAR (GDQ)								
-	-	1 34 6	1205	1245	ET303	DHT	SML	0

FROM GENEINA SUDAN (EGN) +0200

APT GENEINA 5mls/8kms. Check-in 30mins except SD 60.

From	To	Days	Dep	Arr	Flight No.	Acft	Class	Stops
EL FASHER (ELF)								
-	-	1	1325	1415	SD413	F50	Y	0
KHARTOUM (KRT)								
-	-	4	0955	1320	SD411	F50	Y	1
-	-	1	1325	1645	SD413	F50	Y	1
NYALA (UYL)								
-	-	4	0955	1045	SD411	F50	Y	0

FROM GENERAL ROCA ARGENTINA (GNR) -0300(-0200 From 21 October)

APT GENERAL ROCA Check-in AR 60mins.

From	To	Days	Dep	Arr	Flight No.	Acft	Class	Stops
BUENOS AIRES (BUE)				AEP-JORGE NEWBERY				
-	-	2	1450	1920 AEP	LD209	F27	S	2
-	-	2 4 67	1540	1725 AEP	AR8642	F28	Y	0
COLONIA CATRL (CCT)								
-	-	1	1320	1350	LD208	F27	S	0
CUTRAL CO (CUT)								
-	-	1	1320	1525	LD208	F27	S	2
LA PLATA (LPG)								
-	-	2	1450	1845	LD209	F27	S	1
MAR DEL PLATA (MDQ)								
-	-	2	1450	1720	LD209	F27	S	0
NEUQUEN (NQN)								
-	-	1	1320	1435	LD208	F27	S	1
S C BARILOCHE (BRC)								
-	-	1	1320	1750	LD208	F27	S	5
SAN MARTIN (CPC)								
-	-	1	1320	1700	LD208	F27	S	4
ZAPALA (APZ)								
-	-	1	1320	1600	LD208	F27	S	3

FROM GENEVA SWITZERLAND (GVA) +0200(+0100 From 30 September)

APT GENEVA 3mls/5kms N of city centre. Check-in 30mins except AH, KM, KU 90, LO, LZ, MS, TW 60, AI, IR, LY, MK, RJ 2hrs, OA, RK 45, SV 3hrs, FV 20.

STR RAIL
SBB Service from Geneva (Cornavin Station). Journey Time 6mins.
Geneva Airport Railway Station is part of the Swiss Inter-City network.
TROLLEYBUS
TPG Service 10 from City Centre (Bel-Air and Cornavin Station). Journey Time 20mins.

From	To	Days	Dep	Arr	Flight No.	Acft	Class	Stops
AALBORG (AAL)								
-	3Aug	345	0725	0930 CPH	SR406 /SK406	100	FCYML	0
			1110 CPH	1155	DX207 /SK207	M80	YMB	0
13Aug	-	12345	0725	0930 CPH	SR406 /SK406	100	FCYML	0
			1110 CPH	1155	DX207 /SK207	D9S	YMB	0
-	-	1234567	1915	2115 CPH	SK618 /SR618	D9S	CMBGK	0
			2215 CPH	2300	DX221 /SK221	M80	YMB	0
AARHUS (AAR)								
4Aug	-	1234567	0725	0930 CPH	SR406 /SK406	100	FCYML	0
			1300 CPH	1335	DX241 /SK241	D9S	YMB	0
13Aug	-	12345	0725	0930 CPH	SR406 /SK406	100	FCYML	0
			1055 CPH	1130	DX239 /SK239	D9S	YMB	0
-	-	1234567	1915	2115 CPH	SK618 /SR618	D9S	CMBGK	0
			2225 CPH	2300	DX259 /SK259	M80	YMB	0
ABERDEEN UK (ABZ)								
-	-	12345	0745	0920 AMS	SR788	M87	CYML ♦	0
			1100 AMS	1215	UK855	146	CML	1
-	-	1234567	0840	0920 LGW	BA735	73S	CM	0
			1100 LGW	1330	DA134	146	YML	1
-	-	1234567	0905	0945 LHR	BA723	757	CM	0
			1320 LHR	1450	BA5910	320	M	0
-	-	12345	0905	0945 LHR	BA723	757	CM	0
			1210 LHR	1335	BA5908	73S	M	0
-	-	7	1020	1150 AMS	KL320	737	CMBLS	0
			1250 AMS	1400	UK841	146	CML	1
-	-	1234567	1220	1255 LHR	BA725	757	CM	0
			1600 LHR	1725	BA5912	320	M	0
-	-	1234567	1620	1655 LHR	BA729	320	CM	0
			1955 LHR	2120	BA5916	320	M	0
-	-	12345 7	1620	1655 LHR	BA729	320	CM	0
			1800 LHR	1930	BA5914	320	M	0
ABIDJAN (ABJ)								
5Oct	-	5	1240	1735	RK031	D10	FJY	0
-	28Sep	5	1340	1735	RK031	D10	FJY	0
-	29Sep	6	1350	1750	SR256	D10	FCYML	0
6Oct	-	6	1350	1850	SR256	D10	FCYML	0
TRANSFER CONNECTIONS								
-	-	1	0815	0920 CDG	SR722	M80	FCYML	0
			1100 CDG	1635	UT809	D10	FJY	1
-	-	5	0855	1010 BRU	SN792	73S	CYBK	0
			1225 BRU	1950	SN421	310	CYBH	1
-	-	4	0915	1020 CDG	AF961	737	CM	0
			1215 CDG	1830	UT803	D10	FJY	1
-	-	6	0915	1020 CDG	AF961	737	CM	0
			1200 CDG	1735	UT805	74D	FJY	1
-	-	4	1315	1500 MAD	IB551	72S	CMLK	0
			1730 MAD	2255	IB855	AB3	FCYM	1
-	-	5	1945	2035 NCE	AF1995	72S	CM	0
			*0030 NCE	*0400	UT801	D10	FJY	0
-	-	2	2045	2150 CDG	AF969	737	CM	0
			2250 CDG	*0605	UT831	D10	FJY	2
-	-	4	2045	2150 CDG	AF969	737	CM	0
			2355 CDG	*0405	UT305	74D	FJY	0
-	-	7	2045	2150 CDG	AF969	737	CM	0
			2359 CDG	*0715	UT807	D10	FJY	2
12Sep	19Sep	3	2045	2150 CDG	AF969	737	CM	0
			2355 CDG	*0410	UT815	D10	FJY	0
ABU DHABI (AUH)								
-	-	7	0745	0920 AMS	SR788	100	FCYM ♦	0
			1135 AMS	2155	KL549	310	CM	1
-	-	3	0815	0920 CDG	SR722	M80	FCYML	0
			1030 CDG	2250	AF156	AB3	FCY	2
-	-	7	0815	0920 CDG	SR722	M80	FCYML	0
			1030 CDG	2115	AF162	AB3	FCY	1
-	-	1 45	0830	0910 LHR	SR830	310	FCYML	0
			1030 LHR	2245	BA125	767	FJM	1
-	-	3 6	0830	0910 LHR	SR830	310	FCYML	0
			1030 LHR	2310	BA125	767	FJM	1
-	-	1	0915	1020 CDG	AF961	737	CM	0
			1115 CDG	2125	AF150	AB3	FCY	1
-	22Sep	6	1020	1150 AMS	KL320	737	CMBLS	0
			1320 AMS	2205	KL543	310	CM	0
-	-	3	1020	1150 AMS	KL320	737	CMBLS	0
			1315 AMS	2355	UL566	L10	FCYB	1
-	-	4	1020	1150 AMS	KL320	737	CMBLS	0
			1300 AMS	2325	KL805	747	FCM	1
-	-	5	1020	1150 AMS	KL320	737	CMBLS	0
			1300 AMS	*0005	UL564	L10	FCYB	1
-	-	7	1020	1150 AMS	KL320	737	CMBLS	0
			1350 AMS	*0035	UL564	L10	FCYB	1
-	-	2 4	1100	1215 FRA	LH1855	737	FCMTK	0
			1330 FRA	2320	LH630	310	FCDMB	1
-	-	7	1100	1215 FRA	LH1855	737	FCMTK	0
			1350 FRA	2359	LH628	AB3	FCDMB	1
-	-	2 4	1105	1155 ZRH	SR164	D10	FCYML	0
			1240 ZRH	2230	SR374	310	FCYML	1
-	-	7	1105	1155 ZRH	SR198	74D	FCYML	0
			1240 ZRH	2230	SR374	310	FCYML	1
-	-	5	1115	1310 WAW	LO296	TU3	YML	0
			2030 WAW	*0735	LO467	TU5	YMKL	2
-	-	3 7	1330	1845 AMM	RJ128	310	FCY	0
			2145 AMM	*0130	RJ602	310	FCY	0
10Aug	14Sep	5	1350	2035 CAI	MS772	AB3	FY	1
			*0100 CAI	*0640	MS892	AB3	FY	1
-	-	6	1445	1945 CAI	SR348 /MS348	310	FCYML	0
			*0130 CAI	*0615	MS914	AB3	FY	0
-	-	3	1455	1625 AMS	KL322	737	CMBLS	0
			1720 AMS	*0155	KL839	74M	FCM	0
-	-	1	1510	1850 ATH	OA136	73S	FYM	0
			2050 ATH	*0350	OA345	AB3	FYM	1
-	-	3	1510	1850 ATH	OA136	73S	FYM	0
			2050 ATH	*0545	OA345	AB3	FYM	2
-	21Sep	5	1705	1810 CDG	AF971	737	CM	0
			1925 CDG	*0705	AF158	AB3	FCY	2
ACAPULCO (ACA)								
-	27Aug	1	1315	1500 MAD	IB551	72S	CMLK	0
			1710 MAD	2000 MEX	IB979	747	PCYMK	0
			2215 MEX	2305	MX729	72S	Y	0
-	30Aug	4 7	1315	1500 MAD	IB551	72S	CMLK	0
			1710 MAD	2000 MEX	IB967	747	PCYMK	0
			2215 MEX	2305	MX729	72S	Y	0
2Sep		4 7	1315	1500 MAD	IB551	72S	CMLK	0
			1710 MAD	2000 MEX	IB967	747	PCYMK	0
			2230 MEX	2325	MX729	72S	YBQMV	0
3Sep	-	1	1315	1500 MAD	IB551	72S	CMLK	0
			1710 MAD	2000 MEX	IB979	747	PCYMK	0
			2230 MEX	2325	MX729	72S	YBQMV	0
ACCRA (ACC)								
	29Sep	6	1350	1940	SR256	D10	FCYML	1
6Oct		6	1350	2040	SR256	D10	FCYML	1
TRANSFER CONNECTIONS								
-	-	1 5	0745	0920 AMS	SR788	M87	CYML ♦	0
			1200 AMS	1830	KL585	D10	FCM	1
-	-	3	0745	0920 AMS	SR788	M87	CYML ♦	0
			1200 AMS	1830	KL587 /GH587	D10	FCM	1
-	-	2	1040	1130 ZRH	SR655	M80	FCYML	0
			1230 ZRH	1640	SR248	310	FCYML	0
-	-	5	1105	1155 ZRH	SR126	74D	FCYML	0
			1250 ZRH	1855	SR264	310	FCYML	1
-	-	5	1340	1735 ABJ	RK031	D10	FJY	0
			2050 ABJ	2140	GH545	DC9	FY	0
-	-	4	1750	1825 LGW	BA739	73S	CM	0
			*0040 LGW	*0605	BA079	L10	FJM	0
ADANA (ADA)								
-	-	6	1215	1605 IST	TK918	727	Y	0
			1920 IST	2045	TK672	727	Y	0
-	-	1 4	1220	1730 IST	TK920	310	CY	1
			1920 IST	2045	TK466	310	Y	0
ADDIS ABABA (ADD)								
-	-	2 6	0710	0830 FRA	LH1851	737	FCMTK	0
			1015 FRA	1955	LH590	AB3	FCDMB	1
-	-	2	1445	1945 CAI	SR346	310	FCYML	0
			*0330 CAI	*0830	ET725	72S	FSML	1
-	-	4	1510	1840 ATH	OA136	727	FYM	0
			*0200 ATH	*0800	ET745	72S	FSML	1
-	-	7	1510	1850 ATH	OA136	73S	FYM	0
			*0200 ATH	*0800	ET775	72S	FSML	1
-	-	1	1720	*0120 JED	SR292	D10	FCYML	1
			*0630 JED	*0830	ET629	72S	FSML	0
-	-	1	1825	1950 FCO	SR612	M80	FCYML	0
			*0115 FCO	*0800	ET711	767	FJSML	0
-	-	6	1825	1950 FCO	SR612	M80	FCYML	0
			*0115 FCO	*0800	ET761	767	FJSML	0
-	-	3	1845	2005 FRA	SR544	M80	FCYML	0
			2230 FRA	*0800	ET731	767	FJSML	1
-	-	5	1845	2005 FRA	SR544	M80	FCYML	0
			*0030 FRA	*0815	ET751	767	FJSML	0
-	-	7	1845	2005 FRA	SR544	M80	FCYML	0
			*0030 FRA	*0815	ET771	767	FJSML	0
ADELAIDE (ADL)								
-	-	7	1620	1655 LHR	BA729	320	CM	0
			2030 LHR	‡0615	BA9	747	FJM	3
-	-	2	1815	1900 ZRH	SR691	310	FCYML	0
			2030 ZRH	*1730 SIN	SQ35	743	PJY	1
			*2250 SIN	‡0640	SQ227	74D	PJY	0
-	-	7	1820	1905 ZRH	SR941	100	FCYML	0
			2030 ZRH	*1730 SIN	SQ35	743	PJY	1
			*2215 SIN	‡0915	SQ225	747	PJY	1
-	-	3	1835	2005 AMS	SR794	M80	FCYM ♦	0
			2235 AMS	‡0525 MEL	KL843	747	FCM	2
			‡0715 MEL	‡0755	TN22	72S	FJYB	0
-	-	7	1835	1915 LHR	SR836	M80	FCYML	0
			2030 LHR	‡0615	BA9	747	FJM	3
-	-	5	1905	1935 LHR	BA731	757	CM	0
			2215 LHR	‡0705	BA9	747	FJM	2
-	-	5	2000	2035 LHR	SR838	M80	FCYML	0
			2215 LHR	‡0705	BA9	747	FJM	2
AGADIR (AGA)								
-	23Sep	7	1430	1555	AT963	72S	YBM	0
30Sep	-	7	1430	1755	AT963	72S	YBM	1
5Oct		5	1720	1945	AT935	72S	YBM	0
	3Aug	5	1820	1945	AT935	72S	YBM	0
10Aug	31Aug	5	1820	1955	AT935	737	YBM	0
7Sep	28Sep	5	1820	1945	AT935	72S	YBM	0
TRANSFER CONNECTIONS								
-	-	3	1610	2015 CMN	AT995	737	YBM	2
			2110 CMN	2210	AT411	737	Y	0
-	-	7	1615	1720 CDG	SR726	M80	FCYML	0
			1940 ORY	2220	AT751 /AF751	74L	FYBM	1
AT 751 Plane change at intermediate stop								
-	-	7	1815	1905 CMN	AT937	72S	FYBM	0
			2120 CMN	2220	AT751	737	FYW	0
-	-	3	1900	2000 CMN	AT933	737	FYBM	0
			2110 CMN	2210	AT411	737	Y	0
-	-	5	1900	2000 CMN	AT933	737	FYBM	0
			2100 CMN	2155	AT407	72S	YW	0
AJACCIO (AJA)								
-	14Oct	7	1415	1520	AF1991	320	M	0
TRANSFER CONNECTIONS								
-	-	1 3	1425	1520 MRS	SR762	100	FCYML	0
			1700 MRS	1750	AF2509	72S	Y	0
-	-	2 4	1425	1520 MRS	SR762	100	FCYML	0
			1840 MRS	1930	AF1503	72S	Y	0
-	-	5	1425	1520 MRS	SR762	100	FCYML	0
			1700 MRS	1750	AF1509	72S	Y	0
-	-	6	1425	1520 MRS	SR762	100	FCYML	0
			1650 MRS	1740	IT249	AB3	Y	0
-	-	7	1425	1520 MRS	SR762	100	FCYML	0
			1830 MRS	1920	AF1503	72S	Y	0
ALBANY NY USA (ALB)								
-	-	1234567	1045	1520 JFK	PA119	310	FCYBM	1
			2230 JFK	2320	PA4878	DH7	YBMQ ♦	0
-	4Aug	6	1125	1550 JFK	TW831	747	FCYBQ	1
			1815 JFK	2015	TW7797	BE1	YBQM ♦	1
TW 831 -Plane change at intermediate stop								
-	-	1234567	1125	1550 JFK	TW831	747	FCYBQ	1
			2010 JFK	2135	TW7788	BE1	YBQM ♦	1
TW 831 -Plane change at intermediate stop								
11Aug	-	6	1125	1550 JFK	TW831	747	FCYBQ	1
			1815 JFK	2050	TW7797	BE1	YBQM ♦	2
TW 831 -Plane change at intermediate stop								
ALBUQUERQUE (ABQ)								
-	-	1234567	1125	1550 JFK	TW831	747	FCYBQ	1
			1823 JFK	2248	TW179	767	FCYBQ	1
TW 831 -Plane change at intermediate stop								
TW 179 -Plane change at intermediate stop								
ALEXANDRIA EG (ALY)								
-	-	23 6	1100	1215 FRA	LH1855	737	FCMTK	0
			1400 FRA	1905	LH676	737	FCDMB	0
ALGHERO (AHO)								
-	-	1234567	1825	1950 FCO	SR612	M80	FCYML	0
			2145 FCO	2240	BM112	DC9	YHMTL	0
ALGIERS (ALG)								
-	29Sep	1 34 6	1310	1405	SR226	M80	FCYML	0
1Oct	-	1 34 6	1310	1505	SR226	M80	FCYML	0
30Sep	-	2 567	1445	1640	AH2043	73S	FY	0
-	29Sep	2 567	1545	1640	AH2043	73S	FY	0
TRANSFER CONNECTIONS								
-	-	6	1550	1740 TUN	TU701	72S	YB	0
			2120 TUN	2140	TU706	737	Y	0
ALICANTE (ALC)								
-	-	1234567	1355	1515 BCN	SR666	M80	FCYML	0
			1635 BCN	1730	IB721	72S	CM	0
-	-	1234567	1840	2035 MAD	SR654	M80	FCYML	0
			2240 MAD	2335	IB753	72S	CM	0
-	-	1 3 5	1855	2015 BCN	IB561	72S	CMLK	0
			2255 BCN	2350	IB409	72S	CY	0
-	-	2 4 67	1855	2015 BCN	IB561	72S	CMLK	0
			2250 BCN	2350	IB667	72S	CM	0
AMMAN (AMM)								
30Sep	30Oct	3 7	1230	1845	RJ128	310	FCY	0
7Oct	-	3 7	1230	1745	RJ128	310	FCY	0
-	26Sep	3 7	1330	1845	RJ128	310	FCY	0
TRANSFER CONNECTIONS								
-	-	1	0905	0945 LHR	BA723	757	CM	0
			1200 LHR	1915	RJ112 /BA112	310	FCY	0
-	-	5 7	0905	0945 LHR	BA723	757	CM	0
			1145 LHR	1900	RJ112 /BA112	310	FCY	0
-	22Sep	6	1015	1120 CDG	AF963	737	CM	0
			1400 CDG	2140	AF144	AB3	FCY	1
-	-	1	1015	1120 CDG	AF963	737	CM	0
			1230 CDG	1830	AF136	AB3	FCY	0
-	-	3 7	1100	1215 FRA	LH1855	737	FCMTK	0
			1400 FRA	1925	LH652	AB3	FCDMB	0
-	-	4	1100	1215 FRA	LH1855	737	FCMTK	0
			1340 FRA	1915	LH660	737	FCDMB	0
-	-	2 4	1125	1210 ZRH	SR929	100	FCYML	0
			1310 ZRH	2010	SR358	M80	FCYML	1
-	-	3	1215	1320 CDG	SR724	M80	FCYML	0
			1440 CDG	2220	AF142	AB3	FCY	1
-	-	5	1310	1755 ATH	OA134	727	FYM	1
			2015 ATH	2245	OA313	73S	FYM	0
-	-	7	1510	1850 ATH	OA136	73S	FYM	0
			2015 ATH	2245	OA313	73S	FYM	0
AMSTERDAM (AMS)								
-	-	12345	0745	0920	SR788	M87	CYML ♦	0
-	-	7	0745	0920	SR788	100	FCYM ♦	0
-	-	1234567	1020	1150	KL320	737	CMBLS	0
-	-	1234567	1455	1625	KL322	737	CMBLS	0
-	-	1 6	1835	2005	SR794	100	FCYM ♦	0
-	-	234 7	1835	2005	SR794	M80	FCYM ♦	0
-	-	5	1835	2005	SR794	M87	CYML ♦	0
Need a hotel in AMS? You'll find more than 70 in your copy of ABC Worldwide Hotel Guide.								
TRANSFER CONNECTIONS								
-	-	1234567	0601	0640 ZRH	SR610	M80	FCYML	0
			1020 ZRH	1150	KL312	737	CMBLS	0
-	-	123456	0700	0740 ZRH	SR921	M80	FCYM ♦	0
			1020 ZRH	1150	KL312	737	CMBLS	0
-	-	12345	0800	0850 ZRH	SR923	SF3	YML ♦	0
			1020 ZRH	1150	KL312	737	CMBLS	0
-	-	123456	0905	1015 LUX	LG362 /LX362	EM2	MK	0
			1205 LUX	1315	LG781	F27	MK	0
-	-	12345	1235	1325 ZRH	SR937	100	FCYML	0
			1445 ZRH	1615	KL314	737	CMBLS	0
-	-	67	1305	1345 ZRH	AH2042	73S	FY	0
			1445 ZRH	1615	KL314	737	CMBLS	0
-	-	6	1315	1400 ZRH	SR931	100	FCYML	0
			1445 ZRH	1615	KL314	737	CMBLS	0
-	-	12345 7	1615	1705 ZRH	SR935	SF3	YML ♦	0
			1905 ZRH	2035	KL316	737	CMBLS	0
-	-	1 4	1720	1815 ZRH	SR292	D10	FCYML	0
			1905 ZRH	2035	KL316	737	CMBLS	0
-	-	12 6	1725	1810 ZRH	SR205	M80	FCYML	0
			1905 ZRH	2035	KL316	737	CMBLS	0
ANCHORAGE (ANC)				ANC-INTERNATIONAL				
-	29Sep	2 4 6	1105	1225 ANC	SR164	D10	FCYML	1
2Oct	-	2 4 6	1105	1325 ANC	SR164	D10	FCYML	1
TRANSFER CONNECTIONS								
-	-	3	0830	0910 LHR	SR830	310	FCYML	0
			1030 LHR	1025 ANC	BA5	747	FJM	0
-	-	5	0830	0910 LHR	SR830	310	FCYML	0
			1200 LHR	1155 ANC	BA5	747	FJM	0
-	-	6	0830	0910 LHR	SR830	310	FCYML	0
			1125 LHR	1120 ANC	BA5	747	FJM	0
-	-	2 5 7	0855	1010 BRU	SN792	73S	CYBK	0
			1300 BRU	1200 ANC	SN261	D1M	CYBH	0
-	-	5 7	0905	0945 LHR	BA723	757	CM	0
			1200 LHR	1155 ANC	BA5	747	FJM	0
-	-	6	0905	0945 LHR	BA723	757	CM	0
			1125 LHR	1120 ANC	BA5	747	FJM	0
-	-	45 7	1015	1120 CDG	AF963	737	CM	0
			1320 CDG	1235 ANC	AF274	74M	FCY	0
ANKARA (ANK)				ESB-ESENBOGA				
-	-	6	1010	1545 ESB	SR322	M80	FCYML	1
TRANSFER CONNECTIONS								
-	-	1 4	0925	1015 ZRH	SR111	74D	FCYML	0
			1140 ZRH	1545 ESB	SR320	M80	FCYML	0
-	-	6	1215	1605 IST	TK918	727	Y	0
			1730 IST	1825 ESB	TK146	310	Y	0
-	-	1	1220	1730 IST	TK920	310	CY	1
			1825 IST	1920 ESB	TK898	727	Y	0
-	-	4	1220	1730 IST	TK920	310	CY	1
			1825 IST	1920 ESB	TK148	DC9	Y	0
ANNABA (AAE)								
-	17Sep	1	1310	1405 ALG	SR226	M80	FCYML	0
			1800 ALG	1850	AH6004	73S	Y	0
-	20Sep	4	1310	1405 ALG	SR226	M80	FCYML	0
			1655 ALG	1745	AH6004	73S	Y	0
24Sep	-	1	1310	1405 ALG	SR226	M80	FCYML	0
			1615 ALG	1705	AH6002	72S	Y	0
ANTALYA (AYT)								
-	-	7	1800	2340	TK948	727	Y	1
TRANSFER CONNECTIONS								
-	-	7	0710	0835 FRA	LH1851	737	FCMTK	0
			1235 FRA	1655	LH1596	737	FCMTK	0
-	-	6	1215	1605 IST	TK918	727	Y	0
			1945 IST	2050	TK482	DC9	Y	0
-	-	1	1220	1730 IST	TK920	310	CY	1
			1845 IST	1950	TK480	DC9	Y	0
-	-	4	1220	1730 IST	TK920	310	CY	1
			1945 IST	2050	TK482	DC9	Y	0
ANTANANARIVO (TNR)								
-	-	3	1215	1320 CDG	SR724	M80	FCYML	0
			1435 CDG	*0550	AF477 /MD477	74M	FCY	2
-	-	6	1830	1920 ZRH	SR184	D10	FCYML	0
			2040 ZRH	*0915	MD053	74M	FJY	1
ANTIGUA (ANU)								
-	-	1	0710	0830 FRA	LH1851	737	FCMTK	0
			1030 FRA	1330	LH514	D10	FCMBK	0
-	-	4	0710	0830 FRA	LH1851	737	FCMTK	0
			1030 FRA	1330	LH522	D10	FCMBK	0
-	-	2	0830	0910 LHR	SR830	310	FCYML	0
			1115 LHR	1435	BA257	747	FJM	0
-	-	2	0905	0945 LHR	BA723	757	CM	0
			1115 LHR	1435	BA257	747	FJM	0
-	-	3	0905	0945 LHR	BA723	757	CM	0
			1345 LGW	1655	BA255	747	FJM	0
-	-	7	1220	1255 LHR	BA725	757	CM	0
			1430 LHR	1750	BA257	747	FJM	0
ANTWERP (ANR)								
-	-	1234567	1020	1150 AMS	KL320	737	CMBLS	0
			1300 AMS	1335	KL397	EM2	CMB	0
-	-	12345	1455	1625 AMS	KL322	737	CMBLS	0
			1910 AMS	1945	KL399	EM2	CMB	0
ARUBA (AUA)								
-	-	1	0745	0920 AMS	SR788	M87	CYML ♦	0
			1200 AMS	1550	KL759	D10	FCM	0
-	-	2	0745	0920 AMS	SR788	M87	CYML ♦	0
			1120 AMS	1510	KL781	D10	CM	0
-	27Aug	1	1020	1150 AMS	KL320	737	CMBLS	0
			1510 AMS	1850	KL783	747	CM	0
-	28Aug	2	1020	1150 AMS	KL320	737	CMBLS	0
			1540 AMS	1920	KL785	747	CM	0
-	-	2	1835	2005 AMS	SR794	M80	FCYM ♦	0
			2310 AMS	*0305	KL741	D10	FCM	0
-	-	4	1835	2005 AMS	SR794	M80	FCYM ♦	0
			2145 AMS	*0140	KL751	D10	FCM	0
-	-	6	1835	2005 AMS	SR794	M80	FCYM ♦	0
			2355 AMS	*0350	KL755	D10	FCM	0
ASUNCION (ASU)								
-	-	4	1840	2035 MAD	SR654	M80	FCYML	0
			*0125 MAD	*1020	IB987	D10	PCYMK	2
ATHENS GREECE (ATH)								
-	-	1234567	1115	1500	SR314	M80	FCYML	0
-	28Sep	5	1310	1755	OA134	727	FYM	1
30Sep	-	1234567	1410	1750	OA136	73S	FYM	0
-	26Sep	1 3 7	1510	1850	OA136	73S	FYM	0
-	29Sep	2 4 6	1510	1840	OA136	727	FYM	0
Need a hotel in ATH? You'll find more than 60 in your copy of ABC Worldwide Hotel Guide.								
TRANSFER CONNECTIONS								
-	-	1 34 6	0925	1100 VIE	OS212	M80	CYML	0
			1140 VIE	1500	OS873	M80	CYML	0
-	-	1234567	1110	1230 FCO	AZ411	M80	CYML	0
			1530 FCO	1825	AZ484	DC9	CYML	0
-	-	12 4567	1605	1725 FCO	AZ409	M80	CYML	0
			1830 FCO	2125	AZ486	AB3	CYML	0
-	-	3	1605	1725 FCO	AZ409	M80	CYML	0
			1830 FCO	2125	AZ724	M80	CYML	0
ATLANTA (ATL)								
30Sep	-	1234567	1025	2108	TW831	747	FCYBQ	2
TW 831 -Plane change at intermediate stop								
-	26Sep	1 3	1105	1655	SR120	D10	FCYML	1
1Oct	-	1 3	1105	1755	SR120	D10	FCYML	1
-	29Sep	1234567	1125	2108	TW831	747	FCYBQ	2
TW 831 -Plane change at intermediate stop								
TRANSFER CONNECTIONS								
-	7Aug	12345 7	0710	0820 MUC	SR552	100	FCYML	0
			1100 MUC	1500	DL33	L15	FCYBM	0
-	-	123456	0710	0830 FRA	LH1851	737	FCMTK	0
			1140 FRA	1520	DL15	L15	FCYBM	0
-	-	1 4	0710	0830 FRA	LH1851	737	FCMTK	0
			0955 FRA	1325	LH438	747	FCMBK	0
-	-	7	0710	0835 FRA	LH1851	737	FCMTK	0
			1140 FRA	1520	DL15	L15	FCYBM	0
8Aug	-	12345 7	0710	0820 MUC	SR552	100	FCYML	0
			1045 MUC	1515	DL33	763	FCYBM	0
18Aug Only		6	0710	0830 FRA	LH1851	737	FCMTK	0
			0945 FRA	1325	DL4149	L15	FCYBM	0
-	-	1234567	0840	0920 LGW	BA735	73S	CM	0
			1100 LGW	1455	DL11	L15	FCYBM	0
-	-	1234567	0840	0920 LGW	BA735	73S	CM	0
			1245 LGW	1650	BA227	D10	FJM	0
-	-	1234567	0840	0920 LGW	BA735	73S	CM	0
			1305 LGW	1700	DL19	L15	FCYBM	0
-	-	12 4567	0855	1010 BRU	SN792	73S	CYBK	0
			1140 BRU	1625	SN531	747	FCYBH	1
-	-	1234567	1020	1150 AMS	KL320	737	CMBLS	0
			1350 AMS	1720	DL39	L15	FCYBM	0
-	-	123 567	1020	1150 AMS	KL320	737	CMBLS	0
			1330 AMS	1645	KL621	74M	FCMB	0
-	-	2 4 6	1105	1155 ZRH	SR164	D10	FCYML	0
			1300 ZRH	1655	SR120	D10	FCYML	0
-	-	12345 7	1125	1210 ZRH	SR929	100	FCYML	0
			1300 ZRH	1655	SR120	D10	FCYML	0
ATLANTIC CITY (AIY)				ACY-INTERNATIONAL				
-	-	1234567	1125	1550 JFK	TW831	747	FCYBQ	1
			1910 JFK	2015 ACY	TW7567	CS2	YBQM ♦	0
TW 831 -Plane change at intermediate stop								
AUCKLAND (AKL)								
-	-	1	0830	0910 LHR	SR830	310	FCYML	0
			1435 LHR	‡0600	BA9	747	FJM	3
-	20Aug	1	0905	0945 LHR	BA723	757	CM	0
			1215 LHR	1515 LAX	BA283	747	FJM	0
			2010 LAX	‡0615	TE5	747	PJYBM	1
-	-	2	0905	0945 LHR	BA723	757	CM	0
			1215 LHR	1515 LAX	BA283	747	FJM	0
			1945 LAX	‡0630	TE5	747	PJYBM	1
27Aug	-	1	0905	0945 LHR	BA723	757	CM	0
			1215 LHR	1515 LAX	BA283	747	FJM	0
			1945 LAX	‡0615	TE5	747	PJYBM	1
-	-	2 4 7	1020	1150 AMS	KL320	737	CMBLS	0
			1350 AMS	1605 LAX	KL601	747	FCMB	0
			1915 LAX	‡0645	AA2725	D10	PCYBM	1
AA 2725 -Plane change at intermediate stop								
-	-	2	1020	1150 AMS	KL320	737	CMBLS	0
			1350 AMS	1605 LAX	KL601	747	FCMB	0
			1945 LAX	‡0630	TE5	747	PJYBM	1
-	-	1	1220	1255 LHR	BA725	757	CM	0
			1435 LHR	‡0600	BA9	747	FJM	3
-	-	34	1220	1255 LHR	BA725	757	CM	0
			1730 LHR	‡0730	BA11	747	FJM	2
-	-	45 7	1225	1300 LGW	BA737	73S	CM	0
			1725 LGW	‡0615	TE1	747	PJYBM	1
-	-	4	1310	1835 HEL	AY876	M80	CMBK	1
			1905 HEL	*1315 SIN	AY902	D10	CM	1
			*1455 SIN	‡0730	BA11	747	FJM	1
-	-	5	1310	1835 HEL	AY876	M80	CMBK	1
			1920 HEL	*1455 NRT	AY914	D10	FCM	0
			*2030 NRT	‡0945	TE34	747	PJYBM	0
-	-	34	1340	1415 LHR	SR832	310	FCYML	0
			1730 LHR	‡0730	BA11	747	FJM	2
-	-	6	1435	1555 FRA	LH1857	737	FCMTK	0
			1800 FRA	‡0615	LH6498	747	MBK ♦	1
-	-	6	1435	1555 FRA	LH1857	737	FCMTK	0
			1800 FRA	‡0615	TE19	747	PJYBM	1
-	14Sep	5	1455	1625 AMS	KL322	737	CMBLS	0
			1720 AMS	*1430 SIN	KL837	74M	FCM	1
			*1730 SIN	‡1000	TE28	767	JYBMH	1
-	-	1	1455	1625 AMS	KL322	737	CMBLS	0
			1720 AMS	*1430 SIN	KL837	74M	FCM	1
			*1920 SIN	‡0920	TE26	767	JYBMH	0
-	-	4	1455	1625 AMS	KL322	737	CMBLS	0
			1720 AMS	*1415 SIN	KL835	747	FCM	1
			*1920 SIN	‡0920	TE26	767	JYBMH	0
-	-	6	1455	1625 AMS	KL322	737	CMBLS	0
			1720 AMS	*1415 SIN	KL835	747	FCM	1
			*1940 SIN	‡0940	TE26	767	JYBMH	0
21Sep	-	5	1455	1625 AMS	KL322	737	CMBLS	0
			1720 AMS	*1430 SIN	KL837	74M	FCM	1
			*1930 SIN	‡1115	TE22	767	JYBMH	1
-	-	6	1830	*1635 SIN	SR184	D10	FCYML	2
			*1940 SIN	‡0940	TE26	767	JYBMH	0
-	-	3	1835	2005 AMS	SR794	M80	FCYM ♦	0
			2235 AMS	‡0800 SYD	KL843	747	FCM	3
			‡1000 SYD	‡1450	QF43	747	PJYBK	0
-	-	1	1850	*1510 SIN	SR188	D10	FCYML	1
			*1920 SIN	‡0920	TE26	767	JYBMH	0
AUSTIN (AUS)								
-	-	1234567	1045	1520 JFK	PA119	310	FCYBM	1
			1729 JFK	2148	PA475	72S	FYBMQ	1
-	-	1234567	1125	1550 JFK	TW831	747	FCYBQ	1
			1720 JFK	2124	TW801	72S	FCYBQ	1
TW 831 -Plane change at intermediate stop								
BAGHDAD (BGW)				SDA-SADDAM INTL				
3Oct	-	3	1215	2000 SDA	IA276	72S	FY	1

Single transfer with change of airport at London

The next example shows a change of airport in London: the flight from Oslo (FBU) arrives London Gatwick (LGW) and departs London Heathrow (LHR).

Double transfer via Copenhagen and Amsterdam

In the third example the flight departs Oslo and continues via Copenhagen (CPH) and Amsterdam (AMS) to Paris (CDG).

Single transfer via Brussels

This is the fourth example.

Now read this page again.
   Look for the flight departing Oslo at 1410 hours. From which airport does it depart? FBU = Fornebu.
   Name the airport of arrival = CDG = Charles de Gaulle (Paris).
   Give the flight number AF 1135 (Air France).
   What type of aircraft is used? 737 = Boeing 737.
   What are the validity dates? None are shown so the flight operates continuously until further notice.
   What are the days of operation? every day 1, 2, 3, 4, 5, 6, 7.
   Is a thrift class of travel available on that flight? No, C = Business class and M = coach/economy class.
   On a transfer connection flight for a flight departing Oslo at 1415 supply the flight number used between Amsterdam and Paris = KL 333 (Royal Dutch Airlines).
   On the flight from Oslo at 1540 hours via Brussels to Paris is the FBU/BRU section a non-stop flight? No, one (1) stop is made.

Exercise 4

Please study the 'Quick reference section – how to use' page again. Then turn to the extract from the *ABC World Airways Guide* giving details of flights from Geneva. Remember: all flight times shown in the *ABC Guide* are local times. Try the following:

(a) What is the distance between Geneva airport and the city centre?
(b) Describe transport arrangements between Geneva city and airport, together with travelling times.

(c) Your client would like a direct flight from Geneva to Amman on Sunday 9 October. Give details: flight number; times; aircraft type; class of travel available; number of stops en route.

(d) Your client feels that arrival in Amman may be too late for his appointment. Can he travel on Saturday 8 October? Explain your answer.

(e) If your client accepts the Sunday flight, what is the latest time to check in at the airport?

(f) It is not possible to fly direct from Geneva to Auckland (AKL); there is a change of aircraft at other European cities. Give the names and the three-letter codes of those cities.

(g) Your client would like a direct flight from Geneva to Ankara. Please give details, including the check-in time at the airport.

Minimum connecting times

When passengers transfer from one flight to another, a minimum amount of time must be allowed. Sometimes passengers have to go through immigration. The baggage must be transferred, and may need to be cleared by customs. Weather conditions can cause late arrivals. Passengers may also have a change of airport to accomplish before arriving at the final destination. Aircraft may need attention. All the many reasons for missing a flight should be considered when reserving connecting flights. In Chapter 15 there is a client who misses his connecting flight in Paris because insufficient time is allowed between ORY and CDG airports (you know those airport codes now!).

EXPLANATORY NOTES

1. DOM=between domestic flights
   INT=between international flights
   DOM to INT=domestic flights to international flights
   INT to DOM= international flights to domestic flights
   On-line =between flights of the same carrier
   Interline= between flights of different carriers

2. Three letter city/airport codes are used where appropriate.
   To decode refer to pages 36-41.
   Inter-airport connections are shown as follows
   ORD to/from MDW   2.40

3. Two character airline designators are used where exceptions to the standard MCTs have been agreed between specific airlines.
   To decode refer to pages 14-15.

4. All MCTs are shown in hours and minutes.

5. The following rule will be used when Minimum Connecting Times are applied to International flights serving more than one city in the same country.
   Flights will be considered Domestic arrivals only if they have already made a landing within the same country and if full traffic rights exist for that carrier between the two ports in that country. Otherwise, arrivals will be considered International. Flights will be considered Domestic departures only if they will make another landing within the same country and if full traffic rights exist for that carrier between the two ports in that country. Otherwise departures will be considered International.

In addition, the following exceptions to International Domestic status also apply. Cities where the exceptions apply are marked with appropriate note letter immediately after the status.
   MANCHESTER (MAN)
   DOM(e)   30

a) Flights betwen Alaska, Bermuda, Vancouver, Toronto, Montreal, Winnipeg, Hawaii, Nassau (except flights stopping at Freeport), Puerto Rico, U.S. Virgin Islands and the Continental United States are considered Domestic.

b) Europe means the area comprised of the following countries, Albania, Algeria, Andorra, Austria, Belgium, Bulgaria, Canary Islands, Czechoslovakia, Denmark, Finland, France, Germany, Gibraltar, Greece, Hungary, Iceland, Republic of Ireland, Italy, Liechtenstein, Luxembourg, Malta, Monaco, Morocco, Netherlands, Norway, Poland, Portugal (including Azores and Madeira), Romania, San Marino, Spain, Sweden, Switzerland, Tunisia, Turkey (in Europe and Asia), United Kingdom, U.S.S.R. (west of the Ural Mountains), Yugoslavia.

c) Air France and Swissair flights to/from Geneva are Domestic.

d) Conections to STT and STX are considered Domestic. Connections from STT and STX are considered International.

e) Flights to the Republic of Ireland, Jersey, Guernsey and Alderney are considered Domestic, and flights from these points are considered International.

The information on minimum connecting times for every airport in the world can be found in the Blue Book of the *ABC Guide*. Please read the 'Explanatory notes' extract from the Blue Book. The important points are: 'domestic' means flights within the one country; 'international' means flights from one country to another; 'on-line' means a transfer from one flight

CALCUTTA (CCU)		
DOM		30
DOM to INT		2.00
All to AI		3.00
AI	1.10	
INT to DOM		2.00
AI	1.10	
INT		1.30
All to AI,		2.00
AI	1.10	
CALGARY (YYC)		
DOM		45
AC (Between flts 1500-1799)	20	
AC other flts, CP other flts	30	
CP btw flts 500-599	10	
CP btw flts 1100-1297	15	
DOM to INT		45
DOM to USA		1.00
DL	20	
USA to DOM		1.15
CO to CP		1.00
DL	20	
USA to INT		1.15
INT to DOM		1.30
AC	1.15	
INT to USA		1.30
INT		1.30
DL	30	
CALI (CLO)		
DOM		20
AV	30	
DOM to INT		50
INT to DOM		1.00
INT		1.30
AV	1.00	
CAMAGUEY (CMW)		
DOM		30
CAMDEN (CDH)		
DOM		20
CAMPBELL RIVER (YBL)		
DOM		20
CP	10	
CANBERRA (CBR)		
DOM		30
AN to/from EW		15
AN, TN	15	
CANCUN (CUN)		
DOM		20
DOM to INT		45
INT to DOM		1.00
CAPE GIRARDEAU (CGI)		
DOM		20
CAPETOWN (CPT)		
DOM		30
DOM to INT		1.00
INT to DOM		1.00
INT		1.00
CARACAS (CCS)		
DOM		30
DOM to INT		2.00
LV, VE to SR		1.45
LV, VE to VA		1.30
VA	45	
VE	30	
INT to DOM		2.00
SR to LV, VE		1.45
VA to LV, VE		1.30
VA	45	

of an airline to another flight of the same airline; and 'interline' means a transfer from one flight of an airline to a flight of another airline.

Exercise 5

Please read the explanatory notes again for minimum connecting times. Think about whether a journey is domestic or international, and then give the minimum connecting times in Cape Town for the following journeys. We will say the flights are interline. Study the extract minimum connecting times (MCT), reading the details under the heading Capetown (CPT).

(a) JNB–CPT–DUR.
(b) ELS–CPT–MAD.
(c) LON–CPT–DUR.
(d) CAI–CPT–SYD.

The three-letter codes not found in the European extract are: JNB Johannesburg; ELS East London; CAI Cairo; DUR Durban; SYD Sydney.

Answer to Exercise 5

(a) Johannesburg to Cape Town to Durban: domestic, 30 minutes.
(b) East London to Cape Town to Madrid: domestic to international, 1 hour.
(c) London to Cape Town to Durban: international to domestic, 1 hour.
(d) Cairo to Cape Town to Sydney: international to international, 1 hour.

Exercise 6

Try this one without help. The city is Barcelona (BCN).

(a) Madrid (MAD)   Barcelona   Alicante (ALC)
(b) Gerona (GRO)   Barcelona   Lisbon (LIS)
(c) Brussels (BRU)   Barcelona   Alicante (ALC)
(d) Athens (ATH)   Barcelona   Glasgow (GLA)

We have to look for many factors that can affect MCT, for example, the airline used, the flight numbers, whether the 'on-line' or 'interline' and the actual journey. The most simple and straightforward examples have been chosen here.

Exercise 7 – MCT Adelaide

Let's try another one: this time Adelaide (ADL).

(a) Perth (PER) Adelaide   Sydney (SYD)
(b) Melbourne (MEL)   Adelaide   Singapore (SIN)
(c) Hong Kong (HKG)   Adelaide   Perth (PER)
(d) Tokyo (TYO)   Adelaide   Auckland (AKL)

Times

We are going to talk about time differences and elapsed flying times. However, first it is essential that we are familiar with the 24-hour clock. The 24-hour clock and its equivalent a.m. and p.m. times are as follows:

0100   1 a.m. (early hours of the morning) and so on, e.g.
0700   7 a.m. (morning) and so on to
1200   12 noon (midday) then
1300   1 p.m. and so on, e.g.
1900   7 p.m. (evening) and so on to
2359   one minute to midnight
0000   12 midnight
0001   one minute past midnight

International Time Calculator

Standard Clock time is shown in hours and minutes fast (+) or slow (−) of G.M.T.(Greenwich Mean Time). Amended Standard Clock Time used when D.S.T.(Daylight Saving Time) is applied is shown with its effective period.

Country or Area	Standard Clock Time	Daylight Saving Time	DST effective period
AFGHANISTAN	+4.30		
ALBANIA	+1	+2	25 Mar 90–29 Sep 90
ALGERIA	+1		
ANDAMAN IS.	+5.30		
ANDORRA	+1	+2	25 Mar 90–29 Sep 90
ANGOLA	+1		
ANGUILLA	−4		
ANTIGUA AND BARBUDA	−4		
ARGENTINA	−3	−2	21 Oct 90–02 Mar 91(E)
ARUBA	−4		
ASCENSION IS.	GMT		
AUSTRALIA **			
Australian Capital Territory	+10	+11	28 Oct 90–02 Mar 91(E)
Lord Howe Island	+10.30	+11	28 Oct 90–02 Mar 91(E)
New South Wales	+10	+11	28 Oct 90–02 Mar 91(E)
Northern Territory	+9.30	*	
Queensland	+10	+11	28 Oct 90–02 Mar 91(E)
South Australia	+9.30	+10.30	28 Oct 90–16 Mar 91(E)
Western Australia	+8	*	
Tasmania	+10	+11	28 Oct 90–16 Mar 91(E)
Victoria	+10	+11	28 Oct 90–16 Mar 91(E)
AUSTRIA	+1	+2	25 Mar 90–29 Sep 90
AZORES	−1	GMT	25 Mar 90–29 Sep 90
BAHAMAS	−5	−4	01 Apr 90–27 Oct 90
BAHRAIN	+3		
BANGLADESH	+6		
BARBADOS	−4		
BELGIUM	+1	+2	25 Mar 90–29 Sep 90
BELIZE	−6		
BENIN	+1		
BERLIN WEST	+1	+2	25 Mar 90–29 Sep 90
BERMUDA	−4	−3	01 Apr 90–27 Oct 90
BHUTAN	+6		
BOLIVIA	−4		
BOTSWANA	+2		
BRAZIL **			21 Oct 90–09 Feb 91(E)
Fernando de Noronha	−2	−1	
East, all coast and Brasilia	−3	−2	
West	−4	−3	
Amapa	−3	*	
Amazonas,Rondonia and Roraima	−4	*	
Territory of Acre	−5	*	
BRITISH VIRGIN IS.	−4		
BRUNEI DARUSSALAM	+8		
BULGARIA	+2	+3	25 Mar 90–29 Sep 90
BURKINA FASO	GMT		
BURUNDI	+2		
CAMEROON	+1		
CANADA **			01 Apr 90–27 Oct 90
Exceptions: The Province of Saskatchewan and some Canadian cities do not adopt DST			
Newfoundland Island	−3.30	−2.30	
Atlantic Time	−4	−3	
Eastern Time	−5	−4	
Central Time	−6	−5	
Mountain Time	−7	−6	
Pacific Time	−8	−7	
Yukon Territory	−8	−7	
CANARY IS.	GMT	+1	25 Mar 90–29 Sep 90
CAPE VERDE	−1		
CAROLINE IS.	+12		
CAYMAN IS.	−5		
CENTRAL AFRICAN REP.	+1		
CHAD	+1		
CHATHAM IS.	+12.45	+13.45	07 Oct 90–16 Mar 91
CHILE	−4	−3	14 Oct 90–09 Mar 91
CHINA	+8	+9	15 Apr 90–15 Sep 90
CHRISTMAS IS.(INDIAN OCEAN)	+7		
COCOS IS.	+6.30		
COLOMBIA	−5		
COMOROS	+3		
CONGO	+1		
COOK IS.	−10		
COSTA RICA	−6		
COTE D'IVOIRE	GMT		
CUBA	−5	−4	01 Apr 90–13 Oct 90
CYPRUS			
Ercan	+2	+3	25 Mar 90–29 Sep 90
Larnaca	+2	+3	25 Mar 90–29 Sep 90
CZECHOSLOVAKIA	+1	+2	25 Mar 90–29 Sep 90
DENMARK	+1	+2	25 Mar 90–29 Sep 90
DJIBOUTI	+3		
DOMINICA	−4		
DOMINICAN REP.	−4		
EASTER IS.	−6	−5	14 Oct 90–09 Mar 91
ECUADOR	−5		
Exceptions: Except Galapagos Is.			
EGYPT	+2	+3	01 May 90–30 Sep 90
EL SALVADOR	−6		
EQUATORIAL GUINEA	+1		
ETHIOPIA	+3		
FALKLAND IS.	−4	−3	09 Sep 90–20 Apr 91(E)
FAROE IS.	GMT	+1	25 Mar 90–29 Sep 90
FIJI	+12		
FINLAND	+2	+3	25 Mar 90–29 Sep 90
FRANCE	+1	+2	25 Mar 90–29 Sep 90
FRENCH ANTILLES	−4		
FRENCH GUIANA	−3		
GABON	+1		
GALAPAGOS IS.	−6		
GAMBIA	GMT		
GAMBIER IS.	−9		
GERMAN DEMOCRATIC REP.	+1	+2	25 Mar 90–29 Sep 90
GERMAN FEDERAL REP.	+1	+2	25 Mar 90–29 Sep 90

Country or Area	Standard Clock Time	Daylight Saving Time	DST effective period
GHANA	GMT		
GIBRALTAR	+1	+2	25 Mar 90–29 Sep 90
GREECE	+2	+3	25 Mar 90–29 Sep 90
GREENLAND **	−3	−2	25 Mar 90–29 Sep 90
Scoresbysund	−1	GMT	
Eastgreenland and Mesters Vig.	GMT		
Qanaq and Thule	−4	*	
GRENADA	−4		
GUADELOUPE	−4		
GUAM	+10		
GUATEMALA	−6		
GUINEA	GMT		
GUINEA BISSAU	GMT		
GUYANA	−3		
HAITI	−5	−4	01 Apr 90–27 Oct 90
HONDURAS	−6		
HONG KONG	+8		
HUNGARY	+1	+2	25 Mar 90–29 Sep 90
ICELAND	GMT		
INDIA	+5.30		
INDONESIA **			
West Zone	+7		
Central Zone	+8		
East Zone	+9		
IRAN	+3.30		
IRAQ	+3	+4	01 Apr 90–30 Sep 90
IRELAND	GMT	+1	25 Mar 90–27 Oct 90
ISRAEL	+2	+3	25 Mar 90–25 Aug 90
ITALY	+1	+2	25 Mar 90–29 Sep 90
JAMAICA	−5		
JAPAN	+9		
JERUSALEM	+2	+3	25 Mar 90–25 Aug 90
JOHNSTON IS.	−10		
JORDAN	+2	+3	27 Apr 90–04 Oct 90(E)
KAMPUCHEA	+7		
KENYA	+3		
KIRIBATI **	+12		
Canton Is. and Enderbury Is.	−11		
Christmas Is.	−10		
KOREA D.P.R.	+9		
KOREA REP.	+9		
KUWAIT	+3		
LAO P.D.R.	+7		
LEBANON	+2	+3	01 May 90–15 Oct 90
LEEWARD IS.	−4		
LESOTHO	+2		
LIBERIA	GMT		
LIBYA	+1	+2	01 Apr 90–30 Sep 90
LIECHTENSTEIN	+1	+2	25 Mar 90–29 Sep 90
LOYALTY IS.	+11		
LUXEMBOURG	+1	+2	25 Mar 90–29 Sep 90
MACAU	+8		
MADAGASCAR	+3		
MADEIRA IS.	GMT	+1	25 Mar 90–29 Sep 90
MALAWI	+2		
MALAYSIA	+8		
MALDIVES	+5		
MALI	GMT		
MALTA	+1	+2	25 Mar 90–29 Sep 90
MARIANA IS.	+10		
MARQUESAS IS.	−9.30		
MARSHALL IS. **	+12		
Kwajalein	−12		
MARTINIQUE	−4		
MAURITANIA	GMT		
MAURITIUS	+4		
MEXICO **			01 Apr 90–27 Oct 90
General	−6	*	
Lower California and North Pacific Coast	−7	*	
Baja California Norte	−8	−7	
MICRONESIA	+12		
MIDWAY IS.	−11		
MONACO	+1	+2	25 Mar 90–29 Sep 90
MONGOLIA	+8	+9	25 Mar 90–29 Sep 90
MONTSERRAT	−4		
MOROCCO	GMT		
MOZAMBIQUE	+2		
MYANMAR	+6.30		
NAMIBIA	+2		
NAURU	+12		
NEPAL	+5.45		
NETHERLANDS	+1	+2	25 Mar 90–29 Sep 90
NETHERLANDS ANTILLES	−4		
NEW CALEDONIA	+11		
NEW ZEALAND	+12	+13	07 Oct 90–16 Mar 91
NICARAGUA	−6		
NIGER	+1		
NIGERIA	+1		
NIUE	−11		
NORFOLK IS.	+11.30		
NORWAY	+1	+2	25 Mar 90–29 Sep 90
OMAN	+4		
PAKISTAN	+5		
PALAU	+9		
PANAMA	−5		
PAPUA NEW GUINEA	+10		
PARAGUAY	−4	−3	21 Oct 90–02 Mar 91(E)
PERU	−5	−4	31 Dec 90–13 Apr 91(E)
PHILIPPINES	+8	+9	21 May 90–31 Aug 90
PHOENIX IS.	−11		

*–The Standard Clock Time shown is retained all year in this area/time zone. †–Subject to confirmation. ‡–Lord Howe Island subject to confirmation. (E)–Estimated effective dates ..**–Multi zone country. To establish the local clock time of individual cities in this country, refer to the Departure City information in the Quick Reference Schedules section.

By using the 24-hour clock we eliminate mistakes or uncertainty as to whether we mean a.m. or p.m. For example, 8 o'clock might be morning or evening; with the 24-hour clock, clearly 0800 is morning and 2000 is evening.

Standard time

The world is divided into 24 time zones, each of 15° longitude, with the Greenwich Meridian being point zero (GMT). The time used in each country, whether it is the time of the corresponding time zone or a modified time, is fixed by law. For this reason it is called legal time; it is generally known as standard time or local time. Certain countries, for economic reasons, modify their legal time for part of the year, especially in summer.

Time difference

Please study the extract 'International time calculator' from the *ABC Guide*. Here you will see listed the name of the country, whether its legal time is plus or minus GMT, and whether the time is modified (if so, the dates are given under DST (daylight saving time)). If you look at the country Albania you will see that its legal time is plus 1 hour, except between 25 March and 29 September when its time is plus 2 hours.

Try another example. This time for Peru. Their legal time is minus 5 from Greenwich Mean time (GMT) and between 31 December and 13 April they adjust their time to minus 4 hours. The letter (E) has a note at the end of the page explaining those dates are not definite but estimated dates i.e. they could change within a day or so nearer the time. You will notice that when a country adjusts its legal time it is usually by one hour only.

It is now 1500 hours (3 p.m.) in Tokyo on 22 December; what time is it in Copenhagen?

You could be asked this or a very similar question. How to find out? Look for Denmark as Copenhagen is in Denmark and look for Japan as Tokyo is in Japan. Denmark's standard time is GMT + 1 hour (between 25 March and 29 September, GMT + 2 hours). Japan is GMT + 9 hours. It is therefore 9 − 1 = 8 hours earlier in Denmark than in Japan. Subtract 8 hours from 1500 hours to arrive at 0700 hours in Denmark on 22 December.

It sometimes helps to draw the face of a clock and move round the dial to assist with the calculations. Or use fingers and toes!

Let's try another one. It is 0800 hours in Athens on 12 October; what is the time on Barbados? Check the international time calculator: Greece is + 2 hours and Barbados is − 4 hours. You *add* 4 and 2 together (2 − (−4) = 2 + 4) (if Greece is 2 hours ahead of Barbados there must be a 6 hour difference between the two countries) to make it 6 hours earlier in Barbados than it is in Greece. Then deduct the 6 hours from 0800 hours in Athens to reach the answer that is 0200 hours (2 a.m., early hours of the morning) in Barbados.

To establish a time difference between two places, use the following rules. Think about them carefully.

1 Where both signs are the same, i.e. + and +, or − and −, you must *deduct* the smaller figure from the larger figure, as we did in the first example.
2 Where the signs are not the same, i.e. − and +, or + and −, you must *add* the two figures together, as we did in the second example.

Average Journey Times Between Major Cities

From / To	ADDIS ABABA	ANCHORAGE	ANTANANARIVO	ATHENS	AUCKLAND	BANGKOK	BEIRUT	BOGOTA	BOMBAY	BUENOS AIRES	CAIRO	CARACAS	CHICAGO	COPENHAGEN	DAKAR	DELHI	FRANKFURT	HONG KONG	HONOLULU	JOHANNESBURG	KARACHI	KINSHASA	LAGOS	LIMA	LONDON
ADDIS ABABA									05 55		05 20						10 10				04 20	06 15	07 40		10 55
ANCHORAGE													06 50	08 30			10 30		05 40						08 40
ANTANANARIVO																									
ATHENS	07 40					11 00	01 45		06 50		01 45			03 50		10 00	03 10	12 00		13 15	05 50	09 40	05 30		03 55
AUCKLAND									18 35									11 20	08 55						29 25
BANGKOK				11 40					04 25		12 05			15 40		03 55	14 25	03 00			04 50				16 25
BEIRUT				01 55							01 25			06 30			05 50						06 25		06 30
BOGOTA										09 30		01 45					14 35							03 05	13 10
BOMBAY	05 45			07 20	17 45	04 30	06 45									01 40	10 15	07 50			01 40		12 30		11 40
BUENOS AIRES								08 10				06 40		18 45	09 25		17 30	36 30						05 30	17 05
CAIRO	04 50			02 05		11 30	01 20							05 20		07 35	04 55				06 05		06 20		05 20
CARACAS								01 50		06 55							11 30							06 05	10 00
CHICAGO		07 40		14 25										08 30			10 15		10 10						07 35
COPENHAGEN		08 35		03 45		15 50	06 10			19 35	05 10		09 10			13 05	01 25			14 15	07 20		08 30		01 45
DAKAR										10 05												10 20	07 35		05 35
DELHI				07 50		03 50			01 45		08 05			13 50			09 25	07 00			01 50				12 55
FRANKFURT	08 40	10 35		03 00		13 35	05 25	15 35	09 15	09 25	04 40	12 30	09 50	01 20		08 45		17 10		14 20	08 40		06 25	18 45	01 30
HONG KONG				14 30	12 05	03 00			07 20							07 00	17 05		10 20	15 40	07 35				18 00
HONOLULU		06 35			08 55								09 20					11 10							17 35
JOHANNESBURG				13 05										14 40			14 25	15 35				03 35			14 20
KARACHI	04 20			06 40		04 50			01 30		06 35			08 00		01 50	09 05	07 25							11 05
KINSHASA	06 05			09 45											10 20					03 30			02 40		
LAGOS	08 50			05 30			05 50		13 40		06 10			08 20	06 55		06 10					02 35			07 25
LIMA								03 10		04 55		06 05					17 40								15 10
LONDON	09 35	08 55		03 40	27 05	15 40	04 25	15 00	10 20	18 05	04 50	10 35	08 30	01 45	08 10	11 25	01 25	15 40	18 40	13 25	10 25		07 20	15 45	
LOS ANGELES		06 15		18 50	14 50	21 45		08 10	27 10	16 15		07 10	04 00	11 40		25 55	13 10	17 15	05 30		20 20			09 00	11 15
MADRID				03 55			06 05	10 30		14 40	05 50	09 00		03 05			02 45			11 35		06 30	04 55	15 00	02 05
MANILA				16 30		03 15			08 10		15 05		17 40	20 55		08 15	19 05	01 45	10 50		09 55				20 30
MAURITIUS			01 40						06 30		14 30						14 45			05 25					14 10
MEXICO CITY								04 20	27 50	10 05		05 45	03 45			27 20	12 55				26 50			05 20	13 10
MIAMI								04 20		12 30		03 25	03 05				09 25		11 40					06 50	08 10
MONTREAL				10 30						18 30			02 10	06 45			07 10							09 35	06 10
MOSCOW	11 50		18 30	05 05		13 00	05 00		09 35		05 25			03 00	10 25	06 25	03 10				05 45	16 20	12 25		03 45
NAIROBI	01 50		03 55	05 50					07 10		04 40			10 15	11 40		08 10			03 50	06 50	04 20	05 25		09 50
NEW YORK		07 50		09 00	20 30	24 40		06 25	18 50	14 45	13 40	05 05	02 25	07 35	07 25	18 50	08 45	22 20	13 00	15 55	20 00		13 15	09 00	06 35
PAPEETE					07 05																				
PARIS	09 40	09 20	13 35	03 05		14 55	04 15	14 00	11 15	17 40	05 00	11 00	11 10	01 50	06 40	10 15	01 15	17 50		13 00	10 50	07 55	06 25	16 50	01 00
PERTH				17 45	07 30	06 30			09 10									10 00		12 40					19 30
RIO DE JANEIRO								06 40		03 45		06 20		14 05	05 15		13 00			09 15			07 40	05 45	12 25
ROME	06 10		13 20	01 50		12 50	03 00	15 35	08 35	16 20	03 15	11 45		03 15	05 40	09 10	01 55	15 35		13 30	09 50	06 20	06 15		02 40
SAN FRANCISCO		06 10		15 30				09 25		19 50	19 50		04 00				13 30	15 15	15 10					10 25	11 30
SAN JUAN								02 50				01 30	06 20											06 55	08 00
SANTIAGO								07 15		01 55		06 45			12 10		21 30	32 55						03 45	18 45
SINGAPORE				13 35	09 35	02 10	14 55		05 30					18 05		05 25	16 45	04 30	14 50		07 25				15 55
SYDNEY				23 20	02 50	11 50			15 20								25 40	09 25	10 20	18 20					25 15
TEHRAN				04 00		08 20			04 00		03 50			05 40		03 25	05 30	11 20			02 35				07 10
TOKYO		06 30		20 40	12 30	07 50			14 20		20 10		12 30	17 35		12 30	20 50	04 50	07 05	21 25	13 30			20 10	20 35
TORONTO				11 00						15 15			01 40	07 35			07 35		09 35					07 30	06 55
VANCOUVER										02 10			04 10				10 35	15 00	06 00					10 50	10 20
WASHINGTON		09 25								16 30			02 00											09 25	06 30

From / To	LOS ANGELES	MADRID	MANILA	MAURITIUS	MEXICO CITY	MIAMI	MONTREAL	MOSCOW	NAIROBI	NEW YORK	PAPEETE	PARIS	PERTH	RIO DE JANEIRO	ROME	SAN FRANCISCO	SAN JUAN	SANTIAGO	SINGAPORE	SYDNEY	TEHRAN	TOKYO	TORONTO	VANCOUVER	WASHINGTON
ADDIS ABABA								12 30	01 50			11 40			07 20										
ANCHORAGE	06 10									06 55		09 15				05 30						07 20			
ANTANANARIVO				01 45				17 05	03 00			14 00			13 55										
ATHENS	19 50	04 15	15 40				11 35	04 50	05 45	10 55		03 10	16 50		01 55	17 30			13 20	22 25	03 30	19 45	12 30		
AUCKLAND	15 50										06 10	31 10	08 45						11 45	03 15		13 00			
BANGKOK	19 40		03 05					12 40		26 15		15 55	06 20		13 40				02 20	11 25	08 50	07 25			
BEIRUT		06 35						05 10				04 35			03 20										
BOGOTA	07 55	11 15			04 25	03 45				06 25		12 50		06 35	16 20	10 05	02 45	07 10							
BOMBAY	24 30		08 10	06 40	29 45			10 10	06 20	21 35		12 25	09 05		08 55				05 40	14 50	04 05	14 00			
BUENOS AIRES	15 05	13 30			11 20	11 30	15 45			14 10		15 50		03 30	14 55	21 35		02 15					15 30	18 15	16 20
CAIRO		06 25	15 20	14 05				04 15	04 35	14 45		05 05			03 50						03 35	20 00			
CARACAS	07 30	08 25			05 50	03 25				04 40		09 55		06 10	11 10		01 30	06 20							
CHICAGO	04 15		19 35		04 15	02 45	01 55			02 10		08 45				04 30	05 55					13 35	01 20	04 55	01 40
COPENHAGEN	12 15	03 10	20 05				07 40	03 00	10 00	08 30		01 50		14 35	03 10				17 35		05 15	17 35	08 25		
DAKAR								10 00	11 45	07 55		06 30		05 20	06 00			12 30							
DELHI	22 40		08 05		28 00			08 20		21 40		11 05			10 20				05 30		03 35	11 30			
FRANKFURT	13 55	02 45	18 35	14 00	14 15	10 10	08 10	03 10	08 20	08 55		01 10		13 50	01 50	11 30		23 15	16 10	24 05	05 45	20 05	08 30	10 55	
HONG KONG	18 00		01 45							20 20		18 55	10 30		16 35	14 10		31 00	04 35	09 20	11 15	04 25		13 30	
HONOLULU	05 15		11 10							11 25						04 50			17 00	11 15		07 55	11 30	05 40	
JOHANNESBURG		12 00		04 55					03 45	17 15		14 10	11 10	10 30	13 25					16 00		21 00			
KARACHI	24 15		09 40		28 25			06 10	07 20	21 50		11 25			10 40				08 05		03 00	12 35			
KINSHASA		06 35						16 40	04 15			08 05			06 40										
LAGOS		04 55						12 05	05 25	13 55		06 20		07 50	06 20										
LIMA	08 20	15 30			15 55	06 20	09 40	26 15		09 55		15 50		05 35		11 35	07 00	03 35				24 30	07 50	11 05	08 45
LONDON	12 00	02 00	19 10	14 55	14 40	09 00	07 05	03 35	09 35	07 15		01 00	18 20	13 00	02 35	13 15	09 00	20 30	15 30	24 20	07 30	19 55	07 50	10 40	07 35
LOS ANGELES		13 10			04 00	05 50	06 20			05 45	08 05	12 15		15 00	15 40	01 10	07 55	11 30	20 40	19 00		12 55	04 25	02 45	05 45
MADRID					13 25	08 55	07 20	06 20	07 20	08 00		01 45		10 20	02 10		08 15	17 35			08 45	20 55			11 05
MANILA										21 25		20 55			17 30	18 30			03 10	08 05	15 45	04 30			
MAURITIUS								19 55	05 00			15 50	06 40		13 00					11 30					
MEXICO CITY	03 55	03 25				04 00	04 30	18 25		05 55		11 55		12 45		05 15	04 30					16 15	04 20	05 10	06 35
MIAMI	05 50	08 55			03 50		03 45			02 45		09 00		09 10		06 25	02 20	10 34					04 45		02 25
MONTREAL	06 40	06 20			05 00	04 55		09 05		01 15		06 30		15 25	08 10	07 20		14 50					01 05	06 35	02 45
MOSCOW		06 40		21 10	19 05		10 15		11 55			03 55			04 10				13 10		03 35	09 40			12 35
NAIROBI		08 25		04 50				10 30		20 50		09 25			07 25										
NEW YORK	06 10	07 00	24 25		05 40	02 50	01 10		20 35			06 25		10 00	08 05	06 45	03 30	14 30	26 10	25 15		16 00	01 25	06 45	01 00
PAPEETE	07 55																	10 00		10 30					
PARIS	13 05	01 50	09 25	15 40	12 45	09 15	07 25	03 45	08 55	07 10				12 05	01 55			20 55	16 25	25 40	06 00	17 05	09 25		07 10
PERTH				07 35											20 50				05 00	04 45					
RIO DE JANEIRO	15 45	09 35			12 50	08 55	11 30			09 30		11 25			12 05	17 05		06 10				28 50			
ROME	17 25	02 15	16 45	12 35			09 15	04 05	07 05	09 05		01 55	19 50	13 00			11 55		15 10	24 40	04 25	20 10	10 25		11 15
SAN FRANCISCO	01 10		17 45		05 00	05 50	06 35			06 10		13 15		14 40	16 00		09 10	14 05	19 55	16 30		12 45	05 30	02 10	06 20
SAN JUAN	09 00	07 25			04 40	02 20				03 40					11 00	09 40									
SANTIAGO	12 15	16 15				10 35	14 40			14 20	12 10	19 05		05 30		15 25							12 50	15 30	14 20
SINGAPORE	18 55		03 15					15 05		24 00		16 50	04 55		15 50	18 55				07 40		08 25			
SYDNEY	17 35		08 20	13 15						20 40		26 40	05 35		25 45	15 20			08 20			09 25	23 20	17 50	
TEHRAN		08 55	12 55					03 45				06 50			05 00							13 50			
TOKYO	11 50	20 30	04 40		14 55			10 20		14 35		16 50		26 00	21 00	10 10			08 30	09 20	15 40			08 25	
TORONTO	04 55				04 30	04 15	01 05			01 20		08 45			09 25	05 35	07 40	12 45		22 40				05 35	02 20
VANCOUVER	02 45				05 00		05 35			06 30						02 10		04 40		19 00		09 40	04 45		
WASHINGTON	06 20		22 50		05 55	02 20	02 35	11 35		01 00		06 20			10 30	06 25		13 05				16 30	02 25		

Journey Times (Concorde)

LONDON—NEW YORK	03 40	PARIS—NEW YORK	03 45
LONDON—WASHINGTON	04 20		

Some larger countries, such as the USA, Brazil, Australia and the USSR, do not have the same standard time throughout the country. Details of their times are published in the *ABC Guide*.

Let's try one more together then calculate the following three by yourself.

It is 1500 hours in Nairobi. What is the time in Casablanca? Nairobi, Kenya = plus 3 hours. Casablanca, Morocco = GMT so Nairobi is 3 hours ahead of Casablanca = 1500 hours in Nairobi minus 3 hours = 12 noon in Casablanca.

Exercise 8

(a) On the 2 April it is 1800 hours in Amsterdam. What is the time in Hong Kong?
(b) On 3 July it is 1000 hours in Buenos Aires. What is the time in Blantyre?
(c) On 25 December it is 2100 hours in Auckland. What is the time in Beirut?

Exercise 9

(a) The time of travel is January: depart Athens (ATH) 1420 hours; arrive Dhaka (DAC) 0430 hours (early hours of next day).
(b) The time of travel is July: depart Copenhagen (CPH) 0805 hours; arrive Bahrain (BAH) 1840 hours.
(c) Time of travel is April: depart Kuala Lumpur (KUL) 1155 hours; arrive Paris (PAR) 2030 hours.

Journey time

By reading the *ABC Guide* extract 'Average journey times between major cities', you will have a good idea quickly of the approximate flying times between two cities. To read this chart look at the cities at the top of the page: Addis Ababa, Anchorage and so on. Then line the city of your choice with the city listed on the left edge of the page. The actual flying time between Addis Ababa and Moscow is 11 hours and 50 minutes, and between Anchorage and New York 7 hours and 50 minutes. This chart is very useful but you will need to work out individual journeys which are not listed.

To find the actual flying time for a journey where the city of departure has a time difference from the city of arrival, you will need to convert both times into GMT. The procedure is as follows:

1 Establish the departure and arrival times in local times. These are the times published in the timetables. For example, a particular flight in August departs Rome 1415 hours local time and arrives Port au Prince 1915 hours local time.
2 Look at the international time calculator to establish the time variance to GMT. Rome (Italy) is at GMT + 2 (DST 25 March to 29 September). Rome is 2 hours ahead of GMT. Port-au-Prince (Haiti) is at GMT − 4. Port-au-Prince is 4 hours behind GMT.
3 Convert the local times to GMT. For Rome, 1415 hours converted to GMT (−2 hours) is 1215 hours. For Port-au-Prince, 1915 hours converted to GMT (+4 hours) is 2315 hours.

4 Now that you have both departure and arrival times in GMT, it is easy to work out the actual flying time. This is from 1215 hours to 2315 hours GMT; that is, 11 hours.

Exercise 10

(a) The time of travel is October; depart Beijing (BJS) China at 0740 hours; arrive Karachi (KHI) Pakistan at 1220 hours (same day).
(b) The time of travel is June; depart Frankfurt (FRA) 1355 hours; arrive Lagos (LOS) 1925 hours.

International Date Line

Please look at a map for Fiji and Hawaii in the Pacific Ocean. They are not a great distance from each other, and yet there is a 22 hour time difference. This is because Fiji is at the eastern extreme of the time zones (GMT + 12) and Tahiti is at the western extreme of the time zones (GMT − 10). You could say that when we travel across the International Date Line, going from the eastern hemisphere to the western hemisphere, we *gain* a day; travelling from west to east we lose a day.

Passport, visa and health regulations

Passengers travelling to overseas countries need to have valid travel documents. These usually concern passports, visa requirements and health regulations (vaccinations etc. required). Full details can be found in the *ABC Guide to International Travel*, and we shall be looking at extracts from this directory in a moment. The *ABC Guide* contains general information on passports and visas; definitions of organizations, for example the Arab League, the Commonwealth, the European Community, the International Labour Organization, the European Free Trade Association; monetary areas, such as the French franc and sterling areas; World Health Organization maps showing infected areas; airport duty-free shops (we don't want to make any slip-ups there!); and country by country details on regulations.

Passports

Extreme care should be taken when checking a passenger's documents of identity, in particular the validity and the exit, transit and destination requirements.
    To give the correct information we have to understand the terminology of the different types of passport:

AREAS OF MALARIAL RISK

Map reproduced by courtesy of the World Health Organisation

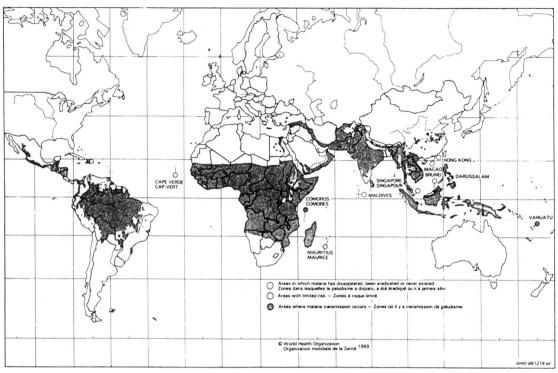

Areas in which malaria has disappeared, been eradicated or never existed
Zones dans lesquelles le paludisme a disparu, a été éradiqué ou n'a jamais sévi

Areas with limited risk — Zones à risque limité

Areas where malaria transmission occurs — Zones où il y a transmission de paludisme

© World Health Organization
Organisation mondiale de la Santé 1989

WHO 881219 bl

GIBRALTAR

Local Time:GMT +2 (From 30 Sep GMT +1)
Capital: Gibraltar
Area Of The World: Western Europe (southern tip of Iberian Peninsular)
Language: English, Spanish
Electricity:220/240V AC 50Hz
Int. Direct Dialling Code:350
Driving Licence: International or National
BBC World Service:

	KHz		
Morning	9410	7150	6195
Daytime	15070	12095	9760
Evening	12095	9410	7325

Currency: Gibraltar Pound (GIP) (Sterling accepted)
    Notes: £1, 5, 10, 20, 50.
    Coins: £5, £2, £1, 50p, 20p, 10p, 5p, 2p, 1p.
Business Hours:
Banking:0900-1530 Mon-Thur. 0900-1530 & 1630-1800 Fri.
Office:0900-1300 & 1500-1800 Mon-Fri.
Shops:1000-1900 Mon-Fri. 1000-1300 Sat.
Emergency Services: Police & Ambulance: 199; Fire: 190

Passport/Visa

Passports: Required by all except seamen in possession of valid Seaman Book provided they are on duty. British subjects (U.K. or Colonies) may use a British Visitor's Passport in lieu of a passport. Nationals of EC national identity card except Portugal and Spain.
Visas: Required by stateless persons and nationals of the following countries: Afghanistan, Albania, Argentina, Bhutan, Bulgaria, Chad, China People's Rep., Cuba, Czechoslovakia, Djibouti, Egypt, Ethiopia, German Dem. Rep., Hungary, Iran, Iraq, Jordan, Korea People's Dem. Rep., Lebanon, Libya, Mauritania, Mali, Mongolia, Morocco, Poland, Romania, Somalia, Sudan, Syria, Tunisia, U.S.S.R., Viet Nam Dem. Rep., Yemen Arab Rep., Yemen Peoples Dem. Rep., and stateless persons.
Residence and Employment: Persons must obtain prior permission from the Government of Gibraltar (nationals of EC countries are exempted).

Customs

Currency
Import: No restrictions but must be declared on arrival.
Export: No restrictions- up to the amount imported and declared
Import Allowances:(a) 200 cigarettes or 100 cigarillos (max. weight each of 3 gr.) or 50 cigars or 250 gr. tobacco. (b) Spirits, liqueurs or cordials. 1 lit. or 2 lit. of fortified or sparkling wine or 2 lit. of table wine. (c) Perfume 50 gr. and 0.25 lit. toilet water. No relief is afforded to any person under the age of 17 years in respect of the above goods. Other goods:articles of any description to the value of £32.
Note: Members of a crew of a ship or an aircraft shall not be afforded relief unless he pays off from his ship or aircraft or proceeds on leave for a period of more than 5 days.

Air Travel

International Airport: Gibraltar (North Front) 1ml/2kms. Bus, taxi, courtesy coaches.
Airport Tax:£5.00 per seat paying passenger included in the published fare.

Climate

Gibraltar	Jan	Feb	Mar	Apr	May	Jun	Jul	Aug	Sep	Oct	Nov	Dec
Temp°C Max		20	20	22	26	28	32	33	34	32	27	23	21
Min		3	3	7	8	11	13	16	19	14	10	8	5
Humidity % am		81	80	83	83	81	80	79	80	82	83	84	83
pm		66	63	67	58	57	54	60	60	61	64	68	67
Rainfall (mm)		152	98	106	59	25	4	1	3	23	55	114	120

Health

Vaccination Certificates Required: No vaccinations are required.
Immunisation Recommended: Typhoid, Polio

Public Holidays

1990: Jan 1 New Year's Day; Mar 12 Commonwealth Day; Apr 13 Good Friday; Apr 16 Easter Monday; May 1 May Day; May 28 Spring Bank Holiday; Jun 18 Queen's Birthday; Aug 27 Late Summer Bank Holiday; Dec 25, 26 Christmas.

Business And Social Hints

British social conventions apply on most occasions. However there are also strong mediterranean influences.

Citizen   A person who owes allegiance to a country's government. Citizenship can be obtained by birth or naturalization.

National   A person who owes allegiance to a government, with his passport declaring him to be a national but not a citizen of that country. People generally become nationals of a government by treaty, international mandate (e.g. UN), right of discovery, or conquest.

Alien   A person in a country of which he or she is not a citizen. He could be an immigrant, a non-immigrant or a resident.

Non-immigrant   An alien who enters a country temporarily as a tourist or for business.

Tourist   A temporary visitor staying at least 24 hours in the country visited.

In transit   A person in transit is passing through a country. He may be in transit on the same aircraft or changing flights, but he is not allowed to leave the international area of the airport.

Stateless   A stateless person is outside the country of his or her nationality, and is unable or unwilling to obtain a passport because the country no longer exists, or because for justifiable reasons he or she no longer owes allegiance to the government in power.

Visas

A visa is an entry in a passport made by a consular official of the government to indicate that the bearer has been granted authority to enter or re-enter the country concerned. The granting of a visa, however, does *not* guarantee entry. The main types of visa are tourist, transit, immigrant and diplomatic.

Health requirements

We need to check the validity of vaccinations. For example, cholera is valid for 6 days to 6 months, and yellow fever for 10 days to 10 years. The *ABC Guide to International Travel* lists the countries with infected areas.

Study the map for malaria infected areas in the world. Read the notes on the map explaining areas (○) in which malaria has disappeared; (◎) areas where risks still exist; (●) infected areas. Then complete Exercise 11. From studying the map please answer the following questions.

Exercise 11

For clients travelling to the following countries should they protect themselves against malaria?

Country	No risk	Limited risk	Definite risk
Australia	√		
Mauritius			
Brazil			
Peru			
Madagascar			
Lesotho			
Zaire			
Algeria			
Turkey			
South Yemen			

Should your client be travelling to, or passing through a country where a malaria risk exists, they are advised to take anti-malaria tablets 10 days beforehand, whilst in the area and afterwards. Particular note is drawn to the need for continuing treatment at least a month after leaving the area. It is advisable to obtain medical advice before being vaccinated, inoculated or taking preventative medicine.

International travel example: Gibraltar

Please study the extract from the *ABC Guide to International Travel*. The country is Gibraltar.

A map has been given, plus a description of the area of the world: Western Europe, at the southern tip of the Iberian Peninsular. We are given the local time (GMT + 2); during the winter from 30 September the local time is GMT + 1. We are given the name of the capital of Gibraltar; the languages spoken; the electricity voltage; the international direct dialling code; driving licence requirements; radio frequencies for the BBC World Service (tourists and business travellers like to keep up to date); currency; business hours; and emergency service telephone numbers.

For passport and visa information, we need to be clear that passports are required by *all* persons (except seamen on duty and in possession of a valid Seaman Book). British subjects may use a British Visitor's Passport; these are valid for one year and can be obtained from a post office (unlike the 10-year passport, they are not valid for all countries). Nationals of EC countries can use their national identity card, except nationals of Portugal and Spain. (The European Community countries are Belgium, Denmark, France, Germany, Greece, Ireland, Italy, Luxembourg, The Netherlands, Portugal, Spain and the United Kingdom.) All stateless persons, and nationals of those countries listed, require a visa. To reside permanently or to work in Gibraltar, permission must be obtained from the government of Gibraltar unless the person is a national of an EC country.

For customs information, we are advised of any restrictions of goods or money to take into and out of the country. Concerning air travel, we are advised that the airport is called North Front, how far it is from the city, (1 mile/2 kilometres) and that transport is available. There is an airport tax but it is included in the published air fare.

We are given details of the climate. For health requirements, no vaccinations are required but immunization against typhoid and polio is recommended (not compulsory). Public holiday dates have been given. Most importantly, there are some business and social hints. For Gibraltar the business and social hints are simple, but those for some countries may advise on dress or on how to greet people. Perhaps business cards must be used by business travellers, and appointments made well in advance.

Exercise 12

Take time to read the Gibraltar details again. Then please study the details given on Greece, and answer the following questions:

(a) What currency is used in Greece?
(b) Your client is going to a Greek island, and wishes to use the banks to change his travellers' cheques. Advise the client when banks are closed.

GREECE

Local Time:GMT +3 (From 30 Sep GMT +2)
Capital:Athens
Area Of The World:South East Europe
Language:Greek, some English, Italian, French
Electricity:220V AC 50Hz
Int. Direct Dialling Code:30
Driving Licence:International (foreign by citizens of Austria, Belgium, Germany Fed. Rep. and U.K.
BBC World Service:

	KHz		
Morning	12095	9410	6180
Daytime	18080	15070	6180
Evening	12095	9410	6180

Currency: Drachma (GRD)
Notes:GRD:50, 100, 500, 1000, 5000
Coins:GRD1, 2, 5, 10, 20, 50
Business Hours
Banking:0800-1400 Mon-Fri. National and General Bank, Constitution Square 0900-2000 Mon-Sat (closed Mon, Thur 1400-1530, Fri 1330-1500)
Shops:Summer :0800-1430 Mon, Wed. Sat. 0800-1400 & 1730-2030 Tue, Thur & Fri. Winter: 0900-1700 Mon. Wed. 1000-1900 Tue. Thur. Fri. 0830-1530 Sat.
Emergency Services:Police: 100 (all large cities. 109 Athens suburbs);   Fire: 199 (Athens); Ambulance: 166 (Athens)

Passport/Visa

Passports:Required by all except:Holders of Laissez-Passer (provided with a Greek visa) issued together with U.N. Military Identity Card (with movement or leave order) issued by a NATO country. National Identity Card:Nationals of Austria, Belgium, France, Germany Federal Rep., Italy, Luxembourg, Monaco, Netherlands ("Toeristenkaart"), Portugal, Spain, Switzerland, United Kingdom (British Visitor's Passport). Passport expired maximum of 5 years:Nationals of Austria, Belgium, France, Luxembourg, Netherlands, Portugal, Spain and Switzerland. Seaman Book:nationals of any country (travelling on duty
Visas:Required by all except:Nationals of Greece. Nationals of the following countries:(a) For a maximum stay 3 months: holders of British passports with on the fron cover "United Kingdom of Great Britain and Northern Ireland" or "Jersey" or "Guernsey and its dependencies" or "Isle of Man", in which the holder is described as "British Subject, Citizen of the United Kingdom, Islands and Colonies" (however, if passport issued in Hong Kong max. stay of 1 month permitted). Nationals of Andorra, Argentina, Australia, Austria, Bahamas, Barbados, Belgium, Canada, Cyprus, Denmark, Finland, France, Gambia, Germany Federal Rep. Grenada, Iceland, Ireland Rep.,Israel, Italy, Japan, Korea Rep., Liechtenstein, Luxembourg, Malta, Mexico, Monaco, Netherlands, New Zealand, Norway, St. Kitts & Nevis, San Marino. Spain, Sweden. Switzerland, Uruguay U.S.A. and Zimbabwe. (b) For a maximum stay of 2 months: Brazil, Bolivia, Chile, Colombia, Costa Rica, Dominican Rep., Ecuador, El Salvador, Macau, Malawi, Morocco, Nicaragua, Paraguay, Peru, Portugal, Seychelles, South Africa Rep., and Tanzania. (c) For a maximum stay of one month:Tunisia. Holders of diplomatic passports, accredited to Greece, provided they are visa exempted on mutual basis.
Notes:(a) Students studying in Greece require a visa. (b) Nationals of Africa, Asia and South America (except Israel, Korea Rep. and Tunisia) wishing to extend their stay must hold a medical certificate issued by the Health Centre of Ministry of Health and proof of sufficient funds to cover the period of intended stay.
Transit:Visa not required by those continuing their journey to a third country within 48 hours, providing that they are holding tickets with reserved seats and valid documents for their onward journey. It is, however, up to the discretion of the immigration authorities whether or not a passenger is allowed to leave the airport.
Re-entry Permit:Required for returning alien residents of Greece, who are not exempt from visa requirements. Returning nationals of Turkey residing in Greece must hold in addition to a re-entry permit a consular visa (prior to their return) for re-entry into Greece.

Customs

Currency
Import:Local limit GRD 100.000. Foreign:Foreign banknotes unlimited; amounts exceeding US$1000 must be declared on arrival.
Export:Local limit GRD 20.000. Foreign:Up to amount imported and declared. It is advisable to export Greek currency in denominations of a maximum GRD 5.000.
Import Allowances:(for passengers 18 years of age or over). Passengers arriving from inside EC countries not tax free. (a) 300 cigarettes or 150 cigarillos or 75 cigars or 400 gr. pipe tobacco. (b) 1.5 litre of alcoholic beverages over 22° or 4 litres of alcoholic beverages of max. 22° and 5 litres of still wine. (c) 75 gr. of perfume and 0.375 litre toilet water. Gift articles (may not include electronic devices) up to a total value of GRD 55.000. Children under 15 years up to GRD 17.000. Passengers arriving from outside EC countries or inside EC countries tax free:(a) 200 cigarettes or 100 cigarillos or 50 cigars or 250 gr. pipe tobacco. (b) 1 litre of alcoholic beverages or 2 litres of wine. (c) 50 gr. perfume and 0.25 litre toilet water. Gift articles (may not include electronic devices) up to a total value of GRD 7.000.
Prohibited:plants with soil. Windsurfboards; unless a Greek national residing in Greece guarantees that it will be re-exported.

Air Travel

International Airports:Athens (Hellinikon) 6mls/10kms. Bus, taxi. Iraklion 3mls/5kms. Bus, taxi. Thessaloniki 10mls/16kms. Coach, taxi. Corfu (Kerkyra) 1ml/2kms. Coach, taxi. Rhodes (Paradisi) 10mls/16kms. Coach, taxi.
Airport Tax:Not applicable.

Climate

Athens	Jan	Feb	Mar	Apr	May	Jun	Jul	Aug	Sep	Oct	Nov	Dec
Temp °C Max	12	13	16	19	25	29	32	32	28	23	18	14
Min	6	6	8	11	16	19	22	22	19	16	11	8
Humidity % am	77	77	74	70	66	61	53	53	60	73	77	79
pm	62	61	54	47	44	40	32	33	38	52	60	63
Rainfall (mm)	61	38	37	22	23	14	6	7	15	50	56	70

Health

Vaccination Certificates Required:Yellow Fever if arriving within 6 days from or via endemic areas. Exempt are infants under 6 months and those not leaving the airport.

(c) Does a national of India staying in Greece for 3 weeks require a visa?

(d) Does a national of Tanzania staying for 10 weeks require a visa?

(e) Your business client will be purchasing goods, and plans to take US$2000 for this purpose. Will there be any restrictions?

(f) If the same business client does not succeed with the business transaction, will there be problems getting the US$2000 out of Greece when returning to America?

(g) Give the distance between the airport and the town centre on the island of Rhodes.

(h) Yellow fever vaccination is compulsory if the client is arriving within 6 days from or via an endemic area. How can you find out which are the endemic areas?

Special services for passengers

Almost anyone can travel by aircraft, providing arrangements have been made beforehand. Each airline sets out the regulations and conditions of booking for each circumstance. Thus it is important to check with each airline being used on the journey, to abide by their regulations and to make prior arrangements. We are going to point out a few general conditions.

Special arrangements can be made for various categories of client. The travel consultant needs to consider the following questions.

Young flyers

What is the minimum age a child may travel alone?
What is the maximum age?
At what age is the child considered an adult?
What are the formalities (completion of forms)?
Who will be taking the child to the airport?
Who will be meeting the child on arrival?

VIPs

What security arrangements should be made?
How many in the party?
What are their special requests?
What can the airline offer in special services?
What are the formalities?

Special meals

What type of food is required: baby food, vegetarian, Moslem, Hindu, kosher, medical? What are the formalities?

Invalid and infirm passengers

Can passengers ascend and descend the aircraft steps?

Are they completely immobile?
Is a wheelchair required?
Is the passenger a stretcher case?
Will any medical apparatus be required?
Has the passenger a medical certificate confirming fitness to travel?
What are the formalities?

Expectant mothers

Does the expectant mother have a medical certificate confirming fitness to travel?
What is the limit on the number of weeks of pregnancy accepted by airlines?
What are the formalities?

Escort services

What types of escort are there: child escorts, medical escorts, legal escorts?
What would they do?
How much would they pay?
What are the formalities?

Making a reservation

Most airlines produce excellent manuals and information brochures. It is necessary to obtain *all* the material from each airline and take time to read and understand it? Have you no time? Then take the books home to read! Query any point you do not fully understand with your manager. After a few months the travel language will seem familiar to you. You will be able to find the relevant regulations quickly, and you will grow in confidence.

Free baggage allowance

Your clients will need to know how much baggage they can take with them on to the aircraft. This information can be found in the *Air Transport Manual.* Many airline carriers also provide a quick reference chart for you to follow.

Generally the free baggage allowance will depend on the class of travel and the route. For some journeys the piece system is used, and for other routes the weight system is used.

You would also need to advise your clients on restricted articles, i.e. items not allowed on board an aircraft.

Airport information

Manuals and information booklets are provided for you to give accurate information on the facilities available at airports.

BETWEEN/ AND	fare basis	GBP OW	GBP RT	AP	min/ max stay	period	res bkg cde	rule	Rtg
LONDON									
AMSTERDAM	YSX	–	108		SU/3M	all year	L	103	
	YPX	–	139		SU/3M	all year	B	100	
	YBD	–	157		–/1Y	all year	B	898	
	YS	108	216		–/1Y	all year	S	524	
	C	125	250		–/1Y	all year	C		
	YZZ	61	122		–/1Y	all year	M	708	
	YCD	–	95	14	SU/3M	all year	L	844	
ATHENS	YLISO	143	286		–/1Y	01 Apr –30 Jun 01 Oct –31 Mar	L	802	
	YHISO	149	298		–/1Y	01 Jul –30 Sep	L	802	
	YLXSX	–	237		SU/1M	01 Nov –06 Dec 06 Jan –14 Mar	L	103	
	YLWSX	–	248		SU/1M	01 Nov –06 Dec 06 Jan –14 Mar	L	103	
	YQSX	–	283		SU/1M	07 Dec –05 Jan 15 Mar –06 Apr	L	103	
	YJXSX	–	207		SU/1M	16 Apr –17 May 28 May –24 Jun	L	103	
	YJWSX	–	218		SU/1M	16 Apr –17 May 28 May –24 Jun	L	103	
	YKXSX	–	224		SU/1M	07 Apr –15 Apr 18 May –27 May 25 Jun –05 Jul 10 Sep –31 Oct	L	103	
	YKWSX	–	235		SU/1M	07 Apr –15 Apr 18 May –27 May 25 Jun –05 Jul 10 Sep –31 Oct	L	103	
	YHXSX	–	251		SU/1M	05 Jul –07 Sep	L	103	
	YHWSX	–	269		SU/1M	05 Jul –07 Sep	L	103	
	YQPX	–	317		SU/3M	07 Dec –05 Jan 15 Mar –06 Apr	B	100	
	YLXPX	–	259		SU/3M	01 Nov –06 Dec 06 Jan –14 Mar	B	100	
	YLWPX	–	269		SU/3M	01 Nov –06 Dec 06 Jan –14 Mar	B	100	
	YJXPX	–	229		SU/3M	16 Apr –17 May 28 May –24 Jun	B	100	
	YJWPX	–	241		SU/3M	16 Apr –17 May 28 May –24 Jun	B	100	
	YKXPX	–	252		SU/3M	07 Apr –15 Apr 18 May –27 May 25 Jun –05 Jul 10 Sep –31 Oct	B	100	
	YKWPX	–	264		SU/3M	07 Apr –15 Apr 18 May –27 May 25 Jun –05 Jul 10 Sep –31 Oct	B	100	
	YHXPX	–	292		SU/3M	05 Jul –07 Sep	B	100	
	YHWPX	–	310		SU/3M	05 Jul –07 Sep	B	100	
	YLE2	–	357		SU/6M	01 Apr –30 Jun 01 Oct –31 Mar	M	587	
	YHE2	–	414		SU/6M	01 Jul –30 Sep	M	587	
	YLE1	–	400		SU/6M	01 Apr –30 Jun 01 Oct –31 Mar	M	587	
	YHE1	–	459		SU/6M	01 Jul –30 Sep	M	587	
	YB	232	464		–/1Y	all year	S	507	
	C	312	624		–/1Y	all year	C		
	YLZZ	140	280		–/1Y	01 Apr –30 Jun 01 Oct –31 Mar	M	708	
	YHZZ	147	294		–/1Y	01 Jul –30 Sep	M	708	
	YLCD	–	237	14	SU/3M	01 Nov –06 Dec 06 Jan –14 Mar	L	844	
	YJCD	–	206	14	SU/3M	16 Apr –17 May 28 May –24 Jun	L	844	
	YQCD	–	283	14	SU/3M	07 Dec –05 Jan 15 Mar –06 Apr	L	844	
	YKCD	–	224	14	SU/3M	07 Apr –15 Apr 18 May –27 May 25 Jun –05 Jul 10 Sep –31 Oct	L	844	
	YHCD	–	251	14	SU/3M	06 Jul –09 Sep	L	844	
BARCELONA	YLXSS	–	95		SU/1M	05 Nov –13 Dec 02 Jan –07 Feb	V	827	
	YLWSS	–	112		SU/1M	05 Nov –13 Dec 02 Jan –07 Feb	V	827	
	YJXSS	–	120		SU/1M	01 Oct –27 Oct	V	827	
	YJWSS	–	130		SU/1M	01 Oct –27 Oct	V	827	
	YKXSS	–	122		SU/1M	28 Oct –04 Nov 25 Dec –01 Jan 08 Feb –21 Mar	V	827	
	YKWSS	–	135		SU/1M	28 Oct –04 Nov 25 Dec –01 Jan 08 Feb –21 Mar	V	827	
	YHXSS	–	167		SU/1M	14 Dec –24 Dec 22 Mar –31 Mar	V	827	
	YHWSS	–	184		SU/1M	14 Dec –24 Dec 22 Mar –31 Mar	V	827	
	YLXBS	109	–	1	–/1Y	02 Jan –07 Feb 05 Nov –13 Dec	B	867	
	YLWBS	130	–	1	–/1Y	02 Jan –07 Feb 05 Nov –13 Dec	B	867	
	YTXBS	137	–	1	–/1Y	25 Dec –01 Jan 08 Feb –21 Mar 28 Oct –04 Nov	B	867	
	YTWBS	148	–	1	–/1Y	25 Dec –01 Jan 08 Feb –21 Mar 28 Oct –04 Nov	B	867	
	YJXBS	123	–	1	–/1Y	01 Apr –13 Jun	B	867	
	YJWBS	133	–	1	–/1Y	01 Apr –13 Jun	B	867	
	YLXSX	–	120		SU/1M	02 Jan –07 Feb 05 Nov –13 Dec	L	103	
	YLWSX	–	141		SU/1M	02 Jan –07 Feb 05 Nov –13 Dec	L	103	
	YTXSX	–	148		SU/1M	25 Dec –01 Jan 08 Feb –21 Mar 28 Oct –04 Nov	L	103	
	YTWSX	–	159		SU/1M	25 Dec –01 Jan 08 Feb –21 Mar 28 Oct –04 Nov	L	103	
	YJXSX	–	133		SU/1M	01 Apr –13 Jun	L	103	
	YJWSX	–	143		SU/1M	01 Apr –13 Jun	L	103	
	YKXSX	–	153		SU/1M	14 Jun –11 Jul 16 Sep –27 Oct	L	103	
	YKWSX	–	172		SU/1M	14 Jun –11 Jul 16 Sep –27 Oct	L	103	
	YHXSX	–	167		SU/1M	12 Jul –15 Sep	L	103	
	YHWSX	–	198		SU/1M	12 Jul –15 Sep	L	103	
	YQXSX	–	210		SU/1M	14 Dec –24 Dec 22 Mar –31 Mar	L	103	
	YQWSX	–	231		SU/1M	14 Dec –24 Dec 22 Mar –31 Mar	L	103	
	YLXPX	–	141		SU/3M	02 Jan –07 Feb 05 Nov –13 Dec	B	100	
	YLWPX	–	162		SU/3M	02 Jan –07 Feb 05 Nov –13 Dec	B	100	
	YQXPX	–	247		SU/3M	14 Dec –24 Dec 22 Mar –31 Mar	B	100	
	YQWPX	–	268		SU/3M	14 Dec –24 Dec	B	100	

RU = Refer Rule

BETWEEN/ AND	fare basis	GBP OW	GBP RT	AP	min/ max stay	period	res bkg cde	rule	Rtg
LONDON									
BARCELONA	YQWPX	–	268		SU/3M	22 Mar –31 Mar	B	100	
	YTXPX	–	171		SU/3M	25 Dec –01 Jan 08 Feb –21 Mar 28 Oct –04 Nov	B	100	
	YTWPX	–	181		SU/3M	25 Dec –01 Jan 08 Feb –21 Mar 28 Oct –04 Nov	B	100	
	YJXPX	–	153		SU/3M	01 Apr –13 Jun	B	100	
	YJWPX	–	163		SU/3M	01 Apr –13 Jun	B	100	
	YKXPX	–	171		SU/3M	14 Jun –11 Jul 16 Sep –27 Oct	B	100	
	YKWPX	–	197		SU/3M	14 Jun –11 Jul 16 Sep –27 Oct	B	100	
	YHXPX	–	202		SU/3M	12 Jul –15 Sep	B	100	
	YHWPX	–	233		SU/3M	12 Jul –15 Sep	B	100	
	YLE	–	264		SU/6M	01 Apr –30 Jun 01 Oct –31 Mar	M	587	
	YHE	–	304		SU/6M	01 Jul –30 Sep	M	587	
	YB	159	318		–/1Y	all year	S	507	
	C	193	386		–/1Y	all year	C		
	YLZZ	85	170		–/1Y	26 Mar –05 Apr 16 Apr –17 May 28 May –12 Jul 17 Sep –27 Oct	M	708	
	YHZZ	127	254		–/1Y	06 Apr –15 Apr 18 May –27 May 13 Jul –16 Sep	M	708	
	YLXCD	–	109	14	SU/3M	02 Jan –07 Feb 05 Nov –13 Dec	L	844	
	YLWCD	–	130	14	SU/3M	02 Jan –07 Feb 05 Nov –13 Dec	L	844	
	YTXCD	–	143	14	SU/3M	25 Dec –01 Jan 08 Feb –21 Mar 28 Oct –04 Nov	L	844	
	YTWCD	–	156	14	SU/3M	25 Dec –01 Jan 08 Feb –21 Mar 28 Oct –04 Nov	L	844	
	YJXCD	–	123		SU/3M	01 Apr –13 Jun	L	844	
	YJWCD	–	133		SU/3M	01 Apr –13 Jun	L	844	
	YQXCD	–	199	14	SU/3M	14 Dec –24 Dec 22 Mar –31 Mar	L	844	
	YQWCD	–	221	14	SU/3M	14 Dec –24 Dec 22 Mar –31 Mar	L	844	
	YKXCD	–	136	14	SU/3M	14 Jun –11 Jul 16 Sep –27 Oct	L	844	
	YKWCD	–	162	14	SU/3M	14 Jun –11 Jul 16 Sep –27 Oct	L	844	
	YHXCD	–	157	14	SU/3M	12 Jul –15 Sep	L	844	
	YHWCD	–	220	14	SU/3M	12 Jul –15 Sep	L	844	
BASLE	YLAP2	–	137	14	SU/3M	01 Oct –13 Dec 08 Jan –31 Jan 01 Apr –31 May	L	403	
	YHAP2	–	159	14	SU/3M	14 Dec –07 Jan 01 Feb –31 Mar 01 Jun –30 Sep	L	403	
	YLAP	–	184	14	SU/3M	01 Oct –13 Dec 08 Jan –31 Jan 01 Apr –31 May	B	400	
	YHAP	–	197	14	SU/3M	14 Dec –07 Jan 01 Feb –31 Mar 01 Jun –30 Sep	B	400	
	YLSX	–	184		SU/3M	01 Oct –13 Dec 08 Jan –31 Jan 01 Apr –31 May	L	103	
	YHSX	–	197		SU/3M	14 Dec –07 Jan 01 Feb –31 Mar 01 Jun –30 Sep	L	103	
	YLPX	–	228		SU/3M	01 Oct –13 Dec 08 Jan –31 Jan 01 Apr –31 May	B	100	
	YHPX	–	242		SU/3M	14 Dec –07 Jan 01 Feb –31 Mar 01 Jun –30 Sep	B	100	
	YLBT	–	125		SU/1M	01 Nov –13 Dec 08 Jan –31 Jan	*	TOP	
	YHBT	–	133		SU/1M	14 Dec –07 Jan 01 Feb –31 Mar	*	TOP	
	YB	146	292		–/1Y	all year	S	507	
	C	173	346		–/1Y	all year	C		
	YZZ	86	172		–/1Y	all year	M	708	
	YLCD	–	137	14	SU/3M	01 Oct –13 Dec 08 Jan –31 Jan 01 Apr –31 May	L	844	
	YHCD	–	159	14	SU/3M	14 Dec –07 Jan 01 Feb –31 Mar 01 Jun –30 Sep	L	844	
BERGEN	YAP	–	194	14	SU/3M	all year	L	400	
	YPX	–	277		SU/3M	all year	B	100	
	YLBT	–	195		SU/1M	01 Apr –31 Oct	*	TOP	
	YHBT	–	207		SU/1M	01 Nov –31 Mar	*	TOP	
	YB	200	400		–/1Y	all year	S	507	
	C	242	484		–/1Y	all year	C		
	YZZ	96	192		–/1Y	all year	M	708	
	YCD	–	194	14	SU/3M	all year	L	844	
BERLIN	YAP2	–	164	7	SU/3M	all year	L	403	
	YAP	–	206	7	SU/3M	all year	B	400	
	YPX	–	231		SU/3M	all year	B	100	
	YGV6	–	270		6N/1M	all year	*	336	
	YB	160	320		–/1Y	all year	S	507	
	C	205	410		–/1Y	all year	C		
	YMT	–	199		SU/3M	all year	L	832	
	YZZ	96	191		–/1Y	all year	M	708	
	YZZRT	–	128		1N/6M	all year	V	718	
	YCD	–	148	14	SU/3M	all year	L	844	
BILBAO	YLXSS	–	95		SU/1M	05 Nov –13 Dec 02 Jan –07 Feb	V	827	
	YLWSS	–	112		SU/1M	05 Nov –13 Dec 02 Jan –07 Feb	V	827	
	YJXSS	–	120		SU/1M	01 Oct –27 Oct	V	827	
	YJWSS	–	130		SU/1M	01 Oct –27 Oct	V	827	
	YKXSS	–	122		SU/1M	28 Oct –04 Nov 25 Dec –01 Jan 08 Feb –21 Mar	V	827	
	YKWSS	–	135		SU/1M	28 Oct –04 Nov 25 Dec –01 Jan 08 Feb –21 Mar	V	827	
	YHXSS	–	167		SU/1M	14 Dec –24 Dec 22 Mar –31 Mar	V	827	
	YHWSS	–	184		SU/1M	14 Dec –24 Dec 22 Mar –31 Mar	V	827	
	YLXBS	109	–	1	–/1Y	02 Jan –07 Feb 05 Nov –13 Dec	B	867	
	YLWBS	130	–	1	–/1Y	02 Jan –07 Feb 05 Nov –13 Dec	B	867	
	YTXBS	137	–	1	–/1Y	25 Dec –01 Jan 08 Feb –21 Mar 28 Oct –04 Nov	B	867	
	YTWBS	137	–	1	–/1Y	25 Dec –01 Jan 08 Feb –21 Mar	B	867	

* = Contact Group Sales

BRITISH AIRWAYS

100 PEX

Application Y RT/Single open jaw
Special Events: Can be used to Belgium, France, Irish Rep, Netherlands.
Fares Only apply if purchased before departure.
Children Pay 67% *Infants* Pay 10%
Period of Application Date of outbound travel determines fare.
Min/Max Stay See fares tables.
Extension of validity not permitted.
Stopovers Not permitted.
Routing/Transfers International travel: Direct flights.
Transfers permitted at London for UK addon constructed fares.
Constructions Permitted with addons.
Combinations Permitted with Domestic fares/other fares which permit combinations
Res/Payment/Ticketing Must be completed at same time.
Ticket must show confirmed Res. for entire journey.
Form of Payment: NON REF/PEX.
Conditions of Sale Sticker: Required.
Refund for Cancellation/No Show Before day of departure, 50% refund. Any other time, no refund.
Upgrading: To F,C,Y,YB,YBD or YE fare permitted but fare must be recalculated from origin and cancellation charge will apply if upgraded ticket is subsequently cancelled.
Rebooking/Rerouting Not permitted.
Agents/Tour Conductors Discounts Not permitted

Exceptions

FRANCE
Periods of Application
LON/MAN - NCE Peak Season:
Midweek (X): Mo-Th Weekend (W): Fr-Su
Min Stay LON-PAR - Same day travel permitted on Sat/Sun.
For travel midweek in one direction and weekend in the other, charge half midweek/half weekend outbound seasonal fare.
Constructions Not permitted with French add-ons

GERMANY
Routing/Transfers One domestic transfer, in UK or Germany, is permitted in each direction.

GREECE
Periods of Application
Midweek (X): Mo - Th. Weekend (W): Fr - Su
For travel midweek in one direction and weekend in the other, charge half midweek/half weekend outbound seasonal fare.

IRISH REPUBLIC
Children Pay 50%
Min Stay LON-DUB: Same day return travel permitted on Sat.

ITALY
Constructions Not permitted with Italian add-ons.

SCANDINAVIA
Combinations Permitted with Domestic fares/Scandinavian Construction Fares/Full sector fares for travel on Braathens within Norway

SPAIN
Children Pay 67% Applicable only for travel on BA sectors
Periods of Application
Midweek (X): Mo-Th Weekend (W): Fr-Su
For travel midweek in one direction and weekend in the other, charge half midweek/half weekend outbound seasonal fare.

103 SUPERPEX

Application Y RT/Single open jaw
Fares Only apply if purchased before departure.
Children Pay 67% *Infants* Pay 10%
Period of Application Date of outbound travel determines fare.
Min/Max Stay See fares tables
Extension of validity not permitted
Stopovers Not permitted.
Routing/Transfers International travel: Direct flights. Transfers permitted at London for UK addon constructed fares.
Constructions Permitted with addons.
Combinations Permitted with Domestic fares.
Res/Payment/Ticketing Must be completed at same time.
Ticket must show confirmed Res. for entire journey.
Form of Payment: NON REF/SPEX.
Conditions of Sale Sticker: Required.
Refund for Cancellation/No Show Before day of departure, 50% refund. Any other time, no refund.
Upgrading: To F,C,Y,YB,YBD or YE fare permitted but fare must be recalculated from origin and cancellation charge will apply if upgraded ticket is subsequently cancelled.
Rebooking/Rerouting Not permitted.
Agents/Tour Conductors Discounts Not permitted

Exceptions

FRANCE
Min/Stay Same day travel permitted on Sat/Sun.
Constructions Not permitted with French add-ons

GREECE
Period of Application
Midweek (X): Mo-Th. Weekend (W): Fr-Su
For travel midweek in one direction and weekend in the other, charge half midweek/half weekend outbound seasonal fare.

IRISH REPUBLIC
Children Pay 50%
Between BHX/MAN and ORK/SNN: one transfer is permitted at DUB

PORTUGAL
Application Open jaw is permitted between Spain and Portugal.

SPAIN
Application Open jaw is permitted between Spain and Portugal.
Children Pay 67% Applicable only for travel on BA sectors
Periods of Application
Midweek (X): Mo-Th Weekend (W): Fr-Su
For travel midweek in one direction and weekend in the other, charge half midweek/half weekend outbound seasonal fare.
Routing/Transfers International travel: Direct BA flights. Transfers permitted at LON for UK addon constructed fares.

SWITZERLAND
Constructions Not permitted with Swiss add-ons

NETHERLANDS
Res/Payment/Ticketing If used for IT, Res/Payment/Ticketing need not be completed at the same time.

277 GROUP IT UK - USSR

Min Group Size 10 passengers
Min Stay Applies from date of arrival in the country of turnaround.
Rebooking/Rerouting After departure: Not permitted

284 INDIVIDUAL IT UK - USSR

Min Stay Applies from date of arrival in the country of turnaround.

312 GROUP IT UK - HUNGARY

Min Group Size 9 adult passengers

We need to advise our clients on how to change planes, and how to get from one terminal to another. Give the correct terminal used by the airline carrier in question. Advise on car parking facilities and cost. Advise on public transport from the airport. Advise on information desks, banks, business centres, baggage security, left and lost baggage, post offices, nursing, mothers' room, public telephones, restaurants, bars, lounges, travellers' welfare (staffed by social workers), medical services, porters and trolleys, customs formalities, duty-free shops – and so on.

Air fares

As this book is explaining life in a travel agency, and the many aspects of work to be processed, there is not sufficient space to give details of the complex subject of air fares. This chapter is meant to be an introduction, and only the surface has been scratched.

Just to give you an idea of the knowledge required before quoting a fare to your client, we have published an extract from the British Airways fares book. In particular, the column GBP/ OW gives the fare quoted in pounds sterling for a one-way journey. The column GBP/RT gives the fare quoted in pounds sterling for the return journey.

Please look at the fares from London (in bold type) to Amsterdam (in light type). Three one-way fares and eight return fares are quoted. Which one should you choose? It can depend on season, class of travel, minimum and maximum length of stay, and many other booking conditions which we will study later. From London to Athens, six one-way fares and 33 return fares are quoted. From London to Barcelona, ten one-way fares and 15 return fares are quoted.

Let's take a closer look at the London to Amsterdam fare.

Column 1 gives the city of departure from London to cities listed in alphabetical order, showing fares *from* London *to* Amsterdam, Ankara, Athens, Barcelona, and so on.

Column 2 Fare basis, means the fare code to be used when issuing the airline ticket. Do you remember we spoke about standardization? Another travel personnel would be able to look at the airline ticket and see immediately the type of fare used because this fare basis code would be entered in the 'fare basis' box on the airline ticket.

Column 3 GBP ow/ shows the one way fare.

Column 4 GBP RT shows the return fare.

Column 5 AP means deadline for advance purchase fares. Look down this column and you will see the number 14. This means this type of fare has to be booked and paid for 14 days before departure. (Count from day before departure e.g. 14 days AP deadline. Passenger wants to travel on Thursday 17 August bookings must be confirmed by Thursday 3 August.)

Column 6 MIN/MAX stay means the minimum and maximum validity. The SU beside first fare Amsterdam minimum means the passenger cannot return before the Sunday after departure. So if your client departed on Thursday 12 March, the return journey could not be made until Sunday 15 March. MAXIMUM STAY, the first fare shows 3M. This means 3 months validity. The 3 months are calculated from day of departure.

Column 7 PERIOD. This gives the dates for seasonal fares, our first fare is valid all year but looking along this column you will see some of the published fares are valid only during the summer months 1 April–31 October for example.

Column 8 RES BKG CODE. This means the code to use when making the reservation. They apply only to British Airways reservations however, other airlines may use different codes.

Column 9 RULE. Tells us to refer to the complete rule in the first fare: it is rule number 103.

Column 10 RTG means routing, when a (D) is shown it is telling us the fare is based on the most (D) direct route.

Let's look at that rule 103 Superpex on p. 152. Looking at the rule column you will notice that rule 103 applies to many fares and destinations, not just the London to Amsterdam fare. This fare applies to Y = economy. RT = return and single open jaw. An open jaw trip consists of travel which is essentially of a round trip nature with the exception that the outward point of arrival and the inward point of departure are not the same. For this European rule open jaw must begin in the same country.

Example:

LONDON

AMSTERDAM

ROTTERDAM
OPEN JAW AT DESTINATION

BIRMINGHAM

LONDON

AMSTERDAM
OPEN JAW AT ORIGIN

FARES: have to be purchased before departure.

CHILDREN: we are advised children pay 67 per cent and infants pay 10 per cent of the fare. Generally infants are considered to be under 2 years and children under 12 years. Anyone 12 years and over is considered adult. This can vary with different areas of the world and so you would need to check the age regulation in the air tariff.

PERIOD OF APPLICATION: Our fare to Amsterdam is valid all year but if a validity date is given the date of outward travel determines the fare. The passenger may be returning on a date that falls within a different season.

STOPOVERS. Not permitted. Passenger must not break the journey.

ROUTING TRANSFERS. Direct flights must be used. However, if the passenger is travelling from, let's say, Edinburgh, London, Amsterdam and a special fare has been used for the Edinburgh to London flight, a break of journey is allowed in London to transfer from one flight to the next only.

CONSTRUCTIONS. Permitted with add-ons. Taking the last example, instead of paying the full fare from Edinburgh to London, we are allowed to use a specially reduced 'add-on' fare because the passenger is 'adding on' the Edinburgh to London flight to the London to Amsterdam flight. That specially reduced 'add-on' fare cannot be used alone.

COMBINATIONS. Only permitted with domestic fares, that means journeys from within the United Kingdom.

RES/PAYMENT/TICKETING. The reservation, payment and ticket issue must be made at the same time. The flights must be confirmed (not waitlisted) for the entire journey. Form of payment refers to this box on the actual air ticket in the form of payment box we must write NON REF/SPEX NON REFUNDABLE SUPERPEX. The rule also says conditions of sale sticker required. The airlines publish the main points of the conditions attached to these discounted fares, usually on a large roll of sticky labels so you would peel one off and place it on the cover of the ticket (not the ticket wallet). This reminds the passenger of the rules.

REFUND FOR CANCELLATION/NO SHOW. No show means passenger didn't arrive at the airport to check-in. A refund of 50 per cent of the fare will be made if cancelled before day of departure, otherwise no refund will be made. The passenger can upgrade (exchange the ticket for a more expensive fare to the same destination). If after upgrading to a higher fare carrying few restrictions and then the passenger decides to cancel, the original superpex cancellation conditions apply.

REBOOKING/REROUTING. Not permitted, cannot change the reservation.

AGENTS/TOUR CONDUCTORS DISCOUNTS not permitted. Sorry travel consultants, a discount on this type of fare is not permitted.

Finally we have listed the exceptions that apply to certain countries. For the Netherlands if we were planning an IT (inclusive tour) the reservations, payment and ticketing need not be done at the same time.

Let's try one of those fares to Barcelona. Check the details on the London to Barcelona RT = return fare GBP (£) 141.00.

First of all the Fare Basis Column = YLXPX. Let me explain. Y = economy. L = low season, X = midweek travel Monday to Thursday. (W = weekend travel, Friday to Sunday) PX = pex fare, (a discounted fare carrying booking conditions.)

You will notice this fare has the SU/3M = minimum and maximum stay rule. SU = passenger may not return before Sunday after departure (must stay the Saturday night) and maximum stay is 3 months, calculated from day of departure. For period we have been given 2 Jan–7 Feb and 5 Nov–13 Dec, so this fare is valid during those dates. When making the reservation we would book code B and the rule that we must read is number 100. Compare the rules with the rule number 103 Superpex. Many of them are the same, can you spot any differences?

Special events. This fare can be used for special events in Belgium, France, Irish Republic and The Netherlands, this would involve organizing a group tour to the event and we would need to read the full definition of 'special event' in the Air Transport Information and Ticketing Manual under the heading Inclusive Tours – General Regulations.

Let's read the exceptions for Spain as our fare is to Barcelona. We are advised children pay 67 per cent applicable only for travel on British Airways (BA) sectors. You would check with any other airline being used.

Finally read the (X) midweek travel and (W) weekend travel note. For travel mid week in one direction and weekend in the other direction charge half mid week/half weekend outbound seasonal fare. For example, London to Barcelona YHXSX (economy high season mid week super pex) GBP 167.00 YHWSX (economy high season midweek super pex) GBP 198.00 period of travel 12 July–15 September. So bearing in mind these are return fares, if our client travelled London to Barcelona Tuesday 9 September and Barcelona to London on Sunday 14 September we would charge half the midweek fare GBP 83.50 and half the weekend fare GBP 99.00 total GBP 182.50.

However if the passenger was returning Barcelona to London at a weekend but the date falls under a different season, the rule says charge the seasonal fare for the outward bound travel as this season determines the fare. Once we have learned the meaning of the fare basis codes we can quickly identify the type of fare and after practice will become familiar with the rules attached to each fare.

An explanation of the codes can be found in the Air Tariff.

What happens if the fare for a journey has not been published? It would be impossible to publish every combination, we would then have to calculate the fare ourselves. The computer can do simple calculations for us, but is not programmed to calculate every possible permutation. Also a computer system has been known to 'go down' which means a breakdown in transmission, and we would therefore need to calculate the fare manually. For this we would use the mileage system, and there are three elements involved in the application of the mileage system: they are as follows:

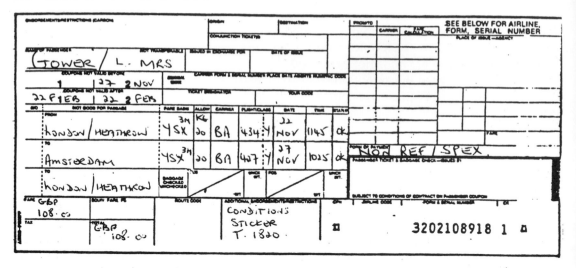

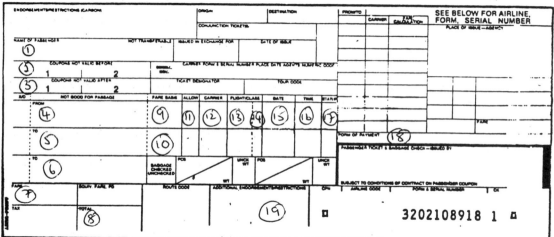

1 Maximum permitted mileage (MPM)
2 Ticket Point Mileages (TPM)
3 Excess Mileage Surcharges.

Maximum permitted mileages are the maximum number of miles a passenger is allowed to travel en route between two particular points at the direct fare.

IATA produce manuals providing all the information on airfares, rules, constructions, ticketing and maximum permitted mileage between cities.

Ticket point mileages (TPM) are used to compute the total mileage of the flown journey.

Excess Mileage surcharges. If the TPM for a desired routing exceeds the MPM published in connection with a fare, a surcharge becomes necessary. We are provided with a chart which indicates the amount to charge in percentages ranging from 5 to 25 per cent.

Let's study an example. We will say a client wishes to travel New York, Paris, Copenhagen, Nice, Milan, Vienna, Rome, Cairo (check your atlas to follow the routing). We have checked the MPM in the Air Tariff manual and for a journey from New York to Cairo the MPM is 6730 (air miles). The next step is to use the pages in the manual giving the *actual* flown miles between each city en route – the TPM computation.

New York–Paris	3,628
Paris–Copenhagen	637
Copenhagen–Nice	861
Nice–Milan	157
Milan–Vienna	400
Vienna–Rome	482
Rome–Cairo	1,329
Total	7,494

Since the sum total TPMs for the above journey exceeds the MPM of 6730 allowed between New York and Cairo a surcharge becomes necessary. We would check the Excess Mileage Percentage Table and find this would be a 15 per cent increase on the published fare.

This really is a very basic outline.

We started by reading a fare from London to Amsterdam. Let's now try issuing an airline ticket for a passenger travelling from London Heathrow airport to Amsterdam using the YSX fare of GBP 108.00 return. We will say the ticket is for Mrs L. Gower, travelling on BA 434 London to Amsterdam on 22 November at 1145 hours returning on BA 427 Amsterdam to London on 27 November at 1025 hours.

1 Name of passenger.
2 Not valid before box – passenger is not allowed to return before the first Saturday. In this case we will say the 22 November is a Tuesday our client could not return until Sunday 27 November.
3 Check the fare again, you will see it is valid for 3 months, passenger is leaving on the 22 November the ticket expires on the 22 February.
4 From London – always write the name of the airport if the city is served by more than one.
5 To Amsterdam.
6 Back to London.
7 The fare GBP 108.00.
8 The total GBP 108.00 we will not discuss tax or equivalent amount paid here.
9 Fare basis YSX3M this is the superpex valid 3 months.
10 Fare basis again.
11 Baggage allowance 20 kilos.
12 The carrier (in this case British Airways).
13 Flight number.
14 Class of travel Y.
15 Date of travel.
16 Time of flight.
17 Status – ok means this flight is confirmed.
18 Form of payment – do you remember the ticketing condition in rule 103? We were instructed to write NON REF/SPEX.
19 Additional endorsements, here we would indicate placing the conditions sticker on to the ticket.

There are many other aspects to learn when issuing airline tickets and it would be impossible to explain it all in a book this size covering so many other aspects of work at a travel agency. However, calculating fares and issuing airline tickets is a large part of our work and it is essential to do a proper airline course and gain recognized qualifications.

To make the reservation, you have a choice of telephoning the airline carrier or making the reservation with one of the many computer systems such as Travicom Skytrack, Galileo or Sabre. Making the reservation by computer is quick and trouble free as the computer is linked directly with the airline reservation system. A vast amount of information can be obtained in addition to making the reservation, and an immediate print out confirming the booking is available. The usual information about the passenger should be obtained before processing the reservation such as name (correct spelling) ages of any children, seat preference, smoking or non-smoking, (seats can often be booked on your computer) and of course you will realize by this time that it is essential to provide your client with full information regarding the fare. Many discounted fares carry a cancellation penalty and reservations may not be changed.

We really do have a wealth of information at hand in the travel and tourism industry. Manuals explain step by step how to do the job in hand. It *does* take a long time to feel really comfortable with those manuals. In addition, the travel and tourism industry is constantly changing; the agent has to keep up to date with fares, conditions, ticketing instructions, destinations, hotels, restaurants and climate. It is a lovely feeling, when you are asked a difficult question, to be able to find the answer quickly – and it is a lovely feeling to be learning something new every day. There are not many jobs around that offer the satisfaction and variety of a working life in the travel and tourism industry.

Exercise 13

This exercise uses information given in this chapter.

(a) Give details of a flight departing Geneva on a Monday at 1725 hours for Amsterdam.

(b) On flight number OA 134 travelling from Geneva to Athens, how many stops are made en route?

(c) Where would you find information on the IATA traffic conference areas?

(d) A passenger is travelling from Toronto via Calgary to New York. What is the minimum connecting time in Calgary?

(e) A passenger is travelling from Madrid via Calgary to Vancouver. What is the minimum connecting time in Calgary?

(f) Give the standard clock time for Chile on 3 December

(g) Give the standard clock time for China on 22 October.

(h) What is the average flying time between Mexico City and Tokyo?

(i) What is the average flying time between Hong Kong and New York?

(j) Is Madagascar an area of malarial risk?

(k) Is Libya an area of malarial risk?

11 Insurance

Summary

In this chapter we are going to discuss:

- general benefits of travel insurance;
- understanding an insurance policy;
- awareness of the exclusions;
- how to calculate the cost of insurance;
- exercises and assignments to complete.

There are many different types of insurance available. We can insure our homes against fire or theft. We can insure a car against damage. We can have life insurance, making a provision for our dependants in the event of our death. If we are organizing an event to take place in the open, we can insure against rain ruining the event; we can't *stop* the rain from falling, but loss of earnings can be compensated! Pianists insure their hands, film stars insure their legs – the opportunities for insurance are endless.

Coverage

We are going to discuss holiday insurance, and the need for this insurance within the travel and tourism industry. Insurance is a system which enables people who suffer a loss or accident to be paid financial compensation for the effects of that misfortune. Let's think about the type of misfortunes likely to happen whilst on a holiday or business trip, and the insurance coverage required: The rates vary according to areas, domestic, Europe and worldwide. Travellers to countries outside Europe (worldwide) will pay a higher premium than travellers within Europe or travelling domestically.

Medical expenses In the event of sickness, medical expenses can be *very* high in most countries. It would spoil your client's holiday to have to worry about meeting these expenses.
Cancellation charges As the date of departure draws closer, so cancellation charges become greater. In the event of your clients cancelling their travel arrangements for 'reasons beyond their control', the insurance company will pay those charges.
Curtailment This is when the client has travelled to the destination but has had to return home early.
Personal liability This indemnifies you for your legal liability in respect of accidental injury to third parties or an accidental damage to their property during the period of travel or holiday.

Personal baggage   Considering the volume of traffic in the tourism industry, very little baggage is actually lost, stolen or damaged. Comedians like to joke 'I went to Florence but my baggage went to Sydney!', and if this really does happen to your clients they will tell you it isn't very funny! Even small items can be expensive to replace, and a change of clothing is definitely necessary!

Personal accident   The risk of personal accident is greater when on holiday than when following one's usual routine. Young people skiing or mountain climbing, elderly people dancing the night away – we often tend to put a lot of energy into enjoying ourselves on holiday!

We can say that insurance offers *peace of mind* to the traveller.

Terminology

Let's make sure we are clear on some insurance terminology:

Premium   The amount of money a person pays to be insured.

Insurer   The company which receives the premiums. This money goes into a common fund and is paid to clients who have suffered a misfortune and made a claim. There is no refund for persons who have not needed to make a claim.

Policy holder   The person who pays the premium for the insurance.

Policy   The legal document providing written evidence of the contract between the insurer and the policy holder.

Claim   A request by the policy holder for payment under the terms of the policy.

Exclusion   An event that is specifically *not* covered by the terms of the policy; often found in small print on the insurance company's brochure. It is *essential* that these exclusions are understood. It is too late after the event has happened to tell your client the circumstances that are excluded from the policy.

Choosing a policy: TravelGuard

Which insurance policy should you choose? There are many insurance companies on the market, and it will take time to compare best value for money. You are looking for a policy that answers your client's needs, and a company that will settle claims quickly and accurately and will not have to be endlessly chased. Some tour operators provide their own insurance cover for their clients; often this is compulsory and many retail agents act as agents for a specific insurance company, selling their own policies. Should the client *not* have insurance cover, and an expensive circumstance does take place and the traveller does not have the money to pay, what happens then? It is unlikely that a hospital or a tour operator will leave the client stranded. The client would have to guarantee payment of any services received on arrival home, or arrange for a friend or relative to send the payment urgently, but this could take time. The situation can be actioned immediately if the client is protected by insurance.

We are now going to study TravelGuard insurance. At the time of writing, TravelGuard is the only retail policy to be approved by the Association of British Travel Agents (ABTA). There are several TravelGuard schemes available, and you would need to read the brochure on each scheme to be able to offer the most suitable one for your clients' needs. The schemes are as follows:

TravelGuard Gold offers 'all round de luxe cover for today's traveller'. The cost for up to 31 days in the UK is £8.60, Europe would be £23.20 and worldwide £45.00.

TravelGuard Family is the 'cost effective cover for the whole family'. One premium covers husband and wife (or recognized common law partners) travelling with their dependent children under the age of 16 years at the date of departure. The premium to cover the whole family for up to 31 days in the UK is £19.20, Europe would be £46.40 and worldwide £103.30.

TravelGuard Annual is year-round travel insurance for business and leisure. By paying just one annual premium of £115, the policy holder can travel as many times and to any part of the world as he/she chooses.

CoachGuard travel insurance is for people travelling by sea or land. The cost for up to 31 days in Europe is £14.30.

The rates are given as examples of the different types of travel insurance available and are for training purposes only. We are going to study the TravelGuard Gold insurance policy. Before doing so, let's be clear about certain terms.

A *broker* is any insurance agent that arranges matters for a client. The *insurer* for the TravelGuard policies is Accident & General Limited; in this case, Accident & General are also principal brokers. The *underwriters* for TravelGuard Gold are Municipal General Insurance and Royal Insurance UK. Underwriters share the risks. The word 'underwriter' originated from marine insurance; when a merchant was prepared to accept part of the risk, he would write his name under the details of the risk with the proportion of the sum insured which he accepted.

The *loss adjuster* in this policy is Claims International Limited, which deals with all claims from customers with TravelGuard insurance. When a claim form is received by Claims International it is immediately entered on their computer under the claimant's name and address; it is then given a claim reference number. Any correspondence sent to the claimant will have this reference number on, and it should be quoted on any response in writing or by telephone. We have to remember that it is the claimant's name and address that is relevant, and this may not be the same as the insured person (the lead name on the booking form).

TravelGuard Gold brochure

Please read the TravelGuard Gold brochure. Take time to study the information under the various headings.

The provision for medical emergencies is very important for clients. Here they will have the services of Mondial Assistance, who provide a 24-hour emergency medical telephone service. Medical repatriation will be arranged where necessary, using an air ambulance service whose planes can accommodate stretchers, beds and accompanying medical staff.

Look closely at the premiums. Note the free insurance for children under 2 years. Note also that persons aged 70 years or more pay treble premiums for travel outside the UK or Europe. As a travel consultant you would need to ensure that your clients have read the brochure and noted these clauses. It is very difficult to guess the age of a client; to attempt this can easily offend! So be sure your client is aware, and he or she will then supply the details in confidence.

The all round deluxe cover for today's traveller

Loss of deposit or cancellation Up to £3,000

Most travellers forfeit some or all of the money they have paid in advance if they have to cancel a booking. TRAVELGUARD GOLD covers cancellation for most causes beyond your control.

Curtailment Up to £3,000

TRAVELGUARD GOLD provides reimbursement up to the limit shown above providing a proportionate reimbursement of the total holiday cost, based on each day of holiday you have lost, if you have to return home early on medical advice, because a close relative in the United Kingdom or Channel Islands falls seriously ill during your absence or if you are hospitalised outside the United Kingdom or Channel Islands.

Medical and other expenses UNLIMITED

Our experience in the past has shown the need for a substantial amount of medical cover, combined with an effective emergency medical/repatriation service. We believe that providing cover unlimited in amount best meets these requirements. You are not excluded because of age or a bad health record. Providing that you are not travelling against a doctor's advice, or for the purpose of obtaining treatment or have been given a terminal prognosis, you are covered irrespective of your previous medical history.

Hospital inconvenience payment Up to £500

You will receive £20 per day (maximum £500) if you are hospitalised outside the United Kingdom. This amount is paid IN ADDITION TO medical and hospital bills reasonably incurred.

Personal baggage Up to £1,000

One of the most common risks when travelling is the loss, theft or damage of personal baggage although the financial loss is not as potentially frightening as medical a result of strike/industrial action. Providing the withdrawal lasts continuously for only two days you may claim £50 for each day you are affected (maximum £300).

Delayed or missed departure Up to £100 or up to £3,000 cancellation option

Hanging around at an airport because your plane is delayed can be costly as well as inconvenient, TRAVELGUARD GOLD goes a long way towards meeting the problem.
If departure or arrival of your aircraft or sea-vessel is delayed by at least 12 hours on the outward or return journey you may claim £20 for the first 12 hours delay and £10 for each 12 hours thereafter (maximum of £100).
Alternatively, if you wish to cancel altogether after 12 hours such delay, you may claim back the cancellation charges levied by the tour company.
Moreover, if you miss your flight as a result of accident or mechanical failure of the car in which you are travelling or public transport failing to deliver you to the airport on time, you can claim up to £1,000 (£500 for European flights) for the cost of an alternative flight to your booked destination. Naturally, it is a condition of this section that you allow yourself a reasonable amount of time when setting out from home.

Legal expenses up to £50,000

TRAVELGUARD GOLD will pay for legal costs and expenses incurred in the pursuit of legal proceedings for compensation and/or damages arising directly from injury or death during the travel or holiday. We also provide a telephone helpline for advice and guidance whilst abroad or on your return to the U.K.

For medical emergencies

Most claims can wait to be settled on the traveller's return. However, medical emergencies can arise abroad. Consequently, TRAVELGUARD GOLD provides through Mondial Assistance a 24 hour emergency medical telephone service (reverse charge calls are allowed) so that you can obtain help and advice. Obviously the help given will be adapted to circumstances, but medical repatriation will be arranged where necessary and if you are hospitalised, you or the hospital may contact Mondial Assistance to obtain confirmation on direct settlement of bills under the terms of this policy.

bills. Previous claims experience indicates the above limit is usually enough to cover most eventualities.

Delayed Baggage £100

We know how frustrating it is to be left with only the clothes you stand up in on arrival at holiday destination if your luggage is delayed or misdirected by the carrier (e.g. airline). TRAVELGUARD GOLD allows you a flat amount of £100 towards the purchase of emergency clothing or toiletries if the delay lasts for at least 12 hours. You do not even have to produce receipts for items bought, and this payment does not affect any claim you have in addition against the carrier.

Personal money Up to £300

TRAVELGUARD GOLD pays up to the limit shown above for loss of personal money. (Limited to £200 for cash).

Personal liability Up to £2,000,000

To indemnify you for your legal liability in respect of accidental injury to third parties or accidental damage to their property, during the travel or holiday.

Personal accident Up to £25,000

This section of the policy will pay a lump sum benefit in respect of each insured person, as a result of accidental bodily injury causing death (benefit up to £5,000), loss of an eye(s) or limb(s) or permanent total disablement.

Tour organiser failure Up to £3,000

Should an unbonded ABTA travel agent, ABTA tour operator or carrier (airline, bus company, etc.) fail to fulfil its travel obligations due to financial failure TRAVELGUARD GOLD refunds your pre-paid monies.

Withdrawal of services Up to £300

Normally most people are happy with their hotel but all countries are now being affected by industrial disputes. TRAVELGUARD GOLD gives some recompense should you suffer a substantial withdrawal of services (e.g. waiter services, swimming pool, water facilities etc.) as

Your premiums

THESE PREMIUMS ARE VALID FOR ALL INSURANCES ISSUED UP TO 31st DECEMBER 1991.
THIS INSURANCE IS VALID FOR ISSUE TO RESIDENTS OF THE U.K. AND THE CHANNEL ISLANDS ONLY.

GEOGRAPHICAL LIMITS – Definitions: **U.K.** shall mean the United Kingdom of Great Britain and Northern Ireland and the Isle of Man. **Europe** shall mean the U.K. as defined, the Channel Islands, The Republic of Ireland, the Continent of Europe west of the Ural Mountains, any country or island with a Mediterranean coastline, Iceland, Madeira, the Azores and the Canary Islands. **Worldwide** shall mean anywhere in the world.

AREA	U.K.	EUROPE	WORLDWIDE
Up to 4 days	£6.40	£13.55	£38.00
5 to 10 days	£6.40	£15.95	£38.00
11 to 17 days	£8.60	£17.55	
18 to 31 days	£8.60	£23.20	£45.00
Each additional week. (max 3 months in all)	£2.50	£6.20	£14.50

PREMIUM NOTES
1. TREBLE PREMIUMS MUST BE PAID BY PERSONS AGED 70 OR OVER AT DEPARTURE DATE. **(EXCEPT FOR TRAVEL WITHIN UK OR EUROPE).**
2. HALF PREMIUMS FOR CHILDREN UNDER 16 YEARS OF AGE AT DEPARTURE DATE.
3. FREE INSURANCE FOR CHILDREN UNDER 2 AT DEPARTURE DATE UNDER THE ACCOMPANYING ADULTS POLICY.
4. WINTER SPORTS INSURANCE – DOUBLE PREMIUM.
5. SCUBA-DIVING INSURANCE – DOUBLE PREMIUM.

Your Travelguard Gold Agent

This insurance is valid for issue to residents of the United Kingdom and the Channel Islands only and for holidays/trips commencing in the United Kingdom and the Channel Islands only. Insurance must be effected before departure from the United Kingdom and the Channel Islands.

INSURED PERSONS (state Mr, Mrs, Miss)	PLEASE TICK APPROPRIATE BOX				PREMIUM PER PERSON
	Under 2	2-15	16-69	70 & over	
1					
2					
3					
4					
5					
TOTAL PREMIUM					

(N.B. No refund of premium is allowed once the insurance has been effected)

GEOGRAPHICAL AREA (Tick Box)

☐ U.K.   ☐ EUROPE   ☐ WORLDWIDE

☐ WINTER SPORTS   or   ☐ SCUBA DIVING

Cover needed

Period of Insurance **(max 3 months in all)** . . . . days

from . . . . .19 . . . .

ADDRESS OF FIRST NAMED INSURED PERSON

. . . .

. . . .

. . . .

. . . .

SIGNED ON BEHALF OF ALL INSURED PERSONS

. . . .

Date . . . .

WARRANTY: It is warranted that no Insured Person is travelling against the advice of a medical practitioner or for the purpose of obtaining medical treatment or where a terminal prognosis has been given.

THE FULL TERMS AND CONDITIONS OF TRAVELGUARD GOLD ARE INCORPORATED IN THE POLICY ISSUED, WHICH ALONE CONSTITUTES THE CONTRACT OF INSURANCE BETWEEN THE INSURED PERSON(S) AND THE INSURER. A SPECIMEN POLICY IS AVAILABLE FROM YOUR AGENT UPON REQUEST.

The following is a summary of the exclusions applicable to TRAVELGUARD GOLD.

GENERAL EXCLUSIONS
(1) Winter Sports and Scuba diving (unless the appropriate premium has been paid);
(2) War and kindred risks;
(3) Nuclear hazards;
(4) Human Immunodeficiency Virus (HIV), and/or any HIV related illness including AIDS;
(5) Property more specifically insured;
(6) Professional sports and/or rugby league or union.

LOSS OF DEPOSIT AND CANCELLATION
(1) Government regulation or act (other than compulsory quarantine);
(2) Currency restriction;
(3) Failure of the tour operator or provider of transport or accommodation to fulfil the holiday travel booking;
(4) Disinclination to travel;
(5) Financial circumstances of the Insured Person, or of any person on whom the holiday plans depend (other than redundancy which qualifies the Insured Person for payment under current redundancy legislation);
(6) Strikes or labour disputes;
(7) Delay in commencement of holiday;
(8) Surcharges levied increasing basic brochure prices.

PERSONAL ACCIDENT, MEDICAL EXPENSES, HOSPITAL INCONVENIENCE & CURTAILMENT
(1) Accidents on two wheeled vehicles of over 250cc;
(2) Medical treatment in the U.K;
(3) Non-essential treatment or surgery;
(4) Medication known to be required or continued outside the U.K;
(5) Extra charges for single or private-room accommodation except where medically necessary;
(6) Racing, motor sports, hang gliding, mountaineering, pot-holing, (unless the appropriate premium has been paid), any aerial activity or aviation other than as a fare-paying passenger in a certified multi-engined aircraft on a licensed passenger flight;
(7) Suicide, self-inflicted injury or illness, insanity, venereal disease, alcohol or drugs, self-exposure to needless peril;
(8) Pregnancy where the expected date of confinement is less than 2 months after the date of return;
(9) Expenses incurred more than 12 months after the accident or illness.

BAGGAGE AND PERSONAL MONEY
(1) Delay or confiscation by Customs or other official(s);
(2) Contact or corneal lenses or damage to fragile articles;
(3) Business goods or samples;
(4) Normal wear and tear, gradual deterioration or mechanical or electrical breakdown, moth or vermin;
(5) Theft or loss not reported to the police within 24 hours.

PERSONAL LIABILITY
(1) Injury to employees
(2) Liability to members of an Insured Person's family;
(3) Liability arising out of:
(i) Any wilful, malicious or unlawful act
(ii) The carrying on of any trade, profession or business
(iii) Ownership or occupation of land or buildings (other than any temporary residence)
(iv) Ownership, possession or use of vehicles, aircraft, watercraft or firearms;
(4) Liability assumed by an Insured Person by agreement;
(5) Legal costs from any criminal proceedings.

TOUR ORGANISER FAILURE
This section applies only to holidays/trips booked through members of ABTA or directly with properly licensed tour operators, coach operators, airlines, shipping lines and railway companies.

DELAYED OR MISSED DEPARTURE
Strike or industrial action which was in existence or for which a commencement date had been publicly announced at the date of application for this policy.

LEGAL EXPENSES
(1) Any claim brought against a tour operator, travel agent or carrier;
(2) Legal expenses incurred prior to the granting of support by the Insurer.
Note: The Insurer shall have complete control over the legal proceedings and the appointment of a solicitor.

EXCESSES
The first **£25** of any claim is not covered in respect of baggage, money or cancellation claims (excluding loss of deposit only), and for medical and curtailment claims other than when the Insured Person is detained in hospital outside the U.K. up to the end of the holiday/trip the first **£50** for Worldwide holidays/trips and the first **£25** for European holidays/trips unless a recovery is made under the EEC Reciprocal Health Agreement.

What Travelguard Gold means to you

Sections 1-12 of the policy are underwritten by Municipal General Insurance Ltd. MGI Ltd is part of the Municipal Insurance Group which has assets in excess of £1 billion and is a member of the Association of British Insurers. Section 13 is underwritten by Royal Insurance (UK) Ltd.

The range of cover provided by TRAVELGUARD GOLD policy is very comprehensive. It has thirteen separate sections covering many and various areas of possible loss at a competitive premium.

Accident and General Ltd, the brokers who administer TRAVELGUARD GOLD have for many years been one of the leading specialists in travel insurance.
The TRAVELGUARD GOLD claims settling agents are also specialists in this field. They understand the modern traveller's problems and the need for speedy settlements of claims.
All of these factors ensure that TRAVELGUARD GOLD is probably the BEST travel insurance available.

Specially arranged by:
ACCIDENT & GENERAL LTD.,
Black Lion House, 45 Whitechapel Road,
London E1 1DU.
Tel: 071-377 6131

RECIPROCAL HEALTH AGREEMENT
Travellers to European Common Market countries are strongly advised to obtain from the local Department of Health and Social Security Office Form CM1. On returning this to the Department completed they will be issued with form E111 which will entitle them to certain free health arrangement in Common Market countries. For full details please obtain leaflet No SA30 from your local Department of Health and Social Security Office.

TravelGuard

GOLD

WE'VE COVERED THE WORLD

Accident & General

Some elderly clients are very proud of having reached a good age and encourage complimentary remarks, but others prefer to keep quiet about it; you will have to assess this type of situation when the time comes!

How do you know which countries are in Europe and which are considered worldwide? Read the geographical limits: definitions are clearly given.

The application form is nice and simple. Just follow the information requested on the form.

Section 1 = Personal Accident. Section 2 = Medical and other expenses, etc. When reading the very small print on *cover and limits* and *exclusions* in full, they will relate to each section number. The brochure only gives a summary of the exclusions.

The exclusions are very important. Conditions and exclusions can vary between companies and here we can see a summary of TravelGuard's. To see all the exclusions we need to read the policy. At this stage we must become familiar with the way the policy is numbered, because the exclusions will refer to each section by number.

TravelGuard Gold policy

Study the full policy. Take your time; reread if you are unsure, think about it, try putting the explanations into your own words. You will have the opportunty in a moment to answer some questions that could easily be asked of you during an ordinary day at a travel agency, when selling travel insurance. Space prevents explaining the many conditions and exclusions but a few will be highlighted.

Note the following on the policy:

Extensions   Insurance policies can be extended, as long as the original policy has not expired. All you need to do is collect the extra premium necessary. If a policy has already expired, an extension is not possible.

Validity   This particular insurance cannot be issued to a customer travelling from abroad to the UK. The insurance should not be sold to a non-UK resident. For example, the customer should have lived in the UK for at least six months and be returning after the holiday to reside in the UK.

Refunds   If a tour operator alters a holiday and offers cancellation with full refund, then a refund of premium can be made. Otherwise, refunds are not allowed except in extenuating circumstances, and in these cases it is always best to check with Accident & General Limited.

Change of departure date   If a tour operator alters a holiday then this is allowed on the insurance. Ask for the original policy document from the customer and reissue. If the insurance was issued the previous year, you should alter the departure date on the original sales receipt and policy document and initial as authorized.

Increase of cover   This is not possible under the TravelGuard policies. Valuables like jewellery, cameras, video equipment etc. should be insured under the customer's household all-risks policy.

Dangerous activities   Sports such as hang gliding and mountaineering are not covered as they are considered hazardous adventures. Scuba and skin diving are not covered unless the customer had paid double the premium.

Luggage   It is appreciated that any settlement is only based on indemnity, which takes into account prior wear and tear, and not replacement value. The insurance company does not pay for any journey or expenses incurred in the replacement of the items.

TRAVEL INSURANCE

Arranged by:
Accident & General Limited
Black Lion House, 45 Whitechapel Road, London E1 1DU
Tel: 071-377 6131
Underwritten by:
MUNICIPAL GENERAL INSURANCE LTD. – Sections 1-12
ROYAL INSURANCE (UK) LTD. – Section 13

POLICY No. G91/ 0000000

This Policy provides details of your TRAVELGUARD GOLD cover arranged by Accident & General Ltd.
AFTER READING THIS POLICY CAREFULLY, PLEASE RETAIN IT SINCE IT MUST BE PRODUCED IN THE EVENT OF A CLAIM.

GEOGRAPHICAL LIMITS – DEFINITIONS: U.K. shall mean:- the United Kingdom of Great Britain and Northern Ireland and the Isle of Man, **Europe** shall mean the U.K. as defined, the Channel Islands, the Continent of Europe west of the Ural Mountains, any country or island with a Mediterranean coastline, Iceland, Madeira, the Canary Islands, the Azores and the Republic of Ireland. **Worldwide** shall mean anywhere in the world.

SUMMARY OF COVER AND LIMITS (per person)

Section 1 PERSONAL ACCIDENT	Section 2 MEDICAL AND OTHER EXPENSES	Section 3 HOSPITAL INCONVENIENCE BENEFIT	Section 4 LOSS OF DEPOSIT OR CANCELLATION	Section 5 CURTAILMENT	Section 6 DELAYED OR MISSED DEPARTURE	Section 7 PERSONAL BAGGAGE	Section 8 DELAYED BAGGAGE	Section 9 PERSONAL MONEY	Section 10 PERSONAL LIABILITY	Section 11 TOUR ORGANISER FAILURE	Section 12 WITHDRAWAL OF SERVICES	Section 13 LEGAL EXPENSES
Benefits up to £25,000	Unlimited	£20 per day up to £500	£5,000	£5,000	Various (as detailed overleaf)	£1,000	£100	£300	£2,000,000	£5,000	£50 per day up to £300	Up to £50,000

NB: SECTION 2 DOES NOT COVER TREATMENT OR AID OBTAINED IN THE U.K. (EXCEPT AS PROVIDED UNDER ITEM 3)
IMPORTANT:
(1) THIS POLICY IS NOT VALID FOR TRAVEL OR HOLIDAYS EXCEEDING 3 MONTHS. (2) THIS POLICY IS NOT EFFECTIVE UNLESS VALIDATED BY AN APPROVED ISSUING AGENT. (3) THIS POLICY IS NOT VALID IF ISSUED AFTER 31-12-91. (4) THIS POLICY IS VALID FOR ISSUE TO RESIDENTS OF THE UNITED KINGDOM AND THE CHANNEL ISLANDS ONLY FOR TRIPS COMMENCING IN THE UK OR THE CHANNEL ISLANDS ONLY. (5) ONCE THE POLICY HAS BEEN ISSUED NO REFUND OF PREMIUM IS ALLOWED.

Agents Validation:

Initial: | Date of Issue:

Insured Persons (state whether Mr/Mrs/Miss)	Under 2	2-15	16-69	70 & over	Premiums per Insured Person	Tick box for Geographical Area of cover:
1					£	☐ U.K. as defined
2					£	☐ Europe as defined
3					£	☐ Worldwide
4					£	Tick if cover for ☐ Winter Sports or
5					£	☐ Scuba Diving included

Total Premium £

Period of Insurance (max 3 months in all)
_____ days from _____ 199_

WARRANTY: The Insured Person(s) warrant(s) that to the best of his/her knowledge and belief no Insured Person is travelling contrary to the advice of a Medical Practitioner or for the purpose of obtaining medical treatment or where a terminal prognosis has been given.

Address of first named Insured Person ....
....
....

The Insurer may decline liability for a claim notified more than 31 days after the expiry of this Policy.

IMPORTANT: Any loss or damage to personal baggage whilst in the custody of the carriers (airline, bus company, etc.) must be notified immediately in writing to such carriers but in any event within three days and a report obtained.

Any loss of money or personal baggage must be reported to the police within 24 hours of the discovery of the loss and a written report obtained. If an airline is involved a Property Irregularity Report must be obtained.

CLAIMS: Any occurrence or loss which may give rise to a claim should be advised immediately to:
Claims International Limited   **Tel: 081-680 5142**
(Scheme No. 15)   **Telex: 916290 CIL G**
279 High Street   **Fax: 081-760 0298**
Croydon CR0 1QH
London, United Kingdom

This document must be submitted when making a claim. If medical attention is received for injury or sickness you should obtain a Medical Certificate showing the nature of the injury or sickness and if possible pay and obtain receipted accounts.

PERIOD OF INSURANCE: Under Section 4 (Loss of Deposit or Cancellation) and Section 11 (Tour Organiser Failure) insurance is effective immediately this Policy is issued and under Section 4 terminates on commencement of the planned holiday or trip. Under all other sections insurance commences when the Insured Person leaves his/her domicile in the British Isles and terminates on his/her return to such domicile at the end of the holiday/trip or expiry of the number of days specified in the Schedule, which ever is the earlier. Extension of the cover for up to one week is automatic if necessitated by public transport delays. Application must be made to Accident & General Limited for any other extension, such extension will become effective only upon acceptance by Accident & General Limited who will also advise the additional premium required, such acceptance being conditional upon the receipt of any relevant additional premium. In consideration of payment of the premium the Insurer agrees to provide insurance for the Insured Person in terms of this Policy.

FOR AND ON BEHALF OF THE INSURER

24 HOUR MEDICAL EMERGENCY SERVICE
A 24 hour emergency aid centre operated by MONDIAL ASSISTANCE is available so that the Insured Person may request help in the event of a MEDICAL EMERGENCY overseas covered under Section 2.
EMERGENCY 24 HOUR TELEPHONE NUMBER 081-686 1666
TELEX 266705
FAX NUMBER 081-686 1707
When contacting this service please quote TRAVELGUARD GOLD and give any information requested.

LEGAL ADVISORY SERVICE
A Legal Advisory Service Operated by CareAssist is available so that the Insured Person may request advice and guidance on any private legal or related problem arising from or out of the journey covered under Section 13.
The service is available from 0900hrs to 2100hrs (UK time) weekdays if the Insured Person is calling from abroad and on a 24-hour basis if dialling from the United Kingdom.
The telephone number is 021 (21 from abroad) 233 0666.
When contacting this service please quote Scheme No. AGA/ES/17118/014 and your Policy Number.

CLAIM NOTIFICATION: To CLAIMS INTERNATIONAL LTD. please send me the necessary forms as I wish to notify a claim under the following Section(s).
(please tick the appropriate box(es)).

Section 1	Personal Accident	☐	Section 7	Personal Baggage	☐	Please send forms to:
Section 2 or 3	Medical Expenses Hospital Inconvenience	☐	Section 8	Delayed Baggage	☐	Name ....
			Section 9	Personal Money	☐	Address ....
Section 4, 5, or 6	Loss of Deposit Cancellation Delayed/Missed Departure or Curtailment	☐	Section 10	Personal Liability	☐	....
			Section 11	Tour Organiser Failure	☐	....
			Section 12	Withdrawal of Services	☐	....

Policy recommended by the Travel Agents Council of the Association of British Travel Agents for sale during 1991.

COVER & LIMITS

SECTION 1 – PERSONAL ACCIDENT

This insurance shall pay the following benefit if during the Period of Insurance the Insured Person sustains bodily injury caused by external, violent, and visible means (or by exposure resulting from a mishap to an aircraft or vessel or conveyance in which the Insured Person is travelling), which solely and independently of any other cause within twelve calendar months from the date of the accident causing such injury results in:

1. Death **£5,000**
2. Loss of one or more limbs or one or more eyes **£25,000**
3. Permanent Total Disablement **£25,000**

Benefit for an Insured Person under 16 years of age at the date travel commences is limited under Benefit (1) to **£1,000** and under Benefit (2) to **£15,000**. Benefit (3) is not applicable to persons under 16 years of age. Loss of an eye means total and irrecoverable loss of all sight in such eye. Loss of a limb means loss of a hand or foot by physical severence at or above the wrist or ankle. Permanent Total Disablement means total disablement from engaging in or attending to any occupation whatsoever for at least twelve months from the date of injury and at the end of that time being beyond hope of improvement. In no event shall the insurer's liability exceed payment for more than one benefit as above.

SECTION 2 – MEDICAL AND OTHER EXPENSES

This Insurance shall pay each Insured Person in respect of:

1. Medical hospital and treatment expenses (including cost of EMERGENCY dental treatment only for the immediate relief of pain), additional accommodation and travelling expenses (including such additional expenses of a relative or friend required on medical advice to travel to or remain behind with or accompany the Insured Person), necessarily incurred outside the United Kingdom as a direct result of accidental bodily injury sustained by or sickness of the Insured Person occurring during the Period of Insurance.
2. The transfer of the Insured Person's body or ashes in the event of death to the United Kingdom or the Channel Islands (excluding funeral and interment costs) or alternatively to pay up to **£1,000** towards the cost of burial or cremation expenses outside the United Kingdom or the Channel Islands.
3. Emergency medical transportation up to **£1,000** each Insured Person within the United Kingdom to alternative medical facility nearest to the Insured Person's home or home address deemed to be required and so directed by medical advice only as a direct result of accidental bodily injury sustained by or sickness of the Insured Person occurring during the Period of Insurance.

Note: This insurance does not cover any expense incurred by the Insured Person more than 12 months after the occurrence of the accident or sickness to which the claim refers.

SECTION 3 – HOSPITAL INCONVENIENCE BENEFIT

This insurance shall pay **£20** per complete 24 hours up to a maximum of **£500** in all each Insured Person in the event that the Insured Person is admitted to hospital outside the United Kingdom as an in-patient due to accidental bodily injury or sickness sustained outside the United Kingdom during the Period of Insurance.

SECTION 4 – LOSS OF DEPOSIT OR CANCELLATION

This insurance shall pay up to **£5,000** each Insured Person in the event of loss of irrecoverable deposits or charges paid in advance or contracted to be paid for the benefit of the Insured Person only in the event of necessary and unavoidable cancellation of the planned holiday/trip due to causes beyond the control of the Insured Person (subject to the exclusions) and of which the Insured Person had no knowledge at the date of effecting this insurance.

SECTION 5 – CURTAILMENT

This insurance shall pay up to **£5,000** each Insured Person in all in respect of:-

1. The proportional amount of the irrecoverable pre-paid expenses of the planned holiday/trip following curtailment of the holiday/trip:-
   (a) by return of the Insured Person to his/her permanent domicile or place of residence in the British Isles unavoidably necessitated by the death, serious injury or illness (occurring during the Period of Insurance) of the Insured Person or his/her spouse, parent, parent-in-law, child, brother, sister, grandparent, close business associate or travelling companion resident in the British Isles,
   (b) as a result of hi-jack of the conveyance in which the Insured Person is travelling;
   (c) as a result of an Insured Person being detained in hospital outside the United Kingdom for the remaining duration of the holiday/trip.
2. The additional accommodation and repatriation costs necessarily and unavoidably incurred by the Insured Person for returning direct to the British Isles earlier than planned as a result of death, serious injury or illness (occurring in the British Isles during the Period of Insurance) of the Insured Person's spouse, parent, parent-in-law, child, brother, sister, grandparent, or close business associate.

SECTION 6 – DELAYED OR MISSED DEPARTURE

1. In the event that the outward or homeward departure or arrival of the aircraft or sea vessel in which the Insured Person had arranged to travel is delayed by at least 12 hours from the time specified in the official itinerary supplied to the Insured Person this insurance shall pay:-
   (a) **£20** for the first full 12 hours delay and **£10** for each full 12 hours delay thereafter (the delay being calculated from the departure or arrival time of the aircraft or sea vessel specified in the official itinerary) up to a maximum of **£100** per Insured Person.
   or (b) Up to **£5,000** in respect of irrecoverable deposits or charges paid in advance or contracted to be paid for the benefit of the Insured Person only in the event of cancellation of the holiday/trip by the Insured Person.
2. In the event that the Insured Person arrives at the point of international departure too late to commence the booked holiday/trip as a result of failure of public transport services or due to an accident or mechanical failure involving the car in which the Insured Person is travelling, this insurance shall pay up to **£500** (**£1,000** outside Europe) for additional travel and accommodation expenses necessarily incurred by the Insured Person in order to reach his/her booked destination.

N.B.: The Insured Person is entitled to compensation under only 1(a) or 1(b) or 2.

SECTION 7 – PERSONAL BAGGAGE

This insurance shall pay up to **£1,000** each Insured Person (**£500** in respect of children under 16 years of age) in respect of loss of or damage to baggage the property of the Insured Person (not hired, loaned or entrusted to him/her) taken or purchased on the holiday/trip (including clothing and personal effects worn or carried on the person, suitcases and like receptacles) occurring during the Period of Insurance.

N.B.: This insurance shall pay the intrinsic value of the lost or damaged articles or the cost of repair whichever is the lesser. If any article is proven to be beyond economical repair, a claim will be dealt with under this policy as if the article had been lost. Insurer's liability is limited to **£200** (**£100** in respect of children under 16 years of age) in respect of any one article, pair or set. However, in respect of cameras, photographic equipment, radios, cassettes and videos, telescopes and binoculars, antiques, jewellery, watches, furs, precious stones and articles made of or containing gold, silver or other precious metals, the Insurer's liability is limited to **£200** in all each Insured Person (**£100** in all in respect of children under 16 years of age).

SECTION 8 – DELAYED BAGGAGE

This insurance shall pay a benefit of **£100** each Insured Person for emergency purchase of essential items of clothing or requisites consequent upon temporary deprivation of baggage of at least 12 hours from the time of arrival at destination on the outward journey due to delay or misdirection in the delivery by the carrier.

N.B.: An Insured Person cannot claim under both Sections 7 and 8 for the same loss.

SECTION 9 – PERSONAL MONEY

This insurance shall pay up to **£300** each Insured Person (**£100** in respect of children under 16 years of age) in respect of loss of personal money cash, bank or currency notes, cheques, traveller's cheques, postal or money orders, travel tickets, passports, petrol coupons or credit vouchers) whilst on the person of, carried by the Insured Person or left in an approved safety deposit box during the Period of Insurance. Losses of sterling are limited to the amount permitted by currency regulations in force at the date of commencement of travel or **£200** whichever is the lesser. Liability is limited to **£200** (**£50** in respect of children under 16 years of age) in respect of actual cash (i.e. coins or bank notes).

SECTION 10 – PERSONAL LIABILITY

This insurance shall pay up to **£2,000,000** each Insured Person in respect of Indemnity in respect of legal liability of the Insured Person for accidental injury to Third Parties and/or accidental loss of or damage to Third Party property.

SECTION 11 – TOUR ORGANISER FAILURE

This insurance shall pay up to **£5,000** in all each Insured Person in respect of:-

1. The Insured Person's holiday/trip being necessarily and unavoidably cancelled prior to his/her departure from the U.K. due to bankruptcy/liquidation of any tour organiser, travel agent or transportation company as defined under Note A below on which the booked trip depends, in respect of deposits or charges paid in advance by the Insured Person which are forfeited by the Insured Person, or
2. The Insured Person's holiday/trip being curtailed due to bankruptcy/liquidation as set out in 1, whilst the Insured Person is on the booked holiday/trip. The Insurer will pay a pro-rata proportion of the booked holiday/trip cost (up to a maximum of **£2,500**).

Note A: Cover under this Section is only applicable to holidays/trips booked through a member of the Association of British Travel Agents or booked directly with a CAA or ABTA licensed tour operator or a properly licensed coach operator, airline, shipping line, or railway company. The Insurer being subrogated to full rights of recovery from third parties or any other source to the full amount of deposits or charges paid. No claim will be admissible in cases where a bond or financial guarantee as required by ABTA is already in force.

SECTION 12 – WITHDRAWAL OF SERVICES

This insurance shall pay **£50** (up to a maximum of **£300** in all each Insured Person) for each complete 24 hours during which the Insured Person suffers a Substantial Withdrawal of Services (as defined below) at a hotel where the Insured Person is staying, as a result of industrial action or strike providing that such withdrawal exists continuously for at least 48 hours during the Insured Person's holiday/trip.

DEFINITIONS: Substantial Withdrawal of Services shall mean:-

a) the withdrawal of all water facilities in the Insured Person's room, or
b) the withdrawal of all electricity facilities in the Insured Person's room, or
c) the withdrawal of waiter services at meals, or
d) the withdrawal of kitchen services of such a nature that no food is served, or
e) the withdrawal of swimming pool facilities such that the pool is rendered unusable, or
f) the withdrawal of all chambermaid services.

N.B.: The Insured Person must submit written confirmation from the tour operator or hotel to substantiate a claim under this Section.

SECTION 13 – LEGAL EXPENSES

This insurance shall pay for legal costs and expenses incurred by the Insured Person up to a maximum of **£50,000** in the pursuit of legal proceedings by the Insured Person for compensation and/or damages directly arising from or out of injury or death to the Insured Person during the Period of Insurance.

CONDITIONS

1. In the event of an occurrence which may give rise to a claim written notice shall be given to the Insurer immediately. All certificates, information and evidence required by the Insurer shall be furnished at the expense of the Insured Person or his/her legal representatives.
2. No person is entitled to admit liability on behalf of the Insurer or to give any representation or other undertaking binding upon them. The Insurer may at its own expense take proceedings in the name of the Insured Person to recover compensation from any Third Party in respect of any indemnity provided under this Insurance and any amount so recovered shall belong to the Insurer.
3. In the event of the death of the Insured Person, the Insurer shall have the right to have a post-mortem carried out at its own expense.
4. No refund of premium is allowed once the insurance has been effected.
5. The Insured Person must exercise reasonable care to prevent accident, injury, loss or damage. Failure to do so will prejudice his/her right to claim under this Policy. The Insured Person shall take all ordinary and reasonable precautions for the safe-keeping of the property insured under Sections 7 and 9 and take such steps for the recovery of the property as if he/she were not insured.
6. In the event of a fraudulent claim being submitted by the Insured Person or anyone acting on his/her behalf or with whom they are in collusion, all benefits under this policy shall be forfeited.
7. The construction, validity and performance of this insurance shall be construed in all respects in accordance with United Kingdom jurisdiction.
8. The Insured Person may not transfer his/her interest in this insurance.

EXCLUSIONS –
APPLICABLE TO ALL SECTIONS
This insurance does not cover:-

1. Loss directly or indirectly occasioned by, happening through, or in consequence of winter sports or scuba diving (unless the appropriate premium has been paid).
2. Loss directly or indirectly occasioned by, happening through or in consequence of war, invasion, acts of foreign enemies, hostilities (whether war be declared or not), civil war, rebellion, revolution, insurrection, military or usurped power or confiscation or nationalisation or requisition of or destruction of or damage to property by or under the order of any Government or local authority.
3. Loss directly or indirectly occasioned by, happening through, or in consequence of nuclear fission, nuclear fusion, or radio-active contamination.
4. Any claim arising directly or indirectly from any injury, illness, death, loss, expense or other liability attributable to HIV (Human Immunodeficiency Virus) and/or any HIV related illness including AIDS (Acquired Immune Deficiency Syndrome) and/or variations thereof however caused.
5. Loss in respect of any property more specifically insured or any claim which but for the existence of this insurance would be recoverable under any other insurance.
6. Incidents which may give rise to a claim not notified direct in writing to the Insurer or its claim settling agents within 31 days of the expiry of this insurance.
7. Claims increased by the Insured Person's own act or omission.
8. Claims arising as a result of the Insured Person engaging in professional sports and/or rugby league or union.

SECTIONS 1, 2, 3 and 5 – PERSONAL ACCIDENT, MEDICAL AND OTHER EXPENSES, HOSPITAL INCONVENIENCE BENEFIT AND CURTAILMENT
This insurance does not cover:-

1. Losses arising from accidents on two-wheeled vehicles of over 250 c.c. as passenger or driver.
2. Treatment or aid obtained in the United Kingdom (other than as provided under item 3) or medical expenses recovered under a reciprocal health agreement.
3. Surgery or medical treatment which in the opinion of the medical practitioner treating the Insured Person can be reasonably delayed until the Insured Person's return to the United Kingdom.
4. Medication which at the time of departure is known to be required or to be continued outside the United Kingdom.
5. The additional cost of single or private room accommodation at a hospital or nursing home except where the medical practitioner treating the Insured Person deems it necessary for the Insured Person to occupy such accommodation.
6. Loss directly or indirectly occasioned by, happening through, or in consequence of accidents whilst engaged in racing, motor rallies and competitions, hang gliding, mountaineering (reasonably requiring the use of ropes or guides), pot-holing, underwater activities requiring the use of artificial breathing apparatus, except when the appropriate premium has been paid, or aerial activities or aviation (other than as a fare-paying passenger in a duly certified multi-engined passenger-carrying aircraft flown in the course of licensed operations for the transportation of passengers by air by a properly licensed crew).
7. Loss directly or indirectly occasioned by, happening through, or in consequence of suicide or wilfully self-inflicted injury or illness, insanity, venereal disease, being under the influence of alcohol or drugs (other than drugs taken in accordance with treatment prescribed and directed by a registered medical practitioner, but not for the treatment of drug addiction), self-exposure to needless peril (except in an attempt to save human life).
8. Claims arising from pregnancy (unless the expected date of confinement is more than two months after the Insured Person's return from the booked holiday).
9. In respect of Section 2 only other than when the Insured Person is detained in hospital outside the United Kingdom up to the end of the holiday/trip.
   (a) the first **£50** of each and every claim each Insured Person for Worldwide holidays/trips.
   (b) the first **£25** of each and every claim each Insured Person for European holidays/trips except where a recovery is made under the EEC Reciprocal Health Agreement.
10. In respect of Section 5, 1(a), (b) and 2 only – the first **£25** of each and every claim each Insured Person.

SECTION 4 ONLY – LOSS OF DEPOSIT OR CANCELLATION
This insurance does not cover:-

1. The first **£25** of each and every claim each Insured Person (except for claims for Loss of Deposit only).
2. (a) Government regulations (other than in respect of compulsory quarantine) or currency restriction or act.
   (b) Omission or default of provider of transport or accommodation or of an agent through whom the travel arrangements were made.
   (c) Disinclination to travel.
   (d) Financial circumstances of any Insured Person (arising from other than loss of his/her employment due to redundancy qualifying for payment under current redundancy payment legislation).
   (e) Strikes or labour disputes.
   (f) Expenses payable by the Tour Operator, Hotel or Airline.
   (g) Delay in commencement of holiday.
   (h) Surcharges levied by the Tour Operator increasing basic brochure prices.
3. Directly or indirectly arising from failure to notify travel agent, Tour Operator or provider of transport or accommodation immediately it is found necessary to cancel the travel arrangements.

SECTION 6 ONLY – DELAYED OR MISSED DEPARTURE
This insurance does not cover:-

1. Claims arising from the failure of the Insured Person to check in according to the official itinerary supplied to him/her and obtain written confirmation from the carriers (or their handling agents) of the number of hours delay and the reason for such delay.
2. Claims arising from the failure of the Insured Person to allow a reasonable period of time when setting off from home to ensure arrival at the airport or port on time under normal circumstances.
3. The first **£25** each and every claim each Insured Person of any claim under Section 1(b).
4. Claims arising directly or indirectly from withdrawal from service (temporary or otherwise) of an aircraft or sea vessel on the recommendation of a Port-Authority or the Civil Aviation Authority or any similar body.

SECTIONS 7 and 9 – PERSONAL BAGGAGE AND PERSONAL MONEY
This insurance does not cover:-

1. (a) Loss or damage due to delay or confiscation by Customs or other official(s).
   (b) Loss of or damage to stamps, documents (other than those specifically mentioned in Section 9) or contact or corneal lenses or damage to fragile articles.
   (c) Business goods or samples.
   (d) Normal wear and tear, gradual deterioration or mechanical or electrical breakdown or derangement, moth or vermin.
   (e) Loss or damage whilst in the custody of an airline or other carrier unless reported immediately on discovery and in the case of an airline a Property Irregularity Report obtained.
   (f) Theft or loss not reported to the police (and hotel management if stolen in a hotel) within 24 hours of discovery.
2. The first **£25** of each and every claim each Insured Person under each section.

SECTION 9 ONLY – PERSONAL MONEY
This insurance does not cover:-

1. Shortage due to error, omission, exchange or depreciation in value.
2. Losses not reported to the police within 24 hours of the discovery of loss. A written police report must be submitted to the Insurer.
3. Loss of traveller's cheques not immediately reported to the local branch or agent or issuing authority.

SECTION 10 ONLY – PERSONAL LIABILITY
This insurance does not cover liability arising directly or indirectly from or due to :-

(a) Injury to employees or liability to a member of an Insured Person's family.
(b) Animals belonging to or in the care, custody or control of the Insured Person.
(c) Any wilful malicious or unlawful act.
(d) Pursuit of trade, business or profession.
(e) Ownership or occupation of land or buildings (other than occupation only of any temporary residence).
(f) Ownership, possession or use of vehicles, aircraft, watercraft or firearms.
(g) Liability assumed by the Insured Person by agreement.
(h) Legal costs resulting from any criminal proceedings.

SECTIONS 6 and 12 – DELAYED OR MISSED DEPARTURE AND WITHDRAWAL OF SERVICES

These sections do not cover strike or industrial action existing or for which a commencement date likely to affect the planned holiday/trip had been publicly announced at the date this insurance is purchased by the Insured Person.

SECTION 13 ONLY – LEGAL EXPENSES
This insurance does not cover:-

1. (i) Any claim brought against a tour operator, travel agent or carrier.
   (ii) Legal expenses incurred prior to the granting of support by the Insurer.
   (iii) Any claim reported more than 130 days after the commencement of the incident giving rise to such claim.
   (iv) Any claim where the Insurer considers the Insured Person's prospects of success in achieving a reasonable benefit are insufficient.
2. The Insurer shall have complete control over the legal proceedings and the appointment of a solicitor.

RECIPROCAL HEALTH AGREEMENT

Travellers to European Common Market countries are strongly advised to obtain from their local Department of Health and Social Security Office Form CM1. On returning this to the Department completed they will be issued with Form E111 which will entitle them to certain free health arrangements in Common Market countries. For full details please obtain leaflet No SA30 from your local Department of Health and Social Security Office.

ABTA Endorsement 1991 TravelGuard Gold

Goods lost or stolen Should the incident happen whilst the goods are entrusted with the carriers (air, land or sea operators) then this must be reported to them, and a property irregularity report or the carrier's confirmation obtained. In other instances the matter should be reported to the police, and a written report obtained to forward with any claim. Without this the claim could be prejudiced.

Money It should be appreciated that the loss adjuster requires some quantification in support of the amount lost or stolen. The length of holiday, and the day on which the money was lost or stolen, must be taken into account. The insurers are always subject to audit, and have to satisfy not only themselves but other bodies that the claim has been correctly determined.

Hospital benefit This only relates to the person confined to the hospital and during the holiday period, and not after the original return date.

Cancellation When you have a party booking and one member drops out by way of an insured contingency, it is not necessarily accepted that the whole party can then cancel. Cover relates to *necessary* cancellation. Often when there are two or more persons or couples involved and one person or couple cancels, there is normally no reason why the remaining clients cannot travel. Cancellation due to redundancy is covered only if the customer is being made redundant under the terms of the Employment Protection Act; his or her employer should be able to advise on this.

When a client cancels a package holiday there will be loss of money: either the initial deposit paid or a percentage of the total cost of the holiday. Details are published in the Tour Operators brochure under Booking Conditions – cancellation charges. The closer to the date of departure the cancellation is made, the higher the cancellation charges.

We will imagine your client has cancelled the holiday 26 days before departure date and the cancellation charges are 60% of the total holiday costs. We will say the holiday cost £500. 60% of £500 = £300 cancellation charges.

For the client to cancel the holiday officially they must confirm their instructions in writing. The Tour Operator will then send the customer (via the travel agent if the reservation was originally made with a travel agency) an invoice showing the cancellation charges of £300 and a refund of the balance of £200. This invoice together with a completed claims form and supporting document is sent to the insurance company who then considers the claim and if the reasons for cancelling agree with the conditions of the insurance policy should effect a refund deducting any excess payment which is usually between £25 and £50.

It is important to advise the client correctly *before* they cancel the travel arrangements that the reasons for cancellation really are due to causes beyond their control. Study the exclusions very carefully, if unsure, then contact the insurance company to obtain the correct information.

Death benefit This is reduced to £1000 for children under the age of 16 years. Section 2 cover is limited to £15,000 for under-16s. Section 3 is not applicable to under-16s. Section 1 Personal accident has three misfortunes listed (a) death; (b) loss of one or more limbs (c) permanent total disablement.

Illness Pre-existing illness is not excluded from the policy as long as the customer is not travelling against doctor's orders. However, people who have a terminal prognosis are not covered.

Medication Medication in use before commencement of the holiday is only covered if lost or stolen. If the traveller does not take enough for the duration of the holiday then replenishing the supply is not covered.

Pregnancy This is not covered under the medical section unless the expected date of confinement is more than two months after the insured person's return from the booked holiday.

Policy excess   These apply per person and not per booking. Under Section 1 of the policy the excess applies to both money and luggage. For example, if the excess is £25.00 and the customer loses a handbag and money, the excess charge will be £50.00.

Limits   In respect of valuable items, the limit applies to the whole of such property. For example, if a customer lost a camera, gold watch and diamond ring valued at £500.00 in all, the maximum amount he or she would receive (under the current policy) would be £200.00.

Bicycles/wheelchairs   These are only covered whilst being transported as luggage, and only up to the limits within the policy. Once they are in use, they are not covered if lost, stolen or damaged.

Skis, boots, poles etc.   These are covered under the winter sports policy but only up to the limits within the policy and when the appropriate premium has been paid, i.e. double.

Issuing a policy

The information required before issuing a policy is as follows: name of insured person; age; area required; total premium; your agency validation (to obtain commission for the booking); your initials; date of issue; client's address; trip duration; date of travel.

Here are some insurance tips for travel agents:

1   Ensure that the cover is what the customer needs.
2   Ensure that the policy you are using is valid for issue and valid for travel dates, and that the customer is eligible to take out the insurance sold to them.
3   Make sure that you give the customer a copy of the policy document.
4   Ask the customer to take the insurance policy with them when they travel.
5   Advise customers that if they have an accident or are hospitalized, they should contact the 24-hour medical emergency service immediately. Tell customers not to delay or look for alternative solutions.
6   If customers have to make a claim, please bear in mind the following:
 (a) They should have acted in a reasonable way to protect their property, i.e. not leave valuables or any other items lying around.
 (b) Insurance policies demand a police report in respect of stolen property; these help substantiate ownership of the items.
 (c) Claims, along with supporting documentation, should be sent off to the loss adjuster as soon as possible after returning to the UK.

Insurance is a specialized field, and you cannot expect to be expert in it. Please do not hesitate to contact the insurance company if in doubt. *Do not guess*; you owe it to your clients to see that the correct information is given to them.

Let's try a few calculations and queries together then try the exercise at the end of this chapter by yourself.

(a)   Two adults travelling to Tenerife for 16 days? Tenerife is in the Canary Islands, which are in Europe, between 11 and 17 days the cost is £17.55 each making a total of £35.10.
(b)   One adult and one child aged 9 years travelling for 41 days to America. Examine the 31 days rate, plus ten extra days (two additional weeks), insurance for one adult for 31 days

cost £45.00 plus £14.50 each additional week (2) making a total £74.00. One child pays half premium £22.50 plus £7.25 each additional week making a total of £37.00.

(c) Two clients have claimed under section 5 curtailment for the total amount of £1300 per person. They had to curtail their holiday in Hong Kong as a close relative fell seriously ill. Will they receive a full refund? No, although the reason for curtailment is valid for worldwide claims a £50 per person excess is deducted.

(d) Your client booked a holiday in January for travel in July, however, in May the client decided to leave his employment and it was three weeks before he could start another job. He now finds he cannot afford the holiday booked to the Far East. If he cancels will he receive a full refund? No. See section four for loss of deposits or cancellations. The exclusion does not cover financial circumstances, only legal redundancy, and this will fall under the heading 'disinclination to travel'. No refund.

(e) Mr and Mrs Searle travelled by car to London Heathrow airport to board a flight to Madrid, allowing 1½ hours longer than the journey actually takes. Unfortunately en route the car developed a mechanical fault. Assistance had to be called and the car was towed to their home. How will the insurance cover help? See section six for delayed or missed departure. The insurance company will pay up to £500 per person (for Europe) towards the cost of another flight to Madrid as Mr and Mrs Searle allowed ample time for the flight. Proof of the mechanical breakdown plus a completed claims form would be submitted to the insurance company. Will an excess be deducted? No, please read the notes on excess – delayed or missed departure is not listed.

Exercise 1

In addition to supplying the answer to the following, please indicate where the information was found.

(a) Your client has suffered a great loss of money owing to unexpected changes in the rate of exchange. Will your client be covered up to £150.00 for the loss?

(b) Your client was involved in a fight at a disco one night whilst in Spain, when he and several other young men were badly injured. Is your client covered by insurance under the personal liability section?

(c) Your client was unlucky enough to catch a virus whilst on board a cruise, and he spent five days in the ship's hospital until he was well enough to return to the cabin. The infection spread quickly amongst passengers travelling together in a confined environment. Will the medical expenses be covered by the insurance?

(d) Name the geographical limit for Leningrad.

Exercise 2

Calculate the cost for the following family travelling to Kenya, duration 28 days: Mr and Mrs Rautio, ages 41 and 39; Mr and Mrs Partanen, ages 72 and

70; Miss Rautio, aged 12. Whilst on holiday Mr Rautio will spend part of the holiday scuba diving.

Assignment 1: travel insurance

You have a client who is travelling independently from London to Morocco and will be on holiday for 21 days. The client is hesitating over taking insurance and does not understand the benefits. Write an explanation for your client.

Assignment 2   (taken from past COTAC examination paper)

Explain the benefits of insurance to your client, covering the following points and demonstrating examples: medical expenses, personal money, personal baggage, medical emergencies, personal liability.

Assignment 3   (taken from past ICM examination paper)

Explain the meaning of insurance.
Explain the following terms: premium; exclusion; claim.

Assignment 4

Choose four topics from sections 1–13 and write a report on the following for each section: the benefits; the exclusions; and give examples of events that could happen when each section of the insurance policy may be required.

12 Handling cash and cheques

Summary

In this chapter we are going to discuss:

- the responsibilities of handling cash and cheques;
- how to record payments;
- points to keep in mind when handling cash and cheques;
- petty cash;
- travel sales analysis;
- cheque clearance procedure;
- acceptance of cheques;
- electronic funds transfer at point of sale (EFTPOS);
- credit and charge cards;
- how to issue foreign currency and travellers' cheques;
- the exchange rate mechanism;
- sample travellers' cheques sales advice to complete;
- exercises and assignments to complete.

Handling cash

During the course of the day at the travel agency we will be handling cash, cheques, credit cards and travellers' cheques. Great care must be taken at all times to avoid mistakes. If there is a discrepancy it can create an uncomfortable atmosphere in the office. By following these guidelines you will be able to minimize errors and avoid embarrassing situations.

The office may not be large enough to employ a cashier solely to deal with the financial transactions. All members of staff may be responsible for the cash. Then the best solution is for each staff member to keep his or her cash in a separate drawer or till, until it is handed over to the person taking overall responsibility (usually the manager). Each till or cash drawer should have only one key in daily use, held by the member of staff responsible; the manager will hold a duplicate key in a safe place. If one person is responsible for his or her own till, more care is likely to be taken as he or she alone is accountable should any money be missing.

The cash should be taken to the bank every day. Choose various times; do not form a pattern, as muggers like regularity! This sounds dramatic but it is very true. Also large amounts of cash left in the safe could tempt a staff member into dishonesty. It may be necessary to pay a visit to the bank several times during the day.

A record of every cash transaction should be made, showing what type of goods or service was purchased.

When would we be handling cash?

We would *receive* cash in exchange for the many products we sell: package holidays, hotel reservations, car rental, insurance, theatre bookings, airline tickets, coach and sea tickets, and so on.

The *outgoing* expenses would be taken from *petty cash*. This is a sum of money, perhaps £100.00, which is used for small expenditures such as tea, coffee, milk, sugar (office refreshments), postage stamps, salaries for the office cleaner and window cleaner, ticket delivery expenses, small shop maintenance expenses, and occasional travel expenses. Petty cash is used for all those small items that crop up during the month that you need to pay on the spot with cash.

For the main outgoing expenses, such as staff salaries, rent, taxes or rates on the office building, heating and lighting bills, a different method of payment would be used. At the moment we are dealing with the actual cash in your travel agency.

Balancing

To help us balance the books correctly and quickly, we need to reduce errors. The most common errors are: incorrect additions; receipts not collected for item purchased; item not entered on sales sheet; unclear figures; and incorrect change given.

When balancing the daily cash or petty cash, try to work away from the atmosphere of constant noise, telephones ringing and interruptions. Find a quiet desk away from the shop counter for reasons of both security and concentration, and hopefully your books will balance first time.

Accounting

A travel company will have its own method of accounting. Perhaps all transactions will be entered immediately on to computers. Perhaps each branch will use a manual method to record transactions, before transferring the information to the computer. As a helpful guide we are going to study a basic method for incoming and outgoing payments.

Please study the travel sales and analysis example. You will see at a glance how much money was received at the travel agency that day, the products purchased and how payment was made. Let's work through the table together. At the top, the branch and date should be completed with your office location and today's date. The sheet number is 7727.

Column 1 contains the invoice number or receipt number. This is the number on the receipt

Travel sales and analysis

Date:

No. 7727

Branch:

Inv. No:	Client	Total	Cash	Account	Details	Air	Tours	Cont. rail	Dom. rail	Hotels	Sea	Insurance	Misc.
731	Brown	300 00	300 00		125 731 (BA)	200 00		30 00		20 00	42 00	8 00	
732	Smith	80 00	80 00		Cosmos		80 00						
733	Reed	124 00		124 00	117 876 (KL)	124 00							
734	Dexter	476 00	476 00		Seaspray		450 00		16 00	20 00	42 00	10 00	
		980 00	856 00	124 00		324 00	530 00	30 00	16 00	20 00	42 00	18 00	

given to your client, at the time payment was made. Column 2 contains the name of the client buying the travel arrangements. Column 3 shows the total amount your client gave you.

Column 4 shows cash payments. In this example a client Brown paid £300.00 in cash, and a receipt or invoice number 731 was given to him. You could work at a travel company that requires finer details, perhaps separate columns to show payment by cheque and credit card. In this example we have just requested cash (which would include cheques and credit card payments) and account.

Column 5 shows account entries. This is when travel documents have been issued to passengers who have an account with your travel agency. They will make one payment at the end of each month. This would apply to business travellers, explained in more detail in Chapter 15.

Column 6 gives product details or references. Columns 7–13 indicate purchase categories. In this case, our client Brown purchased a British Airways (BA) airline ticket number 125731 for £200.00 – but we collected £300.00! Looking further along the sheet, we see that our client purchased a continental rail ticket for £30.00, a hotel reservation for £20.00, a sea ticket for £42.00 and insurance for £8.00, making a total of £300.00.

Column 14 shows miscellaneous items. Here would be entered items not listed separately.

This travel sales and analysis page is an example. The headings and the order of the columns can be changed to accommodate the type of business received at your own office. You may find you need many more headings.

Let's study the next entry. On invoice 732 our client Smith paid £80.00 with cash. This sum was for a Cosmos tour (see the details column), and was obviously a deposit on the tour.

On invoice 733 our client Reed paid £124.00. This has been entered under the account column, which means that Mr Reed is a businessman and that payment will be made at the end of the month. An airline ticket was issued to Mr Reed for Royal Dutch Airlines (KLM); he may have travelled from London to Amsterdam.

On invoice 734 our client Dexter paid £476.00 with cash. A Seaspray holiday was purchased for £450.00 (tours), as well as domestic rail £16.00 and insurance for £10.00.

By studying the totals you can see that £980.00 was received, and the breakdown into each product is clearly identified. The cash and the account columns add up to the total amount. By keeping separate records of all payments made it will be easy to keep up to date with the state of the business. Are sales for insurance decreasing? You can compare this year's figures with last year's, or this month's week figures with last month's week figures. If you know the state of the business and are quick to recognize changes, those changes can be investigated and action taken accordingly.

Exercise 1

Draw up a travel sales and analysis sheet; number it 7728. Enter a branch name and a date. Then enter the following transactions. Add details and purchase categories of your choosing. Complete all totals and check that they tally.

Inv.	Client	Cash	Account
401	Clyde	340.000	
402	Roberts		406.00
403	Lee	124.80	
404	White	641.50	
405	Harper		761.50
406	Williams	81.80	

Exercise 2

Draw up another travel sales and analysis sheet; number it 7729. Transfer the following information in the correct order and calculate the totals:

(i)   Today's date is 12 March 199X and our office is located in Ashford.
(ii)   Ms Jones booked a flight to Paris, and we issued an airline ticket for Air France to the value of £201.00. Insurance for £15.00 was required. Ms Jones paid cash, and the invoice number was 230. The airline ticket number was 057776123.
(iii)   On invoice 231 Mr McCool paid a £200.00 deposit for his family on a Thomson holiday. He paid by cheque – to be entered as cash.
(iv)   Mr Henderson is one of your business clients. His company is AV Electrics and it has an account with your travel agency. On invoice 232 you issued a British Airways ticket number 125 884 132 to Tokyo at £740.000. Mr Henderson needed hotel accommodation in Tokyo, and hotel vouchers to the value of £120.00 were issued. Insurance to the value of £24.50 was also required.
(v)   On invoice 233 the Wright family have booked a Sealink ferry ticket number 1742 to Holland; the cost is £241.00. Hotel accommodation was required, and hotel vouchers to the value of £301.50 were issued plus insurance at £80.00. The Wright family also required special concert tickets in Amsterdam; converted to UK pounds these cost £89.00. Mr Wright paid by cheque.
(vi)   Mrs Marshall has booked a musical tour of Italy. She paid a deposit of £100.00 on a Cosmos holiday, and requires domestic rail tickets that will cost £13.80. Her insurance premium is £12.00, and Mrs Marshall paid by cash. We gave her receipt number 234.

Take your time to enter this information carefully. Double check your work by answering the following questions:

(a) What is the total amount received on 12 March?
(b) Give the payment by cash/cheque totals.
(c) Give the total to be invoiced to the account client.
(d) Which tours did we book, and how much money did we collect for those tours?
(e) Give the total payment collected for insurance.

Petty cash

Float £100.00

Week ending 29 Nov. 199X

Date	Office refreshments		Postage		Salary cleaner		Staff travel expenses		Maintenance expenses		Ticket delivery		Misc.	
24 Nov.	12	40	17	00			4	80	12	00				
28 Nov.			4	00	30	00					4	00	2	50
	12	40	21	00	30	00	4	80	12	00	4	00	2	50
											Total		86	70
											Cash in hand		13	30
											Total		100	00

If you are really happy with your travel sales and analysis sheet, now is the time to check your work with the solution at the back of the book.

Petty cash

Please study the petty cash example. You will find it very straightforward. We have a float (this means money in hand) of £100.00, and we are balancing our books for the week ending (W/E) 29 November. We would only normally balance our books once a week, not every day; hopefully we will not be spending *that* much!

Look along the line dated 24 November, we spent £12.40 on refreshments for the office (tea, coffee, milk, sugar); £17.00 on postage stamps; £4.80 on staff travel expenses; and £12.00 on maintenance expenses, perhaps a small electrical or plumbing job.

On 28 November we spent £4.00 on postage stamps; £30.00 on a payment to the office cleaner; £4.00 on delivering tickets to a client; and £2.50 on miscellaneous, i.e. on some item not listed.

In all for that week we spent £86.70. This left us with £13.30 from the £100.00 float.

Exercise 3

Draw up a petty cash sheet for the week ending 6 December. Your float is £100.00. On 1 December you spent £30.55, and on 5 December £53.00. Decide the details for yourself. Complete the totals.

Exercise 4

Draw up another petty cash sheet, this time for the week ending 13 December. Your float is £100.00. Enter the following expenditure details and check the totals.

8 Dec.	£ 8.40	office refreshments
	£30.00	postage
	£ 9.00	ticket delivery
12 Dec.	£ 5.60	maintenance expenses
	£ 4.45	ticket delivery
	£ 7.30	staff travel expenses

Cheques

A cheque is an order in writing addressed to a bank, signed by the client, authorizing the bank to pay on demand a specified sum of money to a named person or company. But, of course, if there is not sufficient money in the client's account the bank cannot honour the cheque.

You have to keep to very strict rules when accepting a cheque for travel arrangements. If you accept a cheque and hand over the travel documents *before* the cheque has been cleared (i.e. before the bank has paid your travel agency), you could have a situation where your client does not have sufficient funds in the bank account, and the cheque is returned to you *unpaid*. Meanwhile your client is enjoying a lovely holiday, sitting on the beach at Ayia Napa on the island of Cyprus, enjoying the sun, sand and sea, all at the expense of the travel agent. What a horrible thought!

Let's study three days and ten steps in the life of a cheque. When you think of all the events that take place to clear a cheque and receive payment, it makes sense to allow plenty of time for that work to be done.

Day one

1 The customer writes out the cheque to pay for travel arrangements at the travel agency. Let's say the client's bank is Barclays Bank in Brighton, West Sussex.
2 The same day the travel agency pays that cheque into its own account at its own bank, which is the Midland Bank in Brighton.
3 That branch of the Midland Bank collects all cheques paid in that day and sends them to the Midland Bank clearing department.

Day two

4 The cheques are sorted at the Midland Bank clearing department into bank order. Our client's cheque will be included with all other Barclays cheques.
5 The sorted cheques are then taken to the bankers' clearing house in London, where the banks exchange cheques.
6 The Bank of England adjusts the banks' accounts by the difference between the total amounts of the cheques exchanged.
7 Barclays Bank clearing department (our customer's bank) receives the cheque, records its details and sends it with others to Barclays Bank in Brighton.

Day three

8 Barclays in Brighton receives the cheque.
9 The cheque is paid from money in the customer's account.
10 Details are recorded on the customer's statement.

To give you some idea of the enormous volume of cheque traffic, consider the fact that over 10 million cheques pass through the bankers' clearing house every working day.

Usually a travel company will rule that it requires eight days to clear a cheque, and travel documents should not be handed over before that time has elapsed. Another point to bear in mind is that weekend and public holidays will bring delays. Your client can pay for a special clearance at an additional cost; the process of cheque clearance can then be speeded up.

When accepting a cheque we must take special care over the following points:

Correct date   The date must be that on which you accept the cheque. Do not accept a postdated cheque, as this is an indication that there may be insufficient funds. The validity of a cheque is six months from the date of issue. However, we have already discussed the importance of banking cheques and cash every day.

Amount in figures and words   Look carefully at both: they *must* agree.

Travel agency name   Occasionally a client will be unsure as to whom the cheque should be written, the tour operator or the travel agent. If the travel agency is accepting payment, the agency name must appear on the cheque.

Signature   Cheques should always be signed in your presence. See that the signature agrees with the name on the cheque. On joint accounts, usually either signature is acceptable; it is not necessary for both signatures to be obtained. However, single accounts can only be signed by the person named on the cheque; Mr G. Thomson may not sign for Mrs G. Thomson.

Mistakes   Any alterations must be initialled by the person writing the cheque, otherwise the cheque will become void and the bank will return the cheque to you unpaid. A large error would best be corrected by cancelling the cheque and writing another one – perfectly!

Cheque card   Banks issue a cheque card to accompany a cheque book. A cheque card is a guarantee by the issuing bank branch that it will pay cheques up to the amount of £50.00. Once again there are certain points to check when accepting payment. The cheque card must match the cheque. The name of the bank appears on both cheque and card, and the same code number can be seen on both cheque and card. Check the signature on the cheque card with the signature on the cheque, and check the expiry date on the card. When you are happy that all these points are correct, you may accept the cheque. You (not the client) must then write the cheque card number on the back of the cheque.

Stopping payment on a cheque   The occasion may arise when it is necessary to stop payment on a cheque – perhaps the cheque has been lost or stolen. Speed here is required to supply the bank with the following information.

> The cheque number;
> The date it was written;
> The payees' name;
> The amount.

Providing the cheque card number has been entered on the cheque, this information will be entered into the computerized system and the computer will automatically reflect that entry or issue a warning to the customers' own bank.

What happens in the following situation? A booking has been made at the last minute, and the clients *must* have their travel documents today. They do not have a credit card (we will discuss credit cards shortly), and of course you cannot accept their personal cheque. It is not possible to allow the eight days' clearance period, and the value of the travel arrangements are well above the £50.00 guaranteed by the cheque card. The client can pay by cash or providing your clients have sufficient funds in a building society account, they can call at the building society and have a cheque made payable to your travel agency immediately. The cheque will be signed by the building society representative, there will be no need for a supporting cheque card, and there is no need to wait for clearance.

However when the cheque is presented at the travel agency a quick telephone call to the Building Society should be made to confirm the cheque has been issued for this client. The reason for this is that Building Societies do not guarantee payment on any cheques stolen and subsequently represented.

Alternatively, providing there is enough time for the transaction to take place, your clients can accept bank charges to expedite the transfer of the money from their bank account to your travel agency bank account.

Eftpos   Another safe way of collecting money is by the system known as EFTPOS, (electronic funds transfer at point of sale). Basically, EFTPOS machines are card swipe terminals connected to a bank computer. An increasing number of agencies are having these machines installed, and where the cards, known as Switch and Barclay Connect are used, approval can be sought immediately, therefore guaranteeing the funds to the travel agency.

The benefits of Switch and Barclay Connect for the client are;

(a) no cheque to write
(b) no cheque guarantee limit
(c) no need for cash or cheque books
(d) printed details appear on the customer's bank statement in due course.

The benefits for the retailer are;

(a) no eight-day bank clearance required.
(b) quick and simple to process.
(c) payment guaranteed.

When the client makes a payment using this method, the transaction will be processed through an electronic terminal which will produce a receipt. Request the customer to sign the receipt as agreement to the amount. Return the card to the client with a copy of the receipt and it is now safe to hand over the travel documents.

Letter of Credit   Finally the customer could obtain a letter of credit from the bank guaranteeing payment to your travel company.

Bearing in mind the problems that can arise from careless work when dealing with any form of money, if you are ever unsure about the time between payment and the date of travel, or the validity of a cheque or a cheque card, *please* check with your manager *before* handing over any travel documents.

Credit and charge cards

There are many card services in operation. It would be impossible to make a study of them all, so we will outline the basic types of card used to pay for goods and services.

Credit cards

Credit cards offer credit to a preset limit depending on the card holder's income. There may or may not be an annual fee. The card holder can settle each monthly statement in full, or take credit to a preset limit at a monthly interest rate, subject to a specified minimum monthly repayment. So, when the card holder receives the statement confirming the amount that has been spent during that month, he/she has a choice either to pay in full and not pay any interest, or pay a certain amount off the total each month and pay interest for this facility.

The two main credit cards are Access and Visa. Various banks and other organizations act as issuing principals and agents.

Charge cards

These cards offer credit for the period between making purchases and receiving the statement. The card holder is then expected to settle the statement in full. An annual fee is generally charged. Although they are interest free, charge cards offer no credit and a high penalty is imposed on overdue accounts.

The two main examples of this type of card are American Express and Diners Club.

Understanding cards

All credit companies issue leaflets explaining their own conditions of use. It is well worth while collecting these leaflets from banks, post offices, stores etc. and settling down to read them; become familiar with the conditions, and make sure you understand the facts. Some require an annual fee, some offer free insurance; all have certain guarantees. Highlight the main points so that you are able to advise your own clients when necessary.

Let's think about some of the advantages for the card holders, your customers:

1 The convenience of purchasing without either a cheque book and cheque guarantee card or cash.
2 The ability to make purchases by telephone, by giving the credit card number.
3 The ability to draw cash on the card at home and abroad.
4 The facility to use a credit card for purchases or services throughout the world.
5 The flexibility to spread the bills.
6 The ability to make unexpected purchases, perhaps at a sale, making a large saving on the usual price, without using cash.

There are many more advantages: try thinking of various circumstances when *you* would find a credit card convenient.

What are the advantages to the retailer, the travel agent?

1 The agent can offer a complete range of travel services such as car rental, insurance, all travel tickets, holiday and business travel – to be paid immediately by the plastic card!
2 There is no clearing delay as with cheques. Payment is guaranteed providing the usual points are checked.
3 Customers with cards have a great deal of spending power, and this can be to the travel agent's advantage. Payments made to the travel agent by credit card are safer than other forms of payment.

How do credit card companies make a profit?

Many of the credit card companies charge their card holders a small annual fee (£10–£30 per year). Multiply this by perhaps 8 million card holders to give £80 million to £240 million!

On unpaid accounts, credit card companies receive monthly instalments at high interest rates. The companies also charge the retailer a small percentage of the turnover of the business for the privilege of the payment being made by credit card. It is a fact that many customers will choose to shop where the credit card is acceptable rather than pay by cash or cheque. Therefore, as a retailer, if you do *not* accept credit card payments there is a strong possibility of not getting the business.

Checks to be made

First we need to check that the company on whose behalf we are accepting the credit card, i.e. car rental company, tour operator, airline, shipping company etc., will in fact accept that particular credit card. Once we are satisfied on this, we make the following checks:

Validity   Check the expiry date on the card.
Signature   Has the card been signed? Does the signature tally between the card and the sales voucher you will ask the client to sign?
Approval code   On large amounts an approval code must be obtained. Here you telephone the credit card centre, give the card holder's account number and confirm the amount to be debited to his account. The credit card company, when approving the purchase, will give you an approval number to write on the sales voucher.
Sales voucher   For all transactions a sales voucher must be completed and signed by the customer. There are many different styles of sales voucher, but basically the format is the same. Details of goods are entered on the sales voucher, plus the approval code number if required. The customer must sign; this confirms the sale. A copy of the sales voucher is handed to the customer. If reservation and payment by credit card is made over the telephone, then on the line provided for the customer's signature the words 'telephone transaction' or 'M/O' (mail order) should be written. Each copy of the sales voucher is clearly identified for distribution.

Foreign currency

Many travel agencies have their own foreign exchange department. It makes a lucrative contribution to the revenue of the agency, and is very convenient for the customer. Various methods are used for issuing foreign currency and travellers' cheques. We are going to discuss one basic method that is widely used and will be useful knowledge.

Buying and selling rates

When dealing with foreign currency it is important to know the difference between the buying and the selling rates of exchange. Think of it this way. Any retailer will buy something at a certain price and sell it at a higher price in order to make a profit. It is exactly the same for buying and selling foreign currency. Please study the following rates of exchange (once again this is fictitious information; these exchange rates are to be used as an example only):

Country	Currency	We sell	We buy
Austria	schilling	23.74	24.94
Netherlands	guilder	3.80	4.10
Greece	drachma	211.63	310.50
India	rupee	28.00	28.80

A customer enters your travel agency and requests £100.00 worth of Dutch (Netherlands) guilders, as he is going to Amsterdam for the weekend. Because you are *selling* the foreign currency to your client, the rate of exchange to use would be 3.80 (3.80 Dutch guilders to £1.00). Multiply 3.80 by £100.00 to give the amount your client will receive, i.e. 380 Dutch guilders. Perhaps something unexpectedly happened at the last minute and your client had to cancel the trip, and he decided to return the guilders to your agency. You would now be *buying* that foreign currency at the rate of 4.10. So, divide the 380 Dutch guilders by the buying rate of 4.10 to give £92.68. Our client has lost £7.32 on the whole transaction. That profit, like any other profit on goods, will go towards the cost of transacting that piece of business.

Let's try another example. Your client wishes to purchase £200.00 worth of Austrian schillings; how many will she receive? Multiply the selling rate of 23.74 by £200.00 to give 4748 Austrian schillings. Alas! the trip has been cancelled and the currency returned! How much will you return to your client? Divide 4748 Austrian schillings by the buying rate of 24.94 to give £190.37. You have made a small profit of £9.63.

Using the rates of exchange given, practise a few calculations, making up your own examples.

It is important to keep in mind when dealing with foreign currency that many countries impose export and import restrictions. When working in the foreign exchange department of a travel company, you will have this up-to-date information at hand. Also, exchange rates fluctuate, so be very sure that the correct rate is being used for the business transaction.

Exchange rate mechanism

With sterling's entry into the exchange rate mechanism the exchange rate is limited to a +/− fluctuation band of 6 per cent. This will eliminate any sudden and great changes in the exchange rates used by the countries participating in the ERM.

The currencies that have entered the ERM are sterling, deutschmark, French franc, lira, Belgian franc, krona, guilder, punt, and peseta.

Travellers' cheques

So far we have been discussing foreign currency as cash. What are the benefits of taking travellers' cheques on holiday? They are the safest method of carrying money whilst travelling at home or overseas. They can be exchanged for purchases made at shops, restaurants, hotels and airlines throughout the world – just like bank notes. Each cheque has a number of special security features: they are numbered and, providing they have been signed, are self-insured in the event of being lost or stolen.

The procedure for issuing travellers' cheques is as follows:

1 Please study the example of a sales advice, completed for your client Mr Adrian Moore. When Mr Moore requests sterling travellers' cheques to the value of £650.00, you give him a pound sterling sales advice. You ask him to complete his full name and address in block capitals, to add his normal signature in the space provided and to write the date.

2 You would then write the numbers of the cheques being issued to Mr Moore on the sales advice. Please study the sales advice carefully. In this example Mr Moore has purchased 10 cheques at £20.00 each (numbers E173481301 to 310); 5 cheques at £50.00 each (numbers end 011 to 015); and 2 cheques at £100.00 each (numbers end 911 and 912).

3 Total the cheques sold and show this amount in the total sale box.

4 The commission charged on sterling travellers' cheques is 1 per cent. This is to cover the cost of printing, administration costs and insurance against loss or theft. One per cent of £650.00 is £6.50. The final total to collect from Mr Moore is £656.50.

5 When you have received payment, place the travellers' cheques in a wallet and witness your client signing each cheque on the bottom line marked 'signature of holder'. Double check that your client has signed each cheque.

6 Give your client a copy of the sales advice. This is a record of the travellers' cheque numbers, and should be kept in a separate place from the travellers' cheques. Should the

cheques be lost or stolen, the cheque details will be required when making a report to the police.

Travellers' cheques are issued in many currencies, for example Hong Kong dollars, Australian dollars, United States dollars, French francs, Canadian dollars, Japanese yen and German marks.

When cashing the travellers' cheques the client should take his/her passport as identification. Most bureaux charge a handling fee of between 1 and 2 per cent on transactions.

Please study the second example of a sales advice, this time issued to Robert James. Here you can see that Australian dollar travellers' cheques have been issued to the value of $A1740.00, plus 1 per cent commission, total $A1757.40. We need to collect the equivalent amount in pounds sterling. The rate we see is 2.06 Australian dollars to £1.00. So, $A1757.40 divided by 2.06 gives £853.10, to be collected from your client.

Thomas Cook MasterCard Travellers Cheques	Sales Advice/Avis de Vente **Australian Dollars**					
	Cheque Numbers/Numéros des chèques			Quantity Quantité	Denom Coupure	Amount Montant
Selling Agent/Agent Vendeur Code	Prefix	From/De	To/Jusqu'à			
	A24	1798464470		7	$A 20	140.—
	B26	1729320325		6	$A 50	300.—
	Z19	1743214220		7	$A 100	700.—
	023	1794340342		3	$A 200	600.—
Name (print) Nom (en majuscules) ROBERT JAMES					$A	
Address Adresse 114 ORCHARD ROAD				Total Sale Vente Totale		
LONDON SE17.					$A	1740.00
Important: Immediately upon receipt, you must sign each cheque in the space marked "Signature of holder" (at the bottom left hand side). You will only countersign each cheque (at the top left hand side) when you encash it and in the presence of the acceptor. No refund will be made if you have failed to observe these conditions. **I agree to the above and to the Purchase Conditions** printed on the reverse side of this Sales Advice and separately supplied with the cheques, **and I understand the important notice on the back of the Purchaser's Receipt copy of this Sales Advice.**	**Important:** Dès réception, vous devez signer chaque chèque sur la ligne "Signature of holder" (en bas et à gauche du chèque). Ne contresignez chaque chèque (en haut et à gauche) que lorsque vous l'encaissez, et en présence de la personne qui a la charge de l'accepter. Aucun remboursement ne pourra être effectué si vous n'observez pas ces conditions. J'accepte ce qui précède et les Conditions d'Achat figurant au verso de cet Avis de Vente et fournies séparément avec les chèques, et je prends note des importantes dispositions figurant au verso de la copie du Reçu pour l'Acheteur de cet Avis de Vente.			Fee/ Commission 1%	$A	17.40
				Applicable in Australia Stamp Duty	$A	
				Total		
Robert James	Date of Sale/Date de vente				$A	1757.40
Signature of Purchaser/Signature de l'Acheteur	Day/Jour	Month/Mois	Year/Année	Send original to: Thomas Cook Australia Pty. Ltd. Adressez l'original à: G.P.O. Box 990H Melbourne, Victoria 3001 Australia	Rate Cours 2.06	
	24	11	90			853.10
B2250 C 11/89 (French)				Thomas Cook Australia Pty. Ltd., a subsidiary of The Thomas Cook Group Ltd.		

Note that unless your client has large bills to pay, the cheques should be issued in fairly small denominations. One of the main reasons for using travellers' cheques is to avoid carrying large amounts of cash. This is illustrated in Exercise 6.

Exercise 5

A blank sales advice for Japanese yen is shown. Given the following information, write down everything needed to complete the advice, including the total amount in sterling to collect from your client.

Mr Robert Hughes of 44 Heathway, London N7. collected travellers' cheques on 22 October 199X as follows:

Denomination 5000 yen, cheques numbered Y760142701–720
Denomination 10,000 yen, cheques numbered Z156374320–330

MITSUI- Thomas Cook MasterCard Yen Travellers Cheques	Sales Advice／発行通知書					JAPANESE YEN

Selling Agent／販売代理店名	Code コード	Cheque Numbers／小切手番号			Quantity 枚数	Denom. 金種	Amount 金．額
		Prefix／頭文字	From／始番号	To／終番号			
						YEN 5,000	
						YEN 10,000	
						YEN 20,000	
Name(print) お 名前						YEN 50,000	
Address ご住所						YEN 100,000	

Important: Immediately upon receipt, each cheque must be signed in the space marked "Signature of holder" (at the bottom of the cheque) and only countersigned (at the top of the cheque) at the time of encashment and in the presence of the acceptor. Any loss arising from non-observance of these conditions will fall on the holder.
I agree to the above and to the Purchase Conditions (printed overleaf and supplied with the cheques), and understand the notice on the back of the Purchaser's Receipt copy of this Sales Advice.

お取り決め：小切手をお受取りになりましたら、下段の所持人署名 (Signature of holder) 欄にただちにご署名下さい。また小切手をご使用になる際にのみ受取人の面前で上段の副署名欄に副署名をして下さい。以上の取り決め事項の不履行により生じた一切の損失については所持人がその責を負うことと致します。

私は上記取り決め事項及び裏面記載の「ご購入の条件」に同意します。また「発行通知書(お客様控)」裏面に記載されている注意事項を了解致します。

Total Sale 発行金額 合計	¥	
Fee／Commission		
Total	¥	
Rate		

Date of Sale／日 付			Send this original to: The Mitsui Bank Ltd., P.O.Box Tokyo Central 208, Tokyo, Japan.	送付先： 東京都千代田区有楽町1-1-2 三井銀行 国際事務センター
Day／日	Month／月	Year／年		

Signature of Purchaser／ご署名
三井銀行　　　M322 2/89

Denomination 50,000 yen, cheques numbered P443321184–193

Commission is 1 per cent. The rate of exchange is 255.50 yen to £1.00.

Exercise 6

A blank sales advice for sterling is shown. Given the following information, write down everything needed to complete the advice.

Thomas Cook MasterCard Travellers Cheques	Sales Advice/Avis de Vente					Pounds Sterling

Selling Agent/Agent-Vendeur	Code	Cheque Numbers/Numéros des chèques			Quantity Quantité	Denom Coupure	Amount Montant
		Prefix	From/De	To/Jusqu'à			
						Stg £10	
						Stg £20	
						Stg £50	
						Stg £100	
Name (print) Nom (en majuscules)						Stg £200	
Address Adresse						Stg £	

Important: Immediately upon receipt, you must sign each cheque in the space marked "Signature of holder" (at the bottom left hand side). You will only countersign each cheque (at the top left hand side) when you encash it and in the presence of the acceptor. No refund will be made if you have failed to observe these conditions.
I agree to the above and to the Purchase Conditions printed on the reverse side of this Sales Advice and separately supplied with the cheques, and I understand the important notice on the back of the Purchaser's Receipt copy of this Sales Advice.

Important: Dès réception, vous devez signer chaque chèque sur la ligne "Signature of holder" (en bas et à gauche du chèque). Ne contresignez chaque chèque (en haut et à gauche) que lorsque vous l'encaissez, et en présence de la personne qui a la charge de l'accepter. Aucun remboursement ne pourra être effectué si vous n'observez pas ces conditions.
J'accepte ce qui précède et les Conditions d'Achat figurant au verso de cet Avis de Vente et fournies séparément avec les chèques, et je prends note des importantes dispositions figurant au verso de la copie du Reçu pour l'Acheteur de cet Avis de Vente.

Total Sale Vente Totale Stg £	
Fee/Commission Stg £	
Total Stg £	
Rate Cours	

Date of Sale/Date de Vente			Send original to: Adressez l'original à:	Thomas Cook Travellers Cheques Ltd. P.O. Box 36 Peterborough Great Britain PE3 6SB
Day/Jour	Month/Mois	Year/Année		

Signature of Purchaser/Signature de l'Acheteur
B2270 C 10/90 (French)

Thomas Cook Travellers Cheques Ltd., a subsidiary of The Thomas Cook Group Ltd.

Pamela Jones, of 17 Ash Grove, Southport, received her sterling travellers' cheques on 4 May 199X as follows:

Denomination £10.00, cheques numbered A763401–420
Denomination £20.00, cheques numbered S497104–114
Denomination £50.00, cheques numbered R993742–752

Commission 1 per cent. Payment in sterling.

Issuing travellers' cheques

Each time travellers' cheques are issued they must be recorded. Regular checks should be made to ensure that no travellers' cheques are missing from your stock.

The aim is to avoid mistakes, because mistakes cost our company a lot of money, cause our clients a lot of inconvenience, create an unpleasant atmosphere in the office, and waste a lot of time. Let's go through a few golden rules to follow which will help to make life in the travel agency and foreign exchange department reasonably easy!

1 Never leave money unattended. Perhaps you have been called to the telephone. *Stop! Think!* Lock money away first.
2 Do the book work. Remember to record all payments received and outgoing, to issue receipts, to record all travellers' cheques issued. It is always best to do this at the time the transaction was made, not a couple of hours later; in a busy office our memory can let us down!
3 Check all the points discussed in this chapter: correct date, signature, conversion rates, validity, approval code if necessary. Take your time – don't be rushed!
4 Take care. Notes tend to stick together. Did you notice the number of noughts when we issued the Japanese yen travellers' cheques? Several currencies have hundreds of units; it is easy to make a mistake, so care must be taken to count the noughts! It is worth while taking a few seconds longer to write your figures clearly; this could save an hour or so eventually!

Assignment 1

Describe and define the following:

(a) the main differences between credit and charge cards;
(b) 10 points to keep in mind when handling cash, cheques and credit cards;
(c) (i) buying rate of exchange;
    (ii) selling rate of exchange;
(d) the purpose of petty cash.

Assignment 2

Describe and define the following:

(a) the 3 days and 10 steps in the life of a cheque;
(b) how EFTPOS works;
(c) the benefits of credit cards for the
    (i) card holder
    (ii) retailer.

13 Skills

Summary

In this chapter we are going to discuss:

- converting enquiries into sales;
- product benefits for the customer;
- sales techniques in the office;
- controlling the conversation;
- identifying the customers' needs;
- closing the sale;
- after-sales service;
- preparing to use the telephone;
- assignments to complete.

We are going to talk about the skills required to work in a travel agency, and generally when dealing with the public. In this situation life can be fun, stimulating, varied and even exciting – or it can be frustrating, tedious, emotional and a disaster! Which is it to be? Life being what it is, it will probably be a bit of both. However, with training and the right outlook on life we should enjoy more of the former than the latter!

We all develop many skills just by getting up in the morning and tackling each day. If we make our way to a travel agency each morning we can add to those skills. Issuing a ticket, collecting money, giving a receipt, using a computer, using the telephone, finding out information, reading instructions from a manual and understanding them, talking to clients, organizing the day to the best advantage (managing our time), calculating the cost of a journey, advising clients on health and visa requirements, getting on well with our colleagues (not invading their space) – we take all these skills for granted.

How can we convert enquiries into sales?

Selling skills: product benefits

We are trying to sell as many travel products as possible in order to have a profitable travel agency. It is difficult to do that unless we realize the benefits for the customer of the products or services we sell. We cannot use a hard sell approach in a travel agency; we cannot *make* someone buy a holiday if they really do not wish to. However, if the client is unsure of where to travel, or needs many items in addition to say an air ticket, this is where skills are used to do a professional job. A true benefit is a product or service that applies specifically to customers, meeting their individual requirements.

The following sections outline the benefits of the main products sold by travel agencies.

Car rental

The benefits are many. It is often *cheaper* to travel by car than by public transport (4–6 seats in a car). There is the *convenience* of being able to travel when and where the client wishes to go: no waiting around for public transport. All *luggage* can be put into the boot of the car: no heavy cases or samples to carry on public transport. There is the *flexibility* of being able to stop when and for as long as one wishes, choosing the route. *One-way rental* allows the customer to collect the car in one place and leave it at another. *Independence* is vital when public transport is very limited or non-existent. A breakdown in a private car can ruin a holiday, but with car rental from a recognized company there is *continuity*, a wide coverage of offices from which a replacement will be available.

Insurance

Peace of mind is the main benefit that insurance provides. It gives financial assistance to the policy holder in the event of an accident and medical expenses being incurred. Perhaps your clients' baggage has been lost, or they have had to cancel their holiday with charges to pay. It can also cover flight delays. In many countries medical expenses can be astronomical, and if clients require medical attention they will be very pleased that they have the benefits of holiday insurance.

Flights

The benefit of travelling over long distances by air is *speed*. By making the reservations with the travel agency, the client can benefit from the travel consultant's product knowledge. Should the route be a popular one and the aircraft normally fully booked during certain times of the year, the travel consultant would advise the client to book early. Special seating or catering requests can be made. The client could benefit from *cheaper* fares by booking well in advance. The travel consultant can advise on all booking conditions (many will benefit the client), and also on passport, health and visa requirements.

Escorted tours

These may be by air, sea, rail or coach (with an especial variety of coach tours on offer in Europe). There are *no worries*; the tour has an escort or courier, which means that travellers on the tour have someone to organize all the little items as well as to oversee the main construction of the tour. Language, changing money, getting around an unfamiliar district: all these the escort will help. A *prepaid holiday* can be an advantage; the client knows how much the holiday will cost before joining the tour, and just pocket money need be taken. *Companionship* is probably high on the list for many clients; a tour is an excellent way of meeting fellow travellers and enjoying their company, especially for tourists who perhaps would otherwise be travelling alone. *Knowledge gained* on places visited, and the experience of the escort, can benefit the clients; they can go to off-beat places that they would not be able to discover by themselves.

Travellers' cheques

Safety and *security* must be the main benefits for travellers. There is no need to carry large amounts of cash. The travellers' cheques can be changed in most shops, restaurants and hotels, and are self-insured. In the event of them being lost or stolen, they can be immediately replaced. Unused travellers' cheques can be cashed on returning home or kept in readiness for the next holiday; there is no expiry date.

Ferries

To be able to *take a car* on board ship is a great benefit, making it possible for many to travel further afield. The tariffs are very competitive, and at off-peak times this is a *very cheap* way to travel. Sailings are very *frequent*, and there is a choice of shipping companies. It is possible to choose between 20 sailings per day between the United Kingdom and the Continent. *Caravans* can also be taken on board the ferry, to give cheap and independent accommodation on arrival at the destination or en route, for the whole family or for a group of friends travelling together.

Cruises

This is a wonderful way to travel – in style! Again, *companionship* of fellow passengers can be important, as the ship is one's home during the voyage. There is the opportunity to visit *interesting ports of call*, great *entertainment* on board ship, *comfort*, *delicious food*, bracing *sea air*, and so on.

Rail travel

This can be *cheap*. It can also be *fast* on short distances compared with air travel. Consider that airports are located outside cities; reporting time is often one hour before take-off; on arrival at the destination, baggage has to be cleared; and transport has to be taken to a city or a hotel. Rail travel too can be very scenic.

Package holidays

These are different from escorted tours as they may not necessarily have an escort. Passengers may be travelling together as a group only as far as the transport and accommodation is concerned. Some of the benefits remain the same. The client knows the cost of the holiday and has paid for it before departure, making it possible to budget for the holiday. *Cheaper* tariffs are possible because the tour operators are able to buy in bulk. Usually a package will include the main transport, perhaps a flight; airport taxes; transport between airport and hotel; and the accommodation. There is some *companionship*. Passengers boarding the package holiday flight know they are all going to the same destination, and will be divided on arrival between a few selected hotels or apartments. However, this is not to the same extent as on an escorted tour, where the group is definitely travelling together.

Hotel reservations

By booking through the travel agency, information can be obtained on the location, grade, facilities and availability. Perhaps the client has *special requests* that can be actioned. Perhaps the hotel required is fully booked; if so, the travel consultant can quickly recommend another of similar standard and location. Many travel consultants have personal experience of hotels, and certainly they have constant feedback from clients and are therefore in a good position to help with up-to-date information.

Theatre bookings

For the client to book the theatre tickets from the travel agent, the main benefit is *convenience*. The travel consultant can confirm the reservation immediately and write out the theatre ticket. If the show is fully booked, the travel agent can offer an alternative immediately. So customers can save time and money when booking through an agent rather than direct with the theatre.

Special interest holidays

The benefits are sharing a common interest, learning a new skill, improving an existing interest, and travelling as a group with friends and fellow club members. The sense of adventure could be an attraction.

Stopover holidays

These are excellent for travellers on long journeys wishing to make a break in the itinerary to see another part of the world. They are usually used in conjunction with air tickets. On a flight from say Rome to Sydney, many stopovers could be made en route, for example in Delhi, Bangkok and Singapore. Many airlines offer *free accommodation* on those stopover breaks, or *free city sight-seeing tours*. Here the travel agent must keep very well informed, as airline companies are constantly changing their special offers to encourage more business.

Weekend breaks

For clients who are perhaps tired of a cold, grey, dreary winter, a weekend break may be just the right thing to cheer them up. A change of scenery, a weekend with a theme – often this is a pleasant break between work and the annual holiday.

Trade fairs and conferences

For the business traveller in particular, trade fairs and conferences help to keep up to date on movements in the business world. They provide opportunities to meet others with similar business interests. Here the travel agent needs to be right up to date with information on the location of trade fairs, the themes, the accommodation in surrounding areas, and convenient transport arrangements. Again, this can be time and money saving for the customer if the travel agent is well informed.

So! When using our selling skills at a travel agency, we need to think of all the products and services we sell, to consider the many benefits they provide, to offer them to the client when appropriate, explaining those benefits, and to make sure we have up-to-date product knowledge in order to enhance those benefits.

Sales technique in the office

For face to face selling, when the client is sitting or standing opposite you and looking into your eyes, a technique still needs to be developed. Using the rules of *investigating* the client's needs and *listening* to the client, we begin by asking open questions. An *open question* seeks an answer that gives some information. You will then have the beginnings of a conversation on which to build the travel arrangements you hope to make. A *closed question* will receive the response of 'yes' or 'no', making the next step in the conversation harder to take. For example:

Closed question   'Are you travelling alone?' Answer: 'No'.
Open question   'Who will be travelling with you?' Answer: 'My parents and young brothers.'
This can lead on to the question of the ages of the brothers; they may qualify for children's reductions.

Some of the open questions could begin as follows.

Where?

Where would you like to spend your holiday?
Where is the meeting?
Where are you meeting your friends?

Our product knowledge would include up-to-date information on fashionable holiday destinations, special attractions, special and latest reductions, new destinations, and forthcoming and current trade fairs and exhibitions. We would know where up-to-the-minute events, perhaps political, climatic or financial, might require changes to the destination.

When?

When would you like to travel?
When are you returning?

Our product knowledge would include the season of every country and destination, bearing in mind that many countries are so large that the climate varies drastically at the same time of year from one part of the country to the other. When is high season and low season? This will affect availability and cost. This information can be quickly found from the computer or the manuals.

How?

How many people will be travelling?
How do you wish to travel?
How do you wish to pay?

We would need to know the number of clients travelling, to help us with how many seats to book, how many rooms to book etc. We need to know whether their choice is to travel by rail, coach, car, sea or air. We need to know how payment will be made – by cash, cheque or credit card etc.

Why?

Why is this client travelling?
Why does he need to board that flight?
Why have they chosen that destination?

Who?

Who will be travelling with you?
Who will be signing the Booking Form?
Who will be making the payment?

We need to know who will be travelling and sometimes we need to know the relationship as in a spouse fare for example.

We need to know who will be responsible for the party travelling, the person signing the Booking Form must have reached their eighteenth birthday and we need to know who will be making the payment in order to make the receipt to the payee.

What?

What are your interests?
What are your expectations?
What time is your meeting?

We need to know as much as possible about our client's interests and expectations before we can suggest a suitable holiday.

We need to know the reason and deadline for our client's journey in order to offer alternatives and build an acceptable itinerary.

It is important to know why people are travelling – and we are not just being nosey! People travel for many different reasons; if we know why, we are able to offer alternatives should the first choice not be available.

Perhaps they are travelling for educational reasons. Colleges throughout the world, together with the subjects covered and term dates, should be considered as they will affect the travel arrangements. Perhaps our client is travelling for business reasons, and has an important meeting to attend; therefore if the flight requested is fully booked, a later one will not suffice. However, if you know why the business traveller needs that flight, you will be in a position to offer an earlier one that is available.

Is your client seeking the sun? Again, if this is the prime reason for travel the choice is enormous, and a suitable holiday should be possible. Is the client travelling for health reasons? We should have details of the many health resorts, spas and medical schemes available around the world, and make useful and constructive suggestions. Perhaps your clients are visiting friends and relations. Dates may be important here; alternative routings may be necessary to get your clients to a wedding on time.

Throughout face to face selling it is important to demonstrate customer care by smiling, using eye to eye contact, use the customer's name and be genuinely interested. We need to ensure making travel arrangements is an enjoyable thing to do! Never give the customer the feeling that you are 'too busy'.

Telephone techniques

Using the telephone to conduct our business can be an asset. If we are making the call we can prepare what we intend to say; this saves a lot of time and money on the cost of the call. So we need to be organized, to have all relevant papers at hand and our conversation rehearsed if necessary. We certainly need to list the points we wish to cover, otherwise they can be easily forgotten. If the client is not available, keep trying; it is easy to give up when we have many other jobs on the list to do, but keep trying!

Incoming calls can take us by surprise. We could be asked *anything*, so the need to be organized is still very strong. We need to be able to reach the client's booking details, or information on the products we sell or the services we offer. We need a pad and pen at hand to write down essential details.

Often the voice on the other end of the line is the client's first contact with the travel agency, and within a few seconds an impression will have been formed. If we answer a direct line to the public we must introduce our company's name. Usually 'Good morning/afternoon/ evening, XYZ Travel, may I help you?' is successful for the following reasons. If you commence with the name of your company the caller may not hear it, either because it can be clipped or because the caller is not tuned to listen to the first word. The salutation takes care of that problem. Then the name of the company, and the consultant's own name, followed by the question – 'May I help you?', gives the caller the opportunity to ask for a particular department or travel consultant, or perhaps to describe briefly their purpose for calling. If the greeting is too long, the caller is wasting money waiting for you to finish before getting on with the reason for the call.

In those few seconds we have to identify the client's needs and to project the right impression of our company; obtaining the caller's name and using it naturally in conversation makes the call more personal. The voice is the key factor here; it must sound warm and friendly but not emotional. Try to keep a steady pitch; do not sing the words. Practise using words that the customer will understand; do not use travel jargon or slang words. The aim is to *communicate* as easily and as simply as possible. The tone in which we speak the words can alter the meaning of the sentence; it can sound aggressive, sympathetic, sarcastic, un-interested, helpful, hopeful and so on. Volume plays an important part in the call too: too loud, and you sound aggressive; too soft, and the caller has to ask you to repeat everything because he cannot hear you. The pace of the conversation must be considered. Allow time to think, and time for the caller to write down the information you are giving.

A call may take only a few seconds or minutes, and may seem an easy transaction and a natural process. However, by now you will agree that it has to be well planned, organized and practised to be successful.

Let's run through *making* that call again. It's all about preparation:

1 Decide what you are going to say.
2 Make a list of points to be raised.
3 Be ready with relevant papers.
4 Be prepared with alternatives.
5 Have paper and pen at hand.
6 Be organized with all relevant files etc.

If for some reason you are nervous about making that call – go into the back office and have a rehearsal!

Now let's run through *receiving* that call again:

1 Answer calls promptly.
2 Do not leave the caller on hold.
3 Think about the greeting – not too long or too short.
4 Control the tone, pace and volume of your voice.
5 Do not use words that are ugly or hard to understand.
6 Allow thinking and writing time.
7 Aim to communicate simply and easily.
8 Try to sound warm and friendly but not emotional.

Try to remain fresh. This is not easy to do if you have said 'Good morning, XYZ Travel, may I help you?' at least 100 times already today!

If you are in a position where you cannot help, but have to pass the message on, then please do this – and double check that the message has been actioned. Or if you have promised to return a call, please do this as quickly as possible. If you are unable to make contact, keep trying. Many travel companies have lost business because of lax telephone procedures. Clients will not wait; they will book elsewhere.

Closing the sale

So far we have travelled along the path of selling skills by investigating clients' needs and listening to what they have to say. We have made the reservations, offering alternatives if the original request was not available. We have suggested other services; do you remember, we discussed the benefits of the products we sell?

Our next step is to overcome sales resistance! We cannot *make* our clients accept the travel arrangements. However, they have either telephoned our agency or made the effort to call in, and it is reasonable to suppose that the intention to travel was in their minds. So why are they hesitating? Perhaps we didn't *really* listen, and have not offered what the client is really looking for. Perhaps we were not giving enough information about the trip; could that be lack of product knowledge? Did we not really take enough interest in the customer? Perhaps our attention was often diverted by what was going on around us in the shop. Were we too pushy, or perhaps not confident enough?

Now we have won the clients' confidence and sold the holiday, we need to collect payment, complete the booking form and attend to all the other formalities such as passport, health and visa requirements. This is known as closing the sale. But does it end there? *No!*

After-sales service

Having attracted customers to the agency, demonstrated our product knowledge and expertise, gained their confidence and made many sales, we need to *keep* the customers. We would like them to make all their travel arrangements with us every time they travel, and to recommend us to their friends and relations.

There is little point in fighting for business, spending large amounts of money on costly advertising and market research, or racking our brains for new ideas, when we do not look after the business we already have. That business offers us potential future business. The traveller is looking for a reliable, pleasant, efficient travel agent. Once they have found you, they will want to stay: so look after them! Keep them up to date on all the latest information that is relevant, special reductions, country information, special interests for groups and individuals. Keep in close contact before, during and after *their* booking. Remember important occasions such as birthdays, weddings etc., as a comfortable relationship is built over the years. A wedding card or telegram to the bride and groom when you have booked their honeymoon arrangements will mean a lot to them. We need to show that we care – by *really* caring!

Sales summary

Let's go through those steps again:

1 Obtain information from the client: how, why, when, where, who and what.
2 Make recommendations: suggest arrangements that may be suitable, check availability, offer alternatives if fully booked.
3 Remember the benefits of your products and services; offer additional services.
4 Overcome sales resistance, without becoming aggressive! If the clients are not sure, try to dispel their fears.
5 Close the sale by confirming the reservations, collecting a deposit to make them secure, and completing the booking form.
6 After-sales service: keep in touch with the customer. Do not make the booking and then promptly forget about them until six months' time when the balance is due; keep in close contact.

Customer relations

'It is all very well trying to follow these guidelines in theory, but you don't know my customers!'

It is true: some customers are time wasters. It is all part of the day's work, I'm afraid. Experience with providing a public service will often help you to know when clients are genuine or just browsing through the brochures, looking at cheerful photographs, dreaming of sunnier climes during a particularly wet and windy day. Perhaps they have an appointment in half an hour, and a pleasant way to pass the time is at the travel agency. There are many reasons why someone walks into the agency but doesn't buy – and it isn't *always* our fault.

Mostly customers really are very pleasant. If they are booking a holiday it is a happy occasion for them. They need our help, and the whole transaction can be enjoyable for both customer and travel consultant. But we need to be aware that sometimes stronger controls are required, and we must learn how to put them into practice. Don't wait for the customer at the agency – practise on your friends and relations!

You may have a talkative customer (or friend); in fact, once they begin they are very hard to stop. Remember that the person asking the questions is the one in control. Be patient; they must surely take a deep breath sometime. Be ready with a question to steer the conversation in the right direction. It will not be easy because the whole time you must listen and show interest, but be prepared to control the conversation and get on with the job as soon as possible. From the corner of your eye you can see many other customers waiting for attention.

Sometimes customers will be very irritable or suspicious. Try to realize why. Is the service not really what is expected? Are we rushing them? Try to explain everything with confidence – and be patient. Have as much information as possible at hand to show the clients in order to gain their confidence. They may have had a bad experience the last time they made a travel arrangement, and may now be very wary.

Perhaps the customer is rude or angry. Unfortunately there are people who always expect to get everything they want, and they become very threatening when they realize it is not always possible. Keep calm, and try not to take it personally. It is upsetting that you have come up against their problem, but try very hard not to let it show. Be professional; keep detached; try hard to obtain the client's demands; offer as many alternatives as possible. If the client is angry because something has gone wrong, again keep calm for the moment. We will be handling complaints in Chapter 16!

Assignment: comparing agencies   (taken from BTEC Travel and Tourism)

Visit three travel agencies and make a travel enquiry. It has to be the same question to be able to compare the response from each agency. Write a report on your impressions to include the following:

Appearance of the agency   Was it easily recognizable as a travel agency? Did it make you want to go inside? Was it in a good and convenient location?
Interior of the agency   How many staff were there to help? Were the brochures well placed? What computerization was available? Did the staff wear uniforms? How was the office furniture arranged?
Efficiency of service   Were the travel consultants helpful? Were they accurate? Were they knowledgeable? Did you feel you were made welcome?

Finally, the report should include: what customer type were *you*?

Assignment: controlling conversation

Whenever the opportunity arises during the course of a week, practise controlling the conversation. Ask open questions; steer the conversation back to the point. When making telephone calls, either private or business, use control. Follow the points discussed in this chapter and record any changes in your style. Assess the success and failure rates, and analyse why, when and how improvements could be made.

I wonder whether your friends will notice any changes. Ask an open question to find out!

14 Business letters

Summary

In this chapter we are going to discuss:

- the type of letters you may have to write;
- how to compose a letter;
- the curriculum vitae (CV);
- examples for job application letters;
- business letter relevant for travel agency work;
- assignments to complete.

Applying for the job

Perhaps your first really important business letter is to apply for a position in a travel company. Few letters are more difficult to write than the one designed to get you the job you really want. In this letter you really have to sell yourself. It is therefore very important to consider the reader. If the position has been advertised he/she may have hundreds of letters to read, and from these the applicants will be selected who appear to justify an interview. After the interviews a shortlist will be made from which the successful applicant will be selected.

Before giving you a few suggestions and ideas for this letter, let's think about a few basic rules:

Paper   Choose a good quality paper. Plain white is best with matching envelopes. Use black ink or biro as many companies need to photocopy applicants letters and blue is too pale to read. For business letters, write on one side of the page only.

Planning   It is sometimes difficult actually getting started on a letter and so the best way is to write down briefly the points you wish to make, put them into a logical order order so that the subject matter flows, then build on those points. Often a heading will bring the reader's attention to the subject immediately, for example *Completed Application Form – Trainee Travel Consultant*. This could be used when enclosing a completed application form. Never enclose any original certificates or diplomas as they can easily go astray and will be very difficult to replace. So the body of the letter should

(a) state what the letter is about;

(b) continue with the necessary information;

(c) keep to the purpose of the letter, to request an interview perhaps.

Keep the language simple, polite and clear.

Often we can begin a letter by referring to one we have received and this could be as follows, 'Thank you for your letter of 27 March requesting. . . .' We should continue to reply to each topic in the same order of preference.

It can be just as difficult to end a letter as to start, and it is best to avoid all those stereotype expressions such as 'I hope you will consider my application' or 'Looking forward to hearing from you in the near future' it isn't necessary to have a rounding off sentence once the conversation has come to an end. It is often good to end with an action sentence if appropriate for example, 'Please let me know whether Thursday 29 September will be convenient.'

Having finished the text of the letter do you write Dear Sir or the person's name? Generally if you have met the person or have spoken on the telephone you can use the surname, 'Dear Mr Van Der Burgh', if not, 'Dear Sir'. What happens if you are not sure of the sex, then do not write Dear Sir or Madam, but still write Dear Sir. If a woman has signed a letter not giving her title you assume the title is Miss. You can also use the expression Ms which is equivalent of Mrs or Miss but does not distinguish marital status.

Setting out the letter   The name and address of the person to whom you are writing is put at the top left-hand side of the letter above the salutation.

Referencing   The letter should carry the reference number found in the advertisement; this will encourage a speedy reply.

Date   You have a choice! This can be written on the right-hand side of the paper below your own address, or on the left-hand side immediately below the reference. It should give the day of the month, the month, and then the year, e.g. 29 June 199X.

Addressing   As a general rule, if you begin a letter with 'Dear Sir' you should close with 'Yours faithfully'. If you address your letter 'Dear Mr Jones', close with 'Yours sincerely'.

Copies   Always keep a copy of all business letters.

Curriculum vitae (CV)   It is a good idea to attach to your letter of application a brief history about yourself; this is often called a curriculum vitae. This can begin with your date and place of birth, then go on to list details of your education, examinations passed during and after school, and all your previous employment. If you are answering a number of advertisements you can have this information on a separate sheet and have it duplicated.

The curriculum vitae should be typed and be planned as follows:

Personal details.
Name
Address
Telephone number
Date of birth

Details of education
School/college/university
Examinations and qualifications
Current courses

Employment experience
Dates   Name of company   job title

Non-vocational interests

You may like to add the name and address of two referees although this could result in the referees receiving a flood of enquiries! No doubt the application form will request referees and you could give the details then after speaking to the referees individually.

Let's imagine you have seen a position advertised in your local newspaper for the position of trainee travel consultant at a company called Mayflower Travel Services situated at Kings Road, London W8. The contact name of Mr John Reed, Personnel Manager was given in the advertisement. Plan your letter to Mr Reed, writing the headings first. These could be

(a) where you read the advertisement;
(b) the position for which you are applying;
(c) brief outline of your education.

Build up on those headings and write the formal letter. On a separate piece of paper write your curriculum vitae following the guide already provided. When you have completed that, compare your letter with the following example.

```
                                          24 Primrose Court,
                                          London N7

Reference STD/TOUR/JR                     12 March 199X

Mr John Reed,
Personnel Manager,
Mayflower Travel Services,
King's Road,
London W8


Dear Sir,

     With reference to your advertisement in today's ..........
(name of paper) I should like to be considered for the position of
trainee travel consultant. I am nineteen years of age and have just
completed a two year travel and tourism course at .......... (name
of college). I was educated at .......... where I passed my GCSE
with four O levels and three A levels.

     My travel and tourism qualification includes ................
(subjects) and I have enjoyed the work very much.

     I should be available to attend an interview at any time which
is convenient to you.

                    Yours faithfully,




                    (signature)
                    (your name typed)
```

Mayflower Travel Services have replied to your letter offering you an interview on 13 June at 2 pm and requesting you to bring your certificates with you. Write a reply to that letter remembering the following points.

(a) use the reference on Mayflower Travel Services letter;
(b) underline a heading which should detail interview date, time and venue;
(c) keep text short when thanking the person concerned for the invitation to attend an interview and confirm you will attend.

We will say your interview was successful and you have been offered the position of trainee travel consultant. Write a letter in reply to your letter of appointment confirming you will commence work on 1 July. Remember!

(a) use the reference number
(b) you may now use the surname
(c) underline a heading *Letter of appointment to commence work 1 July;*
(d) express thanks for the letter of appointment;
(e) confirm you will commence work on the 1 July;
(f) are you looking forward to joining the company? You may like to say so;
(g) if you used the reader's name you will now close with 'Yours sincerely'.

Preparing business letters

Now you have that job in a travel agency, you may be asked to design a standard business letter. For these you will use the company's paper with its name and address preprinted, usually at the top of the page. A standard letter might be used on the following occasions:

1   Confirmation of travel arrangements.
2   Request for payment.
3   Enclosing travel documents.
4   Change in travel arrangements.
5   A 'welcome home' letter after the holiday.

1 *Confirmation of travel arrangements*

You can design a form giving departure and arrivals details, cost and health and visa requirements, completing the relevant boxes. Or when a computerized confirmation/invoice is received from a tour operator, you can send this to your client with a covering letter.

Dear ....

    I am pleased to enclose the confirmation/invoice for your forthcoming travel arrangements. Please check the details carefully and contact me immediately should there be anything which is not in order.

    Payment of the balance of your travel arrangements will be due not later than .... An order form for travellers' cheques has been enclosed and I will be pleased to assist you with these arrangements. Kindly make cheques payable to Mayflower Travel Services.

    Details of the passport, visa and health requirements for your holiday are shown below. If you should need to obtain a new passport please apply as soon as possible to avoid any delays. We shall be pleased to assist in obtaining your passport, visas and issuing travel insurance which we strongly advise to all our clients.

    If you require any further information, or help with any aspect of your holiday, please contact me without delay.

            Yours sincerely,

            (signature)
            (your name typed)
            Travel Consultant

How about letter 2? Do you find it difficult to ask for money? It could read something like that shown.

2 *Request for payment*

Dear Mr Smith,

As of today's date we have no record of receiving payment of the balance of your holiday account.

If we do not receive this by ...... (give a date) we must assume that you no longer wish to proceed with your holiday and we shall cancel your booking to avoid your incurring further cancellation charges.

Your deposit will be forfeited in accordance with the tour operator's booking conditions.

Yours sincerely,

(signature)
(your name typed)
Travel Consultant

Assignment: business letters

Try writing a letter yourself for each of situations 1, 4 and 5. The best approach is to write down on a separate piece of paper the points you wish to make.

For letter 1, you need to confirm details of the booking, advise the client of the passport, health, and visa requirements, and inform the client of when to pay for the travel arrangements.

For letter 4, try making your own points.

Remember: be yourself; be clear; and keep it simple.

For letter 5 you are really checking that all went well on the holiday and you would like to handle their future travel arrangements. Also, very importantly, we learn a lot from feedback from our clients; they have just been there, they have first-hand knowledge which is invaluable to us, because standards and resorts are constantly changing.

Letter 3 could read something like that shown.

3 *Travel documents enclosed*

Mayflower Travel Services,
King's Road, London W8

SST

29 June 199X

Mr and Mrs R. Jones,
7 Lavender Way,
London E4

Dear Mr and Mrs Jones,

I am pleased to enclose your travel documents for your forthcoming holiday. Please check these very carefully and let me know without delay if there is anything which is unclear.

If you need further information or help with any aspect of your holiday, please do not hesitate to contact me.

I hope that you have a most enjoyable holiday.

Yours sincerely,

(signature)
(your name typed)
Travel Consultant

4 *Change in travel arrangements*

With this letter we are assuming the client has been advised by telephone of the alteration, and the purpose of this letter is to confirm in writing the new arrangements, which have been accepted verbally by the client.

Dear ....

    Further to our telephone call advising an alteration to your travel arrangements, we confirm all details as follows;

Departure/arrival dates:
Flight details:
Accommodation:
Cost:
Additional changes:

    We regret these changes have been necessary for reasons beyond our control, and thank you for your kind cooperation.

                Yours sincerely,

                (signature)
                (your name typed)
                Travel Consultant

5 *Welcome home letter*

Dear ....

    'Welcome home!' I trust that you have returned from a very enjoyable holiday.

    At Mayflower Travel Services we try to ensure that our travel and resort information is accurate. However, the travel industry is constantly changing; therefore any comments made by returning clients are very much appreciated as they help us keep our information up to date.

    I hope you found the services provided at our office to be complete and to your liking. If not, we really would like to know how we can improve. If you have any comments to make please call into the office or write me a line; we will be pleased to hear from you.

    Thank you for choosing to book your travel arrangements with Mayflower Travel Services, and we hope we shall have the opportunity to look after your future travel needs.

                Yours sincerely,

                (signature)
                (your name typed)
                Travel Consultant

15 Business travel

Summary

In this chapter we are going to discuss:

- how business travel differs from retail travel (holiday travel) arrangements;
- giving good service to secretaries;
- providing a good service to business travellers;
- possible business travel problems with solutions;
- meeting the needs of businesswomen;
- assignments to complete.

A travel company will separate business travel from retail travel because the two types of business and the needs of the clients are quite different. With retail travel, holiday-makers will need to go to a travel office that is conveniently situated, possibly in the high street, perhaps near a car park. They will need to browse through brochures, discuss various holidays with the consultant, and take brochures home and chat to the family about the holiday, before returning to the travel agency to make the booking. More discussion will follow before they make the decision to complete the booking form and pay a deposit to secure the reservation. This all takes time and, as you get to know your clients better year after year from booking their annual holidays, the whole process can become a social occasion.

By the term 'business travel' we mean men/women travelling for business purposes whose company will have credit arrangements with your travel agency and payment for the travel arrangements will be negotiated for different periods ranging from 7–30 days and rarely after each travel transaction. This type of travel differs in many ways from retail travel. Reservations are made quickly and confirmed to the client promptly, because the business traveller will need to know immediately whether the flights are confirmed. He/she will have other arrangements to make that will depend upon this information, such as meetings at conference centres and securing hotel accommodation. It often happens that many meetings will be arranged in several countries during the one business trip, and a very complicated itinerary can begin to take shape.

Giving good service to secretaries

Unlike the holiday traveller, who needs a convenient location to make the travel arrangements, most of the business travel reservations will be made over a telephone. After a few months of making these travel arrangements you may feel you know your business traveller very well. You will be familiar with his/her likes and dislikes, for example whether the smoking or non-smoking section of an aircraft is preferred, the standard of hotel required, whether a rented car should be automatic or manual. However, the chances are you will never have met, because all the travel arrangements would have been made through the secretary.

To build a good business travel clientele, we need to give a good service to both the traveller and the secretary. We begin to do this by understanding their needs. Put yourself in the shoes of the secretary: what are her needs? The needs of most secretaries are:

1   To run their work smoothly.
2   To know every detail of their employer's travel arrangements.
3   To be kept up to date.
4   To eliminate errors.
5   To save time.
6   To be in control.
7   To do a professional job, to provide a good service to the employer. We can answer those needs by offering a good service, which will include the following.

Prompt confirmations

As we have said, our business traveller needs to know *immediately* that the reservations are confirmed, so do not delay in giving the information to the secretary. If the reservations are being made on a computer, you will be able to view on the screen the flights that are available and book them at the same time. This can be done whilst the secretary is relaying the itinerary over the telephone, and you would be able to read the information from the screen back to the secretary, confirming the situation immediately. Apart from the savings made on telephone bills by the travel agency (no call back required), the secretary is pleased to know the situation as the reservations are being made. Perhaps the flight required is full, and she will be able to make a decision on an alternative flight that is available.

Correct information

The secretary relies upon the information you give her, so you must ensure the information is correct. The sort of information you will discuss with the secretary will be as follows:

Flight   Provide the timings, days of operation, connecting times with other flights, bearing in mind they are subject to change. The whole itinerary might have to be changed if one airline amends the timings so that connections become impossible for your itinerary. Give the aircraft type, facilities on board, position of seat booked (film viewing, smoking/non-smoking, aisle/window), class of travel, any special requests (vegetarian meals perhaps), reporting times at airport of departure and *en route*, telephone numbers of airlines to reconfirm flights.
Fares   Just because the business traveller is not paying for the travel arrangements, this does not mean that the sky is the limit! Companies are budget conscious, and require the best possible convenience and comfort for the most competitive fares. Keep an eye out for special offers.

Passports, visas, health requirements   You will have details of your client's passport, and will be able to advise on and *obtain* all the necessary visas required for each country. You will sometimes need to obtain them at very short notice, which will test your skill and patience. Advise on health requirements – but don't offer to have the vaccination!

General information   Have up-to-date brochures on cities to be visited, especially a map. Provide current brochures on hotels; be sure of the location in relation to your business traveller's requirements.

The details of the client's likes and dislikes should be entered on a file card or computer, so that you are not asking the secretary for the same information over and over again. Making travel arrangements for her employer will be just one of a hundred jobs she completes each day, and we aim to make the travel side of her work flow as effortlessly as possible.

Other aspects of service

Ticket delivery   As businessmen/women travel at almost a moment's notice, travel documents are seldom posted. A reliable courier service is used. On occasions travel documents are collected at the airport; this is known as ticket on departure (TOD). This facility would be used when there is insufficient time to hand the ticket to your client before the journey to the airport, and he/she would collect the travel document at the airport before boarding the aircraft.

Monthly newsletter   A newsletter circulated to all your business clients can help to keep them up to date with changes in fares, visa regulations, climatic or political changes, and any worthwhile information.

Complete arrangements   Nothing is more irritating for the secretary than booking the flights and hotel accommodation with your travel agency, and then having to book the rail or sea part of the journey elsewhere. If we are offering a good business service it must be *complete*. We will arrange sea, rail, air, and coach reservations; hotel, restaurant and theatre bookings; insurance, car rental and travellers' cheques; interpreters and guide services; and meet and greet service at airports. We should endeavour to respond to any reasonable travel-related request.

Twenty-four hour service   Bearing in mind that our travellers are world travellers, and that hours of business vary throughout the world, we need to provide a 24-hour contact telephone number in the event of an emergency.

Trade fairs, exhibitions and conferences   Keep in touch with what is going on in your client's business world. What does the company produce? Keep your businessman/woman advised on forthcoming trade fairs and exhibitions that may be worthwhile to visit.

Fostering good relations

To help build a good relationship with the secretaries it is a good idea to invite them to your office occasionally to explain how the work is finalized from your side. This will help you to work together.

A way of saying 'Thank you for the business' is to arrange a social occasion from time to time. A fun day out for a group of secretaries can be arranged and will be very much appreciated. If you do decide to organize a special day, this need not be funded entirely by the travel agency. The airline, shipping company, coach company or tour operator concerned might be pleased to offer complimentary tickets; this is a wonderful way for them to advertise their product, and an excellent opportunity for the secretary to experience the type of service she is frequently reserving for the boss. The tourist office of the city being visited may also help with complimentary tickets and useful information, and so a happy day begins to take shape.

Increasing business travel

We have to be constantly eager to increase our travel agency revenue! Perhaps we service 30 businesses in our area, all having an account for their travel arrangements and paying at the end of each month.

Often businesses fail, and we could find ourselves in a very sad financial situation. We must keep our eyes and ears open for news of the businesses in our area, and maintain a close watch on the accounts and the payment for the travel arrangements. Should we find anything amiss, we must advise the travel manager immediately. If two companies spending, we will say £30,000 each on travel arrangements with our agency suddenly go out of business there will be a sudden decrease in our own income.

Increasing business travel revenue is the job of the manager or marketing manager. Many books have been written on that subject alone. As this is a skills book designed for the travel agency trainee, we will explain just briefly how we would go about the task. We need to investigate all the factories, offices and shops in say a 15-mile radius, find out the total number of employees and the number likely to travel frequently, the most likely travel destinations, and the line of business of each company. Discover whether the companies are happy with their existing travel arrangements.

Your next step would be to visit each company, telephoning to make an appointment with the person responsible first, and then make the most of the opportunity to sell your services. Be well prepared with all the details regarding the benefits of using your travel agency (see Chapter 13). You could add to your list of benefits – modern technology to speed reservations, and friendly well-trained staff to serve the business travellers.

Handling business travel problems

What sort of problems are we likely to face? Well, there are the usual problems and frustrations: delays with telephone calls; computer systems going down; the person dealing with the matter in hand has gone on holiday, leaving your problem to wait until he/she returns; and so on. In addition there is a good variety of other problems to unravel. Some of them are self-made, I'm afraid, but by anticipating the possible error we may be able to reduce the number of disasters that unfortunately can happen.

Problem 1

You have booked an itinerary for Mr Kaymar, and part of the journey includes Paris with a change of airport. He arrived at Charles de Gaulle Airport, and departed from Orly Airport. At least four hours should have been allowed to travel between the two airports, but unfortunately you did not allow enough connecting time and Mr Kaymar missed his flight. He had to organize hotel accommodation at Orly Airport, stay overnight and continue his journey the following morning. This meant that he missed part of a very important meeting. On his return he contacted you at the travel agency; he was still furious. He has threatened to remove the account from your company.

Solution

You would need to establish that all this really did happen as reported, because there could be many events that would help Mr Kaymar to miss his flight departing from Paris Orly Airport. The flight arriving into Charles de Gaulle could have been delayed for a variety of reasons (industrial disputes, weather conditions, technical problems etc.). There are many reasons why Mr Kaymar could have been delayed travelling from one airport to the other. Having established that none of these events did take place, you check your record of the reservations. It is quite definite that the connecting time between the two flights was not sufficient. You are left standing with a very red face, and shaking like jelly in your shoes!

Being human we all make mistakes, but this fact does not help Mr Kaymar. He wants to know what you are going to do to put things right. In this particular case you can do nothing to alter the situation; it happened, he missed part of the important meeting, and was also greatly inconvenienced. All you can do is offer some kind of compensation and ask him to give you another chance.

After the apologies, the travel agency would offer perhaps a complimentary weekend away for two, or a reduction from the next travel arrangements made by Mr Kaymar. You would need to assure the client that it would not happen again, and make perfectly sure that it doesn't. Double check every detail of the reservations you finalize. It is unlikely that you would ever make that same mistake again; you probably will never completely forget that 'jelly in the shoes' feeling!

Of course, your travel company will not be able to offer compensation for every mistake that is made. However, when the fault is genuinely with the travel agency, and you wish to keep your client's business, the gesture must be made.

What happens when there is doubt about the mistake: you think you did the right thing, but so does the secretary! Let's look at the next problem.

Problem 2

Mr Anderson travelled from his home in Essex to King's Cross station in London to board the overnight train to Edinburgh, departing at 2240 hours and arriving in Edinburgh at 0620 hours the next morning. The journey from his home to King's Cross station takes about two hours. Mr Anderson has a conference to attend at 1000 hours on the morning of his arrival in Edinburgh. When Mr Anderson arrived at King's Cross station he discovered that no reservation had been made for him, and the train was fully booked. He immediately telephoned his secretary at her home, who assured him that the reservation details were given to you. Mr Anderson decided to return to his home in Essex (hope his wife was happy about that!). The time is now 0830 hours and he should be in Edinburgh, but he is standing on the travel agency doorstep waiting for you to arrive!

Solution

After the initial salutations, you look at the file and discover that the reservations have been made for the following night. At this stage Mr Anderson is not concerned whether his secretary gave the incorrect date or whether you misheard the instructions. His need is to get to the conference in Edinburgh. Offer an alternative. The flight from London to Edinburgh takes one hour and ten minutes. He will miss part of the conference, but it may still be worth while for him to attend. The refund from the rail reservation can be put towards the air fare, and adjustments can be discussed on his return.

Financial problems

One way for the travel agency to relieve some of the financial burden of having many companies with large amounts of money outstanding until the end of the each month is to encourage the business travellers to have their travel arrangements charged to their company credit card. The travel agency will receive commission on the documents issued, but the burden of credit will be borne by the credit card company.

It is a problem when companies either are very slow to pay their dues or are doing their best to avoid paying. If a business is going through a difficult time, the businessman/woman may increase travel activities in the effort to obtain more business, often further afield. This could mean longer and more expensive flights than usual at a time when money is short.

Bad debts are bound to arise at the travel agency. Usually the person responsible – the credit controller, manager or agency owner – will handle the situation, as they have been trained for that unpleasant part of the job, either formally or by life's experience.

At this stage of your career, keep an eye on what is happening around you, be aware of your own agency accounts system, and chat to the manager about any irregularity that may occur.

Meeting the needs of businesswomen

Do the growing number of businesswomen have special needs in addition to those of businessmen? Certainly they have the *same* needs: flexibility with air fares, comfort and convenience, perhaps the services of a secretary at destination, reliable transport, the use of a conference room etc. The businesswoman has to meet the same demands as businessmen, and sometimes more, as many businesswomen have the same responsibilities at the office and full responsibility at home – two full-time jobs!

Even as we approach the twenty-first century, there are many businesswomen who experience a certain amount of embarrassment with everyday needs for which a businessman would not give another thought. For example, personal security is important both in a hotel and whilst travelling to and around the destination. Eating alone in a restaurant can feel uncomfortable. When a woman is waiting for a business associate to arrive at the bar, ten minutes can seem like an hour.

Perhaps there is a lot that could be done by hotels to make life easier for the businesswoman. The travel consultant can help by being aware of the hotels that are improving their facilities with businesswomen's needs in mind. Such hotels might provide hair-dryers and shampoo etc. in the room. They might have rooms for ladies that are self-contained units, with somewhere to relax and eat a meal as well as sleep, but without the high tariff charged for a suite. They might have a business bar/lounge where business travellers can meet away from other clientele.

One way of improving our business travel service is to ask our clients what could be done to make their jobs easier and more enjoyable, and to search for an answer to those needs.

Assignment 1: business travel

You have been asked to write a report for the local newspaper on the business travel service offered by your travel agency. Please write at least 500 words explaining the work you do.

Assignment 2

Describe and define:
(a) how business travel differs from retail travel;
(b) ways of providing a good service to secretaries;
(c) three problems that may occur, providing your own solutions.

16 Handling complaints

In this chapter we are going to discuss:

- guidelines to follow when faced with a complaint;
- some do's and don'ts;
- responding to a letter of complaint;
- trade associations involved with codes of conduct;
- assignment and exercises to complete.

Unfortunately there will be times when we receive complaints. On some of these occasions those complaints could have been avoided if we had finalized our work accurately and thoughtfully. Some of the reasons for complaint will be outside our control, but we will be on the receiving end of the outburst!

There are a million different situations that can initiate a complaint: change of holiday dates; delays at airport; missed flight; inferior standards at hotel; increase in cost of holiday; travel documents incorrectly issued; lack of interest in reservations by travel consultant; and many, many more.

It isn't easy coming face to face with a client who is absolutely furious, and is raising his voice and shaking his fist! What can you do? Put yourself in the client's shoes. He wants the matter put right. Your objective is to keep the business, to defuse the situation and to try to action the problem.

You will need an area away from the main office; a scene becomes disruptive for the other clients and staff members. Be prepared to *listen* without interrupting. Ask the *occasional* question to establish the facts. Make *short* notes; you cannot defuse the situation by writing word for word what the client is saying – his impatience will grow!

Don't give the impression you are rushed. Take as much time as you need. If there is any point you can explain to the client that will help, do so. However, *do not argue* with your client; you are there to establish the facts and to try to correct the situation. Can you offer an immediate alternative? You will not be in a position to make rash promises of compensation. Each complaint will have to be investigated, and the offer of compensation may have to come from the tour operator, airline carrier, shipping company etc.

Let's think about some 'don'ts':

1 Don't lose your temper; it will not help!
2 Don't pass the blame on to someone else, or on to the computer. The client isn't interested in who is to blame; he/she is more interested to know what you propose to do about it!

3 Don't suggest it is the client's fault. It may be partly the client's fault, but this is *not* the time to say so!

4 Don't tell lies. It would be nice to smooth over the truth when we realize we have made a terrible error, but our clients are not silly, and they will realize what actually did happen eventually. It is better to tell them now.

5 Don't take things personally. The client may be very angry, very rude or perhaps very frightened about an incident, and you are the first person to listen. Keep in mind that it is the situation that has become so upsetting, not you personally.

Let's think about some 'dos':

1 Do be as sympathetic as possible. Look and sound sorry for what has happened.

2 Do put yourself in your client's shoes. What would *you* like to be done about the problem?

3 Do ask questions and establish the facts.

4 Do promise to do *something*.

5 Do let clients talk the problem through.

6 Do keep a cool head!

Handling problems and complaints to everyone's satisfaction isn't easy. Although we all know that practice makes perfect, this is one side of the travel and tourism industry where we hope not to get too much practice!

It can be easier to handle a complaint made by letter. One of the assignments at the end of this chapter gives you an opportunity to reply to a complaint letter.

Conciliation and arbitration

What happens if a client is not satisfied with the outcome of a complaint? The first stage for the travel agent is to take the matter up with the tour operator or principal involved. No one likes bad publicity and the complaint will be investigated by the tour operator or principal and if found to be justified, an offer of compensation will be offered to the client. Should the client feel the offer is unfair or insufficient compared to the distress suffered during the holiday the customer may explain their case to the Association of British Travel Agents (ABTA) providing the travel agent or tour operator is a member. ABTA provide a free conciliation service whereby they will investigate the complaint and attempt to resolve the dispute without recourse to law. If the dispute cannot be resolved in this way, the client may pursue the claim through ABTA's arbitration scheme. In this the dispute is adjudicated by a member of the Chartered Institute of Arbitrators, whose decision becomes legally binding on both sides.

With the single European market, there will be many changes in the laws referring to travel and tourism. There will be greater responsibilities placed on the tour operators and travel agents, and tighter control over standards.

There are various associations and offices dealing with the law of the country, to protect the travelling public. Here are just a few:

IATA   International Air Transport Association
UFTAA   Universal Federation of Travel Agents Association
WTO   World Tourism Organization

OFT   Office of Fair Trading
ITT   Institute of Travel and Tourism
CIT   Chartered Institute of Transport
HCIMA   Hotel, Catering and Institutional Management Association

Look in the *Travel Trade Directory* for a full list of societies, associations and trade organizations, and familiarize yourself with the relevant organizations for your work making a note of the areas for which each association is responsible. Each organization will have its codes of conduct or ethics (rules to follow which should minimize complaints). They will cover topics such as reservation procedures, training, issuing of documents, advertising, surcharges and safety.

Use the following guideline when answering questions (a) and (b) taken from an Institute of Commercial Management examination paper.

(a) (i) Have facts at hand.
    (ii) Tell client about the compensation being paid for the inconvenience early in the conversation.
    (iii) Explain the alternative arrangements carefully.
    (iv) Be helpful and caring, remember you represent the customer not the tour operator.
(b) (i) Refer to the list of do's and don'ts.

Question A

You have to tell your client that arrangements have changed. Describe how you would do this.

Question B

You have received a complaint from your client: a mistake has been made and your client is furious. Describe how you would DEFUSE the situation.

Assignment 1: letter of complaint

It can be easier to handle a complaint made by letter. It gives us time to think, investigate and prepare.

You have received the following letter from a Mr R. Arnez. You are employed by a travel agency called Mayflower Travel, and you booked Mr and Mrs Arnez on their holiday to Majorca. Please reply to this letter.

Assignment 2: letter of complaint

A copy of this letter will be sent to the tour operator concerned; however, you will need to list each problem from the letter in order to check that each point is investigated and a satisfactory outcome reached. The client is not looking for a list of reasons or excuses why this happened, but will certainly be looking for compensation. A letter will be written to the clients explaining the action you are taking. It is important not to let the matter drift. It will take time for you to check all details of the booking to see whether any of this could have been avoided from within the travel agency, and whether there is anything you can action now. The tour operator will have to make a full investigation into each complaint and decide on an offer of compensation based on his findings. If your clients are not satisfied with the offer, what will you advise them to do?

```
22 April 199X                                 7 Avon Drive,
                                              London NW4

Mayflower Travel,
PO Box 33,
London NW4

Dear Sir,

Mr and Mrs Arnez, Holiday Number YSO/44/92
Dates: 6 April to 16 April 199X Hotel Luna at Magaluf

     We have just returned from the worst holiday ever experienced.

     Our departure date was changed three times before we eventually
left on 6 April. On arrival at Gatwick Airport we were advised of an
8 hour delay with the flight. No alternative arrangements were made
for us, and we had to wait at the airport for an additional 8 hours.

     On arrival at the Hotel Luna our rooms were not ready, and we
had to wait 3 hours before we could occupy our rooms. The tour
operator representative was nowhere to be seen. The Hotel Luna is
listed as a three star hotel, and yet we had hot water on only 5 of
the 10 days we were there. The food was very monotonous, with very
little choice. We were not advised that extensive building is going
on at a site immediately next to the Hotel Luna, and we could hear
the noise of the building machinery all day and at weekends. We could
not make use of the hotel pool because of the dust from the building
site.

     On arrival at Gatwick at the end of the holiday my case did not
arrive. I completed a loss of baggage claims form at the airport, but
to date have received no news of the case at all.

     I look forward to receiving your reply and to learn what you
intend to do about this disastrous holiday.

                         Yours faithfully,

                         R. Arnez

                         R. Arnez
```

17 Travel agency systems, finance and planning

Summary

In this chapter we are going to discuss:

- one day in the life of a travel consultant;
- incoming and outgoing mail;
- keeping passengers' records;
- the importance of a diary;
- travel agency income;
- travel agency outgoing expenses;
- how computers help with our work;
- the need for security;
- job satisfaction;
- assignments and exercises to complete.

In this chapter we are going to take a typical day at a travel agency as a means of learning about the routine and systems within an agency. Although routines vary according to the size of the office and the number of staff employed, all travel agencies do have a basic way of operating. Sometimes information files and the processing of travel documents are completely computerized; sometimes the systems are partly computerized and partly manual; and sometimes the agency relies on a completely manual system. We are going to discuss a basic system, which will make learning your own travel company's routine easier to follow.

It must be said that an organization is effective only when each person does the job properly, no matter how small the task may be. So it is important that each member of the team follows the rules that are planned for efficiency. A break in the chain means a breakdown of the system, and our aim is for the work to flow smoothly.

Opening up

As you turn the key in the front door lock, you probably have two minutes to run to the alarm system and switch this off before the alarm begins to scream! Or perhaps it is the silent type of alarm system that will alert the local police station without making any noise at the travel agency. In any event, speed is important at this stage, no matter how early in the morning!

Mail

After collecting the mail, you will probably make a cup of coffee. You will then feel fit to open the mail. Date stamp each item; this confirms when it actually arrived on your premises, helping with any possible query later on. The mail should then be read by the manager; this will enable him/her to be in complete control of the transactions taking place within the office.

What sort of mail can we expect to receive?

Tour operators will give details of their tours, including any changes and special offers. Some of these you may like to display in the window, writing them out on a card, or making a big splash to promote a last-minute bargain. Changes could include visa requirements for a particular tour; political situations, perhaps making it unsafe for tourists to visit; weather conditions, affecting transport; cancellation of a departure, or merging with another departure to make a tour a viable proposition; the introduction of a new hotel to a brochure; and so on.

Confirmations, cancellations and changes of travel arrangements, from tour operators, airlines, hotels and other principals

Airline companies will send notification of changes of flight times, withdrawal of flights and fare changes. Fare changes are not always increases; some airlines can offer very good promotional or off-peak reductions in fares. Airlines will notify any new facilities to make a flight more comfortable; details of additional facilities, perhaps free car rental; special reductions on hotel accommodation; ticketing details; instructions to update their manuals; and so on.

Hoteliers will send brochures on their hotels with up-to-date rates. Special rates may be offered over weekends if their main business is gained during the week with the accommodation of business travellers. The situation could be the reverse; a hotel could be announcing its plans to encourage mid-week occupancy.

Clients will make changes in holidays already booked, or cancel their travel arrangements, or perhaps request information about future holiday plans. Some letters from clients may contain complaints regarding poor standards of hotels, loss of baggage, poor service, being misinformed by the travel consultant, flight delays not handled to their satisfaction; hopefully letters of complaint will be rare.

Head office notices If working for a travel company with several offices memos and instructions will be received from the head office and will require actioning.

Each travel consultant will receive the mail that concerns his/her own work. The mail that concerns everyone (update of information) must be circulated to all staff members as quickly as possible. The news sheets must be signed, and working timetables amended where relevant. At the end of each day these papers should be filed in the general files under the correct titles. Speed is important, as each travel consultant needs to be kept up to date immediately. So the daily news must not be allowed to sit on a desk for two or three hours because more pressing work takes priority: read, sign, make adjustments, pass on.

Many travel companies have their own computerized data base providing the latest up-to-date information to their employees. This should be checked several times during the day to ensure all staff members are kept up to date.

The same rules apply to filing the information sheets. If they are not filed at the end of each day, or when every staff member has seen the notice, it will be difficult to find this current information when it is needed. Should an original paper be removed, it should be replaced by a photostat copy. The files should be kept easily accessible to all staff members.

Name				Address/Account			Date	
				Tel. bus.		Res.		
Flight	Class	Date	From	To	Depart	Arrive	Status	

Hotel			Place	From		To		Status

Car rental			Place	From		To		Status

Documents			Number	Value	
Air tickets					
Insurance					
Hotel vouchers					
Car rental vouchers					
Inv./receipts					

General agency files

We will need headings for our files, and in many cases those headings will have subheadings. These files are for general use by all the staff. Just *one* file copy and relevant papers should be kept in the file cabinet. As new papers arrive, the out-of-date papers should be destroyed. Your agency will have files on each airline carrier, shipping company, tour operator and country.

In addition to those files you will need information and often reservation instructions on the following subjects: passports and visas; rail travel; insurance; incentive travel; car rental; accounts; sporting events; trade fairs and exhibitions; refunds and claims; interpreters; credit and instalment plans; charter companies; musical events; and so on. The headings chosen will relate to the type of business your travel agency processes.

Your own files

Card files

As reservation details are received, the travel consultant will open a file for each booking. We usually use the card system for reservations that will not require a lot of correspondence; this applies to business travellers in particular.

Please study the example. Any information can be printed on the booking card – information that is relevant for our own travel agency. In the example, the first entry is for name. Then cames address or company account; the latter is used when the reservation is being made for one of the companies that have an account with your travel agency, and will be paying for the travel arrangements at the end of each month. There follows the date of travel – nice and clear, as you may be looking through many booking cards to find this particular one. Flight details include: class of travel; date of travel; from and to (cities/airports); depart and arrive (flight times); and status, i.e. whether the flight is confirmed or on request. Then there are spaces to enter hotel reservation details and car rental details. The final spaces are to enter documentation details: air ticket number and value; insurance policy number and value; hotel and car rental details. The invoice details are recorded if the client is to pay at the end of the month, and the numbers of the receipts issued if any payments are made.

Very little paper work would be attached to the file card, particularly if the reservations were made by telephone or computer. The status and booking reference would be written on the card, and if the reservation was made by computer then the printout of the reservations would be clipped to the back of the card.

Envelope files

Perhaps the reservation is not so simple. You know there will be correspondence involved. Then you would choose the envelope type of file card to record the reservations and place all the relevant papers in the envelope. Please study the example shown.

Company

Customer ref.

Phone no.   Ext.

Passengers

Address

Load name

A/C code

Passengers

Tickets required by

Date tickets sent

Invoice no.

Outward date

Date

Date

Air reservations

Flight	Class	Date	From	To	Depart	Arrive	Status	Ref.	Visa advice

× Not required   ✓ Required

Health requirements

☐ Small pox   ☐ Malaria
☐ Cholera   ☐ Typhoid
☐ Yellow fever ☐ Paratyphoid
              ☐ Other

Ticket no.

Travellers' cheques and currency

Insurance

Special requests

Hotel reservations

Date	Nights	Town	Hotel	Rooms	Basis	Rate	Status	Ref.

Car hire reservations

Date	Renting location	Driver's name	Car group	Time	Days	Voucher no.	Status	Ref.

Holiday information

Company	Departure point	Date	Time	Days	Status	Ref. / req.

On the front of the envelope is found the company, address, lead name and outward date. The lead name is the name of the person who is head of the group or family travelling, and is the person who has signed the booking form. There may be several passengers travelling together with different surnames, but one of those passengers must take the responsibility of signing any documents on behalf of the rest of the party, and will receive the correspondence and confirmations for the reservations made.

On the reverse of the envelope is a record of the financial history. There are three columns: amount due, amount received, and amount paid out by travel agent. These three columns *must* be completed before handing over any travel documents.

The files should be kept in *date* order, not alphabetical, because each day you must check who is travelling and issue their tickets.

Diary

One of the most important books kept at the agency is the diary. In the diary will be written *everything* you need to remember. Please do not depend upon the brain; it can let you down in times of pressure!

A central diary used by all staff members is useful if an employee is suddenly absent from the office and has not made prior arrangements to deal with the work. Not just ticket issues would be entered into the diary, but everything, such as: chasing up hotel confirmations; obtaining new brochures and sending them to a client who has made the request; checking to find out whether a visa or passport is ready to collect from the consulate; fulfilling a promise to call back; giving ticket numbers to an airline on an agreed date; recording payment dates for holiday balances. Anything that must be done, but has not been done today, has to go into the diary.

Exercise 1

Draw up front and reverse sides of an envelope file similar to those shown. Try completing the file details using the following fictitious holiday information.

Mrs Ann Edmonds and Miss Valerie Wager are travelling together for a European holiday commencing from their home in Sydney. They give details of their home address only, which is 24 Cross Green, Sydney, and their telephone number is 227903. The departure date is 24 July 199X. They will travel on flight number QF009 on 24 July from Sydney to London Heathrow Airport, departing at 1330 hours and arriving London at 0600 hours the next day. The reference for this booking is EV2501and they will be travelling J class.

Their return flight details are QF002 on 29 August from London Heathrow at 1315 hours, arriving Sydney at 2005 hours the next day. The booking reference is DP183 and the ticket numbers to be issued for this flight are 124703962 and 963. Receipt number 971 was issued for payment of this air ticket, and the cost is A$3450.00 per person.

Amount due		Amount received				Amount paid out by travel agent					%	Total
Item	A$	Date	Doc. No.	Item	A$	Date	Doc. No.	Item	A$			A$

Our clients have requested the non-smoking section of the aircraft.

On arrival in London Mrs Edmonds and Miss Wager will stay at the Savoy Hotel for four nights before taking a European coach tour. They will have a twin bedded room on a bed and breakfast basis, and the rate is UK £150.00 per room per night. The rate of exchange to be used is A$2.30 to UK £1. Receipt number 304 was issued for payment of the hotel accommodation, and the booking reference is XYZ.

On 29 July they will take a Coachcruise coach tour of Europe, departing from Victoria, London at 0800 hours. The tour is for 14 days (13 nights). This reservation is confirmed, the reference is LP, and they have requested the front seats of the coach. Receipt number 736 was issued for this coach tour. The cost of the coach tour is A$815.00 per person.

You have checked visa and health requirements. They require visas for Romania and Hungary, and they need smallpox vaccinations.

On completion of their coach tour our clients will return to the Savoy Hotel for one night, then rent a car from Avis RentaCar, group D for eight days. The car will be delivered to the Savoy Hotel at 1000 hours. You have issued voucher number 7984 and have collected a deposit of A$230.00 on receipt number 737. The balance will be collected from the clients by Avis and your travel agency will receive the commission for the whole amount; this will be advised by Avis after the car rental transaction has taken place. The confirmation reference is SP904.

Our clients have taken Carefree Insurance at the cost of A$90.00 each, collected on receipt number 738, and the reference number is AC403.

Travellers' cheques were issued to the value of A$3000 and currency to the value of A$200. Receipt number 739 was issued for this payment. All reservations are confirmed.

The commission rates are as follows: air ticket 9 per cent; hotel 10 per cent (payment made to Savoy Hotel by service order); coach tour 10 per cent (payment made by service order); car rental to be advised (no payment made to Avis until completion of trip); insurance 25 per cent; travellers' cheques and currency 0.02 per cent.

All documents are to be finalized on 13 July. Your clients will collect the travel documents on 14 July with the exception of the travellers' cheques, which will be paid for and collected on 20 July. All other payments were made by the clients on 14 May.

The totals of the payments due and the payments received should tally. At a glance you will be able to see the amount of commission earned on each item and the amount paid to the principal. However, remember that this file will not be closed until the statement from Avis RentaCar has been received, advising the total amount for the car rental and the rate and amount of commission due.

When you have completed both sides of the envelope file to your satisfaction, the answers can be checked at the end of the book.

Technology at the travel agency

We are fortunate in having lots of help to speed our work. We are unfortunate in the fact that the tourist can make reservations by using the computer, without the help of the travel agent! So the computer has a dual role of both friend and foe to us.

What is a computer? It is an electronic general purpose machine (a piece of hardware) which follows a list of instructions called a program (a piece of software) using information (data) drawn from various sources to produce results.

To use the type of computer required to make airline reservations and all the many associated reservations can be mastered on a short course (three or four days) with an airline carrier. Many agencies use computerized reservation systems such as Galileo in Business Travel and Travicom Skytrack in Leisure Shops to make their reservations with airlines. These reservations systems allow the agent access to many different airlines and the computerized reservation companies run their own courses for agents.

The type of computer used to make reservations and view information for holidays, theatre tickets, sea voyages, car rental, hotels, etc. is easy to get to know at the agency with the help of a manual and the instructions on the screen (visual display unit or VDU).

With practice, making reservations by computer will be quick, reliable and accurate. It is good to have the state of the reservation displayed on the VDU, so knowing immediately whether the holiday, flight, car rental etc. is confirmed, fully booked or available, and to be able to make a printed copy of the information, confirming the message on the screen.

Computers can be used to speed documentation by issuing the ticket, the invoice and the itinerary at the same time.

We can use computers to do the accountancy work by programming for the needs of your agency. It can quickly show profits, losses, state of the business, salaries, taxes etc.

So we use computers to provide information and to process the work. Is there anything left for us to do? Yes: at the time of writing, the computer doesn't have feelings! It cannot think about giving a special personalized service. It obeys the instructions we give; the computer is as competent as its operator. Tourists can now make their own straightforward reservations with the computers that are available to them, often in their homes; so when they contact a travel agency they expect a service far superior to any machine.

Don't worry about learning to use a computer. It really is easy once you have mastered the basics. Many manuals and directories are available at the agency to help. Once you become comfortable with the computer you will be *so* pleased with the speed at which you are able to process your work, and with the reduction in paper work.

We have many other aids at the travel agency: telephones, telex machine, fax machine, dictaphone, answering machine, bleepers, photocopier, franking machine (for posting letters, no stamps used), calculators, word processors, typewriters. We really should be efficient with all that help!

Travel agency income

Travel agents gain their income from commission earned on the products they sell. They do not carry any stock as such, but work as mediators between the principal and the customer. In the exercise in this chapter, the coach tour of Europe for the Australian couple cost A$815.00. From this the agency would earn 10 per cent commission, i.e. A$81.50.

It is possible for travel agencies to earn incentive commission. This is a higher rate for being loyal to one or several selected tour operators; after the agency reaches an agreed sales figure, a higher rate will be paid.

Travel agencies can also be part tour operator, producing their own tours and thus receiving the full mark-up. This will be a higher rate than the commission earned from a tour operator.

Charges can be made for services such as obtaining passports and visas. This saves the client a lot of time and trouble, and to be relieved of this chore for a small fee can be worth while from his point of view.

Income is also gained from investment of customers' money between the time it is paid to the travel agent and the time it is paid by the travel agent to the tour operator. The money is deposited at higher interest bank rates. The fluctuation of exchange rates for travel agents dealing in foreign currency can also be advantageous.

Travel agents can offer travel-related goods (hair-dryers, travelling irons, cases etc.) and tourist gifts to boost sales.

Travel agency outgoings

There are salaries, rents, rates, taxes, stationery, advertising, market research, lighting, heating, insurance, maintenance and running costs, telephones and technical equipment, office furniture and many more unexpected expenses. Running a business is similar to, but of course much bigger than, running your own home. Income less expenses equals profit, to save or plough back into the business, the home or both.

What happens if we do not make a profit? Our business fails and we have to close. So the aim is to make a profit and to keep a very strict eye on the health of the business. Make savings where possible; be economical with lighting, heating and stationery. Take care especially with telephones; it is tempting for the travel consultant in Sydney to call a friend in Rome, met whilst on an educational trip to Europe, when the boss is away from the office! The use of computers not only make our work quicker, safer and more convenient, it also saves on telephone calls.

At the end of the day it may seem that a travel agency does not have a large profit margin. However, it must be taken into consideration that the products of the travel agency do not have a high risk value; they belong to the principals. There is nothing to become outdated, as there is with, say, the clothing industry. There are no goods to deteriorate, as with, say, butchers, greengrocers and bakers.

The manager's job will be to forecast future trends. This can be done by keeping a close watch on the travel transactions that have taken place over the past couple of years, by comparing the figures with present sales, and by budgeting for future travel sales. The figures will help to decide what changes are taking place in the marketplace, how fashions are changing, and where to build on strengths and correct weaknesses.

The figures may be taken from the computer, and the state of business can be read in detail from the printout. Alternatively, the totals will be taken from the sales made each day, the receipts issued with the totals, the details of the products sold, the bank statements, and the receipts and bills for every expenditure concerning the agency. This will mean reporting daily figures to the management in order for them to keep up to date and to be able to make constructive decisions.

Security

Because a travel agency is selling valuable services, great care must be given to the handling of cash, cheques and other accountable documents. Probably the most valuable accountable documents held in a travel agency are the IATA airline tickets; these blank tickets are entrusted to the travel agency. All accountable travel documents must be kept in strict numerical order, and locked away in a fire-proof safe. The numbers are entered into a ticket stock book, and the travel consultant must sign acceptance each time a ticket is taken from the stock. The manager should make frequent checks that the correct procedures are being carried out.

Each month a sales return will be completed, when used ticket numbers are entered on an official sheet together with details of the travel transactions. A copy of this will be sent to the principal. For the entire ticket stock, a record must be kept of all accountable documents received; the travel consultant must confirm receipt of the documents to be issued, and report the number of documents issued each month and the serial numbers of the travel documents remaining.

Job satisfaction

So there are many jobs to be done when working in a travel agency, and we can enjoy a lovely variety.

There is some paper work: filing, accounting, banking, writing letters, ticket stock control, completing sales returns, typing itineraries, issuing travel documents – and many more. There is the use of technology: computers, word processors, telephones, photocopiers, telex machines – and many more.

There are the pleasures of meeting people: identifying clients' needs, helping with any travel-related problems, making reservations, communicating with principals – and many more.

We can improve our product knowledge throughout our lives, keeping up to date with current events and changes in the tourism industry, travelling on educational trips to investigate hotels, and experiencing the tourist attractions of Rio, Bali, Kenya, San Francisco, Moscow, Fiji – and many more!

Assignment 1

(a) Name ten tasks that can be performed by the use of computers.
(b) How do travel agents earn their income?
(c) Name ten services offered by a travel agency.
(d) Explain the meaning of code of ethics.

Solutions to exercises

Chapter 2

Exercise 1

(a) No, not within 30 days of departure.
(b) (i) £180.00. (ii) No; this is allowed only when the surcharge is over 10 per cent.
(c) £60.00 per person.
(d) By 56 days or 8 weeks before, that is by 30 August. However, the computer clears a reservation if the payment is not received or the cheque is not cleared by the deadline. So payment made 10 weeks in advance is advised!
(e) 100 per cent.

Exercise 2

Adults 4 April 7 Nights £349.00 × 2	£698.00
First child sharing 15% reduction (£52.35)	296.00
Second child sharing 10% reduction (£34.90)	314.10
Infant £15.00	15.00
Balcony £1.25 per person (not infant) per night: £1.25 × 4 × 7	35.00
	£1358.75

Insurance premium is to be added.

Exercise 3

(a) Pesetas.
(b) Speak to the representative of Enterprise Holidays.
(c) Under 2 years on the date of their return flight.
(d) Friday.
(e)

Adults 27 March 14 nights Club Paraiso £304.00 × 2	£608.00
Unused bed supplement £9.50 per night	133.00
Breakfast (BB) £2.75 per person per night	77.00
Airport surcharge (Newcastle) £22.00 per person	44.00
Insurance £18.00 per person	36.00
	£898.00

There is an unused bed because two people are using a three-person studio.
(f) Payment in full within 8 weeks of departure.
(g) See booking form.

Booking Form — Enterprise WINTERSUN

TO BE RETAINED BY TRAVEL AGENT

HOLIDAY DETAILS

Departure date 27 MAR 199X	Departure Airport NEWCASTLE	Country/Island TENERIFE	Option No: TNRJ70390
No of nights 14	Destination Airport REINA SOFIA	Resort PLAYA de las AMERICAS	Holiday No: BCTFS1112

ACCOMMODATION DETAILS

Hotel/Apartment/Villa   CLUB PARAISO

Two centre: 2nd Resort —	2nd Hotel/Apartment/Villa —

PASSENGER DETAILS

Room Type	Mr/Ms	Initial	Surname	Age if under 12	✓ if cot required	Board basis	Extra facilities	Infants @ £15 each	Total No. in Party
APT	MR	R	ARMSTRONG			BB			2
APT	MRS	S	ARMSTRONG			BB			

CAR HIRE	SPECIAL OFFERS	OTHER REQUESTS
Group:	Singles Holidays ☐	
Resort:	3 weeks for price of 2 ☐	
From: To:	Special board (specify) ☐	
Pickup Point	Other (specify)	

ROOM TYPE CODE	BOARD TYPE CODE	EXTRA FACILITIES CODE
S - Single Q - Quad TW - Twin SU - Suite TR - Triple APT - Apartment	FB - Full board HB - Half board BB - Bed & Breakfast AO - Accommodation only All party members must take the same board arrangements	BAL - Balcony SR - Superior room B - Bath MB - Main building SV - Sea view Other - (Please Specify)

PAYMENT DETAILS

Initial Payment Enclosed   £1031. 00

(Full payment, including insurance premium, if within 8 weeks of departure.)

Holiday deposit $60 per person (excluding infants).
Holiday insurance is arranged automatically unless you or your travel agent have agreed alternative insurance arrangements with us and the appropriate premium will be added to your invoice. Infants (age 2 or under on date of return) pay a standard £15 holiday charge and are insured free. For details of premium and cover, see brochure page 107.
I certify, on behalf of the person(s) included on this form, by whom I am authorised to make this booking, that I/we have read and agree to the Booking Conditions in the above-named brochure, and the conditions of insurance, and that my/our booking is made and is subject to those conditions and that I am over 18 years of age.

Signature *(of lead name)*   R Armstrong

Date   07/02/9X

ENTERPRISE WINTERSUN
Groundstar House, London Road, Crawley, West Sussex, RH10 2TB.

Reservation Help Line: (0293) 519151   Switchboard: (0293) 560777
Group Bookings: (0293) 517866   Tailormade Bookings: (0293) 612122
Telex: 878791 WING G Fax: (0293) 25225

Agents Viewdata
ISTEL –59# FASTRAK SUN   PRESTEL ✳RV2#

TRAVEL AGENT'S STAMP

All holidays in this brochure are operated by Redwing Holdings Ltd., trading as Enterprise Holidays, Registered in England No. 2357936, and subject to availability.

IATA   AITO   ABTA 95301

Exercise 4

The costing table for the Dutch tour is shown.

Description	Fare/rate (UK£, DFL)	Total (DFL)	Gross (UK£)	Commission (%)	(UK£)	Net (UK£)
Transportation						
Air:						
Stansted/Amsterdam/						
Stansted	£120.00		120.00	9	10.80	109.20
Transfers (2)	DFL 25.00	50.00	15.62	10	1.56	14.06
Tours						
Half day (1)	DFL 64.50	64.50	20.15	10	2.0	18.15
Full day (1)	DFL 90.00	90.00	28.12	10	2.81	25.31
Evening (3)	DFL 170.00	510.00	159.37	10	15.93	143.44
Accommodation (nights)						
Hotel Amber (4)	DFL 92.00	368.00	115.00	8	9.20	105.80
Insurance						
Atlas	£17.00		17.00	30	5.10	11.90
			£475.26		£47.40	£427.86
				Mark-up 15%	64.17	64.17
				Profit	£111.57	£492.63
						Sell for
						£492.00

Chapter 3

Exercise 1

(a) 5 p.m.
(b) Rank Organization PLC.
(c) £3.00 per adult, £1.50 per child.
(d) Pages 14–15.
(e) Any of the 33 listed under 'Free fun for everyone'.
(f) Kennels are available at Starcoast World. However, the dog may not be exercised at the holiday centre; only guide dogs for the blind are permitted at the centre itself.
(g) Adults £15.00 × 2 = £30.00. Children £6.00 × 2 = £12.00. Total £42.00.
(h) Subtropical water world of spiralling flumes, rushing rapids, whirlpool and waves.
(i) Eight different food outlets: Chinese, fish and chips, à la carte bistro, cafeteria, pizzeria, bakery, ice cream parlour and fast food servery.

(j) September standard accommodation;

Adults £126.00 × 2	£252.00
Child £63.00 (50% reduction)	63.00
Adults full board supplement £18.00 × 2	36.00
Child full board supplement £9.00	9.00
Insurance £3.00 per adult, £1.50 per child	7.50
	£367.50

(k) (i) Bangor (found under British Rail details).
(ii) Standard return rail fare £17.25 per adult, £8.65 per child: total £43.15.

(l)

Basic cost £132.00 × 20	£2640.00
Less group discount 10%	264.00
	2376.00
Insurance £3.00 × 20	60.00
Total	£2436.00
Cost per person	£121.80

Exercise 2

The booking form is shown.

The costing for the De Silver family is as follows:

County Suites £325.00 × 2	£650.00
Return rail fare £17.25 × 4 adults	69.00
Return rail fare £8.65 × 2 children	17.30
Insurance £3.00 × 4 adults, £1.50 × 2 children	15.00
Total	£751.30
Cost per person	£125.21

Chapter 4

Exercise 1

(a) Fredericton
(b) 8.5 miles or 13.5 km.
(c) 165.
(d) No: Symbol A means accommodation only (EP).
(e) No: the conference room holds a maximum of 350 guests.
(f) Symbol D (MAP).

Butlin's HOLIDAY WORLDS

BOOKING FORM

To make a reservation telephone **0800 222555** or see your Travel Agent. Our staff will give you a provisional booking reference number. Write the reference number in the box below marked Provisional Tel. Ref. We will hold your reservation for 5 days, to give you time to send your booking form and deposit. This booking form is an application for Butlin's Holiday Social Club. Please read the information section carefully before filling in the booking form. PLEASE USE BLOCK LETTERS.

Provisional Tel. Ref. **SCW/019/LPA**

FOR AN IMMEDIATE RESERVATION PHONE: FREE ☎ 0800 222555

1 WHO WILL BE COMING

Please enter the Principal booking name in line 1. Will the Principal please indicate year of last holiday at Butlin's Holiday World.
If there are more than 6 persons, use an additional sheet of paper and attach to the booking form.

	Title	First Name	Surname	Address	Postcode	Husband · Wife · Son · Daughter · Friend	Age on Arrival for room allocation	HH	GC
1	MR	JOSEPH	DE SILVER	44 SEAVIEW ROAD BRIGHTON · SUSSEX	BT136SX	HUSBAND	41		
2	MRS	MARIA	DE SILVER	—— ''		WIFE	40		
3	MISS	ANGELA	DE SILVER	—— ''		DAUGHTER	12		
4	MR	ANTONI	DE SILVER	—— ''		HUSBAND	68		
5	MRS	SOFIA	DE SILVER	—— ''		WIFE	66		
6	MISS	SARA	VICKERY	33 THE DRIVE BRIGHTON SUSSEX	BT147SX	FRIEND	11		

Age on Arrival. *Please indicate the number of people in the appropriate box's*

Senior Citizens ☑ 2   Adults ☑ 2   Children 5-14 ☑ 2   Junior 2-4 ☐   Infants under 2 ☐   No. of Cots required ☐

2 WHICH HOLIDAY

Please tick the appropriate accommodation under your choice of Holiday.

☐ **FULL**   ☐ **HALF BOARD HOLIDAY**   ☑ **SELF CATERING HOLIDAY**

★★★ County Suite with Lounge & Kitchenette ☐
★★★ County Suite ☐   ★★ Standard ☐
★ Budget ☐   Single Person Accommodation ☐
(supplement will apply)

★★★ County Suite ☑   Deluxe Caravan ☐
Snowdon Lodge. Starcoast World only ☐
★★ Standard ☐   ★ Budget ☐

FOR TRAVEL AGENTS

Travel agents must enter the full lead names and address of clients, otherwise bookings cannot be accepted.

Travel Agent's Stamp including ABTA Agency Number

3 WHERE & WHEN

Please tick your Choice of Holiday World then insert your arrival and departure date.

Starcoast World ☑   Somerwest World ☐   Funcoast World ☐
Southcoast World ☐   Wonderwest World ☐

Arrive after 2.00 p.m. Day **01** Month **09** Year **90** X   Depart by 10.00 a.m. Day **08** Month **09** Year **90** X

I enclose Cheque - Please charge to my account* (Authorised Credit Agents only) *Delete not applicable

the amount _____ confirming this booking on behalf of _____
Client's Name _____
ABTA Number _____
Agent's Reference _____

4 TRAVEL SAVERS

The cost of your Ticket will be added to the cost of your holiday. See page 70/71 for details.

National Express ☐   *Please do NOT include children under 5 who are not occupying seats*
British Rail ☑   *Your ticket is valid from 7 days prior to your holiday start date*

Total Number Travelling **6**   Adults 15+ **4**   Children 5-14 years **2**
NE/BR Station of Departure **BRIGHTON**   Date of Travel departure **01.09** 90

FOR OFFICE USE ONLY

FORM	DEP	RJ
BF CODE **61**		DATE REC'D

PTY	SC	AD	CH	INF	JN	COTS	CODE	NO

CODE	AMT	A/P

LKT
RIT MSG
DRY
DH
AL

5 DEPOSIT PAYMENT

Half/Full Board Deposit
No. of Adults   x £15 = £ _____
No. of Children   x £6 = £ _____
Total Amount enclosed   £ _____

Self Catering Deposit
No. of units **2**   x £25 = £ **50.00**
Please enclose the name of your insurer if you do NOT want Travel Insurance arranged by Butlin's Ltd.
I enclose Cheque/Giro order No. **950**
Name & Address if different from Principal Booking Name _____

Credit Card Payment
Please complete the following if you wish to pay by Credit Card.

Tick appropriate box ☐ Access ☐ VISA
Card No. _____
Expiry Date _____
Signature _____
_____ Postcode _____

6 SPECIAL REQUESTS

We regret that these cannot be guaranteed. **2 COUNTY SUITES CLOSE TOGETHER NEAR SWIMMING POOL.**

7 DECLARATION

The principal booking name in (1) above signs on behalf of his/her party and accepts the Conditions of Reservation
Principal Signature **J De Silver**   Daytime Tel. No **070277309**

(g) No: only AX, MC and VI.
(h) In the suburbs.
(i) SB C$ 58–69.
(j) 10 per cent.

Exercise 2

The completed voucher for the Globe Theatre is shown.

XYZ/456 **GLOBE** ▬▬▬ ▬▬▬ **THEATRE**	**GLOBE** ▬▬▬▬ ▬▬▬ **THEATRE** XYZ/456
DRESS CIRCLE	**DRESS CIRCLE**
ADMIT *FouR* PERSONS	ADMIT *FouR*. PERSONS
Wednesday 22 OCT 19xx	*Wednesday 22 OCT 19xx.*
PERFORMANCE: *MATINEE*	PERFORMANCE: *MATINEE*
ROW *G* *8-11* PER SEAT *£ 27·00*	ROW *G* *8-11* PER SEAT *£ 27·00*
NAME OF AGENT	NAME OF AGENT

Exercise 3

(a) (i) Half board (ii) full board (iii) accommodation containing some kind of kitchen facility; also known as studio apartment.
(b) (i) City/commercial (ii) resort (iii) motel.
(c) Juice; toast, roll or pastry; coffee or milk. May be coffee and roll only.
(d) A$110–150.
(e) City centre.
(f) See Chapter 4.

Exercise 4

See Chapter 4.

Exercise 5

See Chapter 4.

Chapter 5

Exercise 1

(a) 11 hours.
(b) No. Extension can only be made at the time of original purchase.
(c) No.
(d) 23 hours.

Chapter 6

Exercise 1

See extracts.

Answers to European quiz

(a) Mon.–Sat. 0900–2000 hours Sun. 0900–1700 hours.
(b) VW Gold 1.6 (A) (3) = Group G (large cars Group E–S) Luxembourg to Italy (Florence is an international key city) Zone 4 = US$400.
(c)

	Unlimited mileage
Group F	LF 19.520.00
CDW LF 425 per day × 7 days.	LF 2,975.00
PA. LF 150 per day (covers both drivers) × 7	LF 1,050.00
	LF 23,545.00
Tax 12%	LF 2,825.40
Total:	LF 26,370.40

	Time and mileage
Group F weekly Lux Franc	LF 9,330.00
LF15.20 per km × 1050 km	LF 15,960.00
CDW LF425 per day × 7 days	LF 2,975.00
PAI LF 150 per day × 7 days	LF 1,050.00
	LF 29,315.00
Tax 12%	LF 3,517.80
Total	LF 32,832.80

(d) No, payment by credit cards only for group F.

(e) Group P – 25 years.
(f) Group F LF 35,000
(g) Yes, Group F Free-sell.
(h) Zone 5 Large Car Group F US$500.

Exercise 2

(a) Zone 4: $300.
(b) Zone 5: $500.
(c) 70 years.

Exercise 3

(a) Group C ESC8400 per day × 3 days	ESC25,200
Kilometres	nil
CDW ESC1200 per day × 3 days	3,600
PAI ESC300 per day × 3 days	900
	29,700
Tax 12%	3,564
	ESC33,264

(b) 23 years.
(c) ESC450,000.

Exercise 4

(a) Group G ML140.00 weekly	ML140.00
CDW ML 2.00 per day × 7	14.00
PAI ML1.00 per day × 7	7.00
	ML161.00

(b) Yes.

Exercise 5

(a) Because Madeira is an island.	
(b) Group C LF13630 for 7 days	LF 13,630.00
Additional day LF1947.14 × 2 days	3,894.28

CDW LF375 per day × 9 days	3,375.00
PAI LF150 per day × 9 days	1,350.00
	22,249.28
Tax 12%	2,669.91
	Total LF 24,919.19

(c) Small car Luxembourg to Italy zone 4 US$ 300.
(d) US$ 714.63 rate of exchange LF34.87 = US$ 1.00.
(e) LF 25,000.
(f) Yes, licence must be held for at least one year only.

Chapter 7

Exercise 1

Standard single fare

Harwich/Hook Holland 12 August Tariff A		Hook Holland/Harwich 27 August Tariff A		
Car/driver	£100.00	£100.00		
caravan	£ 70.00	£ 70.00		
2 adults	£ 60.00	£ 60.00		
1 child	£ 15.00	£ 15.00		
4 berth inside cabin £10.00 per berth × 4	£ 40.00	£ 40.00		
	£285.00	£285.00	Total £570.00	

FareSaver

Out Monday 12 Aug. Night sailing		Return Saturday 27 August		
car/caravan Driver up to 5 passengers	£150.00	£175.00		
4 berth cabin	£ 40.00	£ 40.00		
	£190.00	£215.00	Total £405.00	

When several people travelling together the FareSaver usually becomes the cheaper fare.

Exercise 2

Faresaver 2 day Return

Harwich/Hook Holland		Hook Holland/Harwich		
Car driver D tariff £150.00 Return	£ 75.00	£ 75.00		
2 adults £30.00 each return	£ 30.00	£ 30.00		
	£105.00	£105.00	Total £210.00	

Exercise 3

(a) One Biscayne Tower, Miami, Florida 33131, USA.
(b) Table 758.
(c) (i) Yes, Zurich.
     (ii) Portoferrario, Italy.
(d) (i) Royal Cruise Line.
     (ii) 17,884 gross registered tonnes.
     (iii) 806 passengers.
     (iv) Air conditioned and stabilized.
(e) (i) Car ferry.
     (ii) P & O Ferries.
     (iii) 735 passengers.
     (iv) 4468 gross registered tonnes.
(f) (i) Great Britain to Sweden.
     (ii) DFDS Seaways.
     (iii) Harwich.
     (iv) No: Code B sailings are 15 and 17 June.
     (v) 12 noon next day.
(g) Tuesday, Saturday, Monday.

Exercise 4

(a) Algiers.
(b) Only mountain motorways have toll charges.
(c) No.
(d) 18 years.
(e) Italy, Yugoslavia, Hungary, Czechoslovakia, Germany, Switzerland.
(f) 31 miles per hour.
(g) (i) Two sailings per week.
     (ii) 9 hours.
     (iii) 1000 passengers.
(h) (i) 246
     (ii) Morocco.
(i) (i) 146.
     (ii) France.

Exercise 5

(a) Mr & Mrs K Banda and daughter aged 7 years.
     Harwich to Hook of Holland   Hook of Holland to Harwich.
     Friday 03 July Tariff B   Tuesday 07 July tariff B.

FareSaver

Car and up to 6 passengers £105.00   £80.00
Total Fare £185.00.
compared to standard single fare for the Banda family.

	Harwich to Hook Holland	Hook of Holland to Harwich	
	Friday 03 July tariff B	Tuesday 07 July tariff B	
Car/driver	£ 76.00	£ 76.00	
additional passenger	£ 30.00	£ 30.00	
child	£ 15.00	£ 15.00	
	£121.00	£121.00	Total £242.00

5-day excursion tariff for vehicle and up to 5 occupants: return fare £207.00.
(b) 1200 noon.
(c) 1100 hrs (one hour before sailing)
(d) 5 hours 45 mins.

Exercise 6

(a) Keeps us up to date with latest changes
(b) The Netherlands.
(c) Table 608.
(d) (i) Contact their office in San Francisco, address supplied.
       (ii) No.
       (iii) 104.
(e) (i) 12,600 t.
       (ii) 1600.
       (iii) TT Line.
(f) (i) Brittany Ferries.
       (ii) Plymouth and Santander.
       (iii) 24 hours.
       (iv) £110.00.
(g) (i) *Queen Elizabeth 2.*
       (ii) 286.
       (iii) 16 May.
       (iv) 22 May.

Chapter 8

Exercise 1

See Chapter 8.

Exercise 2

(a) Pisa to Rome, table 355; Rome to Naples, tables 392 and 394.
(b) 2050 hours.
(c) 349.

Exercise 3

(a) Depart Piraeus 1930 hours; arrive Limassol 1400 hours.
(b) Did you read the notes? Code J gives the sailing dates for the full voyage from Ancona to Haifa. Code C shows that the ship arrives in Piraeus on the third day, and code E shows that it arrives in Limassol on the fifth day. The first departure date from Ancona in August is 7 August, making the dates 9 August in Piraeus and 11 August in Limassol.

Exercise 4

(a) M9.
(b) No, he needs service M11.
(c) R1.

Exercise 5

(a) 355.
(b) Yes.
(c) 0945 hours.
(d) The coastal route via Pisa.

Exercise 6

(a) Euston.
(b) Stranraer, Scotland.
(c) Larne.
(d) 2250 hours.

Chapter 9

Exercise 1

(a) £2395.
(b) Main deck, Belvedere deck, Promenade deck, upper deck.

(c) 526; category C; £3050.
(d) Belvedere and Dolphin decks.
(e) £4195 + £3146.25 (75% supplement) = £7341.25.

Exercise 2

(a) (i) Leave ship in Penang on day 6; rejoin ship at Sibolga.
   (ii) Indonesia on day 9.
   (iii) £175.00 per person double, £210.00 single.
(b) 2 days, from 0800 hours on day 15 to 1800 hours on day 16.
(c) Day 13 depart Jakarta; day 15 rejoin ship in Bali.
(d) Value season £2475.00 plus excursion £175.00, total £2650.00 per person; for two persons
   £5300.00.

Exercise 3

(a) No: passports should be valid for 6 months after the date of entry into countries in the Far
   East.
(b) Yes, for India, Turkey and Argentina.
(c) The baggage allowance by air is 20 kg per person. There are no baggage conditions on the
   cruise, although a maximum of two cases is recommended because the 20 kg allowance
   applies for the flight home.
(d) Ocean Cruise Lines.
(e) Anything can happen beyond the control of OCL: strikes, weather conditions, war etc.
   OCL would alter the itinerary for the safety of the passengers.
(f) Yes, if the shipping company is notified in advance. Note that the facilities are not suitable
   in China.
(g) Yes, at extra cost.
(h) The Bahamas.
(i) False: port charges are included.
(j) There is a no-increase guarantee by Ocean Cruise Lines; they will not pass the increase on
   to the passenger.
(k) The balance is due 60 days before departure: in this case, 20 January.
(l) £20 per person amendment fee
(m) The cancellation is in the period 15–28 days before departure; the cancellation charges will
   be 50 per cent of the fare.

Chapter 10

Exercise 1

City	Country	IATA area	Subarea
Bogota	Colombia	1	Mid Atlantic
Bangkok	Thailand	3	South East Asia

Vancouver	Canada	1	North Atlantic
Nairobi	Kenya	2	Eastern Africa
Nicosia	Cyprus	2	Middle East
Los Angeles	USA	1	North Atlantic
Wellington	New Zealand	3	South West Pacific

Exercise 2

City	Country
Madras	India
Istanbul	Turkey
Beirut	Lebanon
Damascus	Syria
Kuala Lumpur	Malaysia
Monte Carlo	Monaco
Manila	Philippines
Colombo	Sri Lanka
Osaka	Japan
Blantyre	Malawi
Chittagong	Bangladesh

Exercise 3

The cities are Vienna, Stockholm, Athens, Belgrade, Madrid, Oslo, London and Geneva. Two possible solutions are shown.

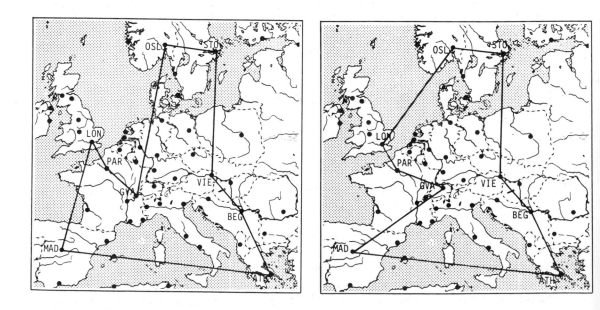

Exercise 4

(a) 3 miles (5 km).
(b) Rail from Cornavin Station takes 6 minutes. Trolley bus from Bel-Air and Cornavin Station takes 20 minutes.
(c) From 7 October depart 1230 hours, arrive Amman 1745 hours. Flight number RJ128. Aircraft is 310, i.e. Airbus A310. Classes of travel: first, business, economy. No stopovers en route.
(d) No. The Saturday flight discontinues on 22 September.
(e) Airline RJ requires check-in 2 hours before: in this case at 1030 hours.
(f) London (LHR), Amsterdam (AMS), Helsinki (HEL), Frankfurt (FRA).
(g) Depart 1010 hours, arrive 1545 hours ESB airport. Flight number SR322. Aircraft is M80, i.e. McDonnell Douglas MD-80. Classes of travel: first, business, economy, thrift discount (F,C,Y,M,L). The aircraft makes one stop en route.

Exercise 6

(a) 30 minutes.
(b) 45 minutes.
(c) 45 minutes.
(d) 45 minutes.

Exercise 7

(a) For an interline flight the minimum connecting time is 30 minutes. For an online flight by AN and TN (Anselt airlines of Australia AN and Australian Airlines TN) the minimum connecting time is 15 minutes.
(b) This is domestic to international; therefore the minimum connecting time is 1 hour 20 minutes.
(c) International to domestic – 1 hour 20 minutes.
(d) This is international – 1 hour connecting time.

Exercise 8

(a) Amersterdam = Netherlands: 2 April plus 2 hours Hong Kong is 6 hours ahead of The Netherlands 1800 hours plus 6 hours = midnight in Hong Kong.
(b) Buenos Aires = Argentina: 3 July is minus 3 hours, Blantyre = Malawi is plus 2 hours (add together, different signs, remember?) there is a time difference of 5 hours. Malawi is 5 hours ahead of Argentina. 1000 hours in Buenos Aires = 1500 hours Blantyre.
(c) Auckland = New Zealand: 25 December is plus 13 hours. Beirut = The Lebanon: plus 2 hours (deduct, the signs are the same) it is 11 hours earlier in Beirut. 2100 hours in Auckland minus 11 hours = 1000 hrs (10 o'clock in the morning, same day) in Beirut.

Exercise 9

   Athens = Greece. + 2 GMT Dhaka = Bangladesh. + 6 GMT
(a) Depart Athens 1420 hours = GMT 1220 hours (− 2 hours)
   Arrive Dhaka 0430 hours = GMT 2230 hours (same day) − 6 hours.
   Actual flying time from 1220 hours to 2230 hours = 10 hours 10 minutes.
(b) Copenhagen = Denmark + 2 hours GMT Bahrain + 3 hours GMT
   Depart Copenhagen 0805 minus 2 hours = 0605 hours GMT
   ıArrive Bahrain 1840 hours minus 3 hours = 1540 hours GMT
   From 0605 hours to 1540 hours = 9 hours 35 minutes.
(c) Kuala Lumpar = Malaysia = + 8 hours GMT Paris = France = + 2 hours GMT. Depart
   Kuala Lumpur 1155 hours deduct 8 hours = 0355 hours (same day) arrive Paris 2030 hours
   deduct 2 hours = 1830 hours. From 0355 hours to 1830 hours = 14 hours 25 minutes.

Exercise 10

(a) China during October is + 8 hours ahead of GMT so the GMT departure time is 0740
   hours. (− 8 hours = 2340 hours the day before)
   Pakistan is + 5 hours ahead of GMT time of arrival 1220 hours − 5 hours = GMT 0720
   hours. The actual flying time is from 2340 hours on Day 1 to 0720 hours on day 2 = 7 hours
   50 minutes flying time.
(b) Frankfurt = Germany: + 2 hours GMT (between Mar–Sep)
   Lagos Nigeria + 1 hour GMT.
   Frankfurt 1355 hours = 1155 hours GMT.
   Lagos 1925 hours = 1825 hours GMT.
   from 1155 hours to 1825 hours = 6 hours 20 minutes flying time.

Exercise 11

Country	No risk	Limited risk	Definite risk
Australia	√		
Mauritius	√		
Brazil			√
Peru	√		
Madagascar			√
Lesotho	√		
Zaire			√
Algeria	√		
Turkey		√	
South Yemen			√

Exercise 12

(a) Drachma (GRD).
(b) Closed after 2 p.m. Monday to Friday, and on Saturday and Sunday. Only the National and General Bank in Athens is open at other times.
(c) Yes.
(d) Yes, 2 months stay is the limit.
(e) Over US$1000 must be declared.
(f) No, money declared on arrival can be exported.
(g) 10 miles (16 km).
(h) By looking at the map provided by *ABC Guide*, with endemic areas shaded.

Exercise 13

(a) Depart Geneva 1725, arrive Zurich 1810, flight number SR 205 (Swissair). Depart Zurich 1905, arrive Amsterdam 2025, flight number KL 315 (Royal Dutch Airlines).
(b) One stop.
(c) Red Book, *ABC World Airways Guide*.
(d) 1 hour (domestic to international).
(e) 1 hour 30 minutes (international to domestic).
(f) 3 GMT.
(g) + 8 GMT.
(h) 16 hours 15 minutes.
(i) 20 hours 20 minutes.
(j) Yes: see map.

Chapter 11

Exercise 1

(a) No: Section 8 exclusion.
(b) No: Section 9 exclusion.
(c) Yes: these circumstances are not listed in the exclusions for Sections 1, 2, 3 and 5.
(d) Europe, west of the Ural Mountains.

Exercise 2

Mrs Rautio	£ 45.00
Miss Rautio half premium under 16 years	£ 22.50
Mr Rautio double premium for scuba diving	90.00
Mr and Mrs Partanen treble premium for 70 years and over 45.00 × 3 = £135.00 × 2	270.00
	£427.50

Chapter 12

Exercise 1

The table shows the basic information required.

Travel sales and analysis

Branch: Date: No. *7728*

Inv. No:	Client	Total		Cash		Account		Details	Air	Tours	Cont. rail	Dom. rail	Hotels	Sea	Insurance	Misc.
401	Clyde	340	00	340	00											
402	Roberts	406	00			406	00									
403	Lee	124	80	124	80											
404	White	641	50	641	50											
405	Harper	761	50			761	50									
406	Williams	81	80	81	80											
		2355	60	1188	10	1167	50									

Exercise 2

The table shows the completed analysis. The answers to the double-checking questions are as follows:
(a) £2137.80.
(b) £1253.30.
(c) £884.50.
(d) Thomson and Cosmos £300.00
(e) £131.50.

Travel sales and analysis

Branch: Ashford   Date: 12 March 199X   No. 7729

Inv. No:	Client	Total		Cash		Account		Details	Air		Tours		Cont. rail		Dom. rail		Hotels		Sea		Insurance		Misc.	
230	Jones	216	00	216	00			057776123 (AF)	201	00											15	00		
231	McCool	200	00	200	00			Thomson			200	00												
232	Henderson	884	50			884	50	125884132 (BA)	740	00							120	00			24	50		
233	Wright	711	50	711	50			Sealink 1742									301	50	241	00	80	00	89	00
234	Marshall	125	80	125	80			Cosmos			100	00			13	80					12	00		
		2137	80	1253	30	884	50		941	00	300	00			13	80	421	50	241	00	131	50	89	00

Exercise 3

The table shows the basic totals required.

Petty cash

Float £100·00   Week ending 6 Dec. 199X

Date	Office refreshments		Postage		Salary cleaner		Staff travel expenses		Maintenance expenses		Ticket delivery		Misc.	
1 Dec.														
5 Dec.														
											Total		83	55
											Cash in hand		16	45
											Total		100	00

Exercise 4

The table shows the completed petty cash sheet.

Exercise 4

Float £100.00

Petty cash

Week ending 13 Dec. 199X

Date	Office refreshments		Postage		Salary cleaner		Staff travel expenses		Maintenance expenses		Ticket delivery		Misc.	
8 Dec.	8	40	30	00							9	00		
12 Dec.							7	30	5	60	4	45		
	8	40	30	00			7	30	5	60	13	45		
											Total		64	75
											Cash in hand		35	25
											Total		100	00

Exercise 5

The completed advice is shown.

Exercise 6

The completed advice is shown.

Thomas Cook MasterCard Travellers Cheques — Sales Advice/Avis de Vente — **Pounds Sterling**

Selling Agent/Agent-Vendeur   Code

Prefix	From/De	To/Jusqu'à	Quantity Quantité	Denom Coupure	Amount Montant
A763401		420	20	Stg £10	200.00
S497104		114	11	Stg £20	220.00
R993742		752	11	Stg £50	550.00
				Stg £100	
				Stg £200	
				Stg £	

Name (print) / Nom (en majuscules)   PAMELA JONES
Address / Adresse   17 ASH GROVE
SOUTHPORT

	Stg £
Total Sale / Vente Totale Stg £	970.00
Fee / Commission 1% Stg £	9.70
Total Stg £	979.70

Important: Immediately upon receipt, you must sign each cheque in the space marked "Signature of holder" (at the bottom left hand side). You will only countersign each cheque (at the top left hand side) when you encash it and in the presence of the acceptor. No refund will be made if you have failed to observe these conditions.
I agree to the above and to the Purchase Conditions printed on the reverse side of this Sales Advice and separately supplied with the cheques, and I understand the important notice on the back of the Purchaser's Receipt copy of this Sales Advice.

Important: Dès réception, vous devez signer chaque chèque sur la ligne "Signature of holder" (en bas et à gauche du chèque). Ne contresignez chaque chèque (en haut et à gauche) que lorsque vous l'encaissez, et en présence de la personne qui a la charge de l'accepter. Aucun remboursement ne pourra être effectué si vous n'observez pas ces conditions.
J'accepte ce qui précède et les Conditions d'Achat figurant au verso de cet Avis de Vente et fournies séparément avec les chèques, et je prends note des importantes dispositions figurant au verso de la copie du Reçu pour l'Acheteur de cet Avis de Vente.

Signature of Purchaser/Signature de l'Acheteur

Date of Sale/Date de Vente — Day/Jour 04 Month/Mois 05 Year/Année 90

Send original to: / Adressez l'original à: Thomas Cook Travellers Cheques Ltd. P.O. Box 36 Peterborough Great Britain PE3 6SB

Rate / Cours

B2270 C 10/90 (French)   Thomas Cook Travellers Cheques Ltd., a subsidiary of The Thomas Cook Group Ltd.

Chapter 16

Assignment 1

The first stage for the travel agent is to take the matter up with the tour operator or principal involved. No one likes bad publicity and the complaint will be investigated by the tour operator or principal and if found to be justified, compensation will be offered to the client. Should the client feel the offer is unfair or insufficient compared to the distress suffered during the holiday the customer may explain their case to the Association of British Travel Agents (ABTA) providing the travel agent or tour operator is a member. ABTA provide a free concilliation service.

Chapter 17

Exercise 1

The front and reverse sides of the envelope file should be as shown.

Company		Address	24 Cross Green	Load name Edmonds	Outward date 24 July 199X

Customer ref.

Phone no. 227903 Ext. Home

A/C code

Tickets required by
Date tickets sent — Date 13 July
Invoice no. — Date 14 July
971-304-736/7/8/9 — Collected

Passengers Mrs A Edmonds   Miss V Wager

Air reservations

Flight	Class	Date	From	To	Depart	Arrive	Status	Ref.	Visa advice
QF 009	J	24 Jul.	SYD	LHR	1330	0600*	OK	EV 2501	Romania
QF 002	J	29 Aug.	LHR	SYD	1315	2005*	OK	DP 183	Hungary

X Not required   ✓ Required

Health requirements

Small pox	✓	Malaria	X
Cholera	X	Typhoid	X
Yellow fever	X	Paratyphoid	X
		Other	X

Ticket no. QF 124 703 962/3

Travellers' cheques and currency
T/C A $ 3000
Currency A $ 200

Insurance
Carefree AC403

Special requests
No smoking area

Hotel reservations

Date	Nights	Town	Hotel	Rooms	Basis	Rate	Status	Ref.	Rate of exchange
25 Jul.	4	London	Savoy	Twin	BB	Per room 150.00	OK	XYZ	2.30
11 Aug.	1	London	Savoy	Twin	BB	Per room 150.00	OK	XYZ	UK£ 750 = A$ 1725

Car hire reservations

Date	Renting location	Driver's name	Car group	Time	Days	Voucher no.	Status	Ref.
12 Aug.	Avis Savoy Hotel	Edmonds	D	10.00	8	7984	OK	904

Holiday information

Company	Departure point	Date	Time	Days	Status	Ref./req.
Coachcruise	Victoria London	29 Jul.	0800	14	OK	LP Front seats

Amount due		Amount received				Amount paid out by travel agent				%	Total
Item	A$	Date	Doc. No.	Item	A$	Date	Doc. No.	Item	A$		A$
Air tickets	6,900 00	14 May	971	QF 12L703962/3	6,900 00	01 Jul	PS741	Air ticket QF	6,279 00	9	621.00
Hotel voucher	1,725 00	14 May	304	Savoy Hotel Voucher	1,725 00	12 Jun	PS 904	Service order	1,552 50	10	172,50
Coachcruise	1,630 00	14 May	736	Tour of Europe	1,630 00	12 Jun	PS 905	Service order	1,467 00	10	163.00
Avis	230 00	14 May	737	Car rental deposit	230 00	01 Jul	798+	Voucher			
Carefree ins.	180 00	14 May	738	Insurance	180 00	01 Jul	AC 403	Policy	135 00	25	45.00
Traveller's cheques	3,200 00	20 Jul	739	T/cheques Currency	3,200 00	00 Jul	739	T/cheques Currency	3,136 00	0.02	64.00
	13,865 00				13,865 00				12,569 50		1065.50

Exercise 2

(a) Displaying availability, amendments, confirming reservations, providing information on climate, flight arrivals, visa requirements, issue travel documents, issue invoices, issue itineraries, book package holidays, book theatre tickets, book car rental, used for accountancy.
(b) From commission earned on the products they sell.
(c) Insurance, package holidays, travellers' cheques, sea, air, rail, coach, hotel, holiday centres, camping, passport, visas, fare calculations. Individual travel arrangements.
(d) The guidelines of ethical behaviour issued by national trade associations dealing with relations between the public, carriers and other industry principals to improve the standards of every aspect of the travel and tourism industry.

Glossary of terms

ABTA	Association of British Travel Agents.
Add-on	A special domestic air fare that may be combined with an international fare.
Agency account number	A reference number given to travel agents by a principal for easy identification.
Balance of payment	The final amount of money due.
Consumer	The customer.
Chapter flights	Aircraft is rented for a specific journey, can be shared by many tour operators.
Comprehensive insurance	A policy that embraces most evantualities.
Check-in	Reporting time prior to departure.
Confirmed	Positive.
Deposit	An initial payment to secure a reservation.
Domestic flights	Flights within one country.
Discounted fares	Fares sold at a reduced price.
En route	During the journey.
Full board	3 meals per day.
Flight schedule	Published times of flight operation.
General Sales Agent	An agent representing a company in a country where the principal does not have a sales office. The General Sales Agent represents many companies and is paid by the companies for this service. It enables travel companies to have representatives throughout the world without actually having their own office.
Half board	2 meals a day usually breakfast and dinner.
IATA/UFTAA	International Air Transport Association and Universal Federation of Travel Agents' Association (address in Chapter 10).
ICM	Institute of Commercial Management (address in Chapter 10).
Inclusive tour	Travel arrangements that include several services for example accommodation, flight, car rental and so on, sold at one price.
International flights	Flight services operating between different countries.
Incentive tours	A travel arrangement given as a reward for achievements.
MCO	Miscellaneous Charge Order, similar to an airline ticket but multi-purpose.
No Show	Non-arrival, passenger does not turn up.
Package Holidays	Travel arrangements packaged and sold as one price.
Producers	Companies that have a product to sell, also known as
Principals	For example, hotels, airlines, car rental companies, shipping companies and so on.
PAX	Abbreviation for passengers.

Retailer	The sales outlet for travel goods the retailer is the travel agent.
Round trip	The term means travel from one point to another and return by any air route for which the same normal all year through one way fare of the same class applies from the point of origin.
Schedule flights	Flights that are published and will operate regardless of number of passengers. Usually the national airline.
Spouse fare	A discounted fare for a husband or wife, travelling together.
Third Party Insurance	Insurance against damage to someone else or their property.
Volume of traffic	Amount of business, activety, people and so on.
Validity	Time limit minimum validity and maximum validity.
Wholesaler	The tour operator, packaging the services together.
Wait-listed	Waiting for the reservation to be confirmed.

Index

ABC Car Ferry Guide, 73, 75–80
ABC Holiday Guide, 5
ABC International, 129
ABC Shipping Guide, 73, 83–9, 111–13
ABC World Airways Guide, 130–4
 aircraft types, 132
 average journey time between major
  cities, 142
 flight information, 132–4
 international time calculator, 140
ABC Worldwide Hotel Guide, 37, 38, 39–40
ABTA National Training Board, 122
Access, 181
Accident & General Limited, 161
Accounting, 172–7
After-sales service, 197–8
Airline reservations, 122–50, 190
 air fares, 153–7
 airport information, 150
 double transfer via Copenhagen and
  Amsterdam, 136
 free baggage allowance, 150
 hotel reservations, 41
 minimum connecting times, 137–9
 reservation making, 150–8
 single transfer, 134
  via Brussels, 136
  with change of airport at London, 136
 special services for passengers, 149–50
Airport information, 150
Airtransport Ticketing Handbook, 48
American plan (AP) food service, 37
 modified (MAP), 37
American Express, 181
Ameripass, 52–3
AMTRAK, 93
Antiques holiday, 31
Application for job letter, 201–3
Archaeology holiday, 31
Athletics holiday, 31

Average journey time between major cities,
 142, 143

Balancing books, 172
Bandido's Club, 25
Bargain breaks, 48–9
Beauty holiday, 32
Bird watching holiday, 31
Botany holiday, 31
British Rail, 94–6
Broker, 161
Business letters, 201–8
 application for job, 201–3
 change in travel arrangements, 207–8
 welcome home, 205
Business travel, 209–16
 financial problems, 214
 good service to secretaries, 209–12
 handling problems, 212–14
 increasing, 212
Businesswomen's needs, 214–15
Butlin's brochure, 22–5

Cabana, 36
Camping site, 36
Caravan site, 36
Car ferries, 73–91, 191
 ABC Car Ferry Guide, 73, 75–9
 ABC Shipping Guide, 73, 83–9
 car lengths, 74
 motorists' information, 74–5
 reservation making, 89–91
 routings, 74
 Sealink, 80–3
Car rental, 58–72, 190
 age restriction, 60
 central billing, 70
 costing, 64–8
 deposit, 60
 direct billing, 70

driving licence, 60
Europcar, 63–8
fuel consumption, 59
groups of car, 59
insurance, 60–1
model, 61
petrol, 60
rates, 59
rates of exchange, 61
taxes, 61
vouchers, 69–70
Cash handling, 171–2
Castles holiday, 31
Central reservation office, 40
Central reservation system (CRS), 41
Charge card, 180–1
Cheque, 177–80
 stopping payment, 179
Cheque card, 179
City hotels, 36
Claims International Limited, 161
CoachGuard, 161
Coach tour, 52–5, 56–7
 European, 54–5
 organization, 52–4
Complaints handling, 216–19
 arbitration, 217–18
 conciliation, 217–18
Conferences, 13, 193
Customer relations, 198–9
Continental breakfast, 37
Continental plan (CP) food service, 37
Conservation control, 199–20
Cookery holiday, 31
Customer relations, 198–9
Credit card, 180–2
Cruising, 108–21, 191
 clothing, 111
 costs, 109–10
 guides, 111–14
 health and beauty facilities, 111
 illness, 111
 laundry, 111
 life on board, 108–9
 nautical terms, 110
 passengers, 108
  density, 108
 reservation making, 120–1

shore excursions, 111
Spice Islands, 117–18
'stay-a-while' programme, 109
telecommunications, 111
Thomas Cook World of Cruising brochure,
 114–16
tipping, 111

Diners Club, 181
Dinghy sailing holiday, 31
Duplex, 36

English breakfast, 37
Enterprise Wintersun brochure, 5–11
 flight details, 9–11
 holiday costs, 9–11
 making reservation, 11–12
Escorted tours, 190–1
Europcar, 63–7
European one-way rental plan, 65
European plan (EP) food service (room
  only), 37
Eurotunnel, 93–4
Exchange rate mechanism, 183

Fishing holiday, 31
Float, 175
Floating hotel, 36
Flowers holiday, 31
Flycruise, 108
Food holiday, 31
Food service terms, 37
Foreign currency, 182–3
 buying/selling rates, 183

Gambling holiday, 31
Game lodge, 36
Geography of Travel and Tourism, The
  (B. Boniface & C. Cooper), 126
Gibraltar, 145, 147
Golf holiday, 31–2
Greece, 148
Greyhound International, 51, 52–3
Group travel, 13–18
 costing, 15–17
 planning, 13–15
Guest houses (pensions), 36

Health holiday, 32
Health requirements, 146
Holiday centre, 20–31
    choice factors, 21
    see also Butlin's brochure; Starcoast World
Holiday Fellowship Holidays, 32
Horse riding holiday, 32
Hotels, 35–43
    accommodation, 36
    cancellation charges, 41
    central reservation office, 40
    central reservation system (CRS), 41
    commission for travel agent, 43
    consortium, 40
    holiday resort, 36
    informing clients, 38
    representatives, 40
    reservation making, 40–1, 192
    types, 35–6
    vouchers, 41–3
Incentive travel, 13
Incoming tourism, 55–6
Institute of Commercial Management, 122
Insurance, 159–70, 190
    broker, 161
    cancellation charges, 159
    claim, 160
    coverage, 159–60
    curtailment, 159
    exclusion, 160
    insurer, 160
    loss adjuster, 161
    medical expenses, 159
    personal accident, 160
    personal baggage, 160
    personal liability, 159
    policy, 160
    policy holder, 160
    policy issuing, 168–9
    premium, 160
    underwriter, 161
    see also TravelGuard
International Air Transport Association
    (IATA), 121–30
    city codes, 127
    offices, 124
    traffic conference areas, 123, 124
      subareas, 125

International date line, 144
International driving permit, 60
International time calculator, 140

Keep fit holiday, 32

Legal time, 141
London airport codes, 127
Loss adjuster, 161

MAGLEV trains, 92, 93
Malarial risk areas, 145, 146–7
Miscellaneous charges order (MCO), 48
Motels, 36
Motor racing holiday, 32
Motor-rail service (car sleepers), 93
Municipal General Insurance, 161
Music holiday, 32

Nautical terms, 110

OAG Worldwide Cruise, 111
Ocean Pearl, 114–16
'Overriding commission' system, 3

Package tours, 3–12, 192
    brochure, 4, 18
      Enterprise Wintersun, *see* Enterprise
        Wintersun brochure
    client's choice factors, 3–4
    'overriding commission' system, 3
Painting holiday, 32
Parachuting holiday, 32
Passports, 144
Pensions (guest houses), 36
Petty cash, 175
Peyton Training Services, 122
Pony trekking holiday, 32
Preferred Customer Card, 69

Rail travel, 92–107, 191
    British Rail, 94–6
    car-sleeper trains, 104, 106
    Eurotunnel, 93–4
    guides, maps, timetables, 96–103
    India, 92
    Japan, 92
    North America, 92

reservations making, 103–5
USSR, 92
Ramblers Holidays, 32
Robinson Crusoe holiday, 32
Room only (European plan food service),
37
Royal Insurance UK, 159

Sealink, 80–3
Shipline Guide, 111
Skiing holiday, 32
Skills, 189–200
Special interest holidays, 31–4
Special Interest Overseas Touring Holidays, 51
Standard time, 141
Starcoast World, 23–31
Children's Clubs, 25
costing holiday, 25–31
Stateless person, 146
Stopover holiday, 47–8, 192–3
Studio apartment (efficiency room), 36
Survival holiday, 32

Tavern, room in, 36
Teamsters Club, 25
Telephone techniques, 196–7
Theatre reservations 43–6, 192
Thomas Cook European Railway and Shipping Timetable, 73
Thomas Cook Overseas Railway and Shipping Services Timetable, 73
Thomas Cook World Cruising, 114–16
Thomson Citybreaks, 49
Ticket on departure, 211
Time difference, 141–3
Trade fairs, 193
Travel agency:
after-sales service, 197–8
closing sale, 197
commission from hotel, 43
comparison of agencies, 199

computerized reservation systems, 228
consumer relations, 198–9
conversation control, 199–200
diary, 225
files, 223–5
card, 223
envelope, 223–5
income, 228–9
job satisfaction, 230
mail, 221–2
open/closed questions, 193–5
opening up, 220–1
outgoings, 229
sales technique, 193–5
security, 230
skills in, 189–200
technology, 228
telephone techniques, 196–7
TravelGuard, 160–4
Annual, 161
CoachGuard, 161
Family, 161
Gold, 161
brochure, 161–3
policy, 164–8
Travellers' cheques, 184–7, 191
Travelmax, 69
Travel Trade Directory, 13, 218

Underwriters, 161

Vaccinations, 146
Visa, 181
Visas, 144

Walking holiday, 32
Weekend break, 193
Whizzy Worlds Club, 25

Yellow fever vaccination, 146
Youth hostel, 36